Palgrave Studies in Literature, Culture and Human Rights

This series demonstrates how cultural critique can inform understandings of human rights as normative instruments that may at once express forms of human flourishing and be complicit with violence and inequality. The series investigates the role of genre and the aesthetic in shaping cultures of both rights and harm. Essential to this work is an understanding of human rights as at once normative and dynamic, encompassing egregious violations as well as forms of immiseration that have not always registered in human rights terms.

More information about this series at
http://www.palgrave.com/gp/series/16248

Katherine Ebury

Modern Literature and the Death Penalty, 1890–1950

palgrave
macmillan

Katherine Ebury
School of English
University of Sheffield
Sheffield, UK

ISSN 2524-8820 ISSN 2524-8839 (electronic)
Palgrave Studies in Literature, Culture and Human Rights
ISBN 978-3-030-52749-5 ISBN 978-3-030-52750-1 (eBook)
https://doi.org/10.1007/978-3-030-52750-1

Cover design: eStudioCalamar
Cover illustration: Mike Abrahams / Alamy Stock Photo

This Palgrave Macmillan imprint is published by the registered company Springer Nature Switzerland AG.
The registered company address is: Gewerbestrasse 11, 6330 Cham, Switzerland

Acknowledgements

I would first like to thank the Arts and Humanities Research Council for funding this project, as well as my colleagues and students at the University of Sheffield, for their friendship and guidance in strange times. There are an enormous number of people that I am indebted to in preparing this book. At Palgrave, I am grateful to my editors, Lina Aboujieb and Alexandra S. Moore, as well as to the editorial board of the 'Palgrave Studies in Literature, Culture and Human Rights Series' and to my anonymous peer reviewers. I also benefited immensely from the work of archival staff at the British Library, the National Library of Ireland, the UK National Archives, the Imperial War Museum and the Marion E. Wade Centre. Special thanks go to my mentor, Christopher Bennett, whose interdisciplinary expertise and patience were always much appreciated, and to my postdoctoral collaborator, Samraghni Bonnerjee (who always gives me a fresh perspective), especially for her work in producing our open access special issue on 'Literature, Law and Psychoanalysis' with the Open Library of Humanities journal. Thanks also to Matthew Thurgood, who worked with me in 2016 on an undergraduate summer research project on Albert Pierrepoint. Part of the project involved working with charities including Sheffield Amnesty and Reprieve on public engagement events and this experience has made a transformative difference both to this book and to me personally; I am especially grateful to Alex Jagger, Christopher Webster and Rhiannon Griffiths, whose contemporary human rights work is always inspiring. Thanks are also due to editors of journals and essay collections who published and helped develop early versions of this research, including Paul Fagan and Ruben Borg; Bob McKay, John Miller and Susan McHugh; Lisa Mendelman and Heather A. Love; Helen Rutherford, Clare Sandford-Couch and Patrick Low. Since 2015 when this project was conceived, the research has proven emotionally and intellectually demanding, as well as beset by industrial action, personal trauma and world crises. I'm therefore immensely grateful for academic friendships with Michelle Witen, James Fraser, Lauren Arrington, Ravit Reichman, Amber Regis, Fabienne Collignon, Maddy Callaghan, Joe Bray, Jonathan Ellis, Laura Lovejoy, Alison Garden, Anne Fogarty, Catherine Flynn, Maebh Long, Adam Piette, Matt Campbell, Adam Hanna, Eugene McNulty, Richard Barlow, Sophie Corser, Katie Mishler, Robert Brazeau, Katherine O'Callaghan, Cóilín Parsons, Sam Slote and many others. Last but not least, my partner, JT Welsch, my parents and my dog also deserve much love and thanks.

Praise for *Modern Literature and the Death Penalty, 1890–1950*

"Through an impressive range of literary works, legal cases, and primary sources, Katherine Ebury's important book offers a fresh and powerful interpretation of how the death penalty changed the modernist literary landscape, and how modernism took up the ethical problems raised by its imposition. Ebury's work sheds light on the submerged juridical and political charge in narrative, connecting it deftly to its historical moment and revealing the intimate ties between literature and law."

—Ravit Reichman, *Brown University*

"Katherine Ebury leads us through a compelling discussion of the death penalty in literature in the first half of the twentieth century, drawing on a rich range of publications, from golden-age detective fiction to memoir to canonical works, such as Richard Wright's *Native Son*. Ebury puts these works into rewarding conversation with key thinkers of the era in sociology, psychoanalysis and legal theory. In doing so, Ebury provides valuable new perspectives on how the death penalty operated as subject and trope within literature and larger discourses of crime and punishment. Chapters on Executioners' life-writing, for example, and the place of animals in thinking about capital punishment, transform our understanding of those discourses in surprising and fruitful ways. *Modern Literature and the Death Penalty, 1890–1950* is essential reading for anyone interested in the place of the death penalty in the Anglo-Atlantic cultural imagination of the twentieth century."

—Katherine Baxter, *University of Northumbria*

"In rigorous and fascinating detail, Katherine Ebury shows the profound influence that literature's responses to the death penalty had on public debates about capital punishment. Ebury's discussion of the ambivalence that authors such as Agatha Christie, Dorothy Sayers, and Elizabeth Bowen had towards to the death penalty shows us new aspects of some of the twentieth century's most influential writers about crime and the psychological subject. With this book, Katherine Ebury breaks new ground, bringing together high modernist and popular literature to show the effect of psychoanalysis on writers' discussion of criminality and capital punishment."

—Lauren Arrington, *Maynooth University*

Contents

CHAPTER 1

Modern Cultures of the Death Penalty

Introduction

This book traces how a psychoanalytic understanding of mind and law are central to the literary understanding of the death penalty from 1890–1950. I also aim to improve our understanding of the centrality of the death penalty to modern culture and the role it played in major twentieth century historical events and literary movements. This introduction will first offer some reflections on the book's design and method, before examining historical details in sections on 'Technologies and Reforms of the Death Penalty', 'Modernism, Psychoanalysis and the Death Penalty' and 'Polemic and True Crime Writing'.

The critical study of literature responding to capital punishment has so far been mainly confined to two main periods: firstly, the nineteenth century, with special attention to William Wordsworth's famous support for and Charles Dickens's famous contestation of the death penalty,[1] and, secondly, contemporary American culture.[2] Beyond these core periods, Michel Foucault's work on punishment famously focuses primarily on eighteenth-century France, while recent edited collections have also been published on histories of execution in Anglo-Saxon England and Renaissance Italy.[3] An emphasis on nineteenth-century and American contemporary literature, and relatedly on the realist novel, determines even Jacques Derrida's grand philosophical project on the death penalty

K. Ebury, *Modern Literature and the Death Penalty, 1890–1950*, Palgrave Studies in Literature, Culture and Human Rights,
https://doi.org/10.1007/978-3-030-52750-1_1

in two volumes.[4] Although Derrida argues broadly that 'literature in Europe over the last three or four centuries is contemporary with and indissociable from a contestation of the death penalty', his key reference points are nonetheless nineteenth-century France and the contemporary American scene, reflecting his delivery of the seminars at the Sorbonne in Paris and University of California, Irvine.[5] Our frequent privileging of the nineteenth-century death penalty is perhaps unsurprising because, as Greta Olson has shown in her recent survey of the field, the nineteenth-century novel is often 'the model for the literary in Law and Literature'; Olson goes on to 'caution against idealizing the realist novel' within the field because of 'the representational techniques and political agendas that the realist novel tends to render invisible'.[6] Previous critics have thus been unable to take substantial account of the impact of psychoanalysis and modernist writing techniques in relation to the public understanding of the death penalty. Further, in response to Olson's caution against exclusive focus on realist novels, I also address a wide range of texts and genres explored throughout this book, including short stories, poetry, canonical modernist fictions, pulp fiction, detective fiction, plays, polemic, criminological and psychoanalytic tracts and life-writing both by condemned persons and by executioners.

My research therefore inserts itself into a specific gap in critical accounts of modernity. Inspired by many historians and historicist critics, I focus on the literary discourses around capital punishment between the late nineteenth century and the mid-twentieth century. Lizzie Seal's work on the cultural significance of the death penalty in twentieth-century Britain was one early provocation for this project, and her recent work with Alexa Neale on racial inequality within penal practice has also informed my thinking.[7] Evie Jeffrey has recently made the case for extending Seal's account to fiction, as a part of rebalancing historical accounts of the death penalty to include 'everyday' rather than 'political' themes, and performs this analysis herself in relation to Josephine Tey's depictions of wrongful conviction.[8] As Jeffrey highlights, and as I also find in my chosen texts, the death penalty was 'a complex and divisive issue, and its presence in detective fiction can be analyzed without necessarily labeling these novels as either pro- or anti-death penalty'.[9] Similarly, Samantha Walton's primary focus on a changing historical paradigm of the insanity defence allows her to have crucial insights into the intersection of treatment and punishment in Golden Age fiction.[10]

I am also indebted to research on modernism and violence by authors including Jonathan Eburne, Sarah Cole, Paul Sheehan and Kai Evers, though this work mostly confines itself to a focus on metaphorical or aesthetic violence and, further, tends not to address punishment.[11] Two recent agenda-setting volumes, Victoria Stewart's *Crime Writing in Interwar Britain: Fact and Fiction in the Golden Age* (2017) and Matthew Levay's *Violent Minds: Modernism and the Criminal* (2019), have been even more important for my approach. These monographs, as Levay puts it, respond to and interrogate equally 'canonical modernists' and 'authors typically neglected by modernist criticism', arguing that 'certain works of crime fiction might be productively understood as examples of popular modernism'.[12] He argues that widening the definition of modernism 'exposes a remarkable degree of overlap between the modernist imperative to reinvigorate past literary forms and crime novelists' affirmation of their work as a sophisticated manipulation of generic convention'.[13] Stewart, similarly, argues that her chosen middlebrow authors 'did not ignore the experiments with the depiction of consciousness that had characterized modernism, and some attempted to incorporate aspects of a modernist aesthetic into their own works'.[14] Although neither Stewart nor Levay is focused on punishment per se, their method has nevertheless proven extremely useful throughout my development of a definitive account of capital punishment as a theme in modern literature. I will show how a focus on the death penalty does indeed reveal a natural convergence of high and popular literature—partly linked to the wide appeal of psychoanalysis and partly explained by the contradictory formal potential of capital punishment—around the problem of writing about this extreme form of justice.

Technologies and Reforms of the Modern Death Penalty

This section of the introduction will examine changes in modern death penalty policy and explore departures from Victorian practice. We see mainly changes in access to information, but there were also technological innovations and refinements: in Britain and Ireland both of these aspects of the twentieth-century death penalty find their origins in the Aberdare Committee (1886–1888), while, as we will see, in the US these changes were more unevenly developed across states, with significant changes from the 1880s traceable to the development of the electric chair. In response to a series of botched executions, Aberdare produced a set of procedures and technologies around the execution process, designing a 'standard scale for drops' which refined William Marwood's procedure to produce a more humane death, as well as a set of standards of training and behaviour which the executioner was expected to adhere to.[15] Assessing the history of capital punishment across the period I am examining, the Gowers Commission (1949–1953) note that from Aberdare onward, 'The authorities had already ceased to give literal effect to the sentence to hang by the neck "till dead", and tried to make death instantaneous by the shock of a long drop'.[16]

After Aberdare, the State also took tighter political control of the administration of capital punishment. Centralised British Prison Authorities aimed to refine and homogenise the process and to suppress uncomfortable or idiosyncratic reflections on the death penalty. Permission for journalists to attend executions was gradually removed, and the number of local prisons at which these punishments could be carried out was progressively reduced. Though the executioner remained a contract worker, the pressure to behave professionally was also stepped up. An Edwardian policy document held at the National Archives called 'The Disclosure of Information by Former Executioners' notes that a person entered into the lists of executioners or assistants 'was required to enter into a bond, the effect of which was to render him liable to forfeit £50 to the Crown if he disclosed…any information or particulars on the subject of his duties as executioner or assistant executioner'.[17] These archives also hold a dated copy of an employment contract for executioners from 1907 which requires them to sleep at the prison on the night before the execution and demands that they 'avoid attracting public attention' for their work.[18] By 1916, a standard form filled out after an execution by the coroner asked for comment on executioner's 'capacity', 'respectability' but also his likelihood of 'bringing discredit upon his office by lecturing or by his granting interviews or causing public scandal'.[19] These were all new restrictions on the executioner compared with Victorian practice. From 1949 executioners were even shown the Official Secrets Act as part of their training, as noted by Syd Dernley in his own memoirs, while the Home Office took legal advice on potential prosecutions of hangmen for revealing details of their work in 1949 and 1956.[20] As I will show, American executioners were a little freer from this culture of secrecy, but their impulse to give testimony was often similarly restrained by social and cultural pressures.

Alongside an increasing secrecy about the whole system and a silence which deepened across the period in question, a bureaucratic approach to the death penalty developed, in which radical questions were generally not asked in the public sphere except by activist groups. These groups included the Society for the Abolition of Capital Punishment (founded 1901), the Howard League for Penal Reform (founded 1921) and the National Council for the Abolition of the Death Penalty (founded 1925). Instead of full debate, then, technical procedures were refined and reforms were instituted. The first full public debate on the civilian death penalty did not take place until quite late in the century, in 1929, and even then, as I will show in Chap. 7, this took most of its energy from more successful reforms of the military death penalty. Indeed, the Gowers Commission (1949–1953)—which assessed the whole period from 1900 to 1950 and as such will be cited frequently here—had extremely limited technical aims, given its closeness in time to abolition in 1965, and was asked only to consider 'whether liability under the criminal law in Great Britain to suffer capital punishment for murder should be limited or modified'.[21] As the Committee noted in their report, 'The natural construction of these words precludes us from considering whether the abolition of capital punishment would be desirable; and the Prime Minister (Mr Attlee) stated in the House of Commons that they were intended to have this effect'.[22] As such the Gowers Commission was mainly noteworthy for the involvement of its most famous member, the novelist Elizabeth Bowen (under her married name, Mrs Cole Cameron), and for its recommendations about a diminished responsibility defence.

The Irish death penalty context was similar to Britain until 1921, and indeed it was closer to England than to Scotland, which had its own local adaptations of capital punishment law and policy. The first draft of the 1922 Constitution of the Irish Free State included an aspiration to abolish the death penalty, but the ensuing turmoil of the Irish Civil War prevented this. Indeed, Gavin Foster notes that in response to the final period of guerrilla Civil War by the IRA, the Free State created oppressive new judicial institutions which, in their recourse to internment, military courts and the death penalty, mirrored the British response to the Easter Rising.[23] After the Civil War, reforms to capital punishment both for murder and treason were debated in The Dàil: in 1925 an amendment was proposed suggesting the substitution of penal servitude as punishment for treason, arguing for the abolition of the death penalty on explicitly anti-colonial grounds.[24] The amendment stated that the Free State 'should not follow the example of Great Britain, which was one of the states now in a majority in maintaining capital punishment'.[25] However, the commitment to the death penalty was affirmed both here in the 1920s and in the 1937 constitution. In a further irony, as before independence, a set of English executioners (primarily Tom Pierrepoint and his nephew Albert) still came to Ireland to perform hangings for the whole period from Irish Independence until the Irish abolition of the death penalty (last execution 1954, abolition 1964). Albert Pierrepoint also describes the only native Irish executioner ever recruited, judging him immediately as a squeamish type: he 'did not think he had the character to be an executioner. He was short and old and timid. When I first took him into the execution chamber his face went as white as chalk'.[26] As Pierrepoint predicted, the Irish trainee was unable to take a full role in his first execution, having apparently forgotten his training or lost his nerve, and was never heard of again.

This lack of an Irish executioner post-1922 likely reflects a wider Irish cultural opposition to the practice of capital punishment; for example, James Berry, in *My Experiences as an Executioner* (1892), describes travelling armed and under the assumed name of 'Ackroyd' to perform executions in Ireland during the Land War.[27] Albert Pierrepoint notes in his autobiography that this was also his Uncle Tom's habit.[28] Albert Pierrepoint also recorded regular protests demonstrating the 'usual resentment that the Irish authorities had asked Englishmen to hang another of their citizens'.[29] There is currently not much historical data available about these protests beyond Pierrepoint's own account of his experience, though Ian O'Donnell discusses how petitions were organised around politically controversial cases.[30] Although Ireland generally lacked its own equivalent to protest groups like the Howard League and the National Council for the Abolition of the Death Penalty, Irish writers and activists such as Eva Gore-Booth often worked with English organisations such as the Committee for the Abolition of the Death Penalty, a branch of the League of Peace and Freedom, to campaign about Irish capital cases.[31] Until Doyle and O'Donnell's recent groundbreaking work on the Pierrepoints and the Irish death penalty, it was not clear how fully the practice was a mere relic of colonialism, as these historians definitively showed that the Irish authorities could not have serviced this violent punishment without the collaboration of the Pierrepoints.[32] Still this fact about the Irish death penalty is not widely known in Irish literary studies; I will address this context again in more detail in Chap. 6, focused on the Easter Rising and its aftermath.

The picture in the US context is more complicated, but a similar bureaucratic approach was in evidence. While some US states, such as Maine (1887) and Minnesota (1911), abolished the death penalty much earlier than many Western nations, at the time of writing many states still practice capital punishment. Around the time of the implementation of the Aberdare reforms in Britain, some northern states began to adopt electrocution as a 'humane' reform as a replacement for abolition. The use of the electric chair often went along with arguments about progress; for example, as I will show in Chap. 3, the executioner Robert Elliott reflected on the 'scientific' value of the modern execution method, arguing that William Kemmler, executed in 1890 as the first victim of the electric chair, 'was dying not alone for the crime he had committed, but for science as well'.[33] Elliott was originally interviewed for the role of executioner not just by the prison warden but also by 'a representative from the General Electric Company'.[34] Later, US states would embrace fashions for other 'modern' methods such as the gas chamber and, eventually, the lethal injection.

While the general public in Britain and Ireland had little access to the details of capital punishment after 1868, the US system retained the tradition of comparatively open representation. Stuart Banner notes that executions after the adoption of the electric chair 'typically limited attendance to no more than twenty or thirty people'.[35] Although this might seem a high number by British standards, most applications from curious members of the public were denied, with the prison authorities instead privileging disinterested witnesses from amongst the general public, as well as the presence of select reporters (practices continued today). The presence of the condemned person's family or the family of the victim was also sometimes permitted.[36] Many southern states retained hanging as the main execution method and so public executions continued there until the execution of Rainey Bethea in Kentucky in 1936, the last 'public' execution in the US. After 1936, executions across the US had to take place either within the walls of the prison or in an enclosure hidden from public view. But prison authorities in the 1930s would sometimes still allow hundreds of witnesses into this enclosed space, and the widespread practice of lynching would keep the memory of public execution alive in America for much longer, as I will discuss in Chap. 8. The American death penalty was also very different to that practised in Britain and Ireland in allowing a wider range of executions for nonlethal offences including rape, whereas in Britain and Ireland this had ceased to be a capital offence in 1841. These capital charges for crimes like rape were rarely enforced for white perpetrators and, as in the case of lynching, were primarily biopolitical instruments used to reinforce segregation.

Alongside these differing historical contexts and a similar emphasis on bureaucracy, in the twentieth century Britain, Ireland and the US shared an increased use of technology to 'humanise' the death penalty and to reduce the psychological effect of the execution on witnesses. To give some examples of safety equipment from Britain and Ireland: leather would be sewn into the rope used for the noose to prevent burns; a chalk cross on the floor would make sure the prisoner was precisely balanced on the trapdoor to prevent their body from swinging on the rope after death; execution chairs could be provided when the prisoner might faint;[37] and special straps were designed to pinion the bodies of amputees and women.[38] In the American system, rubber was also widely used to ensure the safety of those observing electrocutions. The twentieth century also saw improvements to prison design to create separate execution suites, separate from the rest of the institution, stemming from a concern about psychological harm. With the impact of psychoanalysis, to be discussed later, the traumatic effect of executions on other prisoners and on prison officers became widely accepted. New designs for the condemned cell and the space around it dispensed with open air execution in prison yards, or execution sheds outside the main space of the prison, and minimised the distance that a prisoner had to walk to their execution and thus the risk of them panicking, fighting or fainting.[39] The executioner's assistant Syd Dernley noted the careful design of the three doors in the 'drop room' in most prisons, with each door having its own separate purpose: one door allowed the condemned man access from his cell directly into the death chamber, another door led to the post-mortem room where their body would be examined by the coroner, and a last door led to the outside, to allow for speedy burial in the grounds of the prison.[40] This innovation also reduced the impact of an execution on other prisoners held in cells near to the condemned cell.[41] To sum up, in Britain, Ireland and America, the death penalty was maintained in the twentieth century through a mixture of technological refinements, more standardised procedures and increased restriction on public knowledge.

Psychoanalytic Thought and the Death Penalty

Across this book I will show that we cannot overestimate the impact of literary representations of the death penalty informed by psychoanalysis on the public, given that capital punishment could no longer be witnessed after 1868. Both law and literature, as well as the wider culture around them, were profoundly influenced by the developing science of psychoanalysis and the ramifications of this debate extended to capital punishment. As Michal Shapira has explored, psychoanalysis reached Anglophone culture in the 1890s, via the work of F. W. H. Myers, Mitchell Clarke and Havelock Ellis: Ellis had considerable interest in making psychoanalysis useful for criminology from his first book onwards.[42] The nascent science of criminology, represented by publications such Cesare Lombroso's *Criminal Man* (trans. French 1896; English 1911) and Havelock Ellis's *The Criminal* (1890), and early Freudian psychoanalysis were popularised side-by-side during the fin de siècle. This intellectual climate, augmented by modernist anthropology investigating concepts of punishment and revenge in other cultures, had an important influence on twentieth-century debates about the death penalty, both in literary circles and more widely. As we will see in Chap. 7, the experience of extreme violence and shell shock during World War I would further change psychoanalysis, making it more adapted for contesting the death penalty through Freud's new emphasis on the death drive, *thanatos*, taking precedence over the sex impulse, *eros*.[43]

While many aspects of this early criminological and psychoanalytic thinking are positivist and overweening, an embodiment of what Foucault would term a 'will to knowledge', it did also include progressive aspects. Reflecting the progressive aspect of criminology, although Lombroso did not fully oppose capital punishment, he argued against its wide application as well as against the conventional arguments about moral responsibility used to justify it.[44] In *The Criminal*, Ellis, following and intensifying this aspect of Lombroso, would express the hope that capital punishment would be soon abolished. But as an example of a failure of scientific ethics, Elena Past explores how Cesare Lombroso's experiments on living and dead criminals might be compared to forms of torture and desecration, while much criminal anthropology is also tainted by eugenics.[45] Similarly, in relation to this combination of the controversial and the progressive, Freud and his followers also waged a liberal war against the death penalty. However, one of Freud's more important publications from the point of view of the death penalty, *Totem and Taboo* (1913), is contentious today because of the discredited primal horde theory and because of its broad attitudes to the non-Western 'savages' referenced in the volume's title. These aspects of Freud's thought will be directly addressed in Chap. 8.

Nevertheless, with these new developments of a wider public understanding of psychology and the concept of the death drive, from the 1920s onwards Freud's followers would lobby powerfully against the death penalty using psychoanalytic arguments, in works such as Theodor Reik's *The Compulsion to Confess and the Need for Punishment* (1925) and *The Unknown Murderer* (1932) and Hanns Sachs's *Does the Death Penalty Exist?* (1930). Recommending *Totem and Taboo* and Freud's short essay 'Criminals from a Sense of Guilt' (1916), as well as his own *Compulsion to Confess*, Reik argues that 'The results of psychoanalysis reveal possibilities of allaying, channelling and often psychically overcoming the overpowering unconscious feeling of guilt, the real, the underground motor of crime' and concludes by professing on behalf of Freud that psychoanalysis is 'an opponent of murder, whether committed by the individual as a crime or by the state in its retaliation'.[46]

The pathological fear of death which J. B. Pontalis has diagnosed in Freud is an important explanation for his use of Reik to ventriloquise his thoughts on the death penalty; but even in this muted form, Freud's concept of the death instinct, designed as 'a double drive against nature and against the law', has important ramifications in considering capital crimes and capital punishments.[47] Expert testimony based on Freud's work was also being given during trials in the period to ensure that capital offenders might be sent for treatment rather than punishment. By 1922 an article prompted by the Ronald True case, entitled 'Insanity and Crime', notes:

> During the discussion of the Ronald True case frequent allusions were made to the supposed influence of Freudian doctrine on the minds of the medical experts who gave evidence during the trial and of those appointed by the Home Secretary to inquire into the state of the prisoner's mind after his conviction.[48]

The article goes on to summarise the relevance of psychoanalysis for legal practice.[49] Psychoanalysis was indeed central to the True case, who was eventually reprieved for the murder of Gertrude Yates on the ground of insanity due to expert testimony despite being found responsible by the original jury and on appeal. Similarly, a 1923 article reflecting on 'Criminologists' Debt to

Freud' suggests that Freud's theory 'had shown why punishment so often proved futile, had thrown light on many offences, and had opened out a vista of more rational treatment in the future'.[50] By the 1930s, when almost all of the essential UK psychoanalytic infrastructure had been set up, campaigning organisations such as the Institute for the Scientific Treatment of Delinquency were established, supported not just by Freud and Jung but also the literary establishment, with John Masefield and H. G. Wells noted as influential backers of the organization.[51] Even the penal reformer and former conservative M. P. Edward Cadogan, in a comparatively traditional historical survey of crime and punishment, acknowledged that 'we must all acknowledge that in broad general principles we owe a great debt to Freud and the psychoanalysts' in thinking about the source of criminal behaviour in disorders of the mind, in sexual impulses and in childhood trauma.[52] In the US context, there was a similar interpenetration of law, psychoanalysis, literature and anti-death penalty campaigning. For example, Freud was invited to give expert testimony in the sensational Leopold and Loeb trial (1924), and, though he declined due to illness, their lawyer Clarence Darrow was nonetheless an invited speaker at a dinner given in New York for Freud's 75th birthday in 1931 at which much of the legal, psychological and literary establishment were present.

This criminological aspect of the history of psychoanalytic theory has been insufficiently studied within the field of law and literature, but it was one of the ways in which psychoanalysis made a major intervention in culture. This involvement has recently been rediscovered by legal scholars including Anne C. Dailey. Her book *Law and the Unconscious* explores the missed opportunities that twentieth-century culture offered to more fully integrate law and psychoanalysis and considers how we might repair these failures today.[53] Dailey identifies 'the seminal event for law and psychoanalysis' in the American context as 'the publication in 1930 of Jerome Frank's widely read book, *Law and the Modern Mind*', and the 'high water mark of law and psychoanalysis' as the 1967 book *Psychoanalysis, Psychiatry, and Law* by Jay Katz, Joseph Goldstein and Alan Dershowitz. Franz Alexander and William Healy's *Roots of Crime* (1935) and Alexander and Hugo Staub's *The Criminal, the Judge and the Public* (1931) also placed the desire for punishment as caused by unconscious guilt at the centre of their surveys of the justice system.[54] These authors share a similar ambition not simply to deploy psychoanalysis in legal contexts but to go beyond this aim to, as Dailey puts it elsewhere, call attention 'to the unconscious and irrational influences that permeated judicial decision making'.[55] Indeed, many psychoanalysts of the period understood the death penalty to be the product of pathology within the legal system and in culture more broadly.

Psychoanalytic work arguing against the death penalty was frequently introduced into Anglophone culture by modernist literary communities, emphasising the likely extent to which these ideas were accessed by the modernist and middlebrow authors under examination in this book. For example, Reik's *The Unknown Murderer* was first published in an English translation by Katherine Jones in Virginia and Leonard Woolf's Hogarth Press in 1936. The Hogarth Press would also publish Reik's *Ritual: Psychoanalytic Studies* (1931) and his memoir of Freud, *From Thirty Years with Freud* (1942). Reik himself would emigrate to America in 1934 and become part of the American psychoanalytic community, publishing later developments of his theory of crime and punishment such as *Masochism in Modern Man* (1941) with influential literary publishers such as Grove Press and Farrar, Straus and Giroux. Additionally, the extent to which anti-death penalty polemics and criminological tracts written by Freud's followers were read in modernist circles is also shown by the publication by the POOL Group (a publishing enterprise run by H. D., Kenneth MacPherson and Bryher) of Hanns Sachs's related arguments in *Does Capital Punishment Exist?* (1930). Sachs was Bryher's analyst between 1928 and 1932 and wrote extensively about the psychoanalysis of film for the POOL journal *Close Up* (1927–1933).[56] It is unnecessary to prove straightforward one-way influence from psychoanalytic arguments about the death penalty to literary culture in the period, because we know, for example, that Freud read works by Sayers and Christie in the late 1920s and early 1930s, alongside canonical modernist works, while modernist authors consumed both psychoanalytic works and detective fiction.[57] It is enough for my purposes here that the authors examined across my book showed similar interests in the possibilities of psychoanalysis for representations of and responses to the death penalty.

Historicist literary criticism has ultimately been limited by our exclusive focus on what we might call a 'main thread' version of psychoanalysis in much of our research and teaching, focused on a transfer of power from Freud to Lacan. This leads to a neglect of thinkers focused on criminal psychology such as Reik, Sachs, Frank, Katz et al., Marie Bonaparte, Benjamin Karpman and Frederic Wertham. Interestingly, psychoanalysts who were particularly interested in capital crime and racism, such as Karpman and Wertham, who will be discussed in Chap. 8, are even more neglected in literary circles, despite our urgent need for the unearthing of this history. Like Reik, Karpman was against the death penalty and argued that eventually prisons and retributive justice would be entirely replaced by psychoanalytic rehabilitative institutions.[58] Wertham had worked closely with Clarence Darrow in providing expert psychiatric testimony in black capital cases and was often the only psychiatrist who would agree to do so. This book centres these neglected areas of psychoanalysis in literary responses to capital punishment.

Polemic, Literary Activism and True Crime Writing

Across this section, I will consider the varieties of tone and the diverse mix of literary forms and genres used by modern authors in representing capital punishment: this will include a range of affective techniques including sentimentality, melodrama, realistic representation and quasi-scientific detachment. I will discuss authors who actively campaigned against the death penalty in fictional and nonfictional writing, such as Clarence Darrow, Robert McMurdy, Theodore Dreiser and Violet Van der Elst, as well as a range of writers who were critical of capital punishment more indirectly, but still powerfully, such as Oscar Wilde, James Joyce, F. Tennyson Jesse and Richard Wright. There are also a set of writers who are broadly supportive of the principle of the death penalty, with caveats in specific unjust cases, including George Bernard Shaw, W. B. Yeats, T. S. Eliot and Graham Greene. A final grouping might include several writers who are more ambivalent or irresolute in their thinking; at times Agatha Christie, Dorothy L. Sayers, Flann O'Brien and Elizabeth Bowen seem to support capital punishment in biographical statements and narrative patterns, but sometimes the texture of their writing expresses the opposite view, apparently accepting the psychoanalytic critique of the death penalty outlined above. There is a final set of authors who represent the death penalty in sensational ways but whose wider views are unclear, including M. R. James, E. F. Benson and Thomas Hardy.

Here I will also address the inspiration of real cases or 'true crime writing' for literary representations of the death penalty. Within this book, iconic cases of the death penalty which sparked impassioned public debate and which had substantial literary influence will be explored, including the Roger Casement Case (Britain/Ireland, 1916), the Edith Thompson case (Britain, 1923), the Leopold and Loeb case (USA, 1924), the Scottsboro case (1931) and the William Joyce case (Britain/Ireland/USA, 1946). For example, two famous modernist authors recorded their opposed views on the case of Edith Thompson in different ways; Virginia Woolf expressed in her private diary a compassionate opposition to the execution of 'poor Mrs Thompson',[59] while T. S. Eliot's next publication after Woolf's Hogarth Press had printed *The Waste Land* was a letter to *The Daily Mail* in support of Thompson's execution.[60] That Woolf could be friends with both Eliot and the penal reformer Margaret Fry, who visited Thompson before her execution, perhaps explains why she is not substantially part of this book, as capital crime and punishment is not a major preoccupation of hers, despite the importance of the Hogarth press as a psychoanalytic publisher. Several years later the Thompson case had a more literary influence, as Dorothy L. Sayers would write *The Documents in the Case* (1930) and F. Tennyson Jesse would publish *A Pin to See the Peepshow* (1934), while James Joyce would eventually sneak references to the case into *Finnegans Wake* (1939).[61]

As we can see from this case study of Thompson, while modern literary writers organised themselves around the controversy of this trial and execution in a variety of tones and forms, this 1923 context did not produce anything like determined literary activism, either against or in favour of capital punishment in general. The other cases mentioned as shaping the project, including Casement, Leopold and Loeb and William Joyce, were broadly similar in this regard. Indeed, as I have already suggested, despite the lasting power of much of the writing about capital punishment examined by this book, the period from 1890 to 1950 was largely a time of quiescence, where only the gradual reforms of capital punishment seemed possible. In this spirit, the death penalty is often primarily contested through its basic representation, especially in societies in which government practice sought to censor and stereotype the available information. In an age of often austere and disciplined modernism, a literary writer who attempted more than this simple awareness-raising by attempting to represent the death penalty in all of its abject, sentimental, melodramatic reality, such as Theodore Dreiser's *An American Tragedy* (1925) or Richard Wright's *Native Son* (1940), risked having their work labelled 'a heaping cartload of raw materials for a novel, with rubbish of all sorts intermixed—a vast, sloppy, chaotic thing'[62] or a mere 'protest novel', respectively.[63]

As such, the use of fiction for activism was often employed as a side-project to nonfictional writing by those already committed to legal campaigning and death penalty abolitionism. To give a few examples, the famous lawyer and opponent of the death penalty, Clarence Darrow, wrote a sentimental novel *An Eye for An Eye* (1905) about the last hours of a condemned man's life, alongside his criminological writing; the judge Robert McMurdy wrote a well-reviewed abolitionist novel *The Upas Tree* (1912), as well as legal essays, while Violet Van der Elst, a campaigner who used suffragette-style shock tactics, published in 1937 both *On The Gallows*, a combined polemic and memoir, and a work of Gothic short fiction entitled *The Torture Chamber and Other Stories.* Seal has recently unearthed Van der Elst's direct action work from layers of misogynist historiography; in a culture of secrecy and resignation to the death penalty, Van der Elst's sensational demonstrations including the use of music, sandwich boards and skywriting meant that her campaign genuinely raised awareness of the issue.[64] Van der Elst also founded her own publishing company, Doge Press, to circulate her writing and a periodical called *Humanity.* These campaigning writers often share tactics and techniques across the different forms and genres which span their challenge to the death penalty; for example, Van der Elst's chosen fictional form, the short story, mirrors the brief vignettes offered in *On the Gallows* where she reflects on case studies of individual executed criminals that she had attempted to help through her work. Similarly, her polemic *On the Gallows* is as invested in the death penalty as gothic spectacle as her fictional productions; she is particularly attentive to the problem of botched executions,[65] the psychology and deliberate cruelty of juries and judges,[66] torture,[67] and haunting and spiritualism,[68] all aspects that occur in her short fiction. Van der Elst believed that juries in capital cases should not be made up of ordinary citizens but rather artists and psychologists; her fictional and nonfictional work accordingly bears the equal imprint of Freud and Poe.[69]

In all three activist authors, Darrow, McMurdy and Van der Elst, an appeal to the reader's affective response is central to the design of their narratives. For example, Van der Elst's polemic often directs to her reader to feel sympathy, asking of a particular condemned man, 'Cannot you imagine yourself in his place?'. She also includes letters sent to her from condemned men which are designed to provoke emotion based on the authentic experience of these real texts.[70] Similarly, in Darrow's *An Eye for an Eye*, sympathy emerges from the relationship between the condemned man, Jim Jackson, whose unpremeditated murder of his wife comes primarily from poor social conditions, and his friend Hank (a surrogate for the reader) who has visited him the night before his execution and to whom Jim's confessions are directed. Their whole conversation takes place against the realistic backdrop of the noise of the scaffold being built outside.[71] For Hank, Jim's story humanises condemned men, and the criminal population at large. He reflects that their chat means 'I don't think I'll ever feel the same about the fellers that go to jail and get hung'.[72] Some of Jim's arguments against the death penalty are supposedly influenced by the speech of a penal reformer who had previously come to the prison; in fact, this fictional reformer is Darrow himself, as the novel borrows some of its didactic thrust from a real speech that Darrow gave at the Chicago prison in 1902.[73] Darrow's novel stayed in print into the 1920s and was influential on more famous texts including Upton Sinclair's *The Jungle* (1906) and Dreiser's *An American Tragedy*; he would recast the impassioned arguments first tested in fiction in his famous summings up of capital cases such as Leopold and Loeb and Ossian Sweet.

Robert McMurdy's *The Upas Tree* is focused on the emotions attending a miscarriage of justice, with his protagonist, the lawyer Beckwith Miller, unjustly condemned to death for the murder of one of his wealthy clients. Miller's innocence is discovered at the last possible moment, when he has already said farewell to his friends and family. As in Darrow's text, sympathy for the condemned is mostly evoked through the reactions of witnesses and loved ones, especially Miller's wife, who almost loses her sanity as a result of their ordeal. McMurdy's title and preface places a powerful emphasis on affect; the apocryphal upas tree, which 'visited with death every creature that remained within its shadow' and provided poisons for use in war and the death penalty, was 'the tree of sorrows, watered only by the tears of men'.[74] But McMurdy also includes several pages of metafictional first-person polemic against the death penalty which Miller designed to be both his epitaph and, since he is a lawyer, a criminological tract.[75] Due to its combined emphasis on feeling and on reasoned argument, the novel was positively reviewed in several American legal journals;[76] indeed, the effectiveness of the novel was acknowledged even by the editor of the *Virginia Law Register*, who found it 'dramatic, interesting' despite his 'firm belief' in the 'absolute necessity of the death penalty', while the reviewer at the *Yale Law Journal* liked its content ('thrilling, tense, like a real trial') despite the fact that it was 'badly-written'.[77] Indeed, these contrasting reviews of McMurdy show a broader failure to agree on the quality and value of activist writing in the modernist period. An emphasis on emotion might be easily dismissed by contemporary reviewers and subsequent literary critics on aesthetic grounds as Victorian sentimentalism, which undoubtedly explains the lack of place for books like those of Darrow, McMurdy and Van der Elst in the canon. However, my focus on the death penalty itself as a neglected historical context allows polemic texts like these to regain a place in literary history.

For Olson, the conjunction of law and affect is 'anti-narrative', with a strong emphasis on anti-rationality and embodied feeling: previous law and literature scholarship has used texts to explore arguments about justice and 'has thrived on the evocative power of contingent fictional narratives to counter the legal process's legitimation of itself through references to formalism and abstraction'.[78] When it comes to the death penalty, embodied feeling (fear, sympathy, revulsion) frequently overtakes rational argument targeted at the principle. This short-circuiting of the rational also occurs in striking individual moments within the mainstream of modern literature, as I will show across the present volume, such as the physical symptoms of trauma described by executioners depicting their first experience of capital punishment (Chap. 4); Dorothy L. Sayers's Peter Wimsey's breakdown in response to the death penalty (Chap. 7); and the moment of heartsick fracture between the lawyer Boris Max and his condemned client Bigger Thomas in Richard Wright's *Native Son* (Chap. 8).

The commitment to representing the death penalty in parallel fictional and nonfictional forms in the work of activists is also found across canonical modern writing about capital punishment, including James Joyce's 'Ireland at the Bar' (1907), an early newspaper piece on the unjust execution of Myles Joyce in 1882, and George Orwell's 'A Hanging' (1931) and 'Shooting an Elephant' (1936), on colonial injustice.[79] Joyce and Orwell produce texts about capital punishment in hybrid forms, placed awkwardly somewhere between an essay and a short story in their tone and content. Similarly, a run of reflections in Brian O'Nolan's/Flann O'Brien's *Cruiskeen Lawn* columns in the *Irish Times* record a mix of contradictory thoughts, both real and satirical, about capital punishment via his fictional mouthpiece Myles na gCopaleen.[80] This method would be refined by Rebecca West, in *The Meaning of Treason* on post-war treason trials and *A Train of Powder* (1955), focused on the Nuremberg trials. In this legal reporting about the political death penalty, West transcends the boundary between fiction and nonfiction in producing highly wrought, tightly plotted and dramatic reflections on the trials of war criminals, which are as intense as any novel, undermining Truman Capote's claim to have invented the 'nonfiction novel' for his unique challenge to the death penalty, *In Cold Blood* (1966).[81]

Chapter Summaries

My focus on literature in *Modern Literature and the Death Penalty, 1890–1950* is organised in two sections: 'Conceptual Approaches' and 'Conflict'. In Chap. 2 I will examine a formal feature common to many narratives of the death penalty: the extended confession of the murderer, a form of narrative which in the texts I will examine is produced and conditioned by the rhetoric of the death penalty, if not always by its literal reality. I will also examine the historical context to demonstrate how the legal and penal culture of the period frequently prevented the condemned person speaking about their crime and its punishment. The authors discussed in this chapter, including Flann O'Brien, Agatha Christie, Elizabeth Bowen, Dorothy L. Sayers and Anne Meredith, fill a gap in public access to condemned prisoners' writings by creating imagined confessions of guilt which reflect on the mandatory death sentence and its place in a wider culture.

Chapter 3 on the Gothic death penalty is paired with Chap. 2 and considers some of the same texts, but my primary focus will be the representation of the idea of death itself within modern capital punishment. The lack of visibility of the death penalty in the twentieth century explored in this introduction spurred the public imagination: crueler, more gothic and baroque representations of capital punishment emerge from this very lack of knowledge. I will thus examine three interrelated themes emerging from the exceptionality of the death penalty as a form of punishment: firstly, instances of survival, haunting and commemoration beyond the death penalty; secondly, the impression of 'death-in-life', or feeling dead before execution, expressed in both fictional and nonfictional representations of the death penalty; and, finally, the death drive and 'the suicide plot' in a death penalty context. My particular focus is a psychological understanding of execution as a 'nonexperience' via its gothic and theatrical qualities in literary representations by authors including Elizabeth Bowen, Flann O'Brien, M. R. James, E. F. Benson and Agatha Christie.

Chapter 4 will consider how after the end of public execution the executioner becomes not merely the agent of punishment but a privileged interpreter of it. I will look at case studies of a range of executioners' memoirs including James Berry, John Ellis, Robert Elliott, Syd Dernley and Albert Pierrepoint. I will argue that the consumption of life-writing by executioners was a key means by which readers sought to access sensational direct knowledge of the death penalty. I will first consider these memoirs as testimony, emerging from each executioner's practice of diary-keeping and personal reflection after each execution, and explore how they use writing to process and think through their responsibility for the death of the condemned man. Two further sections will explore on the use of life-writing to represent the embodied mind in the twentieth-century execution, with a focus on both the condemned man and on the executioner.

Chapter 5 will consider the entanglement of animal and human rights in relation to the death penalty. Here I will explore how the use of a parallel between the animal and the condemned man is widespread in both pro- and anti-death penalty discourses: in pro-death penalty arguments, 'mad dog' analogies might be used to support society's right to self-defence through violence, while anti-death penalty activists found animal metaphors useful to provoke sympathy, as well as for suggesting the role of evolutionary determinism in human actions. In the texts I will examine, theories of the 'totem animal' in Freudian psychoanalysis and related anthropology (James Frazer and E. P. Evans) shaped writers' responses to their representation of how criminal and animal bodies might be sacrificed within a system of guilt and punishment. Specific historical contexts will include the involvement of the ASPCA in the development of the electric chair in the 1880s; the Brown Dog affair (1903–1910); Edison's 'execution' of Topsy the elephant in 1903; and James Berry's recollections of similar experiments on animals in the 1890s. In a range of Golden Age detective fiction, we find similar concerns about the meaning of animal deaths (from causes including vivisection, animal cruelty and euthanasia) within narratives about capital crime.

The first chapter of the second section of the book on war and conflict, Chap. 6, will reflect substantially on a specific historical context in the way that writing by Joyce, Yeats and the 1916 revolutionaries converge around the Robert Emmet and Sarah Curran myth of a romantic, nationalistic heroism which welcomes the death penalty. In this sense, I will not seek to demonstrate the 'influence' of the Easter Rising on canonical modernist texts like Joyce's *Ulysses* and Yeats's 'Easter, 1916', but rather to facilitate a dialogue about gender, sexuality and the death penalty theorised through psychoanalytic writing on masochism and evidenced through texts produced by participants in the Rising. Through consideration of nationalist concepts of blood sacrifice and Christ-like iconography, Yeats's theory of a 'vertigo of self-sacrifice', as well as gendered ideas of women's fidelity to their executed men beyond the death sentence, I will consider representations of the death penalty as a source of masochistic pleasure in the context of Irish national struggle. The chapter's ending will highlight key aspects of the changing role of the death penalty through the Irish War of Independence, the Irish Civil War and as far as the Emergency (the Irish name for World War II).

Chapter 7 will consider the trauma of the death penalty alongside war trauma. I will build on Christie Davies's suggestion that the reform and repeal of military and civilian capital punishment ought to be studied together. The 1920s and 1930s saw a cultural processing of the effect of the uniquely widespread use of the military death penalty by British forces during World War I, spurred in particular by A. P. Herbert's novel *The Secret Battle* (1919) and Ernest Thurtle's *Shootings at Dawn* (1924); throughout the interwar years, forms of death sentence were removed, after parliamentary debates which frequently also questioned the value of the civilian death penalty. The first full parliamentary debate on the civilian death penalty took place in 1929, so these debates about the military death penalty undoubtedly had a huge influence on interwar writing in texts by Herbert, Patrick Hamilton and Dorothy L. Sayers. Throughout Sayers's novel series, her detective, Lord Peter Wimsey, finds his shell shock triggered by the death penalty and I will examine how her final novel, *Busman's Honeymoon*, ends with Wimsey's utter psychological breakdown in the face of his actions.

Chapter 8 will reflect substantially on how a racialised death penalty contributes to the psychology of modern literature. In Britain, the domestic logic of the death penalty, including its public safety and deterrence arguments, was underpinned by a need to maintain law and order across the Empire, and the target of this judicial violence was often colonised non-white subjects. Similarly, in the American context, violence against Native Americans and African Americans had been central to the establishment and development of the nation and was perpetuated in the twentieth century by an interdependence between lynching and capital punishment. Reference to psychoanalytic thinking about race and judicial violence, such as the work of Frederic Wertham, Benjamin Karpman and Frantz Fanon, will also problematise Freudian reliance on anthropological thinking. In the first half of the chapter, I will examine how in 1930s representations of the colonial death penalty, authors such as Greene, Orwell and Christie exploit the problem of race primarily to illuminate the psychology of white male central characters. In the second half of this chapter, I will examine literary representations of the American death penalty in the first half of the twentieth century, investigating how a history of slavery and lynching shapes the way black writers represented capital crime and punishment. My particular focus in this section will be on Wright's *Native Son* (1940), but I will also consider how a wider international literary culture identified an intersection between British colonial and American racial violence, as represented by Nancy Cunard's *Negro: An Anthology* (1933).

The final chapter will focus on the World War II experience. Here I will consider representations of civilians who are threatened with the death penalty by legislation including the Emergency Powers (Defence) Act 1939, the Treachery Act 1940 and the Treason Act 1945. Because of the way that the political death penalty reached the mid-century without effective examination, instead, reference to past precedent, and especially to Ireland and the Easter Rising, was an important way that debates about the World War II death penalty were short-circuited during the war. The chapter thus intersects with previous chapters in the 'Conflict' section in representing how the individual's relationship with their nation might be thrown into relief by the death penalty, through themes of sacrifice, fidelity and betrayal. Roger Casement's legacy will be shown to inform texts about the psychology of World War II spies by Rebecca West, Graham Greene, Bowen and Christie. West's nonfictional work and the novels that I will discuss share anxieties around whether the death penalty is an appropriate punishment for 'the enemy within', whether they are a disloyal British citizen or foreign patriot.

My approach here will offer opportunities for transnational thinking about literature and the death penalty in considering Britain, Ireland and the US, especially appropriately given the period's history of international literary movements (such as modernism, surrealism, futurism) and international conflicts (primarily World War I and World War II, as well as colonial warfare and occupation). Ultimately, I aim to explore how studying literature of this period in relation to the death penalty offers opportunities to reshape modernist studies in a more political human rights framework, fitting with recent trends in law and literature research, as well as with New Modernist Studies' expansion of the canon.[82]

Notes

1. See, for example, Laura Poulosky's *Severed Heads and Martyred Souls: Crime and Capital Punishment in French Romantic Literature*, New York: Peter Lang, 2003 and Mark Canuel's *The Shadow of Death: Literature,*

Romanticism, and the Subject of Punishment, Princeton: Princeton University Press, 2007.

2. For example, on nineteenth-century and early twentieth-century American literary activism against the death penalty, see rich work by James Gregory, *Victorians Against the Gallows: Capital Punishment and the Abolitionist Movement in the Nineteenth Century Britain*, New York: I.B. Tauris & Co Ltd, 2012; Paul Christian Jones, *Against the Gallows: Antebellum American Writers and the Movement to Abolish Capital Punishment*, Iowa City: University of Iowa Press, 2011 and John Cyril Barton, *Literary Executions: Capital Punishment and American Culture, 1820–1925*, Baltimore: John Hopkins University Press, 2014. On literature and the contemporary American death penalty, see by Ralph F. Voss, *Truman Capote and the Legacy of* In Cold Blood, Tuscaloosa, Alabama: University of Alabama Press, 2011 and Katy Ryan, *Demands of the Dead: Executions, Storytelling, and Activism in the United States*, Iowa City: University of Iowa Press, 2012.
3. Michel Foucault, *Discipline and Punish: The Birth of the Prison*, New York: Vintage Books, 1995; Jay Paul Gates and Nicole Marafioti, *Capital and Corporal Punishment in Anglo-Saxon England*, Martlesham: Boydell Press, 2014; Nicholas Terpstra, *The Art of Executing Well: Rituals of Execution in Renaissance Italy*, Kirksville: Truman State University Press, 2008.
4. Jacques Derrida, *The Death Penalty: Volume I*, trans. by Peggy Kamuf, Chicago: University of Chicago Press, 2014, and *The Death Penalty: Volume II*, ed. by Geoffrey Bennington and Marc Crépon/trans. by Elizabeth Rottenberg, Chicago: University of Chicago Press, 2017.
5. Derrida, *The Death Penalty: Volume I*, 30.
6. Greta Olson, 'De-Americanizing Law and Literature Narratives: Opening Up the Story', *Law and Literature*, Vol. 22 No. 2 (2010): 338–364 (344, 361).
7. Lizzie Seal, *Capital Punishment in Twentieth-Century Britain: Audience, Justice, Memory*, Abingdon: Routledge, 2014. Lizzie Seal and Alexa Neale, 'Race, Racialisation and "Colonial Common Sense" in Capital Cases of Men of Colour in England and Wales, 1919–1957', 'Special Collection: Literature, Law and Psychoanalysis', *Open Library of Humanities*, Vol. 5 No. 1 (2019) 1–21. https://doi.753org/10.16995/olh.471.
8. Evie Jeffrey, 'Capital Punishment and Women in the British Police Procedural: Josephine Tey's, '*A Shilling for Candles* and *To Love and Be Wise*', *CLUES: A Journal of Detection*, Vol. 37, No. 2 (Fall 2019): 40–50 (42).
9. Jeffrey, 'Capital Punishment and Women', 43.
10. Samantha Walton, *Guilty But Insane: Mind and Law in Golden Age Detective Fiction*, Oxford: Oxford University Press, 2015.
11. On concepts of violence in modernism, see Jonathan Eburne, *Surrealism and the Art of Crime*, Ithaca: Cornell University Press, 2008; Sarah Cole, *At the Violet Hour: Modernism and Violence in England and Ireland*, New York: Oxford University Press, 2012; Paul Sheehan, *Modernism and*

the Aesthetics of Violence, Cambridge: Cambridge University Press, 2013; Kai Evers, *Violent Modernists: The Aesthetics of Destruction in Twentieth-Century German Literature*, Evanston: Northwestern University Press, 2013.

12. Matthew Levay, *Violent Minds: Modernism and the Criminal*, Cambridge: Cambridge University Press, 2019, 5.
13. Levay, *Violent Minds*, 19.
14. Victoria Stewart, *Crime Writing in Interwar Britain: Fact and Fiction in the Golden Age*, Cambridge: Cambridge University Press, 2017, 6.
15. Capital Sentences Committee (Aberdare Committee), *Report of the Committee appointed to inquire into the Existing Practice as to carrying out of Sentences of Death, and the Causes which in several recent Cases have led either to failure or to unseemly occurrences; and to consider and report what arrangements may be adopted (without altering the existing Law) to ensure that all Executions may be carried out in a becoming manner without risk of failure or miscarriage in any respect*, London: Her Majesty's Stationery Office, 1888.
16. Sir Ernest Arthur Gowers et al. *Royal Commission on Capital Punishment, 1949–1953, REPORT, Presented to Parliament by Command of Her Majesty September 1953* (also known as Gowers Commission Report), London: Her Majesty's Stationery Office, 1953, paragraph 247.
17. The National Archives, PCOM 9/2024.
18. The National Archives, PCOM 9/2024.
19. See, for example, The National Archives, PCOM 2331.
20. Syd Dernley with David Newman, *The Hangman's Tale: Memoirs of a Public Executioner*, London: Robert Hale, 1989, 32.
21. Gowers et al. *Royal Commission*, paragraph 13, page 3.
22. Gowers et al. *Royal Commission*, paragraph 13, page 3.
23. Gavin Foster, *The Irish Civil War and Society: Politics, Class and Conflict*, Houndsmills: Palgrave, 2015, 5–6.
24. Anon. 'Defence of the State', *Irish Independent*, 7th May 1925, 7.
25. Anon. 'CAPITAL PUNISHMENT IN IRELAND: Strong Opposition', *The Manchester Guardian*, 7th May 1925, 9.
26. Albert Pierrepoint, *Executioner: Pierrepoin*t, Random Acres: Eric Dobby Press, 2005, 161.
27. James Berry, *My Experiences as an Executioner*, London: Peter Lund & Co, 1892, 137–141.
28. Pierrepoint, *Executioner: Pierrepoint*, 103.
29. Pierrepoint, *Executioner: Pierrepoint*, 109.
30. Ian O'Donnell, *Justice, Mercy, and Caprice: Clemency and the Death Penalty in Ireland*, Oxford: Oxford University Press, 2017, 128.

31. Sonja Tiernan, *Eva Gore-Booth: An image of such politics*, Oxford: Oxford University Press, 2013, 247–250.
32. David Doyle and Ian O'Donnell, 'A Family Affair: English Hangmen and a Dublin Jail, 1923–54', *New Hibernia Review*, Vol. 18, No. 8 (2014): 101–118.
33. Robert G. Elliott and Albert R. Beatty, *Agent of Death: The Memoirs of an Executioner*, London: John Long, 1940, 19.
34. Elliott, *Agent of Death*, 73.
35. Stuart Banner, *The Death Penalty: An American History*, Cambridge (Mass.): Harvard University Press, 2002, 195.
36. Elliott, *Agent of Death*, 168.
37. John Ellis, *Diary of a Hangman*, London: Forum Press, 1996, 22.
38. Pierrepoint, *Executioner: Pierrepoint*, 105 and Ellis, 19.
39. See The National Archives, PCOM 8/185 and PCOM 8/186.
40. Dernley, *The Hangman's Tale*, 34.
41. See, for example, a set of procedural discussions from 1924 on 'Watching Condemned Prisoners', which accepts how difficult the duty was for warders. (The National Archives, PCOM 8/2000).
42. Michal Shapira, *The War Inside: Psychoanalysis, Total War, and the Making of the Democratic Self in Postwar Britain*, Cambridge: Cambridge University Press, 2013, 7.
43. In this context we might consider Foucault's reflection in *The History of Sexuality Volume I* that he could have as easily written about the death penalty as a case study in biopower (trans. Robert Hurley, New York: Vintage, 1978, 137–138). For a theory of the Foucauldian death penalty which is more attentive to *The History of Sexuality* than *Discipline and Punish*, see Michael Meranze, 'Michel Foucault, the Death Penalty and the Crisis of Historical Understanding', *Historical Reflections / Réflexions Historiques* Vol. 29, No. 2 (2003): 191–209.
44. Simon A. Cole and Michael C. Campbell, 'From subhumans to superhumans: Criminals in the evolutionary hierarchy, or what became of Lombroso's atavistic criminals?', *The Cesare Lombroso Handbook*, ed. by Paul Knepper and P.J. Ystehede, Abingdon: Routledge, 2013: 153–154.
45. Elena Past, 'Cesare Lombroso Vivisects the Criminal', *Methods of Murder: Beccarian Introspection and Lombrosian Vivisection in Italian Crime Fiction*, Toronto: University of Toronto Press, 2012: 135–170.
46. Theodor Reik and Sigmund Freud, 'View on Capital Punishment' (1926), in *The Compulsion to Confess: On the Psychoanalysis of Crime and Punishment*, New York: Grove Press, 1961: 469–474 (474).
47. J. B. Pontalis 'On Death-work', *Frontiers in Psychoanalysis: Between the Dream and Psychic Pain*, London: The Hogarth Press, 1981: 184–194 (188–189).

48. T. W. M. 'INSANITY AND CRIME: MEANING OF FREUDIAN DOCTRINE WHAT IT REALLY SAYS', *The Manchester Guardian*, 4th July 1922, 8.
49. More detailed discussion of the Ronald True case occurs in Chap. 7.
50. From our London staff, 'PSYCHO-ANALYSIS AND CRIME: SUBCONSCIOUS MIND THAT STRAYS CRIMINOLOGISTS', *The Manchester Guardian*, 21st November 1923, 10.
51. This essential infrastructure included the London Psychoanalytical Society (1913), British Psychoanalytical Society (1919), the International Psychoanalytic Press and the *International Journal of Psycho-Analysis* (both established 1920), and the Institute of Psycho-Analysis (1924).
52. Edward Cadogan, *The Roots of Evil: Being a Treatise on the Methods of Dealing with Crime and the Criminal During the Eighteenth and Nineteenth Centuries in Relation to Those of a More Enlighted Age*, London: John Murray, 1937, 271.
53. Anne C. Dailey, *Law and the Unconscious: A Psychoanalytic Perspective*, Yale: Yale University Press, 2017.
54. Susan R. Schmeiser, 'Punishing Guilt', 'Special Issue: Legal Analysis', American *Imago*, Vol. 64, No. 3 (2007): 317–337 (326).
55. Anne C. Dailey, 'Preface', 'Special Issue: Legal Analysis', American *Imago*, Vol. 64, No. 3 (2007): 291–295 (291).
56. See Laura Marcus, 'Cinema and Psychoanalysis: Introduction', *Close Up 1927–1933: Cinema and Modernism*, ed. by James Donald et al., Princeton: Princeton University Press, 1998: 241–247.
57. Élisabeth Roudinesco, *Freud: In His Time and Ours*, trans. by Catherine Porter, Harvard: Harvard University Press, 2016, 336.
58. Mary Bosworth, *Explaining U.S. Imprisonment*, London: Sage, 2010, 90–91.
59. Virginia Woolf, *The Diary of Virginia Woolf: Volume II, 1920–1924*, ed. by Anne Olivier Bell, London: The Hogarth Press, 1978, 224–225.
60. Eliot commends the editor of the *Daily Mail* for refusing to depict the executions 'with the flaccid sentimentality of other papers that I have seen, which have been so impudent as to affirm that they represented the great majority of the British people' ('Letter to the Editor', *The Daily Mail*, 8th January, 1923, 8).
61. Vincent Deane, 'Bywaters and the Original Crime', *European Joyce Studies 4: Finnegans Wake: Teems of Times*, ed. by Andrew Treip, Amsterdam: Rodopi, 1994: 165–179.
62. H. L. Mencken, quoted in Peter Orlov, *An American Tragedy: the Perils of the Self-Seeking Success*, Cranbury, NJ: Associated University Press, 1998, 44.

63. James Baldwin, 'Everybody's Protest Novel', *Notes of a Native Son*, Boston: Beacon Press, 1984: 13–23.
64. Seal, *Capital Punishment*, passim.
65. Violet van der Elst, *On the Gallows*, London: Doge Press, 1937, 86–87.
66. Van der Elst, *On the Gallows*, 22–23, 242.
67. Van der Elst, *On the Gallows*, 243.
68. Van der Elst, *On the Gallows*, 32–33.
69. Van der Elst, *On the Gallows*, 41, 49.
70. Van der Elst, *On the Gallows*, 94, 100–101, 158.
71. Clarence Darrow, *An Eye for an Eye*, New York: Duffield and Co, 1920, 14 and 65.
72. Darrow, *An Eye for an Eye*, 210.
73. Clarence Darrow, *Crime and Criminals: An Address Delivered to the Prisoners in the Chicago County Jail*, Chicago: Charles H. Kerr & Company, 1910.
74. Robert McMurdy, 'Preface', *The Upas Tree*, Chicago: F. J. Schulte & Company, 1912, 298.
75. McMurdy, *The Upas Tree*, 298.
76. See, for example, H. M. B. 'Review: *The Upas Tree* by Robert McMurdy', *Michigan Law Review*, Vol. 11, No. 2 (1912): 176–177; J. C. A. 'Review: *The Upas Tree* by Robert McMurdy', *University of Pennsylvania Law Review and American Law Register*, Vol. 62. No.5 (1914): 404–405.
77. The Editor, 'Review: The Upas Tree by Robert McMurdy', *The Virginia Law Register*, Vol. 19, No. 2 (1913): 160; W. M. Lyon Phelps, 'Review: *The Upas Tree* by Robert McMurdy', *The Yale Law Journal*, Vol. 24 No.2 (1914): 172.
78. Greta Olson, 'The Turn to Passion: Has Law and Literature become Law and Affect?', *Law & Literature*, Vol. 28, No. 3 (2016): 335–353. (349, 338).
79. On the execution of Myles Joyce, see Margaret Kelleher's recent *The Maamtrasna Murders: Language, Life and Death in Nineteenth-Century Ireland*, Dublin: University College Dublin Press, 2018.
80. See Katherine Ebury, '"Nothing in the world would save me from the gallows": O'Nolan and the death penalty', in Ruben Borg and Paul Fagan (eds.), *Flann O'Brien: Gallows Humour*, Cork: Cork University Press, 2020.
81. Ralph F. Voss, *Truman Capote and the Legacy of* In Cold Blood, Tuscaloosa, Alabama: University of Alabama Press, 2011, 60–61. Capote does cite West as an influence on *In Cold Blood* but adds that 'at her best (and I think she's remarkable reporter) [she] doesn't do what I'm talking about. I've had this theory that a factual piece of work could explore whole new dimensions in writing that would have a double effect fiction does not have—the very fact of its being true, every word of it true, would add a double contribution of strength and impact' (Capote quoted in Roy Newquist, 'A Rainy Afternoon with Truman Capote' (1964), *Truman*

Capote: Conversations, ed. By M. Thomas Inge, Jackson and London: University Press of Mississippi, 1987: 33–46 (40)).

82. See Greta Olson, 'Futures of Law and Literature: A Preliminary Overview from a Culturalist Perspective', *Recht und Literatur im Zweischenraum/ Law and Literature In-Between*, Bielefield: transcript 2015: 37–69.

CHAPTER 2

Confession and the Self

Introduction

In *Troubling Confessions*, Peter Brooks sums up the different forces at work within the idea of confession in religious, psychoanalytic and legal contexts:

> We worry about the trustworthiness of confessions because the speech-act that begins with the words "I confess" seems to be marked by contradictory intentions and subject to contradictory uses by those receiving this most personal of utterances. We want confessions, yet we are suspicious of them. The law has seen the necessity of attempting to regulate and police confessions: it has tried to establish conditions of the confessional act that guarantee that it has been "voluntarily" made, all the whole authorizing kinds of pressure to confess that run counter to voluntariness. And the law still today—as in medieval times—tends to accept confession as the "queen of proofs".[1]

Brooks is strongly influenced by the thought of Freud's follower Theodor Reik, and Reik will be the guiding spirit in my argument throughout this chapter. E. S. Burt has argued of Derrida's death penalty project that confessional writing has a particular power as an abolitionist challenge to the death penalty: the autobiographical subject 'considers how its private beliefs, practices, interiority and experience harmonise with the state's decisions, so as to bring out the stakes for the subject in the scenes of

K. Ebury, *Modern Literature and the Death Penalty, 1890–1950*, Palgrave Studies in Literature, Culture and Human Rights, https://doi.org/10.1007/978-3-030-52750-1_2

execution'.[2] For Burt, within confession we 'find expression for all the guilty desires and blood-thirsty fascinations, second thoughts, regrets, revolts, relentings or repentings on the death penalty': all those who invest in a position for or against the death penalty experience a recursive moment when they switch into the first person.[3] All these forces are at work in the twentieth-century death penalty, which transforms confession strangely, as we will see, in relation to the mandatory death sentence for the crimes of murder and treason through the culture of biopolitical restriction and secrecy which grew up around this punishment.

In this chapter I will thus examine a formal feature common to many narratives of the death penalty in this period: the extended confession of the murderer, a form of narrative which in the texts I will examine is produced and conditioned by the rhetoric of the death penalty. I will explore this extensive use of confession as a blurring of the 'clue puzzle' detective novel with a modernist, psychoanalytically inflected engagement with the sensational techniques of the psychological thriller. This mode, as Stefano Serafini argues, 'deflected the focus from the rational investigation of the sleuth to the irrational and uncontrollable mind of the criminal'.[4] The relative absence of the direct representation of the death penalty in my chosen texts occurs because several of the narratives examined here will allow the murderer to escape the gallows through suicide, as I will examine in detail in the next chapter. While I will briefly refer to verbal confessions where these are particularly intriguing, what follows will be primarily concerned with the influence of psychoanalysis on written first-person confessions that would lead to the death penalty, whether they are full first-person narratives, as in the case of Agatha Christie's *The Murder of Roger Ackroyd* (1926) and Flann O'Brien's *The Third Policeman* (written 1939, published posthumously 1967) or embedded reflections within third-person narratives, in examples such as Dorothy L. Sayers's *Whose Body?* (1923) and *The Unpleasantness at the Bellona Club* (1928), Elizabeth Bowen's 'The Disinherited' (1934) and in Anne Meredith's *Portrait of a Murderer* (1933). I will close the chapter by examining false confession specifically within Agatha Christie's *Five Little Pigs* (1943) and *Towards Zero* (1944).

These texts will show the unique pressure placed by the death penalty on criminal confession in twentieth-century culture. As Brooks argues, confession is overdetermined because of its traditional importance within religious and secular cultures. A criminal confession might also justify capital punishment when the confessing subject admits their guilt and accepts the penalty for their crime. But these representations of confession are also shaped by two other forces which undermine this apparent sense of justice: (1) the mandatory death sentence for capital crimes, which devalues the form and content of confession as this discourse cannot be used to ameliorate punishment, and (2) the intervention of psychoanalysis in questioning the sincerity of confession and in attacking common sense understandings of criminal motivations and society's retributive impulse.

The Problem of Condemned Prisoners' Writing

This first section of the chapter will focus on Reik as a central, but neglected, theoretical context for examining relationships between confession and capital punishment in the period. Reik's claims about capital punishment, and about punishment more generally, are sourced in theories of confession. Further, the focus of his theory is not merely criminological or penal but specifically targeted at the death penalty: as I highlighted in the introduction, Reik wrote Freud's response to the death penalty in the short essay 'View on Capital Punishment'. In *The Unknown Murderer* (1932), he reflects that modern psychoanalysis has recently discovered 'how little we know of psychological conditions and motives in the psychogenesis of capital crimes'.[5] Reik believes that it is crucial for the psychoanalyst—and he suggests it also ought to be important for a wider society—to value the confession beyond the mere admission of guilt or guilty plea: 'The problem is to lead the criminal to a recognition of his guilt in the psychological sense ("Do you recognize that you are guilty?") and not in the legal sense ("Do you admit to being guilty?")'.[6] Similarly, in *The Compulsion to Confess* (1925), Reik sees repression and the compulsion to confess as related, reciprocal processes, with the will to confess a key cause of the return of the repressed.[7]

Reik identifies masochism as a driver of confession: the confession is simultaneously an appeal for punishment and for forgiveness. He argues that 'In some cases [...] the need for punishment will even be the predominant meaning of the [crime itself]'.[8] Reik seeks to upend a nineteenth-century tradition of criminological thought—criminals do not confess because they are repentant or accidentally betray themselves because they are stupid. Rather criminals wish to be caught on an unconscious level. He argues self-betrayal causes criminals pleasure both in the confession itself and in the punishment through subjection to power. This theory, as Reik intended it to, undermined the principle of deterrence in relation to the death penalty: for criminals, 'a powerful unconscious feeling of guilt existed even before their deeds. This feeling of guilt therefore is not a consequence of the crime. It is, on the contrary, its motive'.[9] In so doing, Reik anticipates by 50 years and more Foucault's paradigm of confession and the incitement to discourse as 'perpetual spirals of power and pleasure'.[10] It was important for Reik to establish confession as simultaneously therapeutic *and* punitive because of his wish to establish psychoanalysis in an abolitionist position in relation to capital punishment: at the end of *The Compulsion to Confess*, Reik imagines a utopian future where all punishment will be replaced by psychoanalysis as a talking cure.[11] By the 1950s, Reik's thought had been assimilated enough into psychoanalytic practice and public discourse that the Royal Commission investigating capital punishment between 1949 and 1953 acknowledged that 'in some very rare cases the existence of capital punishment may act as an incitement to murder on the mentally abnormal'.[12] This is nonetheless a limited application of Reik's ideas, as he believed that such cases were far from rare.

While the compulsion to confess was being positioned as essential to ideas of crime and punishment from a psychoanalytic perspective, the fictional confessions I will discuss in this chapter are intriguing because there was rarely a place for such confession in the court room itself, or indeed anywhere else in culture, in the period in question. While the confession of a murderer, or other criminal, might be a valuable piece of evidence for the police, we should not picture the murderer being given a pen and paper and being told to write a memoir of their life leading up to the crime, no matter how incoherent, irrational or socially unacceptable. Such a confession would instead be the product of careful questioning, and written up as a brief, coherent, factual statement, usually by the police themselves, ventriloquising the culprit's first person. Just as there would be no place for the murderer to express the meaning of his act in the context of his sense of self, as Reik advocated, so there would equally be no place for literary artifice. One influential Golden Age crime novel, Francis Iles's *Malice Aforethought* (1931), includes substantial reflection on the constructed, artificial nature of the police statement. We see Iles's culprit, Dr Bickleigh, give first-person verbal answers to police questions which are gradually transformed into a third-person statement which appears to be voluntarily given, although he experiences coercion. Iles's culprit, Dr Bickleigh, reflects on his interrogation in the moments before he signs the statement:

They had tried to wear him down by keeping him up so late, but again they'd got hold of the wrong man. [...] Dr Bickleigh took the Sergeant's pen from him and bent over the table. He was glowing with triumph. There were one or two awkward juxtapositions in the statement, and a few things which he would have preferred to gloss over or perhaps would have worded differently (in fact the wording all through was absurd; but what could you expect when each single sentence was discussed for several minutes, separately and apart from its context, before being written down?), but nothing to which he could take a real exception.[13]

Iles is careful to show Bickleigh's statement was produced between the hours of 9 pm and 3 am at his home and without legal advice being offered. Bickleigh's request for a break until the following day had been denied by the police: 'It's our rule that statements must be taken straight through without a break'.[14] Bickleigh's mix of superiority and inferiority complexes—which, as Serafini points out, is explicitly diagnosed by Iles's narrator—makes him peculiarly compliant and allows him to believe that he has fooled the police.[15] But Bickleigh nonetheless reflects with clarity that the final sentence of his statement, 'I make this statement quite voluntarily and without being questioned', is, in fact, 'bunkum, of course, just put in to save their faces', even though they had been 'quite reasonable'.[16] The self-betraying statement begins a process which will end with Bickleigh's execution, though, ironically, not for this particular crime.

Reik sees a continuity between earlier cultures of torture and police questioning in the twentieth century, referring to the idea of the 'question by torture'.[17] While he acknowledges that 'The coercion [in recent policing and trial procedure] has now [...] been transferred to such an extent into the psychic realm that it can scarcely be called torture anymore', Reik also believes that the contest between repressive and confessive forces occasioned by the subject being questioned by police or cross-examined by barristers is so painful psychologically for the subject that it remains analogous to torture.[18] In mainstream legal culture John Carter Wood notes that the 1918 Judges' Rules:

expressed an established judicial consensus about questioning: 'voluntary statements' by people in custody were acceptable, but the police were allowed neither to induce them (through threats or promises of lenient treatment) nor to actively question ('cross-examine') prisoners. Only questions "for the purpose of removing ambiguity in what he has actually said" were allowed.[19]

Carter Wood has also shown that anxieties about police procedure around confession and witness testimony, similar to those expressed by Iles in *Malice Aforethought*, persisted: after a series of scandals in the late 1920s, twentieth-century literary culture became alert to the dangers of 'the Third Degree', a concept imported from America to reflect anxieties about the psychological pressure exerted by police interrogation techniques and extended to aggressive cross-examination by barristers during trials.[20] In his 1940s essay 'How Bigger Was Born' explaining the context which informed his novel *Native Son*, which I will discuss in Chap. 8, Richard Wright described how the Third Degree was particularly violent when it came to black suspects:

> After the boy has been grilled night and day, hanged up by his thumbs, dangled by his feet out twenty-story windows, and beaten [...], he signs the papers before him, papers which are usually accompanied by a verbal promise to the boy that he will not go to the electric chair. Of course, he ends up by being executed or sentenced for life.[21]

While these anxieties about 'the Third Degree' extended across different classes of offences and across fields including law, medicine and psychoanalysis, the death sentence itself placed particularly acute pressure on the idea of confession as voluntary or involuntary self-incrimination. This was because, although after 1898 a prisoner was allowed to give evidence in their own defence, in murder trials if they pleaded guilty they would have a very limited opportunity to explain their crime because of the mandatory death sentence. Because of this restriction, in some cases, a confession to capital crime was sometimes considered grounds for an insanity defence.[22] The Gowers Commission note that straightforward confession by the accused was, in the period in question, actively discouraged: 'We understand that in England a plea of guilty is very rarely accepted in murder cases at the present time; and that some judges will never accept such a plea but always insist on strict proof', while in Scotland a guilty plea for murder was not permissible.[23]

But this even-handed discouragement of confession did not always apply in politically sensitive death penalty cases—Ian Cobain notes the example of Henri Lassudry (alias Jose Waldberg), a World War II spy who claimed in last letters written to his family that his barrister had encouraged him to plead guilty under the Treachery Act (1940).[24] Not knowing the mandatory death sentence, Waldberg/Lassudry had hoped to present mitigating evidence, but because of his guilty plea and his trial in-camera he had not been permitted to speak before or after being sentenced to death. As such his sentencing took only three minutes. While similar extenuation had seen another member of the same Abwehr scouting party, Sjoerd Pons, acquitted after a plea of not guilty, Waldberg/Lassudry's belated explanation of the circumstances behind his crime and his plea was not accepted by the Home Secretary as grounds for reprieve. Waldberg/Lassudry had failed to comprehend the drawback of confession to a capital crime in the British system in the period: while confession to other forms of crime would be likely to lead to mitigation of sentence and to greater public sympathy, a confession to capital crimes usually meant a very swift sentencing and execution process.

Similarly, in Rebecca West's *The Meaning of Treason* (1947), to be discussed in Chap. 9, she writes about the execution for treason of John Amery after the court accepted his guilty plea. Amery's motives for pleading guilty to a capital charge are unclear: West groups him among her selection of those traitors who were 'madmen' rather than revolutionaries.[25] His guilty plea was, as West movingly presents it, deeply unsettling for those present at his trial:

> But when the question was put to him he answered, "I plead guilty on all counts", and the trial lasted eight minutes. A murmur ran through the court which was horrified, which was expostulatory, which was tinged with self-pity, for this was suicide. [...] In effect, the young man was saying, "I insist on being hanged by the neck in three weeks' time", and the strength of his desire to die was forcing his weak voice through his shuddering lips and ignoring his pain, which was great, for he was blasted by what he did. He was like an insect that falls on a hot stove and is withered, and what he did felt like an act of cruelty to the whole court. It rejected the life that is in all of us. It could be perceived that the legal tradition whereby a man under a capital charge must be urged by every possible means to plead not guilty is no meddling excess of humanitarianism but is an expression of the fundamental belief of living things in life.[26]

Amery's split self ('his desire to die' versus his embodied and painful wish to live) makes witnesses indignant about retributive justice: they feel that he is 'cruel' in revealing the inflexibility of the law and the M'Naghten Rules in a capital case of treason.[27] In his memoirs the executioner's assistant Syd Dernley describes, with similar incredulity, the case of Patrick Turnage (1950), who again defied established practice by pleading guilty to murder: 'The man was putting the noose around his own neck. There could be no defence now: there was no way that skillful argument could perhaps sway the jury and save him from the drop—there would be no jury. Turnage had decided to be hanged'.[28]

Thus, while the Royal Commission asserted that this practice was generally discouraged, cases such as those of Waldberg/Lassudry's, Amery's and Turnage's showed that it was indeed possible for a criminal to 'decide to be hanged'. Such cases fit within a Reikian masochistic view of confession, despite a legal culture which, as shown in the Gowers Commission report, was supposed to prevent the guilty plea leading to an appearance of hasty and unjust capital procedure. Aside from these legal questions about evidentiary and trial procedure, for practical reasons, the prisoner's legal representation would naturally discourage either an innocence plea or confession after conviction, pending an appeal. Further, there would be no automatic right for the condemned person to make such a statement to the court: they might be allowed to speak, or they might not be.

These tensions about the speech of the condemned man are especially visible in the case of Roger Casement, executed for treason in 1916, who made a memorable statement usually published as his 'Speech from the Dock'.[29] This speech, which will be discussed elsewhere, led to a wider legal debate after the trial about the right of the condemned prisoner to speak and what they might be permitted to say. The Lord Chief Justice was criticised by legal voices, including Sir Harry Poland and Sir Homewood Crawford, for allowing Casement to make his statement. Summing up these arguments in the Notable British Trials series, George H. Knott writes that 'The usual practice before trials, especially for capital sentences, is to allow the prisoner to make a verbal statement before sentence [...] But [...] this is not a right, but a grace or judicial courtesy; and the prisoner has no legal claim to do more than take objection to the verdict and judgement'.[30] In rebuking the Lord Chief Justice, Crawford cited the precedent of the murderer Henry Wainwright (1875) who had 'the reputation of being an eloquent speaker, and was evidently about to exercise his gift', but the judge interrupted him to say, 'I cannot allow you to make a speech' and to ask for a simple answer to the question of sentence.[31] Crawford suggested that the Lord Chief Justice in the 1916 treason trial should have prevented Casement from speaking. The use of the Wainwright precedent in relation to Casement's speech was also designed to build on arguments made during the trial that compared Casement's treason to murder: the official statement released after his execution uses emotive language to reinforce this image, stating that some of the Irish prisoners of war who Casement had attempted to suborn, have since 'died [...] regarding Casement as their murderer'.[32]

Given that the public speech of a condemned prisoner was constrained and contentious, private communications during the period between trial and execution were also often restricted. A 'Standing Order' dating from 19 February 1904 requires that Prison Governors treat the letters of capital offenders differently to those of ordinary prisoners:

> 584A. (1) Great care will be exercised by Governors before passing any letters received or written by a prisoner under sentence of death.
>
> (2) Any such letters will be submitted to the Commissioners should they, in the opinion of the Governor, contain other than quite ordinary matter, or matter which might be of importance to the Secretary of State, as bearing on the case in any way.[33]

While condemned prisoners might well have understood that their letters were being read by the Prison Governor, it is unlikely that they would have suspected how their last letters might be directly used as evidence for or against a reprieve.[34] In rare cases, letters *received* by the prisoner might also be incriminating.[35] 1920s discussions of prisoners' letters instigated by Sir Ernley Blackwell (Under Secretary of State at the Home Office) are preserved in the Prison Commission archive.[36] Blackwell raises the question of limiting the number of letters a condemned man could send: 'At present a prisoner may write any number, throwing a great strain on the Governor who is personally responsible for their contents under S. O. 192, etc'. Blackwell also asks the Prison Commission to consider issuing a warning to the condemned prisoner that 'if any of his correspondence (? Incoming and outgoing) is made use of for press purposes a prisoner should not be allowed to write or receive letters'. The Prison Commission show a more sympathetic understanding of the range of motives and purposes for which a condemned person might enter a correspondence, calling letters 'an emotional outlet', and noting the difficulty of keeping such letters out of the newspapers given the financial pressures involved in a capital case: 'it is not an unknown thing I believe for the defence to be subsidised by the press for the sake of the copy'.[37] In Dorothy L. Sayers's *Strong Poison* (1930), Harriet Vane's defence for a capital crime is supported by 'a certain newspaper' who 'expect a scoop'.[38] The Commission in essence reject Blackwell's proposal, suggesting that the only limits on such letters should be that they are addressed to close friends and family and limited to one letter per day per correspondent. But they do concede the desirability of keeping prisoners' letters secret and avoiding publicity.[39]

It is also uncertain whether condemned prisoners would have realised that their letters could be destroyed outright, rather than merely censored. These 1920s discussions throw up at least one example where a prisoner's last letter might be said to have been unjustly intercepted. Blackwell notes that the last letter written before execution at Wandsworth in 1927 by a prisoner called James Murphy 'contained libellous statements about the evidence of Inspector Hedges': after ascertaining that Murphy had been visited by his wife before his execution, Blackwell kept back the letter and destroyed it.[40] Similarly, we have already noted the suggestion that Casement's 'Speech from the Dock' should have been censored, and while some of the letters written before his execution have survived, at least two of his last letters were destroyed. After his execution at Pentonville, the Prison Governor wrote to the Home Office enclosing letters written by Casement on 27th of July and 1st of August: 'The two letters herewith should I think be stopped. They would probably be used for purposes of agitation in Ireland and America. I posted the third letter. ? suppress them'.[41] The Home Office, via Blackwell who had taken personal charge of the Casement case, responded:

> Casement set himself to write letters to his friends which should be used by them to make a martyr of him. The 1. of 27 July was of this kind. The principal reason used against executing him was that he might become a martyr and it wd. have been impossible to justify the passing of a letter if it had been published as would certainly have been the case.
>
> Miss O'Farrelly refers to the letter of 1 Augt. It is of the same sort but it is treasonable as well. He asks his friends to 'roll away the stone from his grave'. This kind of stuff would go down with people unacquainted with his other writings and the most engrossing pursuit of his life [...]
>
> These letters are clearly of 'objectionable tendency' and are forbidden [...].
>
> And destroy these 3 letters.

While the Prison Governor is clear that Casement's third letter is to his mind unobjectionable and has indeed already been posted, Blackwell's final demand that all *three* letters written by Casement be destroyed is excessive and was by then impossible. Following this thread from

Blackwell's experience of the Casement case to the letters of the 1920s, I suggest that this experience had shaped his attitude to prisoners' writings in general.

It is naturally very difficult to find archival traces of suppressed writing by condemned prisoners. But from the evidence I have found in the very different cases and kinds of writing practiced by Roger Casement (a sensational treason trial involving a knight of the realm, 1916) and James Murphy (an 'ordinary' murder in commission of a robbery, 1927), I conclude that the official withholding and destruction of personal writing by capital offenders was reasonably widespread in the period in question. In Waldberg's/Lassudry's last letters, discussed above in the context of confession and mitigation in relation to a guilty plea, he writes to his mother: 'God knows when you will get this letter. Maybe in a year, or even two'.[42] The question is *when*, not *if*, she will receive the letter: Lassudry does not comprehend that the content of his confession, criticism of the British justice system, means that his letter will be suppressed. As Cobain notes, the letters were not sent to his family but passed instead to MI5 where they were held under seal until they entered the National Archives in 2005.[43] It is noteworthy that these letters, but not Casement's or James Murphy's, were at least preserved, though suppressed, and this seems to be a function of the British Government's anxiety about in-camera trials during World War II: while they were deliberately kept from circulation, Waldman's/Lassudry's letters could also be produced if needed.

As the century progressed, the Official Secrets Act further constrained the publication of life-writing by executioners, while journalists were not permitted at executions: therefore, the confessions of condemned prisoners, whether written or verbal, rarely found an audience. Public knowledge of the lives of condemned prisoners post-sentence was often limited by the Official Secrets Act even in more mundane disclosures, with Cobain noting the 1926 case of 'a retired governor of Pentonville prison [who] was fined £250 under the Act for revealing the details of the last hours of a convicted murderer'.[44] Prison Governors were likewise forbidden from disclosing whether prisoners had confessed on the scaffold or not, even to the Coroner during the inquest on the death.[45]

This British and Irish culture of secrecy and restriction was different to the American context, where journalists and official witnesses would often relay the condemned person's last words. A further difference is the mandatory capital sentence, for the American legal context had then, as today, two degrees of murder. Robert Elliott, the American executioner, notes that condemned people arriving in the execution chamber 'realize that anything they say, be it only a brief farewell, will be published in the newspapers. It is usually obvious that they have carefully planned and memorized their words'.[46] Narratives by condemned prisoners were often freely published in American newspapers and magazines, while they were waiting on death row or after their execution. In James M. Cain's hard-boiled thriller *The Postman Always Rings Twice* (1934), it is eventually revealed that the narrator has all along been producing his narrative for the prison chaplain who will publish his story after his execution.[47]

A wide range of popular and accessible trial transcripts, such as the *Notable British Trials* series and the *Penguin Famous Trials* series, meant that as Victoria Stewart has shown, 'A much larger audience could read about trials, and indeed executions, than could ever have attended either'.[48] However, it is also the case that this audience would have had very limited opportunities to gain knowledge of the crime from the condemned criminal's perspective. As Brooks argues, privacy and secrecy within the penal system 'produces a gap in our knowledge' which 'demands to be filled and activates the interpreter's ingenuity'.[49] Fictional confession therefore filled an appetite for writing about capital crimes and punishments and hid the evidence of a deliberate suppression of nonfictional confessional writing. The public craving for confessional writing by condemned men certainly far exceeded the amount of material allowed to circulate publicly in the culture of the day. But people may have felt that they had greater access to information about capital punishment than they really had, via these surrogate fictional texts. In short, I will argue in what follows that twentieth-century British writers produce fictional texts about the death penalty because of a lack of access to it.

The Compulsion to Confess

As examined in the previous section, there was a great deal of cultural scepticism around the value and meaning of confession, which, despite his emphasis on its importance, was shared by Reik himself. His theory does not imply that confessional utterances and texts can be easily and straightforwardly read and interpreted by the psychoanalyst, especially in criminal cases. He argues that, 'For the perpetrator also, the crime is a traumatic event that has flooded the psychic apparatus… sometimes it takes the criminal years before he knows what he has done and what his deed means'.[50] Similarly, Reik emphasises that a confession must only serve as proof for a criminologist where there is a clear motive, but that even in cases where there is no positive insanity the nature of the unconscious means that the truth of any case may be more complicated. Emphasis on plausible, normal motives suggests a simplistic view of the mind, Reik suggests,

> Without understanding the course of certain ego-agencies, the unconscious need for punishment and the compulsion to confess, certain confessions will, of course, be difficult to comprehend. The criminal himself can say nothing as to the nature of the unconscious processes, the result of which is the confession. This means that he can say nothing that would suffice for their explanation.[51]

Reik argues that this distortion, associated with a view of the crime as 'a traumatic event' that the perpetrator is also somewhat a victim of, may have a palpable effect on the form and content of the confession itself. This section will discuss the effect of a compulsion to confess on real and fictional narratives of capital crime.

Earlier examples of criminal confessions, as Brooks argues, such as the public *amende honorable* or the Newgate Calendar, tended to offer closure: 'In the demand for a final confession by the convicted criminal—who will be executed with or without it—we may recognize society's need to confirm its assignments of guilt and punishment, and, beyond that, perhaps a generalized desire for transparency'.[52] But Carl R. Lovitt notes the unique quality of the writing produced by the condemned man in terms of reader response: 'Confronting greater [reader] resistance than any other category of writers, the confessing murderer must overcome a complete lack of credibility before his assertions can be taken seriously'.[53] Confessions in the period examined by this chapter are perhaps uniquely unsettling, straining at the limits of formal and psychological realism. For example, the gothic, circular narrative of Flann O'Brien's *The Third Policeman* (written 1939), where the narrator turns out to have died soon after his crime without realising it, is an extreme case, but there are many other instances: similarly to O'Brien's text, Christie's *The Murder of Roger Ackroyd* (1926) tempts us to reread from the beginning in the light of the final confessional revelation that our narrator is indeed the culprit. Pierre Bayard writes that *Roger Ackroyd* 'is a book that contains at least two books, explicitly composed for the sake of a rereading'.[54] These formal features hinder the reader's likely sense of closure, and often these confessions did not provide full resolution to the narratives in which they appear. Instead, as the comparatively experimental examples of *The Third Policeman* and *Roger Ackroyd* suggest, destabilising questions about the death penalty and the psychology of the condemned person might be raised by a fictional confession.

Confession often alters the form of the text itself and its style of narration. For example, in Elizabeth Bowen's short story, 'The Disinherited' (1934), a double murderer, whose true name we never learn but who calls himself Prothero, compulsively writes out each night the story of how he murdered his lover in a fit of passion and killed another man in order to assume his identity and escape the death penalty. In Bowen's text, the crime insists upon being processed through confession to the murdered mistress, through an obsessive use of the second-person: 'You said what you'd said before. I saw a red mist where your face was, just a red mist on the pillow. I took the pillow and smothered you'.[55] But what the mistress said in provocation of the man remains repressed and obscure. The repressive impulse works alongside the fear of the death penalty to ensure that this remains auto-confession, as the pages on which Prothero writes his story must be burnt every night: 'rising, an automatic and mindless movement, he flung open the lid of the stove with a pothook and thrust the papers in […] So his nights succeeded each other'.[56] Bowen's story starts in a distanced third-person, which is closest to the perspective of the character Davina (Prothero's employer's niece who has begun a strange flirtation with him); the text then moves into a mix of first- and second-person to give Prothero's perspective on his crime and then returns to the third-person primarily concerned with Davina.

Similarly, Anne Meredith's 'crime story' *Portrait of a Murderer* (1933) begins with a distanced and slightly ironic third-person narration, but early on breaks into the written confession of the murderer, the painter Brand Gray, who has killed his father in a fit of passion. Meredith's text therefore takes the form of the 'crime story' discussed by Sayers as 'psychological studies of the criminal mind'[57] or the 'inverted detective story', a term coined in a 1924 essay by R. Austin Freeman.[58] Brand Gray's killing of his father is of course the classic Oedipal crime, and Freud's complex appears central to Meredith's understanding of Brand's psychology. Indeed, Derrida argues that Freud, in the essay 'The Taboo of Virginity', implies that 'the castration complex' is the cause of unconscious guilt behind both murder and the death penalty.[59] In Meredith's first-person narrative at the centre of *Portrait of a Murderer*, Brand reflects on how he attempted to process the immediate aftermath of the murder of his father through the logic of vengeance and sacrifice central to the talionic law:

> I suppose it isn't a very ordinary situation. Not many men can have murdered their father in a fit of rage; and so it may be difficult for the majority to believe that I simply couldn't understand, couldn't make my mind understand, that is—what had occurred. I repeated over and over again, "He's dead. I've killed him. I'm a murderer. Murderers hang." But it was no use. I couldn't believe it, and presently, through sheer repetition, the words ceased to have any meaning at all, and became as incongruous as any casual collection of letters might, if you stared at them long enough. Even the word "murderer," the word "hang," meant nothing.[60]

Brand will repeatedly use this phrase 'murderers hang' in his narrative as he continues to internally confess his guilt, but this repetition is a marker of his failure to accept the crime and of his fear of the death penalty. There is no progress in his thinking as, nearly a hundred pages later, he repeats the very terms of his initial shock: 'He's dead. I've killed him. I'm a murderer. Murderers hang'.[61] The phrase thus appears to be merely a masochistic repetition compulsion, reflective of the way that, as Reik suggests, 'The unconscious does not forgive; the unconscious is inflexible in its desire to punish, to pay or make pay'.[62]

Although during this first-person narrative Brand establishes a plan to hide his guilt and evade the death penalty, his confession does not offer closure. Brand's narration must therefore make way for a more conventional crime and punishment narrative: Meredith's novel returns to the third-person to follow the police investigation from the more detached perspectives of his siblings and, crucially, his brother-in-law, Miles Amery, a solicitor who informally investigates the crime. Brand's confession, because of his profession as a painter, also takes another form of self-betrayal: on the night he kills his father, he uses the mirror to sketch a picture of his own face, which, throughout the investigation of his crime, he works into his masterpiece, the eponymous portrait of a murderer. Brand reflects when confronted with his crime: 'A picture may lead one man to the Academy and another, it seems, to the gallows'.[63] Miles Amery considers the painting a 'death warrant' but also succumbs to the powerful effect of the image, which Meredith uses to revalue the artist-murderer in a way that neither the written confession nor a legal trial could: 'In the drab futility of the dead man, in the energy of purpose of the murderer,

Brand had achieved a masterpiece'.[64] While Meredith will not allow her murderer to escape the talionic law that demands his death in revenge, her representation of the painting nonetheless echoes Brand's belief that his life is inherently more valuable than his father's life, or the life of Eustace Moore, the man he framed. In response to the picture, Amery himself experiences an impulse to sacrifice Eustace's life for Brand's sake, 'to destroy the envelope and its contents, and let that grey-faced, shuddering creature in a Grebeshire gaol take his chance. It wasn't as if his life was of any value'.[65] In Meredith's psychoanalytic design of the narrative, the picture seems to represent the power, and perhaps even the beauty, of the primal drive to kill associated with the id. Brand is eventually forced to produce the written confession that we have already read and then allowed to commit suicide. Brand does not value his written confession as he values the painting—his last gesture is to ignore the document that Amery is taking away and to sign the painting instead—and similarly the 'Epilogue' to the whole book is from a review of the exhibition in which Brand's painting is identified as its *pièce de résistance*. To sum up, in both Bowen's and Meredith's texts, the first-person confession of the murderer deforms and alters the form of the text surrounding it, but is not felt to be sufficient in itself, and it does not offer the reader narrative resolution. Indeed, several Bowen critics have felt that Prothero's confession is ultimately unsuccessful in its integration into the story given its clash with Davina's perspective.[66] Confession is literally at the centre of each text, but cannot be the metaphorical heart of it: these narratives might thus frustrate or disappoint their readers.

While the confessions of Bowen's Prothero and Meredith's Brand Gray are quite emotional, Reik also argues that the appearance of rational thought in a confession, which might lead to presumption of premeditation and a harsher view of the crime (with less likelihood of a reprieve), could suggest a lack of criminal responsibility via insanity more powerfully than a more conventionally emotional one:

> A criminal who recounts his deed entirely without affect, like a police report, may be compared to a neurotic who tells of the very essence of his disturbance in such a manner than any indication of affect is missing. In such a case, the emotion is often found to be a displaced one. The need for punishment is certainly of determining influence in this displacement of affect.[67]

In a telling example of a pathological, unemotional drive to confess occurs in Dorothy L. Sayers's first Lord Peter Wimsey novel, *Whose Body?* (1923). Her culprit, Sir Julian Freke, is an anti-Freudian psychoanalyst, the author of a telling list of books including—*Some Notes on the Pathological Aspects of Genius*, 1892; *Modern Developments in Psycho-Therapy: A Criticism*, 1910; *An Answer to Professor Freud, with a Description of Some Experiments Carried Out at the Base Hospital at Amiens*, 1919—and, just published as Wimsey investigates the crime Freke is eventually proved to have committed, a new book called *The Physiological Bases of the Conscience*.[68] Freke's crime is the murder of his past love rival, Sir Reuben Levy, which he has been contemplating for many years; I will discuss the details of this crime more in Chap. 5. When Freke is warned of his potential arrest by Wimsey, he is apparently determined to avoid the death penalty through suicide and begins to write a confession in which he claims to have avoided any sense of guilt or emotion.[69] But though he knows he has only a little time to spare before he is arrested, Freke's confession runs to 17 pages in Sayers's novel, including a lengthy post-script. Freke is still confessing, this time to the attempted murder of Wimsey himself, at the time of his arrest:

> No trace would have been left in your body of the injection, which consisted of a harmless preparation of strychnine, mixed with an almost unknown poison, for which there is at present no recognized test, a concentrated solution of sn—At this point the manuscript broke off.[70]

Wimsey reflects on the excessive, dangerous qualities of Freke's confession, which means that despite his intentions, Freke will still suffer death on the gallows, rather than the painless death he supposedly aimed for:

> 'Isn't it queer?' said Lord Peter. 'All that coolness, all those brains—and then he couldn't resist writing a confession to show how clever he was, even to keep his head out of the noose.'[71]

The character of Julian Freke seems expressly designed by Sayers to demonstrate the value of a Freudian psychoanalysis for considering questions of crime and punishment. Despite all his conscious rejection of Freud, Freke shows an unconscious masochistic impulse towards the death penalty which manifests itself as excessive, compulsive confession: he is writing his autobiography, his Last Will and Testament, and his death warrant, all at the same time.

In a few of the texts examined in this chapter, we see a striking flatness and off-handedness of tone and a similar lack of affect to that described by Reik, as each author risks banality in challenging the reader's wished-for experience of the drama of fictional confession. As with Freke, whose name tells us all we need to know, these characters' confessions reflect the need for punishment in their displacement of affect, as well exhibiting features of what Bayard calls a delusional, or paranoid rationality.[72] Opening his narrative, the narrator of Flann O'Brien's *The Third Policeman* confesses immediately, ramblingly:

> Not everybody knows how I killed old Phillip Mathers, smashing his jaw in with my spade; but first it is better to speak of my friendship with John Divney because it was he who first knocked old Mathers down by giving him a great blow in the neck with a special bicycle-pump which he manufactured himself out of a hollow iron bar.[73]

Similarly, closing his narrative, about to commit suicide to save himself from disgrace and the death penalty, Dr Sheppard, the narrator of *The Murder of Roger Ackroyd*, designs his suicide to mirror his 'murder' (through blackmail) of Mrs Ferrars with veronal. But his last recorded words are banal, about cucurbits: 'I feel no pity for her. I have no pity for myself either. So let it be veronal. But I wish Hercule Poirot had never retired from work and come here to grow vegetable marrows'.[74] Sheppard's utterance creates a relationship between himself and his victim in choosing the same drug: repeating the phrase 'no pity' the confession also registers a lack of affective response.

A superficial reading would suggest that neither Christie's nor O'Brien's narrator felt guilt, but instead their fear of the death penalty is figured in their construction and narration of an alternate reality (for O'Brien's narrator this reality is the fantastic world of the Parish, for Christie's the distortions Sheppard introduces into his diary) which both hides and obliquely reveals the crime. Along with this alternate reality, where punishment is threatened but always deferred, each narrator creates a shadow self—when Poirot accuses Christie's narrator, he says not 'you', but 'Dr. Sheppard' committed the crime,[75] when O'Brien's narrator enters the Parish, he loses his name and gains 'a soul', called Joe, who consistently speaks the truth of his guilt to him when he cannot acknowledge it.[76] In these narratives we see a battle between Reikian conflicting forces of repression and confession. Within the idea of confession itself, these narrators vacillate between auto-confession and confession for a broader audience. The narrator of *The Third Policeman* denies his guilt, to himself, to Joe and to others, within the plot of the novel, so that we can picture this as an auto-confession (especially given his beyond-the-grave status). But he is also, at least in the opening, conscious of an audience which may or may not know of his crime and its context ('Not everybody knows [...] but first it is better to speak of').[77] Similarly, while by the end of the narrative Poirot has insisted that Sheppard must finish his story and confess his crime, he initially begins to write without apparent sense of audience, out of an impulse within himself: 'Mrs Ferrars died on the night of the 16–17th September—a Thursday'.[78] From the point of view of a psychoanalytic argument, Samantha Walton and Serafini each argue that Sheppard's split self also has a dangerous effect on the reader: as Serafini summarises, 'Although the detective is ultimately able to outwit and capture the criminal, he cannot actually suppress the deviant self, because the reader's dangerous identification has already taken place'.[79]

In this section I have used Reik's theories to examine 'true' confessions of murder, discourses produced by each narrator through a sense of their condemnation to death, in which the reader is encouraged to accept, gauging the twin representation of self-punishment caused by guilt alongside the demand for retributive punishment demanded by society. In the last section of the chapter, I will consider the psychoanalytic challenge to the death penalty even more directly through a focus on false confessions which might lead to a miscarriage of justice.

The Death Penalty and the Psychology of False Confession

Freud would claim in his 1906 public lecture to future judges that 'in your examination you may be led astray by a neurotic who, although he is innocent, reacts as if he were guilty, because a lurking sense of guilt that already exists in him seizes upon the accusation made in this particular instance'.[80] He asserts that this is true not just in extreme cases, but that many people might confess falsely. Legal practice, especially around confession and interrogation, must therefore aim to 'succeed in distinguishing self-accusing individuals from those who are really guilty'.[81] In 1924 he would update his theory in response to his new sense of the centrality of the death drive,[82] in 'The Economic Problem of Masochism', which argues that an 'unconscious sense of guilt' should be called 'the need for punishment', which is itself the same as masochism and 'identical with' the death instinct.[83] All this allows Freud to assert that 'even the subject's destruction of himself cannot take place without libidinal satisfaction'.[84] Although psychoanalytic critics of Golden Age fiction such as Walton and Serafini have applied these concepts successfully to guilty criminals with a diverse range of mental disorders, the phenomenon of false confession to capital crime has never previously been examined.

In *The Unknown Murderer*, Reik uses the idea of false confession to pick away at 'common sense' notions of crime and punishment, such as the question of why someone would confess to a capital crime that they had not committed, even though this would mean their death. In Reik's view, the person might confess from a specific sense of guilt because they unconsciously *wished* to commit the crime or from a more generalised sense of guilt associated with the Oedipus complex. It is perhaps because of a literary sense of the value of the confessional mode (from Rousseau to today's 'New Sincerity') that public awareness of the concept of false confession has waxed and waned so much. Brooks reminds us that for writers like Moses Maimonides, coming from a different legal and cultural tradition, 'Talmudic law [...] traditionally did not allow confessions from the accused: they appeared contrary to the instinct for self-preservation, something like a product of the death drive'.[85] Certainly, in Talmudic law, no one could be executed simply on their own admission of guilt without other corroborating evidence, because there was too much risk involved. But it is only fairly recently that contemporary legal culture has rediscovered the psychology of false confession.[86]

Indeed, in relation to false confession, Reik further deliberately troubles the boundary between premeditation and accidental action, and between wishing to kill and actually killing:

> If we all unconsciously harbour such evil wishes, if their domain is so extensive that judges sometimes arrive at false conclusions on the strength of them, is there really such a world of difference between the wish and the deed? Is punishment really the proper reaction to a breaking through of the boundary line between the two?...If the man who has only wished to murder is completely innocent while he who has accidentally occasioned it has to suffer the extreme penalty, then the idea of justice becomes quite grotesque.[87]

In relation to this, in F. Tennyson Jesse's *A Pin to See the Peepshow*, her protagonist Julia Starling is condemned to death for her unacted desires. Having lived her whole life mainly through imagination, she writes letters to her lover, Leonard Carr, expressing a fantastic wish to be like Lucrezia Borgia and poison her husband: 'Naturally, she would never really kill anyone, but it would be marvellous to feel that you were what she had read of in books, one of the "great lovers of history"'.[88] Like Edith Thompson, it is for these letters confessing the wish to kill that Julia is condemned to death by her society, as during her lover's murderous assault on her husband she was instinctively appalled: 'She screamed from the moment Leo first hit Herbert'.[89] Leonard Carr likewise did not believe he was taking Julia's fantasies seriously, but did respond to her love letters as incitement to murder on an apparently unconscious level. (Even during his trial, Carr seems not to have realised the meaning of his act.) Ultimately Julia's letters betray her by *appearing* confessional when they are merely fantastic false confessions.[90] Indeed, for Roseanne Kennedy, re-examining Edith Thompson's letters, the truth status of Thompson's own confessional fantasies of killing her husband is 'not to be found in her letters', but only in her relationship with Bywaters as receiver of her confessions (whose own letters are mostly destroyed or missing).[91] Kennedy argues that Thompson's defence barrister's understanding of her letters as a complex mix of reality, fantasy and performance 'would find support from epistolary criticism and theory today'.[92] One of Jesse's core lessons in writing the book is a modernist, psychoanalytic sense of the unknowability of the other person: '"Knowing" anyone is only the getting together of a collection of these little points, or catching a spark as it flies off the surface of the mind struck at a certain angle for a brief flash'.[93] Jesse's other goal is to stress a sense of tragic inevitability, which, as Stewart suggests, is also true of Jesse's criminological work especially in *Murder and Its Motives*.[94] Revealingly, Jesse wrote the beginning of the story with Julia's childhood and then the ending with her execution before constructing any of the main body of the narrative.[95] In short, Julia Starling is a psychological study of a self-betraying character who is designed to be put to death.

As we have seen in Reik's work, psychoanalysis was keen to put pressure on the authenticity and legibility of confession—the extreme case of this is Bayard's reinvestigation of *The Murder of Roger Ackroyd*. He reads the novel against its grain to discredit Sheppard's apparent confession. One of his key questions is a metafictional one: whether Christie understood the ending of her own book and therefore 'tricks' us into accepting a false confession or whether she had fallen under the spell of her own narrator and does not understand her own real meaning. Bayard suggests that the real contest of the novel is between Poirot and Sheppard's sister Caroline, who he identifies as the real killer, as well a figure of the authorial function. For Bayard, Caroline's doctor brother confesses falsely to shield her (successfully) from the suspicions of Poirot and the reader. He concludes that to interpret Sheppard's confession as false is to turn the novel into the story of 'the slow execution of Dr. Sheppard, the victim of Hercule Poirot's murderous delusion'.[96] The most important lesson from Bayard's exercise, whether he convinces us about Caroline or not, is that first-person confessions might not resolve the plot or might multiply uncertainty, especially where the character is speaking to us about crime, trauma, mental illness or all three.

While readers are encouraged to take many examples of confession in Golden Age detective fiction seriously, in a more complicated case, which occurs in *The Unpleasantness at the Bellona Club* (1928), Wimsey is shown the written confession of the shell shocked Captain George Fentiman, who has turned himself in for the murder of his grandfather:

> It was written in a staggering handwriting, much blotted and erased, with words left out and repeated here and there: 'I am making this statement quickly while he is asleep, because if I wait he may wake up and stop me. You will say I was moved and seduced by instigation of but what they will not understand is that he is me and I am him. I killed my grandfather by giving him digitalin. I did not remember it till I saw the name on the bottle, but they have been looking for me ever since, so I know that he must have done it. That is why they began following me about, but he is very clever and misleads them. When he is awake. We were dancing all last night and that is why he is tired. He told me to smash the bottle so that you shouldn't find out, but they know I was the last person to see him. He is very cunning, but if you creep on him quickly now that he is asleep you will be able to bind him in chains and cast him into the pit and then I shall be able to sleep. George Fentiman'.[97]

Here the formal texture of Sayers's writing, and even the way the handwriting of her character is introduced ('staggering', 'blotted', 'erased'), suggests Reikian counterforces of repression and confession. Reik suggests that fantasies of the death penalty confessed to by his patients display a particularly Gothic, Medieval atmosphere, with a particular interest in torture.[98] Fentiman, similarly, has masochistic, Biblical fantasies of punishment, asking the police to 'bind him in chains and cast him into the pit', which, however out of place in a twentieth-century literary environment, do reflect in a distorted mirror the violence of retributive justice. Traumatised by war, and unsure of his mind, Fentiman unconsciously seeks the death penalty as a way out of a life that feels untenable.

The police surgeon smugly diagnoses Fentiman, 'Nervous shock with well-marked delusions [...] A hundred years ago they'd have called it diabolic possession, but we know better'.[99] But the key question posed by Parker, the police detective, is: 'do you think he is under a delusion in saying he murdered his grandfather? Or did he actually murder him under the influence of this diabolical delusion? That's the point'.[100] Parker's question is one of guilt and also, implicitly, whether Fentiman could be executed for his crime. The police surgeon suggests that Fentiman may not be 'permanently insane', but instead currently suffering a 'nerve storm', making it unclear if he might be facing the gallows.[101] Sayers in fact makes the text of this false confession very plausible. Fentiman shows features of trauma and self-division in relation to the crime, marked by the unnerving use of 'I' and 'he' to refer to the confessing self and the self which may have killed, respectively (at times 'he' also refers to the victim, the murdered grandfather). Further, Fentiman's delusion includes specific, though confused, evidence about the crime and its investigation including the method of murder, the clue of the broken medicine bottle and the fact that he was the last to see his grandfather alive. According to Reik, for Fentiman to develop this delusion, he must also, given his plausible motive, a large inheritance, have unconsciously wished to kill his grandfather. Ultimately Wimsey's investigation will disprove this written confession, even though it could easily be part of an end sequence leading to the resolution of the mystery. In Chap. 7, I will examine other cases where war guilt shapes fictional representations of both murder and capital punishment.

Christie's oeuvre also shows her understanding of this psychoanalytic premise of false confession, despite her broad support for the legal system and the death penalty. In the years after the initial translation of Reik's works into English by the Hogarth press, Christie goes through a phase of exploring the narrative implications of false confession, so that we might suspect a direct influence. For example, in *Five Little Pigs* (1943), Poirot reinvestigates an old crime where a character, Caroline Crale, falsely confessed to the murder of her husband for three interlinked reasons:

1. She believed that her sister Angela, who she had disfigured in fit of childhood jealousy by throwing a paperweight into her cradle, was the real culprit.
2. She had unconsciously wished to take revenge on her husband for his adultery.
3. She had consciously considered suicide before her husband's death and unconsciously still wished to die.

Before her death (from illness while in prison) she writes an ambiguous, coded confession to her sister, which can be read as either an admission of guilt or as reassurance that she will take the blame. Caroline sacrificed herself to redeem her act of childhood violence, which she believed was as bad as murder. As Poirot reflects when he learns the truth, 'Because of her belief that she was paying that debt, the ordeal of trial and condemnation could not touch her. It is a strange thing to say of a condemned murderess—but she had everything to make her happy'.[102] Caroline's apparent confession is more legible as rational than Fentiman's, but it is ambiguous enough to lead to a miscarriage of justice and to implicitly question the death penalty.

Christie's next novel, *Towards Zero* (1944), features an even more explicitly Reikian understanding of false confession. It opens with Sylvia, the young daughter of the detective, Superintendent Battle, falsely confessing to a series of petty thefts at her school. Her teacher, Miss Amphrey, who has inadvertently pressured her pupil to confess, has embraced an imperfect, coercive understanding of psychoanalysis. Miss Amphrey's method is to set a word association test for Sylvia, who looked 'guilty—confused', as a psychological experiment: 'I wanted, not to *confront* her with her guilt, but to get her to admit it *herself*'.[103] Her father, knowing his child better, challenges his daughter with his knowledge that her confession is false: 'You're not a thief. You're a very unusual type of liar'.[104] Sylvia retracts her confession with the help of her father, admitting the sense of 'relief' that she felt in agreeing with the teacher that she was guilty.[105] It would be easy to suggest that Battle's methods are old-fashioned compared to the teacher's or that he rejects psychoanalysis wholesale, but he actually asserts a more sophisticated understanding of psychology: to him, Miss Amphrey is a 'half-baked exponent of misunderstood theories', who forces a weaker, unformed subject to betray herself.[106] Amphrey understands the compulsion to confess but believes mistakenly that confessions are always true because of her lack of understanding of the unconscious and of her own power as an authority figure.

Battle will use his personal understanding of these Reikian principles in the course of the crime narrative of *Towards Zero* to contextualise the false confession of Audrey Strange, framed for murder by her ex-husband Neville, in a motiveless crime. Neville's desire to kill Audrey through the murder of another person draws on the special symbolic force of capital punishment, as Battle explains while confronting him: 'Death by itself wasn't enough for Audrey [...] You had to think of some special kind of death, some long drawn out specialized death [...] You couldn't think of anything worse than this—to get her hanged'.[107] Neville breaks down and confesses with 'a strange queer scream' in a 'high whinnying voice', using childish language quite unlike his past rational discourse: 'Curse Audrey—she *shall* hang—you've *got* to hang her—I want her to die afraid—to die—to die...I hate her. I tell you I want her to die...*I want her to be hanged. I do want her to be hanged*'.[108] The reader suspects that any other investigator, without Battle's fatherly experience of his daughter's false confession (and his apparent intuition of Reik's theories), would have believed Audrey's confession, just as any judge and jury would have accepted all the evidence against her. In this sense, Audrey would have been hanged in a miscarriage of justice. She had accepted this death submissively as her fate by confessing. Like Battle's daughter Sylvia, Audrey reflects on the 'relief' that her false confession brought her:

> No more waiting and fearing—it's come. You'll think I'm quite demented, I suppose, if I tell you that when you came to arrest me for murder I didn't mind at all. Neville had done his worst and it was over. I felt so safe going off with Inspector Leach.[109]

Christie's story reveals that, as Brooks argues of contemporary interrogation tactics, coercive psychological methods in fact 'produce false confession because they convince innocent suspects that their situations are hopeless just as surely as they convince the guilty that they are caught'.[110] Audrey's confession, as she reflects in the safety of exoneration, is the product both of a fear of Neville and of a masochistic sense that she was worthy of punishment for leaving the marriage.[111]

If Audrey's madness is her false confession, Neville's is an excessive idea of punishment. As Battle summarises it, the death penalty itself is made to seem pathological: 'Anyone who does you an injury has to be punished—and death to you doesn't seem an excessive penalty for them to pay'.[112] But as Derrida discusses, this logic, identified as 'madness' when the punishment does not fit the crime, has always been at the centre of arguments about the death penalty. A key example is Nietzsche's investigation of the concepts of 'schaden' and 'schmerz' in a framework of money and credit: in place of 'a wife, for example, or a good, or a thing, a body, the creditor is granted a psychic reimbursement, as it were psychic or symbolic. Instead of a thing, instead of something or someone, he will be given [...] a pleasure that consists in the voluptuous pleasure of causing the other to suffer'.[113] At the start of the narrative, Neville has already replaced Audrey by remarrying and has no need of the money he will inherit by the crime: he is in search, rather, of what Derrida calls the 'jouissance' associated with the talionic law of the death penalty. He will force his ex-wife, who has injured him through her bad faith, to feel the pain of the death penalty. At the same time, as Freud writes in 'Three Essays on Sexuality' (1905), 'a sadist is always at the same time a masochist'.[114] Neville also risks the death penalty himself in first committing the murder (revealingly, he kills his surrogate mother) and second in confessing, even though he has chosen this fate for Audrey because it is the worst fate he can imagine, due to a narrow escape from punishment when he committed murder in childhood.

Neville's confession is necessary to save Audrey, because there is so little decisive evidence in the case, but the narrative has taught us to be sceptical of confession, so that Christie's reader might not be fully satisfied: to give us closure, Neville is found to be unfit to plead, never mind to be executed. Despite her avowed belief in the death penalty, Christie's narrative ultimately resists this talionic logic and designs an ending where Neville cannot receive the punishment he planned for his wife. But the idea of the death penalty which Neville's repetitive 'whimpering' speech represents—as a childish, excessive revenge, as a primitive pathological drive, but also as the essence of the death penalty in principle—cannot be fully resolved by Christie's 'happy' ending. Similarly, all the narratives discussed in this section make us doubt the justice of the irrevocable death penalty through the danger posed by false confession.

Notes

1. Peter Brooks, *Troubling Confessions: Speaking Guilt in Law and Literature*, Chicago and London: University of Chicago Press, 2000, 4.

2. E. S. Burt, 'The Autobiographical Subject and the Death Penalty', *The Oxford Literary Review*, Vol. 35, No. 2 (2013): 165–187 (167).
3. Burt, 'The Autobiographical Subject and the Death Penalty', 168.
4. Stefano Serafini, "The Ghost of Dr. Freud Haunts Everything Today": Criminal Minds in the Golden Age Psychological Thriller', *CLUES: A Journal of Detection*, Vol. 37, No. 2, Fall 2019: 20–30 (21).
5. Theodor Reik, *The Unknown Murderer, The Compulsion to Confess: On the Psychoanalysis of Crime and Punishment*, New York: Grove Press, 1961, 27.
6. Reik, *The Unknown Murderer*, 110.
7. Theodor Reik, *The Compulsion to Confess, The Compulsion to Confess: On the Psychoanalysis of Crime and Punishment*, New York: Grove Press, 1961, 212.
8. Reik, *The Compulsion to Confess*, 209.
9. Reik, *The Compulsion to Confess*, 292.
10. Michel Foucault, *The History of Sexuality Volume 1*, trans. Robert Hurley, New York: Vintage, 1978, 45.
11. Reik, *The Compulsion to Confess*, 298.
12. Gowers et al. *Royal Commission*, paragraph 60, page 21.
13. Francis Iles, *Malice Aforethought*, London: Orion, 2005, 262.
14. Iles, *Malice Aforethought*, 255.
15. Serafini, '"The Ghost of Dr. Freud Haunts Everything Today"', 22–23.
16. Iles, *Malice Aforethought*, 262.
17. Reik, *The Compulsion to Confess*, 255 and 276.
18. Reik, *The Compulsion to Confess*, 276.
19. John Carter Wood, '"The Third Degree": Press Reporting, Crime Fiction and Police Powers in 1920s Britain', *Twentieth Century British History*, Vol. 21, No. 4, 2010: 464–485 (474).
20. Carter Wood, '"The Third Degree"', 474.
21. Richard Wright, 'How Bigger Was Born', *Native Son*, London: Vintage, 2000: 1–31 (24).
22. See Doyle and O'Donnell on the case of William O'Shea in Ireland in 1943 ('A Family Affair: English Hangmen and a Dublin Jail, 1923–54', *New Hibernia Review*, Vol. 18, No. 8 (2014): 101–118 (110–111)).
23. Gowers et al. *Royal Commission*, paragraph 557, page 196.
24. Ian Cobain, *The History Thieves: Secrets, Lies and the Shaping of a Modern Nation*, London: Granta, 2016: 261–263.
25. Rebecca West, *The Meaning of Treason*, London: The Reprint Society, 1952, 185.
26. West, *The Meaning of Treason*, 198.
27. West, *The Meaning of Treason*, 198.

28. Syd Dernley with David Newman, *The Hangman's Tale: Memoirs of a Public Executioner*, London: Robert Hale, 1989, 121.
29. Roger Casement, 'Statement by the Prisoner', *The Trial of Sir Roger Casement* ed. by George H. Knott, Edinburgh and London: William Hodge & Company, 1917: 197–204.
30. George H. Knott, 'Introduction', *The Trial of Sir Roger Casement*, xxiv.
31. Knott, 'Introduction', xxiv.
32. Knott, 'Introduction', xxix.
33. The National Archives, PCOM 8/203.
34. The National Archives, HO 45/25843 and PCOM 8/214.
35. Doyle and O'Donnell note the unlucky case of John Fleming (executed in Ireland 1934) who was executed after being sent an incriminating letter from a friend ('A Family Affair', 106).
36. The National Archives, PCOM 8/203.
37. The National Archives, PCOM 8/203.
38. Dorothy L. Sayers, *Strong Poison*, London: Hodder and Stoughton, 2003, 44.
39. The National Archives, PCOM 8/203.
40. The National Archives, PCOM 8/203.
41. The National Archives, HO 144/1637/311643/182.
42. Cobain, *History Thieves*, 262.
43. Cobain, *History Thieves*, 263.
44. Cobain, *History Thieves*, 35.
45. The National Archives, PCOM 8/214.
46. Robert G. Elliott and Albert R. Beatty, *Agent of Death: The Memoirs of an Executioner*, London: John Long, 1940, 115. Elliott includes many of these 'last speeches' by prisoners he executed within his memoirs.
47. Similarly, in the last lines of *Kind Hearts and Coronets* (1949), a dark comedy loosely based on Roy Horniman's *Israel Rank: The Autobiography of a Criminal* (1907), the newly exonerated Louis D'Ascoyne Mazzini, 10th Duke of Chalfont, having narrowly escaped execution, is approached by a reporter from *Titbits* seeking the publication rights to his story. Louis has written out his life story while in prison, which is presented to the film's audience in flashback with his voiceover. Louis confesses that though he is innocent of the crime of which he is accused (the murder of his lover's husband, who actually committed suicide), he has instead killed six members of his family through increasingly baroque means in order to inherit the dukedom and avenge their treatment of his mother. In the rush of his escape from the gallows and his sudden release, when new evidence is finally produced by his lover, Louis has left his confession behind, where it may be read at any moment by the prison authorities. The film concludes with Louis's agonised recognition of his self-betrayal:

'My memoirs? Oh, my memoirs. My memoirs' (*Kind Hearts and Coronets*, Dir. Robert Hamer, Ealing Studios, 1949).

48. Victoria Stewart, *Crime Writing in Interwar Britain: Fact and Fiction in the Golden Age*, Cambridge: Cambridge University Press, 2017, 12.
49. Brooks, *Troubling Confessions*, 12–13.
50. Theodor Reik, *The Compulsion to Confess*, 265.
51. Theodor Reik, *The Compulsion to Confess*, 261.
52. Brooks, *Troubling Confessions*, 160–161.
53. Carl R. Lovitt, 'The Rhetoric of Murderers' Confessional Narratives: The Model of Pierre Riviere's Memoir', *The Journal of Narrative Technique*, Vol. 22, No. 1 (1992): 23–34 (24).
54. Pierre Bayard, *Who Killed Roger Ackroyd?: The Murderer who Eluded Hercule Poirot and Deceived Agatha Christie*, trans. by Carol Cosman, London: Fourth Estate, 2000, 36.
55. Elizabeth Bowen, 'The Disinherited', *Collected Stories*, London: Vintage, 1999, 395.
56. Bowen, 'The Disinherited', 398.
57. Stewart, *Crime Writing in Interwar Britain*, 124.
58. R. Austin Freeman, 'The Art of the Detective Story' *Nineteenth century and after*, May 1924, 718.
59. Jacques Derrida, *The Death Penalty: Volume II*, ed. by Geoffrey Bennington and Marc Crépon/trans. by Elizabeth Rottenberg, Chicago: University of Chicago Press, 2017, 234.
60. Anne Meredith, *Portrait of a Murderer*, London: British Library, 2017, 55.
61. Meredith, *Portrait of a Murderer*, 135.
62. Meredith, *Portrait of a Murderer*, 170.
63. Meredith, *Portrait of a Murderer*, 233.
64. Meredith, *Portrait of a Murderer*, 235.
65. Meredith, *Portrait of a Murderer*, 236, 232.
66. See Stewart, *Crime Writing in Interwar Britain*, 168–169.
67. Reik, *The Compulsion to Confess*, 279.
68. Sayers, *Whose Body?*, London: Hodder and Stoughton, 2016, 135–136.
69. Sayers, *Whose Body?*, 190.
70. Sayers, *Whose Body?*, 204–205.
71. Sayers, *Whose Body?*, 205.
72. Bayard, *Who Killed Roger Ackroyd?*, 85–92.
73. Flann O'Brien, *The Third Policeman, The Complete Novels*, New York: Everyman's Library, 2007, 223.
74. Agatha Christie, *The Murder of Roger Ackroyd*, London: Harper Collins, 2002, 368.
75. Christie, *The Murder of Roger Ackroyd*, 358.

76. 'I knew also that my soul was friendly, was my senior in years and was solely concerned for my welfare. For convenience I called him Joe.' Flann O'Brien, *The Third Policeman*, 240.
77. Flann O'Brien, *The Third Policeman*, 223.
78. Christie, *The Murder of Roger Ackroyd*, 9.
79. Samantha Walton, *Guilty But Insane: Mind and Law in Golden Age Detective Fiction*, Oxford: Oxford University Press, 176. Serafini, '"The Ghost of Dr. Freud Haunts Everything Today"', 25.
80. Freud, 'Psycho-Analysis and the Establishment of Facts in Legal Proceedings' (1906), *The Standard Edition of the Complete Psychological Works of Sigmund Freud, Volume IX*, trans. by Strachey et al., London: Vintage, 2001: 97–114 (113).
81. Freud, 'Psycho-Analysis and the Establishment of Facts', 113.
82. See Freud, 'Beyond the Pleasure Principle' (1920), *The Standard Edition of the Complete Psychological Works of Sigmund Freud, Volume XVIII*, trans. by Strachey et al., London: Vintage, 2001: 7–66.
83. Freud, 'The Economic Problem of Masochism', *The Standard Edition of the Complete Psychological Works of Sigmund Freud, Volume XIX*, trans. by Strachey et al., London: Vintage, 2001: 159–172 (166).
84. Freud, 'The Economic Problem of Masochism', 170.
85. Brooks, *Troubling Confessions*, 62–72.
86. For an excellent contemporary discussion of false confession, see Anne C. Dailey, *Law and the Unconscious: A Psychoanalytic Perspective*, Yale: Yale University Press, 2017.
87. Reik, *The Unknown Murderer*, 154–155.
88. F. Tennyson Jesse, *A Pin to See the Peepshow*, London: Virago, 1988, 265 and 276. For productive close analysis of Edith Thompson's real letters, see Matt Houlbrook's '"A Pin to See the Peepshow": Culture, Fiction and Selfhood in Edith Thompson's Letters, 1921–1922', *Past & Present*, No. 207 (2010): 215–249 and Rosanne Kennedy, 'Affecting Evidence: Edith Thompson's Epistolary Archive', *Australian Feminist Law Journal*, Vol. 40, No. 1(2014): 15–34. On Thompson in general see Lucy Bland, 'The Trials and Tribulations of Edith Thompson: The Capital Crime of Sexual Incitement in 1920s England', *Journal of British Studies*, xlvii (2010).
89. Jesse, *A Pin to See the Peepshow*, 310.
90. Houlbrook, 'A Pin to See the Peepshow', 222.
91. Rosanne Kennedy, 'Affecting Evidence: Edith Thompson's Epistolary Archive', *Australian Feminist Law Journal*, Vol. 40, No. 1 (2014): 15–34, (23–24). See also Margaretta Jolly and Liz Stanley, 'Letters As/Not a Genre', *Life Writing*, Vol. 2. No. 2 (2005): 91–118.
92. Kennedy, 'Affecting Evidence', 27.

93. Jesse, *A Pin to See the Peepshow*, 292.
94. Stewart, *Crime Writing in Interwar Britain*, 63–98.
95. Stewart, *Crime Writing in Interwar Britain*, 86–87.
96. Bayard, *Who Killed Roger Ackroyd?*, 145.
97. Dorothy L. Sayers, *The Unpleasantness at the Bellona Club*, London: Hodder and Stoughton, 2016, 255.
98. Reik, *The Compulsion to Confess*, 288.
99. Sayers, *The Unpleasantness at the Bellona Club*, 256.
100. Sayers, *The Unpleasantness at the Bellona Club*, 256.
101. Sayers, *The Unpleasantness at the Bellona Club*, 256–257.
102. Agatha Christie, *Five Little Pigs*, London: Harper Collins, 2007, 318.
103. Agatha Christie, *Towards Zero*, London: Harper Collins, 2002, 29.
104. Christie, *Towards Zero*, 33.
105. Christie, *Towards Zero*, 33.
106. Christie, *Towards Zero*, 34.
107. Christie, *Towards Zero*, 283–284.
108. Christie, *Towards Zero*, 285.
109. Christie, *Towards Zero*, 291.
110. Brooks, *Troubling Confessions*, 153.
111. Christie, *Towards Zero*, 288.
112. Christie, *Towards Zero*, 283.
113. Derrida, *The Death Penalty: Volume I*, 155.
114. Sigmund Freud, 'Three Essays on the Theory of Sexuality', *The Standard Edition of the Complete Psychological Works of Sigmund Freud, Volume VII (1901–1905)*, trans. by Strachey et al., London: Vintage, 2001: 125–172 (159).

CHAPTER 3

The Gothic Death Penalty

Introduction

In 'Thoughts for the Times on War and Death' (1915), Freud famously wrote that 'It is indeed impossible to imagine our own death; and whenever we attempt to do so we can perceive that we are in fact still present as spectators. Hence the psycho-analytic school could venture on the assertion that at bottom no one believes in his own death, or, to put the same thing in another way, that in the unconscious every one of us is convinced of his own immortality'.[1] Across the first volume of *The Death Penalty*, as Michael Naas expresses it, 'Derrida demonstrates how every claim either for or against the death penalty borrows in some way from a theologico-political heritage informed by Christianity',[2] showing how the death penalty depends on a failure to fully believe in death.[3] Here I will explore how fiction can compensate for a lack of experience of the reality of capital punishment after the end of public execution, but only at the price of making the death penalty, and indeed death itself, transcendental, symbolic, theatrical, unreal or fantastic.[4] Peggy Kamuf argues that literary and theatrical representation of capital punishment 'keeps the secret in the open, in the public domain under the seal of literature and protected free speech in general': but this power to apparently reveal the secret of the death penalty can point both ways.[5] A writer might transgress by designing gothic representations of the death penalty, thereby breaking a cultural covenant of

K. Ebury, *Modern Literature and the Death Penalty, 1890–1950*, Palgrave Studies in Literature, Culture and Human Rights, https://doi.org/10.1007/978-3-030-52750-1_3

secrecy, but they might still be as likely to use this transgression to support capital punishment as to critique it. As I will show, modern authors' revelation of the horror of death penalty might not be an abolitionist practice in itself, instead simply adding to folk myths, traditions and beliefs that had always existed around it. And yet, I must agree that, as E. S. Burt claims, it is only 'the haunted subject who can question the mad dictum of the state that one death can ever be equivalent to another'.[6]

This chapter will therefore examine three interrelated themes emerging from the exceptionality of the death penalty as a form of punishment: (1) instances of survival, haunting and commemoration of the condemned person after their execution; (2) the impression of 'death-in-life', or feeling dead before execution, expressed in narratives of the death penalty; and (3) the death drive and 'the suicide plot' in a death penalty context. My focus is on how a range of literary representations express a psychological understanding of execution as a 'nonexperience' via its gothic qualities. Characters subject to the death penalty will feel dead before their execution and will also survive far beyond their death in different forms of literal and metaphorical haunting. Finally, I will examine representations of the principle of deterrence in relation to the death drive and to suicide.

Ian O'Donnell's work on the length of jury consideration provides historical evidence for a sense of the unreality of capital punishment: he shows that in just 25% of 76 modern Irish death penalty cases did the jury deliberate for three hours or more.[7] In 'almost half of the deliberations of death penalty cases concluded within the hour', while 30% of these cases included jury discussions of less than half an hour.[8] Similar historicist legal work is not currently available for the UK or the US, but reviewing jury consideration in important cases suggests an analogous practice of very brief deliberation. In the celebrated and controversial trial of Dr. Crippen, much of which had turned on expert forensic evidence, the jury took a mere 27 minutes to convict. In Roger Casement's case, where his defence depended on a relatively obscure point of law, the jury deliberated for 55 minutes. In the US context, in the 1906 case of Chester Gillette (the inspiration for Dreiser's *An American Tragedy*), the jury are officially recorded as debating for a more sensible five hours. However, historical review based on the jury's testimony after the trial suggests that they immediately decided he was guilty after the first ballot, but the Foreman 'told the others that it would not seem right if they voted to convict Chester too quickly, because some might say they had acted without proper consideration of all the facts' so they agreed to wait a few hours longer without debating any further.[9] In short, it seems likely that juries, though responsible symbolically for the life or death of the defendant in a capital crime (all the more so as they could recommend mercy even in a guilty verdict), may not have felt that the duty carried substantial affective and ethical weight. The jury's inability to fully accept their responsibility is frequently satirised in Golden Age death penalty fictions such as Raymond Postgate's *Verdict of Twelve* (1940) or Richard Hull's *Excellent Intentions* (1939). Beyond this, though with more exceptions for the diversity of American law, it is generally true that in all systems, as O'Donnell argues of Ireland: 'It took longer to sentence a person for larceny than for murder', as the question of the appropriate punishment was removed by the mandatory death sentence.[10]

Evidence of an aesthetic of unreality in relation to the death penalty is also present in the frequent use of execution technology as theatrical spectacle. As Lizzie Seal has discussed, the retired executioner John Ellis took on the role of the executioner William Marwood in a 1927 true crime play called *Charles Peace*. She argues that Ellis's casting 'made the hanging scene uncomfortably realistic—and was also the reason to go and see the play'.[11] The *Daily Express* noted in a review that 'The people who came to the theatre tonight wanted to see Ellis and the way he did his work'.[12] While Seal describes a certain amount of backlash from the Lord Chamberlain, as well as several MPs and newspapers, for the casting of a real hangman, in general stage execution scenes were often praised and felt to be 'harmless fun', with reviewers frequently reporting audience laughter at the moment of the stage hanging.[13] While, as I showed in the introduction, there were increasing restrictions on public information about executions as the century advanced, some MPs even felt that Ellis's demonstrations of the death penalty might have a deterrent effect, acting like a virtual, non-scandalous return of public execution.[14] Ellis appears to have somehow acquired the model gallows after the play finished its run: by the 1930s, in the period immediately before his suicide, he appeared at fairgrounds with 'a show demonstrating an actual hanging'.[15] This argument that public demonstrations of the death penalty could reinforce the deterrent value of capital punishment directly contradicted the approach of some death penalty abolitionists, who argued that only in undoing the secrecy and complacency associated with the 1868 abolition of the public death penalty could activists achieve full abolition.[16] The next section of this chapter will thus discuss this sense of unreality via reference to instances of survival, haunting and commemoration of the condemned person after their execution.

Survival Beyond the Death Penalty

Owen Davies and Francesca Matteoni argue that, in earlier centuries, 'the ghosts of executed murderers were far less numerous, it would appear, than their victims'.[17] But within modern culture, the ghosts of the condemned became far more central to death penalty narratives. Indeed, these folkloric traditions were discussed by psychoanalysts outside of a purgatorial framework, as part of an exploration of anxieties around the talionic law. For example, Reik argues: 'All these superstitions…testify to a belief in the existence of a magic bond between the murderer and his victim. The murdered man is supposed to be not quite dead and to be able to revenge himself on his murderer'.[18] Public anxieties about being haunted by a condemned person might suggest an unconscious fear that a particular execution was unjust or even sometimes an anxiety that the principle of the death penalty itself might be unfair or dangerous.

In keeping with a greater sense of psychological subtlety in public discourses around haunting, ghosts often become metaphorical or symbolic in texts from the period, reflecting Shoshana Felman's sense that 'a judicial case becomes a legal trauma in its own right and is therefore bound to repeat itself through a traumatic legal repetition'.[19] In these texts there is first the event of the capital crime itself, repeated by the way the trial reenacts and repeats it, followed by the carrying out of judicial execution mirroring the original taking of life. These hauntings are part of the judicial process, but, beyond this, literary re-tellings also repeat and amplify the traumatic content of the crime and its punishment. For example, Elizabeth Bowen's story 'The Cat Jumps' (1934) reveals the way that those executed for capital crimes were felt to haunt the culture they left behind. The story opens with the most banal expression of an executed criminal's legacy in the way Harold Bentley, an executed wife-murderer, is felt to leave his mark behind: husbands forbidden to buy Rose Hill House by wives fearful of femicide look at Bentley's garage and ponder, 'Funny to think a chap who was hanged had kept his car there'.[20] The Wrights (Harold and Jocelyn) eventually buy the house and believe themselves to be modern and enlightened, as they know 'all crime to be pathological, and read their murders only in scientific books'.[21] But the house has an uncanny effect. A sense of tension and haunting builds within the house and the story, as

Bowen echoes the Golden Age crime conceit of entrapment in a country house. The fact that the criminal Bentley and the modern patriarch of the Wrights share a first name creates a strange connection between them, as the executed man becomes a doppelganger who overshadows the household. The 'normal' husband and host Harold Wright eventually unconsciously echoes the words of the murderous Harold Bentley ('Here we are') on finally killing his mutilated wife, triggering panic. In this moment his wife Jocelyn explicitly fears that her husband is possessed by the spirit of the condemned man:

> The Harolds, superimposed on each other, stood searching the room strangely. Taking a step forward, shutting the door behind him. 'Here we are,' said Harold. Jocelyn went down heavily. Harold watched. Harold Wright was appalled. Jocelyn had fainted: Jocelyn never had fainted before.[22]

While there is a limit to how seriously readers should take the gothic elements of Bowen's story given her use of parody and dark humour, her use of free indirect discourse apparently concedes the presence of the two Harolds, living and dead, in the room with Jocelyn. At the start of the passage, which is apparently focalised around Jocelyn, there are two Harolds—but even *after* Jocelyn faints, and her panicked perspective is removed, there persists a deliberate separation between the Harold (Bentley?) who impassively 'watches' Jocelyn and the 'Harold Wright' who is 'appalled'. Bowen's story never uses the word 'ghost' and the reader never witnesses any concrete manifestation of the executed murderer Harold Bentley. While critics have productively read Bowen's use of the gothic in her short stories, it is also crucial to highlight her fixation with the death penalty in this period.[23] In the previous chapter, I discussed 'The Disinherited', but her other thrilling stories touching on capital crimes include 'Recent Photograph' and 'Telling'. Indeed, her interwar interest in crime foreshadows her later representations of the politics of the wartime death penalty and her work on the Gowers Commission investigating capital punishment (to be discussed in Chap. 9).

In contrast with Bowen's oblique hints, more traditional ghost stories by E. F. Benson and M. R. James feature literal hauntings connected with the death penalty. M. R. James's famous ghost story, 'A View from a Hill' (1925) centres on ghosts connected with the legacy of the death penalty. The haunting originates with a pair of field glasses loaned to the protagonist, Mr. Fanshawe, by his host, an unnamed country Squire. These binoculars, originally made by a local antiquarian who has died before the story begins, give Fanshawe a direct view of the violent past of capital punishment. When he climbs a hill with the Squire to familiarise himself with the countryside, Fanshawe witnesses an apparent public execution on Gallows Hill. As Fanshawe describes it,

> There's a largish expanse of grass on the top and your dummy gibbet in the middle; and I thought there was something on it when I looked first [...] That is one of the oddest effects. The gibbet is perfectly plain, and the grass field, and there even seem to be people on it, and carts, or *a* cart, with men in it. And yet when I take the glass away, there's nothing.[24]

This, says the Squire, is impossible: the hill had not been used as a site of capital punishment for many decades. Fanshawe makes a point of visiting the hill to test his vision, which is indeed just thick woodland, as the Squire had said. But exploring the area, Fanshawe immediately feels haunted: 'steps crackling over twigs behind me, indistinct people stepping behind trees in front of me, yes, and even a hand laid on my shoulder'.[25] In the centre of the wood, he stumbles over 'an unholy evil sort of graveyard' where he immediately becomes convinced 'there was someone looking down on me from above—and not with any pleasant intent' and flees the scene.[26]

After Fanshawe's escape, the Squire confirms that Gallows Hill is also a grave site, as these past victims of capital punishment were gibbeted and left unburied: 'There must be a good few of them up there [...] They left 'em there when they fell to bits, I fancy'.[27] This marks Fanshawe's vision as earlier than 1834, when a Statute requiring the use of gibbeting or dissection after the execution of a murderer was repealed; a lasting interest in gibbeting is also shown in other M. R. James stories, such as 'Martin's Close' (1911) and 'The Story of a Disappearance and an Appearance' (1913). The frontispiece of E. F. Benson's *Spook Stories* (1928), some of which I will shortly discuss, also features an image of gibbeting, even though all the stories in that collection are set in the 1920s. Evocations of gibbeting thus reflect a deliberate reawakening of cultural memory by authors and publishers to create a haunting atmosphere.

In James's story, the mysterious field glasses turn out to have been made from boiling the bodies of those men executed on the hill, in keeping with the local antiquarian's wish 'to look through a dead man's eyes' to assist him with his archaeological work.[28] As part of an informal investigation of Fanshawe's experience, the Squire's servant describes seeing the antiquarian apparently summoned him against his will to the wood, where he was eventually found with his neck broken, symbolically mirroring the effect of hanging on the body. The story ends with the field glasses being broken in several ways: first by being taken into a church, then by being dropped, and they are finally 'buried decently' in a belated gesture of respect.[29] The conceit of James's story is that the field glasses (coded as both modern and magical) allow Fanshawe to witness the traditional gothic violence of the death penalty at a time when very few people would ever have seen an execution. But this is not merely a vision of a cruel past, as the condemned men can still haunt and hurt the living. The death of the maker of the field glasses and their belated burial offers a little closure to the story, but James suggests that the space of Gallows Hill will remain unhallowed by its history.

James's story is thus more traditional than Bowen's in its rendering of folkloric ghosts whose violence lingers 'at the spot where they were executed and gibbeted, long after all visible signs of punishment had disappeared from the landscape, with only a place name, perhaps, otherwise to memorialize the execution'.[30] Equally, the treatment of the bodies of the condemned by Baxter alludes to an equally old tradition of treating the criminal body as a trophy with medical and magical properties. Davies and Matteoni discuss how a wide range of these behaviours survived for a much longer period than we might expect: 'into the nineteenth century skull moss and oil of man (a distillation of human bones) were requested from chemists and druggists'.[31] While James presents the antiquarian's behaviour as uniquely transgressive, the real new note in his story is thus his portrayal of the ghosts themselves as dangerous enough to kill. According to Sarah Tarlow in her study of gibbeting: 'An encounter with the living body of a criminal—especially a violent one—is dangerous. The potential risk of physical harm, however, is tamed by execution. The criminal corpse still looks like the thing it was but is rendered inert—harmless—by death'.[32] In Wordsworth's *Prelude*, his childhood self stumbles upon 'a bottom / where in former times / A Murderer had been hung in iron chains'.[33] Wordsworth's poem shows the taming effect of the punishment, of nature and of time passing: 'The Gibbet mast had mouldered down, the bones / and iron case were gone', leaving only the murderer's name written on the turf as though this were a more normal grave-site.[34] But James's story asserts by contrast that such a purification of the site of punishment is impossible, even though in his narrative a much longer time has passed since executions last took place there. This reading of the story fits with Andrew Smith's recent challenge to critics who see no political meaning in James's work.[35] James, as Smith argues, represents a psychoanalytically inflected understanding of 'the presence of a barbarism' within modernity 'that can be recorded and understood, but which cannot be defeated'.[36] James seems quite undecided about the abolition of the death penalty. Even if the death penalty were to be abolished in the world of the story, Gallows Hill would still be a dangerous place, and executing these men has not accomplished the aims of the death penalty: they remain unrepentant and capable of harming the living.

Indeed, from the 1890s onwards there is increased anxiety about the death penalty failing to 'tame' the criminal body and mind in the context of a vogue for the occult. Christine Ferguson notes a debate about capital punishment in the spiritualist magazine *Light*: while some readers of the journal were in favour of capital punishment because of their eugenic beliefs, the journal's editor, William Stainton Moses, argued for the abolition of hanging both on the grounds of principle and because 'dead criminals might be just as dangerous as live ones—their deviance not being immediately effaced by death'.[37] Similarly, as late as 1949, we find the lead story of the *Psychic Journal* advocating the abolition of the death penalty because of the danger posed by executed spirits: surprisingly, this article was preserved in official Home Office files prepared as evidence of public opinion ahead of the work of the Gowers Commission.[38] While in Bowen's and James's oeuvres the ghost of the condemned man remains more or less isolated case, in E. F. Benson's stories the occult effects of execution are in fact his substantial preoccupation: the executed man appears to be the most common type of ghost represented in Benson's work, with the suicide a close second. In a range of ghost stories from across his career, including 'The Confession of Charles Linkworth' (1912), 'The House with the Brick Kiln' (1912), 'The Gardener' (1923) and 'The Hanging of Alfred Wadham' (1934), Benson depicts the gothic death penalty through representations of executed capital offenders continuing to haunt either the space in which their crime was committed (as in Bowen's story) or places and people connected with their execution (as in James's case). Benson's stories combine a realistic understanding of the twentieth-century death penalty—including details about the modern death cell and prison space, the reprieve process and the post-mortem procedure—with occult themes. One of his condemned ghosts (Charles Linkworth) even communicates with the living via the prison telephone. Benson's worldview implies that the threat posed by the condemned person cannot be contained through execution; his ghosts are very visual representations of the death penalty, much more grotesque than Bowen's or James's more intangible presences. For example, in 'The Confession of Charles Linkworth', the eponymous ghost, who seeks release from limbo through a posthumous confession, is marked in his spiritual body by the process of hanging: 'the figure of a man with his head bent over on to his shoulder, so that the face was not visible. Then he took his head in both his hands and raised it like a weight, and looked them in the face. The eyes and tongue protruded, a livid mark was round the neck'.[39] Similarly, in 'The Hanging of Alfred Wadham' the ghost takes the form of 'a face swollen and purple, with tongue lolling from the mouth, and as it hung there it oscillated to and fro'.[40]

Despite this emphasis on the grotesque violence of the death penalty, we can still identify in Benson an underlying orthodox Christian dogma, as in the crucial later story 'The Hanging of Alfred Wadham', which depicts the aftermath of the execution of an innocent man. Benson's unnamed narrator recounts the experience of a Catholic priest, Father Denys Hanbury. The Father claims that ghosts should be avoided because they are devilish tricksters rather than the real dead person and uses the story of Alfred Wadham as an example. As part of his work ministering to condemned criminals, Hanbury had been initially perplexed by Wadham's refusal to confess until an enemy of Hanbury's, Horace Kennion, tells Hanbury under the seal of the confessional that he was the real murderer. Kennion's confession aims only to taunt and torture the priest with the knowledge of a miscarriage of justice. Hanbury explains how he tried and failed to secure a reprieve for Wadham and then gave him absolution and accompanied him to the scaffold. Soon after, he is haunted by the visceral ghost described above, but he cannot believe that Wadham would blame him, as a Catholic, for preserving the sanctity of confession: he feels 'sure knowledge that this apparition could not be of God, but of the devil' and that Wadham's spirit 'had suffered the sacred expiation of martyrdom'.[41] At the end of this story, the unnamed narrator witnesses Wadham's 'diabolical counterfeit', but Hanbury is finally able to exorcise it. He explains that this is because Kennion had recently died by suicide.[42] Still, this denouement suggests a buried doubt about whether Wadham's apparition was a true vengeful ghost or a deceiving demon. If, as Hanbury believed, this was a demon sent to shake the priest's faith and not an tortured innocent man, why would the real murderer's death have any transformative effect? Benson's story allows it to be possible that Wadham was not reconciled to the priest's choice and that the priest is self-deluded about his role in supporting the death penalty. Much about this story and its representation of the horror of a miscarriage of justice in capital cases therefore remains ambiguous.

In these quite different case studies from Bowen, James and Benson, I have explored how the figure of the condemned person still held a great deal of power both in relation to its new psychological effects and to previous folk beliefs. These ghosts have great difficulty entering an afterlife, whether religious or occult, which could justify their punishment. These experiences of the survival of the condemned man as a ghost or evil influence in spaces they had inhabited might appear metaphysical, but they also depend on material survival—of Harold Bentley's house, of the bodies of the condemned men in the field glasses, of the prison spaces where executions took place, of the weapons used for the crimes—and the lasting cultural memory of famous crimes, spectacular punishments and a history where gallows hill was not merely a name. In the next section of this chapter, I will examine the way that death penalty fictions reflect a liminal state between life and death, as the sentence of death poses a unique challenge to the subject's sense of self.

Posthumousness and 'Death-in-Life' in Death Penalty Narratives

In narratives like those discussed in the previous section, I addressed a cultural anxiety about the haunting presence of the condemned prisoner, which intensified as the public ability to witness and to know the death penalty continued to reduce due to governmental restriction and secrecy. Does the executed person *really* die? What kind of death do they die? Can they continue to hurt us? In *The Death Penalty*, Derrida argues that that the death penalty is not a 'punishment' as death cannot be experienced and retold—'the condemned one, once executed, disappears before being able to pay any penalty whatever'.[43] The effect of a death sentence, whether executed or not, might therefore be to make the subject disappear to themselves and make them otherworldly. As Davies and Matteoni discuss, from the Victorian period onwards spiritualist mediums attempted to contact the souls of executed men and women: sometimes the medium wished to establish innocence or guilt, in the case of a famous crime, but often the purpose was to gain direct knowledge of the death penalty itself. For the medium John G. H. Brown, who in 1857 contacted the spirit of William Saville (executed in 1844), an attraction of spiritualism was that it 'offered the prospect of getting a unique personal account of the experience of being executed—from the executed themselves'.[44] In Saville's beyond-the-grave testimony to Brown, he remembers of the process of execution, and survival beyond it:

> I felt the horrible sensation of tottering and trembling on the verge between life and immortality [...] a death-like faintness came over me, and the same moment I experienced the sensation as of a sleeping vision, and all pain, all cares, and all troubles left me. My eyes then appeared to open, and I felt conscious of what had passed, heard the screams which ascended from the crowd below, and felt to secretly smile at their belief of my being dead.[45]

While this impulse to represent the death penalty through problematising death itself thus predates the twentieth century, it intensifies markedly after the end of public execution and with the dawn of psychoanalysis. A particular feature of death penalty narratives in the period in question includes gothic qualities which we might call 'posthumousness', which also found in the last will and testament, but which often present as a kind of autoscopy or out of body experience reflecting their quality as near-death-experience (or, in fact, beyond-death-experience).[46]

Golden Age texts are littered with symbolic references to capital criminals dying through illness or suicide soon after their trial—in these narratives, even if the person was imprisoned or exonerated, their sense of self and their bodily integrity appears to be reduced by the threat of the death penalty. These plots represent an anxiety that the person threatened with the death penalty is no longer a subject or a citizen but also attempt to offer a rhetorical challenge to the principle that 'An execution cannot be told in the first person [...] No one who says I is left to give the crucial testimony on "what happens to one condemned to death" or what the supposedly humanitarian death "feels like"'.[47] In the previous chapter I have already examined the split selves evident in texts such as *The Third Policeman* and *Roger Ackroyd*, which appear to be a version of the same autoscopic tendency, while O'Brien's text also features direct representations of ghosts and haunting. In *Five Little Pigs*, also discussed there, Elsa, the real murderer, confessed to Poirot that in killing Caroline's husband Amyas and allowing her to take the blame, 'I didn't understand that I was killing myself—not him…They didn't die. I died'.[48] In her final moments, Tennyson Jesse's Julia Starling will reflect 'She was dead already, because she had to die at nine next morning'.[49] Similarly, in 'The Disinherited' Bowen represents Prothero experiencing death as he writes his confession: 'The pen rushed the hand along under some terrific compulsion, as though something, not thought, vital, were being drained out of him through the point of the pen', while he feels 'as though he were a ghost—'.[50] Bowen implies that Prothero's death sentence is only deferred while the *real* Prothero is dead already, killed by this compulsive writer who has stolen his name. In short, our readings of the confession texts discussed in the previous chapter are not just generated and deformed by their having been written by a murderer, but specifically written by a murderer who is conscious that he or she is marked for death.

The concept of 'death anxiety' is precisely the ground on which the psychoanalyst Hanns Sachs in his 1931 pamphlet *Does Capital Punishment Exist?* (published by the modernist POOL Group) argued for the abolition of capital punishment:

> I will not maintain that Capital Punishment is not connected with the idea of a deterrant [sic] but this evil is not death but the anxiety of death…The death anxiety punishment is a punishment exclusively from the one point of view as a mere torturing punishment which gives the condemned pain without fulfilling any other condition; and it is just those torturing punishments, very popular in olden times, against which modern criminology has most revolted.[51]

Sachs compares the death penalty to torture in order to suggest that from a psychoanalytic perspective the sovereignty associated with the death penalty—not only to kill us but to make us feel pain and anxiety before death—is excessive, going back to the primitive origins of society explored in Freud's *Totem and Taboo* or *Civilisation and Its Discontents.*

Both fictional and nonfictional instances of 'death anxiety' and loss of self in modern literature can be profitably theorised in comparison with Maurice Blanchot's short prose piece, 'The Instant of My Death', which recounts an apparently autobiographical story of being saved from a Nazi firing squad in a mixture of first- and third-person: in a companion piece, 'Demeure: Fiction and Testimony', Derrida considers Blanchot's (non) experience as a limit-case for philosophical discussions of testimony, violence and death. For Blanchot, the death sentence causes an experience of becoming-dead which persists far beyond the original traumatic experience. Blanchot writes:

> There remained, however, at the moment when the shooting was no longer but to come, the feeling of lightness that I would not know how to translate: freed from life? The infinite opening up? Neither happiness, nor unhappiness. Not the absence of fear and perhaps already the step beyond. I know, I imagine that this unanalyzable feeling changed what there remained for him of existence. As if the death outside of him could only henceforth collide with the death in him. "I am alive. No, you are dead." [...] All that remains is the feeling of lightness that is death itself, or to put it more precisely, the instant of my death henceforth always in abeyance.[52]

The young man of Blanchot's story narrates an experience of being simultaneously alive and dead. The death sentence is deferred but never rescinded in a moment that changes temporality itself in both the translation and the original French: 'the moment when the shooting was no longer but to come' (*Demeurait cependent, au moment où la fusillade n'était plus qu'en attente*), with 'the instant of my death always in abeyance' (*l'instant de ma mort désormais toujours en instance*).[53] Derrida sees the young man of Blanchot's story as dying in a meaningful sense, despite his actual survival, and paradoxically experiencing a moment of immortality: 'in the instant of death, when death arrives, where one is not yet dead in order to be already dead [...], at that instant I am immortal because I am dead'.[54] Here, the difficult syntax and the tangled use of the first-person within both Blanchot's original and Derrida's commentary make us aware of this deferred death sentence as an autoscopic experience.

Blanchot's example, usually classed as testimony rather than fiction, shows how this quality of posthumousness and of death-in-life is also featured in surviving writings by condemned men. Twentieth-century writers often reflected on the anxiety caused by the period between sentencing and execution, during which time the criminal's sense of themselves as a living being was radically reduced. For example, the novelist and journalist James O'Connor wrote a news article in the form of a letter to Albert Pierrepoint which confronts Pierrepoint, and a wider society, about the cruelty of the death penalty. O'Connor had almost been executed after a murder conviction in 1942 but was eventually reprieved: the article's headline, 'Dear Mr. Pierrepoint, you hanged me 1000 times', has qualities of posthumousness and impossible survival. The striking headline is eventually explained as reflecting the death anxiety associated with the delay between the death sentence and the execution: 'Eight weeks I was waiting for you. You hanged me a thousand times in my dreams. I woke up screaming as you put the noose around my neck. But in the end you were cheated, Albert'.[55] Similarly, Roger Casement's famous last letter to his sister Nina illuminates both his death drive, linked to an apparent sense of closeting, and a powerful sense of posthumousness and autoscopy:

> If I could only tell you the whole story, but that too is part of my punishment—of the strange inscrutable fate that has come to me—that I am not only being put to death in the body but that I am dead before I die—and have to be silent and silent just as if I were already dead—when a few words would save my life—and would certainly change men's view of my actions.[56]

It is particularly striking that we find this twin impulse towards confession/testimony and towards a feeling of death-in-life in these cases of the political death penalty represented by Blanchot and Casement because it suggests that the primary cause of the feeling of posthumousness is not the status of being a murderer—but rather these uncanny qualities come from thinking about the death penalty itself. Felman summarises Walter Benjamin's emphasis on 'those whom violence has treated in their lives as though they were *already dead*, those who have been made (in life) without expression'.[57] While Benjamin's arguments are best adapted to the grand scale of war or genocide which they were designed for, some of the qualities he identifies are also present in this nonfictional testimony about the death penalty.

Alongside the concepts of posthumousness and autoscopy I have been exploring, I should close this section by comparing feelings of traumatic affect experienced by those who will suffer the death penalty with the obscure mental illness of Cotard delusion (also called Cotard's syndrome or walking corpse syndrome) which was first described in 1880 as *Le délire des négations* ('The Delirium of Negation') as an affective disorder akin to melancholia.[58] The symptoms of this disease include both a sense of negation of the body, including often a belief in the patient that they have already died, alongside a paradoxical feeling of transcendence and immortality. Reminding us of Freud's general insight in 'Thoughts for the Times on War and Death', Jacques Lacan writes of the victim of Cotard syndrome that 'the being's identification with its pure and simple image takes effect, there isn't any room for change either, that is to say death. That in fact is what their theme is—they are both dead and incapable of dying, immortal—like desire'.[59] Recent thinkers have associated Cotard's syndrome with 'the attitudinal changes brought about by chronic institutionalisation'.[60] The institution under discussion by Trémine and Berrios here is the asylum, but in our case the legal system, and the prison and the mechanisms of execution might provoke the same symptoms, allowing us to examine the psychological effect of the apparent removal of citizenship and personhood from the condemned person. The idea of Cotard's syndrome as the effect of institutionalisation allows us to politicise these questions of self-experience and self-representation and to emphasise the affective unreality surrounding the death sentence in the twentieth century.

The process of the death penalty thus often *produced* the uncanny feelings discussed so far throughout this chapter. For example, in the British system, we might be surprised to learn that the custom of the burial service being read by the prison chaplain *during* the execution continued into the mid-1920s.[61] This aspect of the execution process was felt to be particularly disturbing by Oscar Wilde, as he rendered it in 'The Ballad of Reading Gaol' (1898), based on his experience of anxious identification with Charles Thomas Wooldridge (executed 1896):

> For each man kills the thing he loves,
> Yet each man does not die:
> He does not bend his head to hear
> The Burial Office read,
> Nor, while the terror of his soul
> Tells him he is not dead,
> Cross his own coffin, as he moves
> Into the hideous shed.[62]

The gothic details of the execution are central to Wilde's poem: on the night of the execution, the other prisoners pray for the condemned man, haunted by 'each evil sprite that walks by night', by 'phantoms' and the 'Lord of Death'.[63] Folk aspects of execution culture haunt Wilde's poem, while Christianity appears warped and twisted as the executed man is denied full Christian burial except for the cruel detail of the Burial Service. In the 1920s J. W. Wenham argued that 'since the priest was conducting not a corpse to the grave but a living man to the gallows' this custom was distressing and should be discontinued.[64] Wenham's initial appeal to the Church via the Archbishop of Canterbury fell on deaf ears but the Home

Office eventually agreed that 'the use, before the execution, of passages usually associated with the burial of the dead is open to objection' and protocols were adjusted.[65] While this was a positive development, the change of practice avoided addressing Wenham's central argument about the historic inhumanity of treating a living man as if he were already dead, or the role of the Church in preparing the condemned man to die and thereby maintaining the death penalty.

The unusual features of the writing discussed in this section also offer a way forward in recent critical conversations about the role of affect in the field of law and literature.[66] In these texts, literature provides something fantastic and impossible which depends upon powerful affect, as the 'I' that is subject to the death penalty narrates an experience of death anxiety before and after their literal execution. Even when this feeling of posthumousness or autoscopy is expressed in a nonfictional document, it depends on an 'as if' quality and a suspension of disbelief which belongs to fiction. However, such an emptying out of the legal subject, as the inclusion of grotesque, gothic and fantastic elements, might not necessarily be an abolitionist practice. This style of representation removes much of the symbolic power of the death penalty and could undermine traditional arguments for the death penalty on the grounds of seriousness and deterrence. But we may also suspect this feeling of death-in-life undermines the value of the individual human life and the significance of potential miscarriages of justice. In the final section of this chapter, I will consider the effect of death anxiety on the intersection of suicide, murder and execution, especially within the case studies of Gladys Mitchell's *Speedy Death* (1929) and Agatha Christie's *Curtain: Poirot's Last Case.*

Suicide and Murder in the Golden Age

For Derrida, capital punishment 'finds its place of inscription where it is indissociable from both murder and suicide', and this will be the focus of the chapter's final section.[67] Derrida argues that because for Kant and others the death penalty is a categorical imperative, the executed person consents to it, even if they are not resigned to it: 'Execution is sui-cide. For the autonomy of juridical reason there is only auto-execution'.[68] These aspects of the death penalty might partly explain the fascination with haunting and death-in-life explored earlier. For Derrida, a suicidal impulse makes the executed person both the victim and the master of punishment:

> the one suicided by society ends up no longer really believing in the relation of the death of which he remains the master…He believes it without believing it, whence the feeling of fictional or theatrical unreality, whence the essential literariness attached to these scenes of executioners in frock coats and top hats.[69]

Derrida's concept of the death penalty is directly influenced by Freud's followers such as Sachs and Reik. For example, in 'Does Capital Punishment Exist?', Sachs argues against the death penalty on the grounds that suicidal drives are a cause of murders:

> Psycho-analytical insight demonstrates in an unmistakable way that those whose destructive impulse is directed against the life of others have always an uncommonly high degree of self-destructive tendencies. Experience proves the same, because in many cases just those who have killed others are quite ready to commit suicide. Death, therefore, in the way the Law threatens it, is no evil, and least of all to those on whom its threat is meant to work.[70]

In conceptualising execution as suicide, Sachs and Derrida directly attack the principle of deterrence but also implicitly tap into wider cultural beliefs about suicide as sinful: if the death penalty is close to suicide in its orientation, then it is itself immoral according to the established Christian teaching often used to maintain the death penalty. Davies and Matteoni describe how this functioned in an earlier execution culture:

> Suicide was an act of self-execution, but there could be no public redemption or remorse on the scaffold. Self-murder was the most heinous of sinful crimes. […] This theological position occasionally drove the suicidal to the act of murder in order to be executed by the state, thereby achieving their desire to end their lives and still leave open a possible path to salvation.[71]

Demonstrating the persistence of this view in the context of capital punishment, while giving evidence to the Gowers Commission, the Archbishop of Canterbury, Geoffrey Fisher, was asked whether a person condemned to death could be allowed to commit suicide. Harry Potter summarises his shocked response:

> Not only did the archbishop see suicide as the sin of self-murder, but he also insisted in his reply that it was important that society itself should inflict the

> death penalty, rather than permitting condemned persons to choose how they wished to die.[72]

In executioners' memoirs, cases of attempted suicide, where a great deal of medical attention was required to spare the life of the person so they could undergo trial and execution, are presented as a particular challenge to the executioner's skill (and morale).[73] The American executioner Robert Elliott notes that 'It always seems ironical to me when science is called upon to save a human life so it can be taken a short time later by the statement', not merely in suicide cases but also in cases where an operation was required to facilitate a successful execution at a later stage.[74] For a prisoner to 'cheat the gallows' was 'a major scandal and disgrace', and a whole set of prison procedures were designed to prevent it.[75]

However, the failure of these safeguards is recorded in statistics examined by the Gowers Commission: they note that of 7454 murders in 1900–1950, 1674 suspects committed suicide.[76] This shocking number goes alongside Reik's sense that 'suicide, for instance, ultimately satisfies the murderer's unconscious need for punishment with active assistance from the judiciary' and, as I explained, Sachs also asserted this in his 'Does Capital Punishment Exist?' pamphlet.[77] The Gowers Commission do not further speculate on this figure, or concede that it is a very high number of deaths (22%), but we must acknowledge that these numbers are so high that it would surely have to include innocent people afraid of the process of justice, as well as the guilty who could not come to terms with the death penalty. Within both of these groups, there would undoubtedly be many people who were mentally ill. These forces were recognised, though not addressed, in contemporary culture: for example, in Meredith's *Portrait of a Murderer*, discussed in the previous chapter, Brand Gray's brother Richard, who is a Member of Parliament, plans to commit suicide if suspected of the crime because of the disgrace involved, though he is entirely innocent.[78]

Samantha Walton argues of Golden Age narratives that 'when the detective has scruples about presenting a killer for punishment, suicide is a convenient and painless alternative (for the author, that is). Justice is still done, in the sense that the killer is "executed". They no longer pose a threat to others and narrative closure is achieved through their obliteration'.[79] While Walton's diagnosis is entirely accurate, a focus on connections between the death penalty and suicide (rather than simply on crime) allows us to see tensions in the way that 'executed' is held within her inverted commas. Stewart summarises the use of the suicide plot, but, like Walton, she does not consider in historicist terms how transgressive of legal and Christian norms this was in its day.[80] Further I am the first scholar to highlight how, in the legal culture of the period, assisting in or encouraging suicide was held to be the same as murder and could be punished by the death penalty. The Gowers Commission argue decisively that often the 'incitement to suicide involves as much moral guilt as many heinous murders and ought to remain punishable by death'.[81] I argue that we should resituate the 'suicide plot' common in Golden Age narratives within this complicated context: of a prevalence of suicide in those accused of capital crimes despite cultural stigmatisation of this act and of the legal norms which treated encouraging or assisting suicide as capital offences.

In several of the narratives examined in the previous chapter, the investigator 'saves' the criminal from the gallows through a coerced suicide, blurring the boundaries between suicide, murder and execution. The criminal is not always even spared a version of the 'death anxiety' punishment discussed by Sachs as they are often forced to take a direct responsibility not just for their own death but also for their confession and the exoneration of other possible suspects. Further, historically, the sympathetic criminal in these stories stood a chance at reprieve denied to them by the suicide plot: the Gowers Commission report demonstrates that 'In all, during the past fifty years, some forty-five per cent. of persons sentenced to death have been reprieved in England and nearly sixty per cent. in Scotland'.[82] At best, the Golden Age detective is only saving the confessing criminal from disgrace, suggesting that other factors such as public dishonour and death anxiety are stronger deterrents than the death penalty per se. At worst, in terms of the strict letter of the law, any fictional detective offering the solution described by Walton and Stewart is a murderer.

Therefore, in the sense held by the Gowers Commission that 'incitement to suicide involves as much moral guilt as many heinous murders', many of the investigations of Golden Age detectives end in murder, as well as beginning with it.[83] As we have seen, incitement to and assistance in suicide was a capital crime, not just in terms of the letter of the law but in actual legal and penal practice. That Golden Age writers were aware of this is shown by the direct occasions where detectives engage in acts that are more explicitly coded as murder. In the remainder of the chapter, I will briefly discuss two examples of capital punishment's indissociable connection with both murder and suicide, Gladys Mitchell's *Speedy Death* and

Agatha Christie's *Curtain: Poirot's Last Case*. Both of these texts shockingly violate self-imposed 'fair play' rules for Golden Age fiction that the detective must not be the culprit and, ultimately, subvert relationships between detection and capital punishment.

At the end of Gladys Mitchell's *Speedy Death* (1929), Mrs Bradley, a psychoanalyst-detective investigating her first ever case, is tried and exonerated for the murder of Eleanor Bing, a nymphomaniac who had killed once and attempted other murders at the point where Bradley intervenes. This novel has naturally been read primarily through the lens of queer modernism, because of its concern with gender and sexuality: its other key interest is the death penalty.[84] After Bradley's acquittal (Eleanor's death is hidden as a suicide), she frankly admits to committing this murder in order to save Eleanor from the gallows: she conceptualises this act as a mercy killing, but apparently does not consider whether Eleanor could be brought to justice supported by an insanity defence. Instead of harnessing her psychoanalytic skills as an expert witness in a potential trial, Bradley becomes a detective through identification with the law's retributive power rather than medicine's curative role. Bradley deploys the traditional eugenic arguments supporting the death penalty, rather than a medical rhetoric of euthanasia, to justify her own murder: 'It was what one might term a logical elimination of unnecessary, and, in fact, dangerous matter', as she 'erased [Eleanor], as it were, from an otherwise fair page of the Bing family chronicle'.[85] Though Bradley's profession as psychoanalyst is useful to Mitchell in terms of her characterisation, her detective's position in support of the death penalty places her far from Freud, Reik and Sachs on issues of criminology. That Bradley murders Eleanor with a drug then used in psychological medicine (hyoscine) and which could benefit her if taken in a smaller dose appears to imply Mitchell's belief that psychoanalysis, like writing, is a pharmakon which may kill or cure.

While Mitchell's detective sets out from her very first adventure as a self-confessed murderer-executioner and in subsequent novels such as *The Saltmarsh Murders* (1932) will both criticise capital punishment and call herself as a murderer, in *Curtain: Poirot's Last Case*, Poirot becomes a murderer at the very end of his career and his life. *Curtain* marks posthumousness and gothic stylistic features as essential for thinking about the death penalty—Christie wrote a book which concludes with Hastings (our narrator) reading Poirot's posthumous confession that he has murdered a dangerous man, named Stephen Norton. In admitting his crime to Hastings in a written document, Poirot is thus placed in parallel with Dr.

Sheppard in *Roger Ackroyd* and with the other confessions to capital crimes discussed in the previous chapter.

Christie's design of this ultimate outcome also throws into doubt the use of the suicide plot in earlier Poirot narratives, reflecting the legal understanding of incitement to suicide as a form of murder that I have explored. As in Mitchell's novel, we also find in Christie a deep influence of psychoanalysis but also a similarly profound ambivalence about Reik's abolitionist belief that psychoanalysis could prevent capital crimes: in fact, Norton is a criminal by proxy who applies psychological pressure to induce others to kill. What Norton practices is the opposite of psychoanalysis in its result, but it shares many of the same methodologies: through dialogue, through active listening, he breaks through repression to help his patient/ victim understand their desires. The difference is that he encourages the subject to act upon their instinctive drive to kill, as Poirot reflects, '*to widen a breach instead of repairing it*'.[86] Poirot's understanding of the psychology of murder throughout Christie's series is thus shared by the culprit in this final novel.

Part of the fascination for Norton is with capital punishment itself. It is not enough for him that he encourages murder, but he also wishes victims of his psychological experiment to face retributive justice. Poirot argues that '*he is a sadist. He wants the whole gamut of emotion, suspicion, fear, the coils of the law*'.[87] Is it the same for Poirot? As is clear from examining these passages, there is an implicit parallel in Christie's narrative between Norton and Poirot, as well as between both these characters and Judge Wargrave in the earlier *And Then There Were None* (1939), to be discussed in Chap. 8. Pierre Bayard uses his reading of Christie texts including *Roger Ackroyd*, *Endless Night* and *Curtain* to conclude that 'Interpretation in detective work is first and foremost a death sentence', even beyond those novels where anxieties about capital punishment seem most explicit.[88] In his confession, Poirot recounts how he engaged in a quasi-judicial process in confronting Norton about his actions: he presents the evidence, allows him space to confess and directly conceptualises his plan to kill Norton as an execution ('*I told him that I proposed to execute him*').[89] After the murder, Poirot disguises Norton's death as a suicide, in a symbolic connection with the coerced suicides of the murderers he caught in the past. In his last words, he examines the logic of extrajudicial execution and its intersections with other forms of state killing:

> *As a young man in the Belgian police force I shot down a desperate criminal who sat on a roof and fired at people below. In a state of emergency martial law is warranted. By taking Norton's life, I have saved other lives—innocent lives. But still I do not know…it is perhaps right that I should not know. I have always been so sure—too sure.*[90]

Poirot's arguments, and beyond him Christie's as author, might apply to the justice of death penalty more broadly here: these arguments are not about deterrence but rather about a protective, eugenic logic by which the murderer is removed from the community for the good of others (as in Mitchell's *Speedy Death*). But in contrast to Mitchell's text where Mrs. Bradley insouciantly outlives her crime, the tensions raised by Poirot's confession are only to be resolved beyond the grave, in his appeal to the divine. Poirot writes out his confession and stops taking his heart medication, in a form of suicide or self-imposed execution: '*I prefer to leave myself in the hands of the bon Dieu. May his punishment, or his mercy, be swift!*'.[91] Hastings's last recorded thoughts are shocked ('I have finished reading…I cannot believe it all yet') but tend towards a justification of Poirot's actions.[92] And yet, in the meantime, Poirot has died, a victim of the suicide plot, or divine vengeance.

In this sense, Poirot's actions in *Curtain* allude to the fate of those criminals throughout his career whose suicide he has required and the story appears to speak to public reservations about capital punishment quite powerfully. Beyond its plot, the very process of composition of *Curtain* likewise marks posthumousness, and also the sense of 'emergency' that Poirot identifies, as crucial to Christie's thinking about the death penalty. Christie wrote this novel fearing her own death during the Blitz and kept it for 30 years in a bank vault with a note that it should only be published posthumously. She eventually authorised its publication in the year before her death, 1975, but references to hanging and other period details were kept and not updated. In the meantime, she had written many other Poirot novels. The novel which outs Poirot as a murderer-executioner-suicide is thus in itself posthumous, anachronistic, alternative and atemporal. But in another sense this ending, which suggests that, even for Christie, capital punishment 'is indissociable from both murder and suicide', was inevitable, as she implies by the metafictional gesture of setting the action of *Curtain* at Styles, the country house setting of the very first Poirot novel.[93]

Naas argues, in summarising Derrida, that:

> The scandal of the death penalty consists in this calculation by the other of the instant of my death, a mechanical calculation of the instant that leaves no room for the incalculable future or for the event—even if, though this is another story, such calculation is always a kind of phantasm of control or mastery over the event.[94]

In response, the narratives examined across this chapter have complicated the idea of the other's power over death within the death penalty in at least three ways: firstly I considered the haunting effect of those who were executed in twentieth-century culture; secondly I examined concepts of death anxiety, posthumousness and autoscopy in the psychology of the condemned person; and finally I explored close connections between suicide, murder and capital punishment.

Notes

1. Freud, 'Thoughts for the Times on War and Death', *On Creativity and the Unconscious*, ed. by Benjamin Nelson, New York: Harper & Row, 1965: 222–223.
2. Michael Naas, 'The Philosophy and Literature of the Death Penalty: Two Sides of the Same Sovereign', *The Southern Journal of Philosophy*, Vol. 50 (2012): 39–55 (42).
3. Jacques Derrida, *The Death Penalty: Volume II*, ed. by Geoffrey Bennington and Marc Crépon/trans. by Elizabeth Rottenberg, Chicago: University of Chicago Press, 2017, 49–50.
4. Derrida, *The Death Penalty: Volume II*, 72.
5. Peggy Kamuf, *Literature and the Remains of the Death Penalty*, New York: Fordham University Press, 2018, 59.
6. E. S. Burt, 'The Autobiographical Subject and the Death Penalty', *The Oxford Literary Review*, Vol. 35, No. 2 (2013): 165–187 (181).
7. Ian O'Donnell, 'Table 4.1', *Justice, Mercy, and Caprice: Clemency and the Death Penalty in Ireland*, Oxford: Oxford University Press, 2017, 87.
8. O'Donnell, 'Table 4.1', 87.
9. Craig Brandon, *Murder in the Adirondacks: "An American Tragedy" Revisited*, Utica: North Country Books, 1986, 235.
10. O'Donnell, *Justice, Mercy, and Caprice*, 103.
11. Lizzie Seal, *Capital Punishment in Twentieth-Century Britain: Audience, Justice, Memory*, Abingdon and New York: Routledge, 2014, 70–72.
12. Seal, *Capital Punishment*, 70–72.
13. Seal, *Capital Punishment*, 71.
14. Seal, *Capital Punishment*, 72.

15. Seal, *Capital Punishment*, 72.
16. Harry Potter, *Hanging in judgement: religion and the death penalty in England from the bloody code to abolition*, London: SCM Press, 1993, 138.
17. Owen Davies and Francesca Matteoni, *Executing Magic in the Modern Era: Criminal Bodies and the Gallows in Popular Medicine*, Houndsmills: Palgrave, 2017, 86.
18. Theodor Reik, *The Unknown Murderer, The Compulsion to Confess: On the Psychoanalysis of Crime and Punishment*, New York: Grove Press, 1961, 54.
19. Shoshana Felman, *The Juridical Unconscious: Trials and Traumas in the Twentieth Century*, Cambridge, Mass., and London: Harvard University Press, 2002, 57.
20. Elizabeth Bowen, 'The Cat Jumps', *Collected Stories*, London: Vintage, 1999, 362.
21. Bowen, 'The Cat Jumps', 362.
22. Bowen, 'The Cat Jumps', 369.
23. See Luke Thurston, 'Double-crossing: Elizabeth Bowen's ghostly short fiction', *Textual Practice*, Vol. 27, No. 1 (2013): 7–28 and Thomas S. Davis, 'Elizabeth Bowen's war gothic', *Textual Practice*, Vol. 27, No. 1 (2013): 29–47.
24. M. R. James, 'A View from a Hill', *Collected Ghost Stories*, Oxford: Oxford University Press, 2013: 330–331.
25. James, 'A View', 336.
26. James, 'A View', 336.
27. James, 'A View', 337.
28. James, 'A View', 339.
29. James, 'A View', 342.
30. Davies and Matteoni, *Executing Magic*, 86.
31. Davies and Matteoni, *Executing Magic*, 2.
32. Sarah Tarlow, *The Golden and Ghoulish Age of the Gibbet in Britain*, Houndsmills: Palgrave, 2017, 114.
33. William Wordsworth, *The Thirteen-Book Prelude*, ed. by Mark L. Reed, Ithaca: Cornell University Press, 1991, XI, 290–291.
34. Wordsworth, *Prelude*, XI, 292–294.
35. Andrew Smith, 'M. R. James's Gothic Revival', *The ghost story 1840–1920: A cultural history*, Manchester: Manchester University Press, 2013: 168–185.
36. Smith, 'M. R. James's Gothic Revival', 169.
37. Christine Ferguson, 'Eugenics and the afterlife: Lombroso, Doyle, and spiritualist purification of the race', *Journal of Victorian Culture*, Vol. 12, No. 1 (2007): 64–85 (72–73).
38. Margery Lawrence, 'Abolish the Death Penalty!', *Psychic Journal*, No. 22, May 1948 in The National Archives, HO 45/25084.

39. E. F. Benson, 'The Confession of Charles Linkworth', *The Room in the Tower and Other Stories*, London: Mills & Boon, 1912: 62–86 (85).
40. E. F. Benson, 'The Hanging of Alfred Wadham', *More Spook Stories*, London: Hutchinson & Co. Ltd, 1934: 89–108 (107).
41. Benson, 'The Hanging of Alfred Wadham', 106.
42. Benson, 'The Hanging of Alfred Wadham', 108.
43. Derrida, *The Death Penalty: Volume II*, 50.
44. Davies and Matteoni, *Executing Magic*, 99.
45. Davies and Matteoni, *Executing Magic*, 99.
46. Autoscopy means 'a form of visual hallucination in which a person sees an image of himself outside his own body' (*OED*): this specific term predates the more common 'out-of-body-experience' and 'near-death experience' which were coined in the 1960s and 1970s respectively. The term had its first English usage in *The New York Times* in May 1904.
47. Burt, 'The Autobiographical Subject and the Death Penalty', 173.
48. Agatha Christie, *Five Little Pigs*, London: Harper Collins, 2007, 335.
49. F. Tennyson Jesse, *A Pin to See the Peepshow*, London: Virago, 1988, 402.
50. Elizabeth Bowen, 'The Disinherited', *Collected Stories*, London: Vintage, 1999, 392 and 395.
51. Dr Hanns Sachs, *Does Capital Punishment Exist?*, Territet: POOL Group Pamphlet 1930, 11–12.
52. Maurice Blanchot and Jacques Derrida, *The Instant of My Death/Demeure: Fiction and Testimony*, trans. by Elizabeth Rottenberg, Stanford: Stanford University Press, 2000, 9–11.
53. Blanchot and Derrida, *The Instant of My Death*, 7 and 8 and 10 and 11 in the parallel translation.
54. Blanchot and Derrida, *The Instant of My Death*, 67–68.
55. Press Clippings on Pierrepoint kept by Prison Commission, The National Archives, PCOM 9/2024.
56. Roger Casement, 'Letter from Roger Casement to Nina Casement, 25th July 1916', *Letters of 1916*, ed. by Susan Schreibman, Maynooth University, 2016. Website. [Accessed 20th June 2018].
57. Felman, *The Juridical Unconscious*, 14–16.
58. German E. Berrios, *The History of Mental Symptoms: Descriptive Psychopathology Since the Nineteenth Century*, Cambridge: Cambridge University Press, 1996, 304.
59. Jacques Lacan, *The Seminar of Jacques Lacan: Book II: The Ego in Freud's Theory*, ed. by Jacques-Alain Miller and trans. by Sylvana Tomaselli, New York and London: Norton, 1991, 268.
60. T. Trémine quoted in Berrios, *The History of Mental Symptoms*, 309.
61. The National Archives, HO 45/25843.
62. Oscar Wilde, 'The Ballad of Reading Gaol', *Oscar Wilde: Complete Poetry*, Oxford: Oxford World's Classics, 2009: 152–171 (I, 154).

63. Wilde, 'The Ballad of Reading Gaol', III, 161–162.
64. Potter, *Hanging in judgement*, 118.
65. The National Archives, HO 45/25843.
66. See Greta Olson, 'The Turn to Passion: Has Law and Literature become Law and Affect?', *Law & Literature*, Vol. 28, No. 3 (2016): 335–353 and Daniel Hourigan's response essay, 'Specters and Psychoanalysis in the Turn to Law and Affect', *Law & Literature*, Vol. 31, No. 1 (2017): 1–17.
67. Derrida, *The Death Penalty: Volume I*, 239.
68. Derrida, *The Death Penalty: Volume II*, 67.
69. Derrida, *The Death Penalty: Volume II*, 67.
70. Sachs, *Does Capital Punishment Exist?*, 11–12.
71. Davies and Matteoni, *Executing Magic*, 89–90.
72. Potter, *Hanging in judgement*, 373.
73. For example, John Ellis reflects, in describing the execution of Joseph Deans in 1916 that he had had to take special precautions to prevent wounds from an attempted suicide from reopening (*Diary of a Hangman*, London: Forum Press, 1992, 192); a similar case is also discussed by Ellis in his execution of Robert Upton in 1914 (Ellis, *Diary of a Hangman*, London: Robert Hale, 1989, 230–231); Dernley describes how Piotr Maksimowski (executed 1950) had to be 'patched up' with heavy bandages after a suicide attempt only days before the execution (Dernley, *The Hangman's Tale*, 90).
74. Robert Elliott, *Agent of Death: The Memoirs of an Executioner*, London: John Long, 1940, 111–112.
75. Potter, *Hanging in judgement*, 373.
76. Sir Ernest Arthur Gowers et al. Royal Commission on Capital Punishment, 1949–1953, REPORT, Presented to Parliament by Command of Her Majesty September 1953 (also known as Gowers Commission Report), London: Her Majesty's Stationery Office, 1953, paragraph 58, pages 19–20.
77. Reik and Freud, 'View on Capital Punishment' (1926), in *The Compulsion to Confess: On the Psychoanalysis of Crime and Punishment*, New York: Grove Press, 1961: 469–474 (474).
78. Anne Meredith, *Portrait of a Murderer*, London: British Library, 2017, 163.
79. Samantha Walton, *Guilty But Insane: Mind and Law in Golden Age Detective Fiction*, Cambridge: Cambridge University Press, 2015, 127.
80. Victoria Stewart, *Crime Writing in Interwar Britain: Fact and Fiction in the Golden Age*, Cambridge: Cambridge University Press, 2017, 40, 105.
81. Gowers et al. *Royal Commission*, paragraph 168, page 60–61.
82. Gowers et al. *Royal Commission*, paragraph 606, page 212.
83. Gowers et al. *Royal Commission*, paragraph 168, page 60–61.

84. For excellent work on this strand of *Speedy Death*, see Paul Peppis, 'Querying and queering golden age detection: Gladys Mitchell's *Speedy Death* and popular modernism', *Journal of Modern Literature*, Vol. 40, No. 3 (2017): 120–134 and, on Mitchell's psychoanalytic interests in gender and sexuality, see, Brittain Bright, 'The Unshockable Mrs. Bradley: Sex and Sexuality in the Work of Gladys Mitchell', *Murder in the Closet: Essays on Queer Clues in Crime Fiction Before Stonewall*, ed. by Curtis Evans, Jefferson: McFarland & Company, 2017: 78–92.
85. Gladys Mitchell, *Speedy Death*, London: Vintage, 2014, 308.
86. Agatha Christie, *Curtain: Poirot's Last Case*, London: Harper Collins, 2002, 261, Christie's italics throughout.
87. Christie, *Curtain*, 277.
88. Pierre Bayard, *Who Killed Roger Ackroyd?: The Murderer who Eluded Hercule Poirot and Deceived Agatha Christie*, trans. by Carol Cosman, London: Fourth Estate, 2000, 144.
89. Christie, *Curtain*, 278.
90. Christie, *Curtain*, 283–284.
91. Christie, *Curtain*, 284.
92. Christie, *Curtain*.
93. Derrida, *The Death Penalty Volume I*, 239.
94. Naas, 'The Philosophy and Literature of the Death Penalty', 54.

CHAPTER 4

Justice and Punishment in Executioners' Life-Writing

Introduction

This chapter will discuss a range of executioners' memoirs, considering autobiography as a means of writing about the death penalty for James Berry (1852–1913), John Ellis (1874–1932), Albert Pierrepoint (1905–1992), Syd Dernley (1920–1994) and Robert Elliott (1874–1939). The chapter will first focus on the concept of testimony, considering how the executioner represents their responsibility for death, and then a further two sections will then consider representations of embodiment, both the condemned person's body and the executioner's own physical role, within the remembered and recorded execution scene. As noted in the introduction, after the 1868 Capital Punishment Amendment Act, which abolished the public death penalty in Britain, executions became a private, even a secret, business. As a result of their privileged access, executioners' life-writing in the late-nineteenth and early-twentieth centuries thus came with powerful truth claims about the nature and psychology of punishment. For example, concluding a chapter called 'How Murderers Die' in his own 1892 memoir, James Berry responded to potential criticism of his portrayal of capital punishment by arguing for the ethical value of his frank perspective upon questions of justice:

K. Ebury, *Modern Literature and the Death Penalty, 1890–1950*, Palgrave Studies in Literature, Culture and Human Rights,
https://doi.org/10.1007/978-3-030-52750-1_4

> As one of my objects in writing this book is to give the public a solid basis for the formation of a sound public opinion upon the subject of capital punishment, [...] many of its details should be painful—because they are true. If I glossed over the facts I should signally fail in my duty to my readers, but I have endeavoured, so far as possible, to avoid revolting details.[1]

Similarly, Ellis, writing about the 1923 execution of Edith Thompson, argues that 'The public are entitled to know the truth, and since I was there, and the man in charge, I claim to be best qualified to tell it'.[2] The American executioner Robert Elliott also suggests that the practice of capital punishment demands full public knowledge of the process involved: 'A society that demands the death penalty [...] should know just how the legal killing of a human being is accomplished'.[3] The executioner thus becomes not merely the agent of punishment but an interpreter of it.

Despite the frequent involvement of a ghost writer in this life-writing process, the executioner's autobiographical writing in newspapers or books was often simply a public version of a private quirkier text, the executioner's diary, which was often augmented by a scrapbook or collection of newspaper cuttings. The 'editor'/ghost writer of Berry's memoir describes the writing process as one of conversion from diary to autobiography: 'The narrative and descriptive portion of the work is taken from a series of note-books and a news-cuttings book kept by Mr. Berry', while more discursive chapters were given in note-form or dictated.[4] Similarly, Elliott kept 'a careful record of all my cases. A page—sometimes more than one—is devoted to each': Elliott presents his writing as less a diary and more a record of scientific experiments 'from these accounts, I have been able to reach various conclusions, which I will discuss later'.[5] Albert Pierrepoint's reflections on his father's diary reflect the idiosyncratic investments in life-writing of the man himself, as his execution book contained a record of family births and deaths, useful addresses, and a section on veterinary medicine, all mixed amongst his observations of the men he had executed.[6] The root of Dernley's memoir was a set of 'records' kept in his own form of archival system: 'one brown envelope for each execution; each envelope containing all the newspaper cuttings, the official correspondence and my notes, usually written in the hour between the hanging and the recovery of the body'.[7] Even executioners who did not publish their reflections appear to have had an equivalent of this text: for example, Harry Allen (executioner 1941–1964), who was otherwise circumspect on the topic of his employment, kept a diary of reflections which has never been published and which was sold into a private collection in 2010.[8] The materiality or non-reproducibility of executioners' life-writing might thus explain the marginalisation of this form of writing in literary and historical studies of the twentieth century, especially added to other factors such as collaborative authorship and working-class origin. The unreliability and idiosyncratic nature of these texts have also so far prevented them from being given serious notice by historians, legal scholars, philosophers and literary critics, with a small number of exceptions.[9] Nevertheless, life-writing served a range of complex purposes for these men including the desire to make money and enhance their reputations; a wish to become part of a historical record, especially around controversial cases; an autobiographical impulse, particularly where memoirs were based on diary-keeping; and a wish to record their own response to the judicial, philosophical and legal question of capital punishment.

Testimony and Responsibility in Executioners' Memoirs

If we value the powerful truth claims made by executioners, and their sense of their writing as an historical document, we must classify these texts within the genre of testimony. Indeed, it might be appropriate to define this writing even more narrowly as a form of perpetrator testimony. As Anthony Rowland notes, 'the concepts of victim and perpetrator testimony that have been developed in relation to the holocaust are both relevant and problematized' in other contexts: Rowland's key example is World War II poetic testimony by soldiers, where his particular question is whether to class these writers as victims or perpetrators.[10] They may be 'a reluctant conscript, or subsequently traumatized individual', but their writings may also 'celebrate the killing of German soldiers' and describe violations of the Geneva Convention.[11] Rowland asks whether the term perpetrator testimony should 'only be used in a legal sense, or should critical discussions of literary testimony draw on the dictionary definition of a perpetrator as an instigator of (potentially heinous) acts, which may include—whatever the pertinent definition of criminality—the killing of others in combat?'.[12] I have only to remove the reference to 'combat' to make the question my own. Executioners were breaking no law, and, analogously with soldiers, their violence was required by and sanctioned by the state: for example, Albert Pierrepoint was appointed as an honorary lieutenant-colonel in order to perform executions at Belsen, and he would receive medals for his execution of Nazi war criminals in the aftermath of World War II. And yet, given their status as a contract worker, each executioner chose to perform his role on each individual occasion.[13]

Despite Pierrepoint's honorary post-war inclusion in the army, when he processed his responsibility for capital punishment, he argued that an analogy with soldiers was not appropriate:

> I may add that there is never at any execution the situation where an unwilling executioner is ordered to take an action which he dare not refuse. This would be the parallel to the defence offered by some Germans accused of war crimes, some indeed whom I myself have executed [...] that they were given orders which it would have been contradictory to their oath of loyalty to refuse. No executioner is appointed under sealed orders to perform any execution as directed by his superiors.[14]

But if the comparison with soldiers is rejected by Pierrepoint, how *did* executioners represent their role? The answer is a complex one, as executioners took on a wide range of postures to examine their responsibility for the death of the other at stake within the death penalty. Discourses including the theological, the psychological, the legal and the medical are used to position the executioner within the same structures that surrounded the condemned man. As a writer or storyteller, the executioner generally positions himself as an empowered figure, recalling his active participation in the machinery of justice and, with retrospective distance, interpreting events for the reader as if he were a distanced observer. But the executioner also frequently represents himself as a more involved witness to violence, sometimes even a victim of it. For Burt, this is a general problem of autobiographical writing about the death penalty: 'autobiography has ceaselessly to take on the problem of whether the I is determined by or determines the models it uses to say its experience, and thus whether it is spoken or speaking, victim or executioner'.[15]

Here the blurry distinction between execution and murder leads to a literary question about the nature of executioners' testimony. Ellis, reflecting on the controversial case of Edith Thompson, does offer himself the comfort of the 'following orders' defence: 'Now I was faced with the problem of deciding whether I would accept a request to act as executioner to someone who [...] was thought by a good many people to be innocent. The question troubled me for hours. In the end I decided that it was my duty to obey instructions'.[16] When accused by an under-sheriff (an official witness) of being 'hard hearted' after an execution, Ellis reflected that:

> As an executioner, I don't consider my heart is any harder than those of the jury men who find the accused guilty of murder, the judge who sentences them to death, or the sheriffs and prison officials who arrange the details of the executions. We are all part of the same system of British justice.[17]

Indeed, Ellis (somewhat infamously) chose to travel to witness the trials of several criminals whom he would eventually execute, as part of this self-conscious strategy of extending his responsibility for the death penalty across British society.[18] In an otherwise quite different American system, we find Elliott uttering almost identical sentiments to those of Ellis: beyond ensuring that the sentence is humanely carried out, 'my responsibility for this individual's untimely death is no greater than that of any other member of a society which endorses or condones capital punishment'.[19] Elliott further claimed that he preferred his own role to service on a jury.[20] Elliott also suggested an analogy between the work of the executioner and the work of a soldier, quoting Henri Deibler: '"To kill in the name of one's country is a glorious feat, one rewarded with medals. But to kill in the name of the law, that is a gruesome, horrible function, rewarded with scorn, contempt, and loathing"'.[21]

Even Pierrepoint, who, as we have seen, resented the implication that he was like a soldier, accepted an oblique analogy in rare cases. Reflecting on his role in the Belsen trials, he found the scale of this work reduced his sense of agency, while his belief in the apparent balance of justice and mercy appears slightly shaken:

> Often I did not know what their crimes had been, although I respected the judgement of the courts [...] It was a period of summary justice, martial law, and I do not claim that there was even time or opportunity to introduce any more merciful approach. All I could extend was my own final mercy of a quick death.[22]

As early as his first execution, there is a suggestion that Pierrepoint struggled psychologically to process his responsibility for the death penalty:

> In all my thoughts or day-dreams I had, as it were, gone through all the motions of an execution—always entirely alone except for the prisoner, curiously enough—but in my mind there was never even the suggestion of a noose. I never saw a noose. I was going through a complicated routine, alone, but there was never a noose at the end of the dream. I don't think I had ever thought about it in any waking analysis or rehearsal. Now, in real life, I looked up through the doors in the scaffold floor and saw the noose above me, and iron chains. I accepted it, and arranged it into the routine, but it was a completely new detail. I cannot explain this. I only record it.[23]

Nothing is more symbolic of the British execution system in the period in question than the image of the noose: the fact that Pierrepoint, despite his intimate knowledge of his father's work, was unable to imagine the rope in planning his own career suggests a powerful denial of both the reality of the death penalty and his responsibility for it. Similarly, Elliott, after witnessing his first execution, that of Carmine Gaimari in 1903, writes that he 'could not convince myself that I had actually been present at his death'.[24]

In the context of this anxiety about judicial violence and individual responsibility in the context of perpetrator testimony, the vacillation between different retrospective views of the encounter between condemned man and executioner is frequently reflected in the range of language choices made by the executioner-as-author. Berry mainly described the men and women he executed as 'prisoners', 'murderers' and 'criminals': but more than once, when depicting the detailed process of hanging, often in particularly violent passages, he revealingly called them 'victims'. For example, 'the drop must not be so great as to outwardly mutilate the victim';[25] 'in the earliest days of hanging it was the practice for the executioner to place his noose around the victim's neck, and then to haul on the rope';[26] 'The drop was not so long as to absolutely pull off the victim's head, but it ruptured the principal blood-vessels of the neck'.[27] Similarly, Ellis referred to one of the condemned as a 'poor doomed wretch' and sometimes uses the more general 'wretches' to describe those he executed, suggesting some sympathy with the plight of those subject to capital punishment.[28] While Pierrepoint was always careful to avoid calling the condemned 'victims', he repeatedly used religious language in order to indicate his respect for their humanity: he writes that 'There is only a final relationship which matters: in Christianity this is my brother or sister to whom something dreadful must be done, and I have tried always to be gentle with them, and to give them what dignity I could in their death'.[29]

By contrast, Dernley, with deliberately crude irony, occasionally uses the word 'clients' to describe the condemned.[30] All of these writers refer to their work as 'a craft', connecting it with creativity and skilled labour rather than with violence, killing or crime. Indeed, their writings often imply connections between their work and medical or spiritual care.

All the executioners in this chapter connect their role to cultural questions of legal, cultural and social responsibility. For example, literary references by these unusual life-writers sought to contextualise their role as executioners with reference to a broader society in which, they felt, the majority of members of the public were supportive of their work. For example, Pierrepoint wrote that 'The executioner in Shaw's play *Saint Joan* speaks of his craft as a "highly skilled mystery". That is what I found it to be'.[31] Pierrepoint's family tradition led him down the path of becoming an executioner, but nonetheless he found this quotation by Shaw expressed his experience of his work as empowering, a craft and a mystery. Dernley credits his choice to become an executioner to his childhood reading of Golden Age detective fiction, especially Edgar Wallace:

> I decided to become a hangman when I was eleven years old. It all started when I was browsing among the shelves of the small local library at Mansfield Woodhouse in Nottinghamshire, and, by chance, picked up a book by Edgar Wallace. [...] Wallace had seen a couple of hangings and when he later turned his hand to writing crime thrillers, he made good use of the experience. I was fascinated by the tension and drama of the preparations for the execution and when I closed the covers of the book, I found myself thinking that I could do that...I could be an executioner.[32]

Dernley was thus inspired to create a small personal library of books that spoke to his sense of vocation, amassing a 'very good collection of books on crime and punishment', which he began through the purchase of Berry's memoir.[33] Perhaps as interestingly, Elliott, by contrast, deliberately avoided consuming crime films and books, implying that they have too powerful an effect on his imagination.[34]

Because the confessional form requires constant adjustment of claims about agency, the executioner's position in relation to questions of guilt, power and responsibility is not stable, and might look different from sentence to sentence, as he imagines himself sharing responsibility with others, obeying orders like a soldier, and refusing to acknowledge violence by taking on other models of labour like craft and care. Further, as we will see in subsequent sections, the executioner as life-writer is struggling against the nature of their material: they must translate a mostly silent, intensely physical, and deeply traumatic process into words.

The Body of the Condemned

Gill Plain has argued that the remapping of 'the familiar landscape' of crime writing might be achieved through an analysis of how the body is written as an agent or victim of violence.[35] While Plain is particularly focused on the boundary between 'hard-boiled' and 'soft-boiled' writing, her emphasis on the ability to 'read' the body in relation to violence gains a particular additional valence if we consider that, as we saw in the previous section, executioners were reading these Golden Age texts and partaking of the 'cultural complexity' that she identifies.[36] In this section I will explore an analogous version of the detective's appraising or scientific investigation of bodies by examining the measuring gaze turned upon the condemned person by the executioner. By the twentieth century the criminal body had long been overdetermined by eugenic thinking and, especially, by Cesare Lombroso's early criminological work on the criminal body. Twentieth-century developments of this tendency to study and record the criminal body included fingerprint technology and criminal photography.[37] These ideas shaped both the treatment of capital offenders and the way the death penalty was represented in executioners' life-writing. Criminal measurements were readily converted into physical and mental typologies, and this style of scientific thinking had a direct impact on how executioners understood their trade: for example, in 1889 James Berry had to be disciplined by prison authorities for lecturing on criminal phrenology in a public house in Kidderminster.[38] While many ideas from criminal anthropology had already been discredited by psychoanalysts, including Freud and Reik, who emphasised on how 'normal' minds and bodies were also subject to the same violent impulses, these notions nevertheless continued to shape both fictional and nonfictional writing about justice and punishment.

The fictional texts which I am examining across this project generally have a more stereotyped view of the death penalty, which is not so intensely physical and medicalised as executioners' life-writing. One exception to this is F. Tennyson Jesse's *A Pin to See the Peepshow* (1934), which, although it cuts away from her protagonist Julia Starling's actual execution, still offers a very precise response to the condemned prisoner's body.

Jesse's prison doctor's perspective includes similar grotesque details to those we find in executioners' memoirs: for example, he anticipates examining Julia's body after her death, 'Here he would have the job of testing the heat that had been stilled for ever, of noting at which cervical vertebra the fracture had occurred, even of noting the haemorrhage that might burst forth', and considers how the body of her lover Leonard Carr will be transformed by an involuntary erection: 'nature would take her last ironic revenge in the body of the man who had killed for love, making a final gesture, lewd as a sneer'.[39] Jesse depicts very clearly how the condemned are medically treated before execution including the use of alcohol, bromide and injections: Julia's experience of the prison doctor makes her feel that his questions 'were being asked about a dead body instead of about a living one'.[40] The original *TLS* reviewer, Orlo Williams, felt a sense of resistance to Jesse's realism: 'Julia's dream ends in the Central Criminal Court, in the condemned cell and on the scaffold, the sordid horrors of which are conscientiously piled upon the reader'.[41] For Gerald Gould, *The Observer* reviewer, the scenes of Julia's trial and punishment 'are awful in their reality',[42] while for the anonymous reviewer in *The Times*, Jesse 'piles on the horrors of the closing episode a little unnecessarily'.[43] These contemporary responses to the novel reflect a rejection of Jesse's frank and embodied representation of the death penalty and thus a deliberate denial of the process of capital punishment.[44] This level of insight into the process of execution is rare in a fictional text, and we might wonder where Jesse acquired this level of knowledge: perhaps from her criminological work or from direct interviews.

As discussed in the introduction, after the Aberdare Committee report (1888) a standard table of execution drops was produced by the Home Office. In Marwood's system, and following on from him, the condemned prisoner's weight was the key factor, but records of their age, general health and muscular condition were also believed to be necessary. Therefore the prisoner would not only be weighed before their execution, but the hangman would be allowed to view them directly on the day before their execution (usually through an observation window into the cell or the exercise yard).[45] In the previous section, we saw how executioners often represent their work as a skilled craft, but in describing their execution methods they also often used the language of science. For example, Berry referred to his 'table of drops' as constructed through experiment, experience and calculation on 'a truly scientific basis'.[46] A huge amount of data was created about the condemned person's body, which would be recorded before the execution in the executioner's diary and afterwards in a special coroner's report. In assessing the evidence of execution practice between 1900 and 1950, the Gowers Commission therefore had access to extremely detailed information about the body of the condemned prisoner before and after death. An appendix to their report included records of hangings carried out at Pentonville between 1931 and 1950 with a table which noted the precise effect of execution on the bodies of executed prisoners: including which vertebrae were dislocated; whether the spinal cord was crushed, severed or torn and whether there were signs of asphyxia in the lungs.[47]

Within executioners' memoirs, the condemned person's body was subject to an appraising, reifying gaze, as the executioners experienced their 'victim' primarily as a mathematical, scientific problem. We see this very starkly in the descriptive language used in each case, which were based on original observations and calculations entered into the executioner's diary. For example, James Berry's first execution, the double execution of Robert Vickers and William Innes, seems to have made little impression on him as a personal experience, but he had access to very precise details of measurement: 'The respective weights were 10 stone 4 lbs. and 9 stone 6 lbs., and I gave them drops of 8 ft. 6 in. and 10 ft. respectively'.[48] Similarly, of Frederick Seddon, executed in 1912 after one of the most sensational murder trials of the century, Ellis is precise about physical measurement: 'He was only a medium-sized man. Officially he stood 5 ft. 3 in. in height and 136 lb in weight, but he had a way of proudly holding himself that made you think he was a much bigger man'.[49] After an examination of Josef Kramer, the 'Beast of Belsen', Pierrepoint regretted that he was too 'busy making a note about his physique' to hear how he answered questions about more sensitive topics, such as his religion.[50] Similarly, in a suppressed manuscript, originally planned for publication in the *Empire News*, Pierrepoint focused on the body of Ruth Ellis, noting her loose hair and her 'dab of lipstick' on the execution morning, and on the practical difficulties of hanging a woman.[51] A similar suppressed manuscript exists about the execution of Neville Heath, who Pierrepoint called 'the handsomest murderer I ever hanged' betraying eugenic anxieties in relation to the hanging: 'He was such a splendid physical specimen of manhood that it seemed a pitiful thing to have to hang him'.[52] In his description of Heath, the professional and appraising gaze blurs with an apparently erotic interest:

> He had no soft fat on his body at all. He weighed a spare 171 lbs despite his height of 5ft. 11 inches, and with his clear blue eyes and fair, curly hair, he looked like a tall young god. Yes, even to me, and I am not usually much disturbed by what a man looks like.[53]

In this sense, cultural memory of these famous justice cases is shaped by each executioner's very specific physical impression of the bodies of criminal men and women just before execution. This focus on sensational physical details is also a strategy to avoid reflecting on the executioner's responsibility: to objectify a criminal body is also to divest them of their ethical status as a living subject.

While the American system of electrocution described by Elliot might seem not to require detailed physical data about the condemned person, such information was nonetheless required and produced: 'Certain information about the condemned is necessary to guard against mishaps. I must know his general physical specifications such as his size and height'.[54] In the American system, Elliott noted, sometimes 'experiments' were also conducted during the electrocution: George Ogle examined the body of one condemned man by wearing rubber gloves, noting 'muscular contraction' and alterations to the man's heart rhythm during the execution.[55] On another occasion, a heart monitor was attached to provide a record of the heart's action during electrocution. The body of the condemned person was managed by straps, while both men and women had their hair clipped to allow contact with the electrodes.[56] Elliott's narrative is also full of different kinds of information, especially about the regulation of electricity in each case, its voltage, and for how many minutes and seconds it was turned on: for example, explaining that 'the average number of amperes in an electrocution is eleven' but that resistance in different human bodies might be less or greater.[57] Further, in keeping with the period's eugenic criminological discourse, the body of the executed man, and its resistance or responsiveness to the lethal electricity, was also used as evidence of their moral character. For example, Austin Sarat quotes the *Tribune* on a botched execution in 1898 which required five electric shocks over eight minutes: 'Ferraro was of a brutish nature, and it has been the experience at Sing Sing that men of that stamp offer more resistance to the electric current than those of more delicate composition'.[58] The greater need for scientific knowledge and training meant that Elliott was interviewed for the role of executioner not just by the prison warden, but also by the General Electric Company.[59] Elliott was also keen to correct popular misinformation about the electric chair noting that, for example, 'contrary to popular belief' the lights in the prison 'do not dim when the death chamber switch is thrown' because 'the current for the chair is on a separate circuit' to the central power for the prison.[60]

Increased technological efficiency and smoother execution protocols led to an emphasis on speed. Each executioner linked their professional pride with humane concerns, arguing that speed was necessary to spare the prisoner a cruel suspense. But in each life-writing narrative, the repetitive, compulsive concern with the speed at which a live, guilty person could be transformed into a dead body might begin to have connotations of cruelty, indignity and unseemly haste. These contradictions are especially visible in the more condensed evidence which Pierrepoint gave to the Gowers Commission when asked if the punishment is 'as humane and quick' as possible: 'Yes, I think [hanging] is quick, certain and humane. I think it is the fastest and quickest in the world bar nothing. It is quicker than shooting and cleaner'.[61] Pierrepoint makes claims about speed four times within this short answer ('quick', 'fastest', 'quickest', 'quicker'), alongside just three claims for humaneness (it is 'certain', 'humane' and 'clean'). When asked 'whether the condemned man suffers any pain' in the use of the electric chair, Elliott likewise short-circuited the question by discussing the speed of the method: 'Medical experts declare that unconsciousness is produced in less than one two-hundred-and-fortieth of a second. This, then, is as humane as ordered death can possibly be.'[62]

The executioner was also conscious of a sense of revulsion or anxiety in reflecting upon their own measuring gaze. For example, Albert Pierrepoint builds on his father's legacy of diary-keeping but also wished to depart from his practice: 'When I came to keep my own execution diary I [...] omitted any reference to the condition of the condemned man's neck, which I found a little distasteful to record'.[63] Pierrepoint also felt compelled by the prison authorities to keep measurements that he would not otherwise wish to record, noting the 'strange requirement' to measure 'the stretch of the man's body' after he had been left hanging on the rope for an hour.[64] Pierrepoint experiences revulsion from this particular measurement, perhaps because of a sense of disrespect: 'This was the last ignominy in hanging, a relic from the time when bodies were exposed on the gibbet. I had no heart for it, nor for the careful logging in registers of the dimension of the distortion of the body'.[65] Pierrepoint was uncomfortable answering questions about bodies in front of the two female members of the Gowers Commission, Dame Florence Hancock and Elizabeth Bowen.

(I will discuss Bowen's participation in the Gowers Commission in a later chapter.) Pierrepoint's professional squeamishness, a sense that discussing his work was 'difficult' and 'embarrassing', seems to come less from the aspects of his work that we might expect (e.g. his experience of stripping the body for burial) or even a feeling that women might be opposed to the death penalty.[66] Rather, his anxiety was about the measuring gaze and his rarer memories where the criminal body did not fit into the normal requirements of the system of hanging in which he participated:

> I just do not speak of this sort of thing before women. How far did they want me to go into detail? One of the men I had to execute soon after I started courting Annie was a dwarf. I didn't even tell her I was going on a job, let alone discuss the problems of the length of the coil, the height of the noose, and the drop to be calculated for the abnormal muscular formation of a dwarf.[67]

Pierrepoint was concerned that were he to tell this story, or many others in his repertoire, capital punishment would come to seem grotesque. Other executioners were also alert to how hanging as a form of execution calls for an able, healthy body. There were many ways that normal precautions built into the system could fail: the condemned person might become hysterical or faint on the scaffold;[68] they might have made an earlier suicide attempt which had left damage to their neck and wrists;[69] they might have missing limbs or other disabilities and abnormalities;[70] they might be offered brandy or be prescribed medication that would make their experience harder;[71] they might resist execution by fighting with the warders.[72] Sometimes a mistake might be made in assessing the prisoner's general measurements or condition: these cases could result in decapitation or asphyxiation.[73]

In the American system described by Elliott, many of these risks were present, added to others including power outage[74] and problems when the electrodes caused burning of the body.[75] The effect of electrocution on the prisoner's body might also cause 'a gurgling in the throat' caused by air escaping from the lungs, which, though a reflex action and not necessarily a sign of suffering, was still felt by observers to be particularly grotesque and abject.[76] Prison guards might also be burned when removing the condemned person's dead body from the chair.[77] While these risks could be minimised through the use of special equipment, they could never be fully removed. Sometimes the equipment itself would fail or be misused.[78] In any of these circumstances, rather than the ideal of the scientific, speedy and humane treatment that has been described, an execution might become extremely traumatic for the prisoner, executioner and witnesses. Even a 'normal' execution might sound disturbing when recorded in such detail. Elliott's discussion of a general case of how execution by electricity should work is a case in point: 'The figure in the chair pitches forward, straining against the straps. There is the whining cry of the current, and a crackling, sizzling sound. The body turns a vivid red. Sparks often shoot from the electrodes. A wisp of white or dull grey smoke may rise from the top of the head or the leg [...] An offensive odour generally present'.[79] Elliott describes common physical reactions to the execution scene experienced by witnesses including turning pale, gagging, trembling, crying out or even fainting.[80]

Even when the execution went perfectly, the criminal body then quickly became a problem again in relation to post-mortem and burial. In Britain the executioner's role often required him to move rapidly from retributive to apparently caring modes of behaviour. It was not widely known even in the period in question that the executioner had charge of the condemned person's body after death: he had responsibility to take the body down from the gallows and to strip it for the post-mortem or for burial.[81] Pierrepoint dwells quite movingly on the restorative, affective value of this second phase of his work, in which he assumes the role of doctor, undertaker and priest simultaneously:

> I put the tape measure away, and went below. I stared at the flesh I had stilled. I had further duties to perform, but no longer as executioner. I had been nearest to this man in death, and I prepared him for burial. As he hung, I stripped him. Piece by piece I removed his clothes. It was not callous, but the best rough dignity I could give him, as he swung to the touch, still hooded in the noose. He yielded his garments without the resistance of limbs. If it had been in a prison outside London, I should have left him his shirt for a shroud, and put him in his coffin. In London there was always a post-mortem, and he had to be stripped entirely and placed on a mortuary stretcher. But in common courtesy I tied his empty shirt around his hips. Wade had fixed the tackle above. I passed a rope under the armpits of my charge, and the body was hauled up a few feet. Standing on the scaffold, with the body now drooping, I removed the noose and the cap, and took his head between my hands, inclining it from side to side to assure myself that the break had been clean. Then I went below, and Wade lowered the rope. A dead man, being taken down from execution, is a uniquely broken body

> whether he is a criminal or Christ, and I received this flesh leaning helplessly into my arms, with the linen round the loins, gently with the reverence I thought due to the shell of any man who has sinned and suffered.[82]

Pierrepoint goes so far to state that he is 'no longer' an 'executioner' in the moments following an execution. The tape measure, the stripping of the body, the post-mortem, the stretcher, the details of armpits and hips all suggest the medical doctor. Pierrepoint also constructs the scene more deliberately in religious terms in his references to Christ, to 'reverence', to the man having 'sinned and suffered'. While we cannot be sure which painting he is thinking of specifically, the passage alludes directly to the tradition of the 'Descent for the Cross' (also called 'Deposition from the Cross'). But other details in the scene are more troubling and mark this specifically as a less aestheticized scene of violence: the body of the condemned man is 'uniquely broken', a 'shell' and, perhaps most strikingly, the clothes of the dead man are removed before the noose and the hood. While Pierrepoint attempts to keep his representation of the scene detached, strange traces of sexuality and violence persist.

None of the executioners explain if they are required to have similarly close contact with female executed prisoners after their death. It does seem likely that practices were different. Ellis briefly noted that he helped the matron in putting Thompson's body in her coffin, but he does not further explain how his involvement was required.[83] He also noted that before her execution he was allowed to see her 'in her undies'.[84] While Pierrepoint says he wished to always maintain detachment, he also displays some fetishist behaviour in his use of a 'special strap' to mark a personal interest in the execution. The special strap is

> made of pliant pale calf-leather, no different in design from the straps I normally used, supplied by the Home Office in the box of execution apparatus, but it is personal to me. I have used it only about a dozen times. Whenever I used it I made a red ink entry in my private diary.[85]

Pierrepoint does not list all those whose bodies were treated as special in this way but included John George Haigh, Neville Heath and Josef Kramer as examples.

In Dernley's memoir, there was a notable lack of reference to the gentleness and care regarding condemned bodies that Pierrepoint attempted to show, which is especially stark given that Pierrepoint had trained him.

Dernley is more generally concerned with grotesque details of the body of the condemned in which he maintains an unhealthy interest: for example, he notes that the execution of Timothy Evans was 'the only time I heard the noise' of a man's neck breaking.[86] This focus on how Evans's body was exceptional distracts from the controversial aspect of Evans's established innocence at the time Dernley was writing and distracts the reader from the miscarriage of justice: indeed, Dernley briefly insists on Evans's guilt. Many of Dernley's most frank, troubling reflections on embodiment within the execution process came out of direct conflict with Pierrepoint himself. For example, Pierrepoint briefly told a story within his memoirs of an anonymous assistant making a crude remark while stripping the body.[87] Dernley seems determined, in writing his own story much later, to fill in the gaps in Pierrepoint's narrative and to upset his former mentor's cherished idea of the 'sanctity' of the execution process. Dernley wished to make clear that executioners and their assistants had their share of morbid curiosity, of disgust and sexual deviancy and therefore revisits this story of the inappropriate assistant to reveal himself as the culprit:

> I was stripping the last items of clothing from the body when it became clear that the dead man was…shall I say, well-endowed. "Now that's what I call a magnificent set of vital parts!" I cracked out. No doubt there are a lot of people who will say that it was a very crass and awful remark to make. Certainly it was a very weak joke. All I can say in my own defence is that the atmosphere was so bad that I wanted to say something to break the tension and raise a laugh; it did not. There was no reaction from the screws or Pierrepoint or the stranger.[88]

We can hardly reconcile these conflicting stories with the way Pierrepoint represented his work, as offering dignity in death, or with the medical and scientific claims made by other executioners, but that does not necessarily make Dernley's more violent and unvarnished version untrue. As I will show in the next section, while the body of the condemned person, as well as the executioner's responsibility for violence, was usually managed by execution technologies and procedures, all these executioners are haunted by failures of control.

The Executioner's Body and Mind

The executioner's body might ultimately fail to respond in the ideal ways demanded by the system of capital punishment, or their minds might register a permanent trauma. Just as executioners recorded and measured the bodies and behaviour of condemned men, so the Home Office also archived judgements on the behaviour of men they employed as executioners. Doyle and O'Donnell note the removal of William Willis from the Home Office approved list of executioners due to carelessness, including an anonymous judgement on Willis's character and body as 'fat, clumsy and possibly a little flurried'.[89] The Governor of Pentonville further recorded a moral judgement on Willis's psychology that 'One considers cold calculated callousness as part of an executioner's make up but brutal callousness bordering on blood-lust is not desirable, and this is the impression Willis gave to me'.[90] These files also note that Stanley William Cross and Robert Baxter, both on the official list of executioners in both England and Ireland in the 1920s and 1930s, had 'defective eyesight' that might hinder their work, while detailed medical files and witness statements were kept regarding Thomas Pierrepoint to determine if he was too old for the physical and mental demands of his job.[91]

The Prison Commission additionally kept note of drunkenness by executioners.[92] Doyle and O'Donnell note that the execution of Michael Manning required a special explanation for the Irish Department of Justice about why so much whiskey had been consumed (and not by the condemned man). They include a response from the deputy governor who stated that

> the whiskey was requisitioned by the Medical Officer for issue to those members of the staff whose duty it was to attend at the execution, the removal of the remains from the execution chamber to the hospital for post mortem examination…and the actual burial following the holding of an inquest. This sequence of events […] provide a most undesirable and unpleasant experience for the officials concerned, hence the necessity for requisitioning the whiskey.[93]

The concerns expressed by the authorities about drinking *after* a successful execution suggest not an anxiety about humaneness but rather an aesthetic sense that the execution must be seen to be a decorous and fundamentally normal occasion, indicating an official denial of the fact that an execution might be traumatic for those involved. However, Doyle and O'Donnell are conscious of the ironies of drinking culture around an execution given the widespread role of intoxication as a driver of capital crimes in Ireland at the time (it had been the unsuccessful defence in Manning's own case) and further remind us of Pierrepoint's own role as a publican in the period.[94] The link between killing, whether murder or judicial execution, and alcoholic indulgence is central to this vignette. Beyond this anecdote, in the memoirs, in government records and in public discourse there is a recognition of the necessity of alcohol consumption to facilitate the death penalty.

The trainee executioner might undergo even more abject physical experiences than drunkenness or clumsiness. Again, Dernley is most direct about how the executioner's body might become grotesque or unruly. His account of training to be an executioner immediately foregrounded the disruptive male bodies of those who are attempting to choose this as their profession: in breaks in their training to use the equipment, he and his fellow trainees urinated in the post-mortem room sinks.[95] Further, Dernley frankly admitted his fear of fainting or vomiting at his first execution: 'The first hanging was shattering. As a trainee executioner I was there to watch. I did not have to do anything except stay on my feet and keep my breakfast down'.[96] Elliott likewise felt 'nauseated' during his first execution after focusing too much on the body of the condemned man: 'I saw the body lurch against the straps…Sparks danced about the leg electrode part of the time. Greyish blue smoke rose from the head, and a faint odour of burning flesh reached my nostrils'.[97] While Dernley managed to get through this experience, one of his fellow trainees, Dickinson, had a 'brief and disastrous' career because of his traumatised physical response to his first hanging.[98] After Dickinson's first execution, Pierrepoint offered him a lift home in his car and later told Dernley the story of the journey: Pierrepoint reflected, according to Dernley, 'We were driving back to Manchester. He looked a bit white and he was saying hardly anything. Then all of a sudden he groaned and the bugger was sitting there pissing himself!'.[99] Dernley recounted in a long vignette how Dickinson wet himself three times on the way home to Pierrepoint's disgust: Dickinson resigned and emigrated to Canada shortly thereafter.

The psychological effect of each execution might be even more damaging than the physical symptoms of trauma indicated above. During training, each trainee executioner took on the role of the condemned man at least once, so that other trainees could practice on him. Thus, they had direct experience of the physical and mental effects of execution protocols and of putting themselves imaginatively in the place of the condemned man. Dernley's memoir manifests an intriguing formal breakdown when he is required to do this himself, including the use of ellipses to reflect his sense of panic:

> this time I'm being hanged and the first time it's terrifying. There's the tap on your shoulder...you start to rise and they have your arms behind your back...the straps are on and you can't do a thing, you're helpless...they turn you and there's the noose hanging through in the other room and you're walking towards it...closer...you're in the execution chamber, and the hangman stops you and you're standing on the trapdoor...then it's so dark...hood on the face...things going on that you can't see...something tightening around the legs...noose round the neck...something under the chin...hard to breathe...scuffling.[100]

Here Dernley includes details of the emotional effects of capital punishment on its victims ('terrifying' and 'helpless'), but he is mainly focused on the disturbing effect of its sensory aspects ('the tap on your shoulder', 'the straps', 'it's so dark', 'hard to breathe', 'scuffling'). Elliott recounts a similar psychological reaction when he first sits in the electric chair, long before he becomes an executioner, after an official's wife asked for demonstration: he was 'strapped in' by a guard 'just as he would a person doomed to die'.[101] Although, like Dernley, Elliott was perfectly safe (he was not wearing electrodes and the current was off), nonetheless, a strange sensation engulfed me. I felt so completely helpless. I realized that, no matter how hard I might struggle, I could not free myself. I wondered whether those who had been put to death in this fashion had felt the same way, only, of course, to a greater degree.[102]

Dernley's memory of acting the part of the condemned man is the source of recurring nightmares, suggesting a greater likelihood of serious psychological harm than he is able to acknowledge:

> In the dream it is execution morning and I am the condemned man! The cell door opens...two figures come towards me...my arms are strapped...I see the noose in front of me...they start dragging me towards the gallows...I am screaming for it to stop...and I have woken in a cold sweat! I have had the nightmare twice. The first time they got me as far as the door leading into the execution chamber before I woke up. The second time they actually got me on to the trap. I am hoping they do not come a third time.[103]

These depictions of his experience as a trainee and of his recurring nightmare are the only times Dernley's account departs from strict realistic, even irreverent reporting. Elliott also noted another occasion when he experienced a 'strange sensation' when working as an assistant executioner early in his career. He made the mistake of looking into the condemned man's eyes: 'It was the first time I had ever looked into the eyes of an individual on the brink of eternity. The blaze of those blue eyes held mine. I was as though hypnotized. I could feel the perspiration on my forehead. [...] I could not move. Neither could I take my eyes from his'.[104] Elliott had to blink his eyes to be able to continue the execution: another guard involved in the death penalty also believed that he had been hypnotised by a condemned man, but they were afraid to talk about what happened in case the authorities thought they were 'crazy'.[105]

It is worthwhile, in closing, to return to Rowland's questions about whether a perpetrator can also be a victim in examining more fully the psychological effect of their work on executioners. As early as 1899, there was substantial coverage of the case of Amos Lunt, a former executioner at San Quentin Prison who had to be institutionalised after believing that he was being haunted by the ghosts of the men he had executed.[106] Another exemplary case in the American context was John Hulbert, Elliott's predecessor as executioner, who once fainted in the execution chamber and who committed suicide within two years of his 1926 retirement.[107] In Britain, for subsequent executioners and for popular culture, the story of Ellis is a case study and flash point for thinking about the traumatic effect of executions on an executioner, after his prosecution for attempted suicide in 1924 and final suicide in 1931. In working with volumes of executioners' memoirs held by my home institution, I found that Western Bank Library at the University of Sheffield contains a very unusual copy of Henry Sanson's *Seven Generations of Executioners*, which has been modified by one of its past readers.[108] This mystery 1930s reader has glued a 1932 newspaper clipping about the executioner John Ellis's death by suicide with the date, as well as their own initials, onto the flyleaf of the book. The reader apparently means to record their opposition to capital punishment, by implying that Ellis's tragic end was a judgement on the psychology of his whole profession. Narratives about Ellis's life and death continued to be contested as a way of considering the traumatic effect of the death penalty as long as capital punishment existed in Britain: for example, a large government file from 1956 assesses the likely psychological effect of Edith Thompson's execution on Ellis and other witnesses, considering (but rejecting) the idea that this execution was the cause of his suicide.[109] By the time Dernley started his training in the late 1940s, prospective executioners were not only interviewed by the prison governor and subject to a medical and physical fitness test, but they were also vetted as to their psychological health. In keeping with his refusal to conceptualise himself as a victim, Dernley considers this, revealingly, as a test of his potential sexual pathology, rather than of his psychological soundness and ability to withstand traumatic work: 'He asked me a few funny questions which were obviously probing my psychological state, to make sure I was not a pervert trying to get his thrills with the government's help, and he then went on to give me a medical'.[110] In Dernley's case, the authorities might have been wise to have been even more discerning and inquisitive.

While more visceral, emotional moments occur in each memoir, emphasis should be placed upon the more reflective conclusions in each text, which are often still full of contradictory claims and judgements. Most of these texts, though very conflicted, thus fit a model of perpetrator confession summarised by Carl R. Lovitt:

> Reik and Doody's model of the criminal who confesses to repudiate his crime evidently presupposes that the crime and the confession are incommensurable. According to their conception, the confession reflects the criminal's dissociation from the crime; it purports to show that the writer, like other law-abiding citizen is no longer capable of committing such a crime.[111]

As part of the terms of their employment, no practising executioner was permitted to tell their sensational secrets to the public: in fact, this publishing culture depended on executioners being dismissed from or becoming disillusioned with their profession. To write the texts I have been examining, then, executioners must become confessional writers who retain the memory of their work and yet develop a detachment from it. They must dissociate themselves from capital punishment and from past commitments that they made to governmental and penal authorities to keep their work a secret. But these memoirs also necessarily memorialise themselves in the public mind in the role of executioner. For example, in Elliott's final chapter, he claims that he is not a murderer and does not feel like one, as well as asserting that he is not remorseful and does not fear death. (This text was written when he was critically ill, so he must be conscious that this text will be a personal epitaph.) Nevertheless, the second half of this chapter, revealingly called 'Death is Not the Answer', argued against the death penalty and hopes that one day it will be replaced by life imprisonment. In order to prevent this being too contradictory, Elliott pathologises not the executioner but the public, accusing them of sadism.[112] Pierrepoint also argued against capital punishment, placing his work in the past tense and distancing himself from his past support for the practice: 'I had an ambition, I have it no longer. All the desire is quite gone'.[113] But we should also consider the circumstances of these changes of heart. Dernley's crude judgement on Pierrepoint's claim is nevertheless insightful: 'When you have hanged more than 680 people, it's a hell of a time to find out that you do not believe capital punishment achieves anything!'.[114] Elliott himself had executed 387 people before writing his conclusion that he hoped that the day is coming when 'legal slaying [...] is outlawed throughout the United States'.[115] Dernley remained in favour of execution and argued defensively (despite his nightmares) that his work has left him unscathed. But the close of his memoir still finds him dwelling on how the work had blighted the lives of many of his peers: 'Several [executioners] had unsuccessful and problematical lives when their hanging days were over'.[116] His friend Kirky 'became a very strange old man' who kept a loaded revolver on his wall at home, while Steve Wade 'always did look a haunted man' and 'Even the great Pierrepoint developed some strange ideas in the end'.[117]

Across this chapter we have examined a neglected strand of writing in the form of life-writing produced by executioners, in which those employed to dispense retributive justice offered their testimony about how it worked in practice. Burt has argued of Derrida's work that 'autobiography is a good to place to start to re-think the subject as the subject of the death penalty in a way that might provide a basis for a principled abolitionist argument'.[118] While these writers were not philosophers but rather the personnel of state-sanctioned execution, these autobiographers still often seek out 'a self-reflexive turn' and a perspective in which the death penalty no longer seems necessary.[119] This examination has given us a unique perspective on the scientific, spiritual, medical and literary claims made about the process of capital punishment in the twentieth century, as well as a deeper understanding of the foundation of the death penalty in the interaction of the executioner's body and the condemned man's. While new technologies and procedures aimed to humanise and regulate twentieth century capital punishment, the state would continue to depend on vulnerable and fallible humans to act as agents of death: these life narratives reflect the nature of that dependence as well as a deep ambivalence about the responsibility held by executioners within a broader system of justice.

Notes

1. James Berry, *My Experiences as an Executioner*, ed. by H. Snowden Ward, London: Percy Lund, 1892, 66.
2. John Ellis, *Diary of a Hangman*, London: Forum Press, 1996, 9.
3. Robert G. Elliott and Albert R. Beatty, *Agent of Death: The Memoirs of an Executioner*, London: John Long, 1940, 93.
4. Berry, *My Experiences as an Executioner*, 9.
5. Elliott, *Agent of Death*, 77.
6. Albert Pierrepoint, *Executioner: Pierrepoint*, Random Acres: Eric Dobby Press, 2005, 52–53.
7. Dernley, *The Hangman's Tale: Memoirs of A Public Executioner*, London: Robert Hale, 1989, 195.
8. The diary, together with other personal items, sold for £17,200 to Mike James of the 'True Crime Library' publishing house ('Hangman's effects auctioned', Manchester Evening News, 18th April 2010 https://www.manchestereveningnews.co.uk/news/greater-manchester-news/hangmans-effects-auctioned-972869 [Accessed 13th May 2018]).
9. See, for example, in history, Ian O'Donnell and David Doyle use Pierrepoint's autobiography to give serious consideration to the ramifications of the work in Ireland of Henry and Albert Pierrepoint between 1923 and 1954 in 'A Family Affair: English Hangmen and a Dublin Jail, 1923–54', *New Hibernia Review*, Vol. 18, No. 8. (2014): 101–118 and, in philosophy, Christopher Bennett, 'Considering Capital Punishment as a Human Interaction', *Criminal Law and Philosophy*, Vol. 7, No. 2 (2013): 367–382.
10. Anthony Rowland, 'The Oasis Poets: Perpetrators, Victims, and Soldier Testimony', *Poetry as Testimony: Witnessing and Memory in Twentieth-century Poems*, New York and London: Routledge, 2014: 41–69 (41–42).
11. Rowland, 'Oasis Poets', 41.
12. Rowland, 'Oasis Poets', 42.
13. This is in direct contrast to, say, the French system or some colonial systems, where the executioner was an official salaried employee.
14. Albert Pierrepoint, *Executioner: Pierrepoint*, 77.
15. E. S. Burt, 'The Autobiographical Subject and the Death Penalty', *The Oxford Literary Review*, Vol. 35, No. 2 (2013): 165–187 (180).
16. Ellis, *Diary of a Hangman*, 17.
17. Ellis, *Diary of a Hangman*, 111.
18. Ellis, *Diary of a Hangman*, 73.

19. Elliott, *Agent of Death*, 12.
20. Elliott, *Agent of Death*, 208.
21. Elliott, *Agent of Death*, 204.
22. Pierrepoint, *Executioner: Pierrepoint*, 158.
23. Pierrepoint, *Executioner: Pierrepoint*, 93.
24. Elliott, *Agent of Death*, 46–47.
25. Berry, *My Experiences*, 30.
26. Berry, *My Experiences*, 30.
27. Berry, *My Experiences*, 33.
28. Ellis, *Diary of a Hangman*, 17 and 232.
29. Pierrepoint, *Executioner: Pierrepoint*, 34.
30. Dernley, *The Hangman's Tale*, 200.
31. Pierrepoint, *Executioner: Pierrepoint*, 117. Pierrepoint's choice of *Saint Joan* as inspiration for his work as an executioner is interesting as Alison Garden has explored Shaw's inspiration for the play in the Casement case: it is ironic because we would not expect identification with the executioner in a play like this one (Garden, *The Literary Afterlives of Roger Casement, 1899–2016*, Liverpool: Liverpool University Press, 2020, 108–115). In the historical narrative, the executioner is reported to have claimed that he 'greatly feared to be damned for he had burned a holy woman' (Régine Pernoud, *Joan of Arc by Herself and Her Witnesses*, Lanham: Scarborough House, 1994, 233), while in Shaw's play he is the subject of a dark comedy.
32. Dernley, *The Hangman's Tale*, 13.
33. Dernley, *The Hangman's Tale*, 24.
34. Elliott, *Agent of Death*, 181 and 209.
35. Gill Plain, *Twentieth-century Crime Fiction: Gender, Sexuality and the Body*, Edinburgh: Edinburgh University Press, 2001, 30.
36. Plain, *Twentieth-century Crime Fiction*, 31.
37. For recent critical work on this topic, see, for example, Rex Ferguson, 'Personal Impressions: Fingerprints, Freud and Conrad', *New Formations: a journal of culture/theory/politics*, Vol. 79 (2013): 43–62 and Alyce von Rothkirch, '"His face was livid, dreadful, with a foam at the corners of his mouth": a typology of the villains in Detective Fiction', *Modern Language Review*, Vol. 108 (2013): 1042–1063.
38. Harry Potter, *Hanging in judgement: religion and the death penalty in England from the bloody code to abolition*, London: SCM Press, 1993, 103.
39. F. Tennyson Jesse, *A Pin to See the Peepshow*, London: Virago, 1988, 392–393.
40. Jesse, *A Pin to See the Peepshow*, 370.
41. Orlo Williams, 'A Pin to See the Peepshow', *The Times Literary Supplement*, 11th October 1934, 692.

42. Gerald Gould, 'New Novels: A ROUND DOZEN', *The Observer*, 21st October 1934, 6.
43. Anon. 'New Novels: A PIN TO SEE THE PEEPSHOW', *The Times*, 9th October 1934, 8.
44. Theatrical adaptations of Jesse's novel were repeatedly censored: see, for example, 'To-night's Censored Play', *The Daily Telegraph*, 8th May 1951, 4.
45. See Pierrepoint's evidence to the Gowers Commission, *Minutes of Evidence*, The National Archives, PCOM 9/1773, 8420–8425.
46. Berry, *My Experiences*, 32.
47. 'Appendix to Pierrepoint's Evidence: Coroner's Report', *Minutes of Evidence*, The National Archives, PCOM9/1773.
48. Berry, *My Experiences*, 25.
49. Ellis, *Diary of a Hangman*, 85.
50. Pierrepoint, *Executioner: Pierrepoint*, 147.
51. Pierrepoint, 'Ellis', The National Archives, PCOM 9/1773, 1–11.
52. Pierrepoint, 'Heath', The National Archives, PCOM 9/1773, 1–8.
53. Pierrepoint, 'Heath', 3.
54. Elliott, *Agent of Death*, 101.
55. Elliott, *Agent of Death*, 106–107.
56. Elliott, *Agent of Death*, 59 and 101.
57. Elliott, *Agent of Death*, 99.
58. Austin Sarat et al., *Gruesome Spectacles: Botched Executions and America's Death Penalty*, Stanford: Stanford University Press, 2014, 155.
59. Elliott, *Agent of Death*, 73.
60. Elliott, *Agent of Death*, 99.
61. See Pierrepoint evidence to the Gowers Commission, *Minutes of Evidence*, The National Archives, PCOM 9/1773, 8403.
62. Elliott, *Agent of Death*, 108.
63. Pierrepoint, *Executioner: Pierrepoint*, 52–53.
64. Pierrepoint, *Executioner: Pierrepoint*, 132–133.
65. Pierrepoint, *Executioner: Pierrepoint*, 132–133.
66. Pierrepoint, *Executioner: Pierrepoint*, 183.
67. Pierrepoint, *Executioner: Pierrepoint*, 183.
68. Pierrepoint says in his evidence to the Gowers Commission that he has seen three faints 'at the last minute' during executions, but this is not substantially discussed in his memoirs (*Minutes of Evidence*, The National Archives, PCOM 9/1773). Elliott describes several cases where condemned prisoners became hysterical before or during their execution, as well as the execution of Mary Creighton who was executed while unconscious (*Agent of Death*, 146–149).

69. Suicide cases, where a great deal of medical attention was required to spare the life of the person so they could undergo trial and execution, are presented without apparent sense of irony as a particular challenge to the executioner's skill. See, for example, Ellis (192 and 230–231); Dernley (90); Elliott (111–112).
70. Pierrepoint, *Executioner: Pierrepoint*, 105 and 183. In his career Elliott executed a man whose heart was on the wrong side as well as several one-legged men, while he also reflects on several others who because of fear or illness had to be assisted during what he euphemistically calls 'their last mile' (*Agent of Death*, 101–102 and 118).
71. See, for example, Ellis's reflections on the controversial execution of Edith Thompson who was unconscious when she was hanged (*Diary of a Hangman*, 27–28). Documents held at the National Archive prepared for a parliamentary answer on this execution show Thompson was given hyoscine and morphine, as well as brandy, before her execution against normal practice. It was noted as a medical error to give both stimulants and depressants at the same time (The National Archives, PCOM 9/1983).
72. See, for example, Ellis's recollections of William Palmer who shouted 'I'm not going to allow myself to be murdered without putting up a fight': it took ten warders as well as the executioner and assistant to restrain him enough to facilitate the execution (144). Pierrepoint also includes an account of his execution of a German spy after a trial in-camera: 'Schmidt fought me, fought everybody' (*Executioner: Pierrepoint*, 140). Elliott writes that he considered quitting his training after the execution of Frank White, who kicked and fought while being placed in the chair and who had to be given six separate electric shocks before he died. This execution was so traumatic for those involved that one of the doctors fainted part way through (*Agent of Death*, 48–49).
73. Berry notes of the execution of Robert Goodale in 1885 that, as a result of a miscalculation, 'the jerk had severed the head entirely from the body, and both had fallen together to the bottom of the pit' (*My Experiences*, 64–65). The execution which ended his career occurred in 1891, that of John Conway at Kirkdale Gaol as a result of a disagreement between Berry and the medical officer: 'The result, everyone knows. The drop was not so long as to absolutely pull off the victim's head, but it ruptured the principal blood-vessels of the neck' (*My Experiences*, 33). This failed execution brought in standard procedures for executions and led the Home Office to take much more direct control of the process of execution from local prisons (Seán McConville, *English Local Prisons 1860–1990*, London and New York: Routledge, 1995, 392).
74. Elliott, *Agent of Death*, 97.

75. Elliot, *Agent of Death*, 101–102.
76. Elliott, *Agent of Death*, 49.
77. Elliott, *Agent of Death*, 150.
78. Berry's account of the execution of John Lee in 1885 notes that the trap-doors failed to fall on two occasions and the man's sentence was eventually commuted (*My Experiences*, 59–64).
79. Elliott, *Agent of Death*, 105.
80. Elliott, *Agent of Death*, 168.
81. Despite government papers that suggest prison officers would receive an extra fee of 5 shillings for handling the body, this is a frequent feature of British executioners' memoirs suggesting prison officers generally declined to do this work (see The National Archives, HO 45/25843).
82. Pierrepoint, *Executioner: Pierrepoint*, 133.
83. Ellis, *Diary of a Hangman*, 28.
84. Ellis, *Diary of a Hangman*, 9.
85. Pierrepoint, *Executioner: Pierrepoint*, 164–165.
86. Syd Dernley *The Hangman's Tale*, 81.
87. Pierrepoint, *Executioner: Pierrepoint*, 99.
88. Dernley, *The Hangman's Tale*, 186–187.
89. Doyle and O'Donnell, 'A Family Affair: English Hangmen and a Dublin Jail, 1923–54', *New Hibernia Review*, Vol. 18, No. 8 (2014), 101–118 (104–105).
90. Doyle and O'Donnell, 'A Family Affair', 105.
91. Doyle and O'Donnell, 'A Family Affair', 106 and 109.
92. For example, their records on James Berry include witness accounts of his drunkenness just before the 1891 decapitation incident described above (The National Archives, PCOM 8/191). Henry Pierrepoint's retirement (a formative experience for Albert) is more explicable given files held in the National Archives describing an incident at Chelmsford Prison in 1910 when he arrived drunk and proceeded to assault Ellis, his assistant (The National Archives, PCOM 8/196).
93. Doyle and O'Donnell, 'A Family Affair', 117.
94. Doyle and O'Donnell, 'A Family Affair', 117.
95. Dernley, *The Hangman's Tale*, 35.
96. Dernley, *The Hangman's Tale*, 11.
97. Elliott, *Agent of Death*, 48.
98. Dernley, *The Hangman's Tale*, 47.
99. Dernley, *The Hangman's Tale*, 47.
100. Dernley, *The Hangman's Tale*, 40.
101. Elliott, *Agent of Death*, 40.
102. Dernley, *The Hangman's Tale*, 40.
103. Dernley, *The Hangman's Tale*, 201.

104. Elliott, *Agent of Death*, 56–57.
105. Elliott, *Agent of Death*, 57.
106. Anon. 'Haunted by Ghosts of Men He Hanged', *San Francisco Call*, 86.145. 23rd October 1899, 2; 'The Slow Passing of Amos Lunt' Sausalito News, Vol. 17, No. 31, 31st August 1901, 5; 'The Haunting of Amos Lunt', *San Francisco Call*, Vol. 87, No. 107, 15th September 1901, 5.
107. Elliott, *Agent of Death*, 69 and 88.
108. Henry Sanson, *Memoirs of the Sansons (1688–1847)*, London: Chatto and Windus, 1881. The specific edition I am referring to is held at Western Bank Library, University of Sheffield, with the shelf mark 3B 343.25 (S).
109. The National Archives, PCOM 9/1983. For a legal reading of what the rumours of Thompson's execution meant for the death penalty then and today, see Roseanne Kennedy, 'The Media and the Death Penalty: The Limits of Sentimentality, the Power of Abjection', *Humanities Research Journal Series*, 'Pain and Death: Politics, Aesthetics, Legalities', Vol. XIV, No. 2 (2007): 29–47.
110. Dernley, *The Hangman's Tale*, 30.
111. Carl R. Lovitt, 'The Rhetoric of Murderers' Confessional Narratives: The Model of Pierre Riviere's Memoir', *The Journal of Narrative Technique*, Vol. 22, No. 1, 1992: 23–34 (26).
112. Elliott, *Agent of Death*, 218.
113. Pierrepoint, *Executioner: Pierrepoint*, 211.
114. Dernley, *The Hangman's Tale*, 199.
115. Elliott, *Agent of Death*, 224.
116. Dernley, *The Hangman's Tale*, 198.
117. Dernley, *The Hangman's Tale*, 198–199.
118. Burt, 'The Autobiographical Subject and the Death Penalty', 168.
119. Burt, 'The Autobiographical Subject and the Death Penalty', 168.

CHAPTER 5

Animals and Modern Capital Punishment

Introduction

In the twentieth century, as earlier, parallels and analogies between the animal and the condemned man were widespread in both pro- and anti-death penalty discourses. It will thus be important to consider in this chapter whether the ethical power of such analogies is meaningful if it can be mobilised by both sides of the debate. Overall, the comparison reflects ambivalence about the deliberate sacrifice of an individual life, whether human or animal, within the death penalty. This strand of research is especially timely given an increasing interest in violence across the human-animal divide, as well as the rise of the field of 'Green Criminology'.[1] In the tenth seminar of *The Beast and the Sovereign*, Derrida asserts that 'there is between sovereign, criminal and beast a sort of obscure and fascinating complicity'.[2] Similarly, Derrida elsewhere asks 'whether we can speak of a death penalty inflicted by man on animals, or whether the death penalty is something proper to man'.[3] David Nibert has argued for the entanglement of animal rights and human rights in a model of 'interrelation' that is attentive to the application of political violence and oppression across species.[4] Additionally, Greta Olson's *Criminals as Animals from Shakespeare to Lombroso* (2013) demonstrates how animal metaphors have always been used to denigrate persons identified as criminal in literature, law and science, while Piers Beirne has developed a concept of 'theriocide' (the

K. Ebury, *Modern Literature and the Death Penalty, 1890–1950*, Palgrave Studies in Literature, Culture and Human Rights,
https://doi.org/10.1007/978-3-030-52750-1_5

killing of animals by humans) to sit alongside homicide through readings of animal executions, visual art and modernist drama.[5] In this chapter I will consider first the psychoanalytic theory of the 'totem animal', followed by an assessment of the symbolic use of animal figures in criminological thinking and then consider the practical role of animals in experiments on execution technology. I will finally apply these ideas to a range of Golden Age fictions about capital punishment in which animals are important to the narrative.

Psychoanalysis, the 'Totem Animal' and Animal Executions

Theories of the 'totem animal' in Freudian psychoanalysis shaped writers' representations of the sacrifice of criminal and animal bodies within a system of guilt and punishment. Freud's interest in primitive societies' investments in animals runs parallel to his reflections on the desire to murder. He asserts that the totem animal 'is nothing but a substitute' for the murdered father central to his 'primal horde' theory of the origin of law: 'the original animal sacrifice was already a substitute for a human sacrifice—for the ceremonial killing of the father; so that, when the father-surrogate once more resumed its human shape, the animal sacrifice too could be changed back into a human sacrifice'.[6] For Freud, the impulse to retaliate against this primal murder was the source of many death-dealing behaviours including sacrificial animal killing, human sacrifice, the death penalty and certain forms of suicide:

> The law of talion, which is so deeply rooted in human feelings, lays it down that a murder can only be expiated by the sacrifice of another life: self-sacrifice points back to blood-guilt...Thus we can trace through the ages the identity of the totem feast with animal sacrifice, with theanthropic human sacrifice, and with the Christian Eucharist, and we can recognize in all these rituals the effect of that crime by which men were so deeply weighed down of which they must nonetheless feel so proud.[7]

Reik continues this thought, writing that primitive human societies would use the sacrifice of the totem animal to develop a talionic law which simultaneously expiates and *reenacts* the original crime: 'By participating in the killing and eating of the flesh and blood of the totem animal, all have repeated the old deed and satisfied the instincts which come to expression in the act'.[8] Hanns Sachs would write similarly about sacrifice in primitive societies in his 1930 pamphlet *Does Capital Punishment Exist?*: for Sachs, the death penalty is 'a thought-saving device, and psycho-analysis has taught us that anything which can serve in this way furnishes a high premium of pleasure. The most primitive way in which we can react to anything that has been done to us is the talion principle'.[9]

The death of the totem animal would replace the scapegoat punishment of, at first, a whole community, and then, later, similar sacrifice would eventually be required to remove the guilt of an individual transgressor who had broken taboos such as murder and incest. In short, consuming the animal might replace a specific act of capital punishment, though it does not remove the threat of the death penalty. And indeed, some of the guilt for expiation might persist as the taboo of killing could transfer onto the person who performed the animal sacrifice or human execution: Freud suggests that 'the temporary or permanent isolation of the professional executioner, which has persisted to the present day, may belong in this connection'.[10] These sacrifices cannot eliminate the desire to kill, especially within the Oedipus Complex, even as prohibitions against other forms of killing emerge.[11] In modern society, Freud argues, these impulses are legible in the destruction of a child's powerful initial identification with animals: he argues that a sense of species hierarchy, along with fear of animals and desire to harm them, only sets in with the Oedipus Complex as the direct result of anxieties about parricidal impulses.[12] The model of society described by Freud and his followers thus relies not on the prohibition against killing per se, but rather on a complex system of literal and symbolic animal and human sacrifice.

In the cases of totem sacrifice discussed by early psychoanalysis, the animal stands as a proxy for a human transgressor, but there were also cases where animals were judged to be criminally responsible for their own deeds even into the twentieth century. Such animal punishments and executions were discussed by Sir James Frazer, an anthropologist who had influenced Freud (and some literary thinkers), in a chapter called 'The Ox that Gored' in his *Folklore in the Old Testament* (1919), where he links this practice to the concept of 'blood-revenge' (or talionic law) in many cultures.[13] Each of the cases included by Frazer are not merely random, irrational human acts of retaliatory violence against violent animals: instead, they involved a formal judicial procedure, which would include a legal advocate being appointed on the animal's behalf. Frazer also explores an interesting distinction between how different classes of animal were made subject to the law in Medieval Europe:

> Domestic animals were tried in the common criminal courts, and their punishment on conviction was death; wild animals fell under the jurisdiction of the ecclesiastical courts and the punishment they suffered was banishment of death by exorcism and excommunication.[14]

Frazer believed that the explanation for this distinction is a practical one: 'It was physically impossible for a common executioner, however zealous, active and robust, to hang, decapitate, or otherwise execute all the rats, mice, ants, flies [...] of a whole district; but what is impossible with man is possible and indeed easy with God'.[15] Another related explanation is an ontological one, in that the domesticated animal is held to be closest to the human and is thus tried and punished in a conventional court: Frazer cites the case of a sow executed in 1386 which was led to the gallows dressed in human clothes and wearing the mask of a human face, 'to complete the resemblance to an ordinary criminal'.[16]

Frazer had been influenced by E. P. Evans's earlier text, *The Criminal Prosecution and Capital Punishment of Animals* (1906), which provided a 'Chronological List of Excommunications and Prosecutions of Animals from the Ninth to the Nineteenth Century' including animals from dolphins (Marseille, 1596) to a She-Ass (Vanvres, 1750).[17] While Evans's project has appeared idiosyncratic to those historians and animal studies writers who have previously approached it, Frazer's intellectual interest in animal punishment situates this theme within mainstream thinking about criminal anthropology in relation to capital punishment. The range of methods of capital punishment for animals that Evans discusses is very wide, including decapitation, burning at the stake, being buried alive, hanging and being stoned to death. The last punishment covered by Evans, of a dog in Délémont in Switzerland, dates from the twentieth century, the same year his book was published, while several examples are given from the nineteenth century.[18] Unlike Frazer, Evans sees a direct contemporary relevance in his investigation of animal criminology, using the analogy between humans and animals to critique what he sees as an overuse of the insanity defence in modern societies:

> whereas, a few generations ago, lawgivers and courts of justice still continued to treat brutes as men responsible for their misdeeds, and to punish

> them capitally as malefactors, the tendency now-a-days is to regard men as brutes, acting automatically or under an insane and irresistible impulse to evil, and to plead this innate and constitutional proclivity, in prosecution for murder, as an extenuating or even wholly exculpating circumstance.[19]

Despite the deep influence of psychoanalysis on his work, Evans objects specifically to the role of psychoanalysts in mitigating capital punishment: 'Judicial procedure no longer stops with testimony establishing the bald facts in the case, but admits also the evidence of the expert alienist in order to ascertain to what extent the will of the accused was free or functionally normal in its operation'.[20] Evans's final statement looks forward to a golden age of psychoanalysis, but fails to intuit the explicitly anti-death penalty stance which Freud and his followers would come to hold:

> The hemp cure is always a harsh cure, especially where there is any doubt as to the offender's mental soundness; but in view of the increasing frequency with which atrocious and willful crime shelters itself under the plea of insanity and becomes an object of misdirected sympathy to maudlin sentimentalists, the adoption of radical and rigorous measures in the infliction of punishment were perhaps an experiment well worth trying. Meanwhile, let the psychiater continue his researches, and after we have passed through the present confused and perilous period of transition from gross and brutal mediæval conceptions of justice to refined and humanitarian modern conceptions of justice, we may, in due time, succeed in establishing our penal code and criminal procedure upon foundations that shall be both philosophically sound and practically safe.[21]

While, as I have shown, Freud and Reik undermined rational and emotional distinctions between humans and animals through concepts of sacrifice at the origin of a primitive law, the different use that Evans made of his interests in psychoanalysis and anthropology points already to the insight that drives the next section of this chapter: that animal metaphors were easily mobilised by both sides of the capital punishment debate throughout the twentieth century.

Figurative Animals in Pro- and Anti-Death Penalty Rhetoric

Beyond these scientific and historical discussions of the origins of law and of animal sacrifice and responsibility, animal metaphors were often used in literature and popular culture to support public safety arguments in favour of the death penalty. The most famous writer of the period to use these arguments was George Bernard Shaw, who asserted that dangerous law-breakers must be 'painlessly killed or permanently restrained', and that this 'has no more to do with punishment or revenge than the caging or shooting of a man-eating tiger'.[22] Bernard F. Dukore highlights how Shaw's analogy of the need to kill a dangerous lion dates all the way back to his 1898 play *Caesar and Cleopatra*.[23] Shaw would also bring in a wider range of rhetorical animals to support his argument for a preventative death penalty in a 1947 letter to *The Times*:

> Let me illustrate. Dogs are friends of Man; but an exceptional dog sometimes goes mad and runs amok through the streets, biting and infecting everybody it comes across. Fond as we may be of dogs we must kill it on the spot, by gun or bludgeon. Cobras and adders, perfectly sane and normal, may get loose in a school playground or domestic garden. We break their necks without trial by jury. A fox caught in a poultry yard is liquidated on the spot, though it is only acting according to its nature as we ourselves do when we eat the turkey we have killed the fox for pursuing with the same purpose. Nobody thinks of these liquidations as punishments, nor expiations, nor sacrifices, nor anything but what they really are: sheer necessities. Precisely the same necessity arises in the daily-occurring cases of incorrigibly mischievous human beings. They are vermin in the commonwealth, ferocious wild beasts on our highways, robbers and crooks of all sorts.[24]

Although, as Olson has shown, animal metaphors had long been used in a similar way, in the twentieth century they acquired a specifically eugenic, social Darwinist aspect. Shaw argues that while criminals who are responsive to the state should be reformed and allowed 'not only to read the newspapers but also to marry and breed', 'the criminal you cannot reform: the human mad dog or cobra' should receive instead 'kindly but ruthless judicial liquidation'.[25] Shaw, somewhat unusually for the period, is also in favour of the execution of those suffering from mental illness, asserting simply that 'Dangerous insanity, instead of exempting from liquidation, should be one of the strongest grounds for it'.[26]

As Dukore points out, Shaw also uses animal metaphors in arguing that the death penalty is less cruel than life imprisonment: in a 1945 letter to *The Times* arguing for the execution of Elizabeth Maud Jones, convicted with Karl Gustav Hulten in the 'Cleft Chin Murder Case', he suggests that even death by hanging (the cruelty of which he concedes) is kinder than 'to waste useful lives in caging and watching her as a tigress in the Zoo has to be caged and watched'.[27] The equivalence between a criminal and a 'cobra or a mad dog' would be reused by Shaw in arguing for the *extension* of the death penalty to vitriol throwers and, incredibly, for breach of promise.[28] In Shaw's persistent thinking about analogies between criminals and animals, we find similarities with Evans's ideas about the relationship between crime and animality, as well as the same regressive rejection of the consensus that someone who was not mentally competent should be treated rather than punished. Contradictions are also present in Shaw's own record as a vegetarian and a campaigner against hunting and vivisection, even as he uses animal death as a shorthand for the appropriateness of the death penalty. Shaw was an active member of the Humanitarian League which asserted a strong link between human and animal rights, and the League's ideas are explicitly mangled in Shaw's pro-death penalty arguments.[29]

These eugenic arguments for the death penalty were not only found in humanist, rationalist thinkers like Shaw but were also adopted by more traditional religious discourse. For example, the Very Revd William Inge used 'mad dog', euthanasia and eugenic arguments interchangeably in his writings in support of the death penalty in his *Christian Ethics and Moral Problems* (1930).[30] The same contradictions found in Evans and Shaw also exist in Inge; as in the same volume in which he advocates the death penalty along the lines of the 'putting down' of animals, Inge also criticises early Christians who 'laying so much stress upon a future life, and placing the lower creatures out of the pale of hope, placed them at the same time out of the pale of sympathy, and thus laid the foundation for an utter disregard of animals' which caused the modern cruelty to animals which he roundly condemned.[31] Inge and Shaw therefore, much as Evans had in 1906, also incongruously criticise theriocide while using animal metaphors to leverage the rightness of the death penalty.

Animal images and comparisons are equally crucial within anti-death penalty polemic of the twentieth century: for example, Clarence Darrow includes a chapter of his 1922 polemic *Crime: Its Cause and Treatment* on 'Man as a Predatory Animal', which highlights the influence of both psychoanalysis and evolutionary biology on his thinking. (Darrow would also famously defend the teaching of evolutionary biology in public schools in the 'Scopes Monkey Trial' (1925).) While Darrow's reference points are similar to those of Evans or Shaw, he comes to exactly opposite conclusions. He writes that

> Man, by virtue of his organic nature, is a predatory animal. This does not mean that he is a vicious animal. It simply means that man, in common with the eagle and the wolf, acts in accordance with the all-impelling urge and fundamental instincts of his organic structure. In any conflict between newer and nobler sentiments and the emotions which function through the primeval instincts, he is shackled to the bed-rock master instincts in such manner that they usually win. This is conclusively shown by the history of the race.[32]

Darrow's arguments are thus used to question to the Christian idea that man was created differently from the rest of animal life in being given a conscience and free will. Influenced by Freud, he turns animal metaphors against those who would argue for the 'rationality' and humanity of the talionic law: 'Punishments, even to the extent of death, are inflicted where there can be no possible object except revenge. Whether the victim is weak or strong, old or young, sane or insane, makes no difference; men and societies react to injury exactly as animals react'.[33] In defending Nathan Leopold and Richard Loeb from a capital sentence in 1924, Darrow used this same language of animality, alongside a psychoanalytic view of the child's development, to argue that as minors these criminals were like 'the animal that wants something and goes out and gets it, kills it, operating purely from instinct, without training'.[34] While a child might be gradually taught 'habits that are supposed to be strong enough that they will make inhibitions against conduct when the emotions come into conflict with his duties of life', he argued that in abnormal subjects like Leopold and Loeb, these safeguards would fail.[35]

Darrow's interest in the link between human violence and our animal selves is also reflected in his interest in violence against animals in the design and symbolism of his polemic fiction. In his novel, *An Eye for an Eye* (1905), discussed in the introduction, his murderer Jim Jackson believes that he was brutalised first by his work in the Chicago stock yards ('I never liked that work; I used to see so much killin'[36]). The symbolism of animal sacrifice and meat consumption explicitly overshadows his violent crime: Jackson kills his wife after an argument about his purchase and cooking of meat (he claims, 'it was the beef-steak that brought me here').[37] Although Jackson succeeds in cleaning the crime scene after impulsively killing his wife, blood from the meat wrapper is mistakenly used as evidence against him at his trial: the prosecution confuses animal and human blood as evidence, symbolically linking Jackson's consumption of meat, his wife's murder and his ultimate execution. Towards the close of his narrative, Jackson admits to his friend that he particularly fears the death penalty because he believes that hanging is crueller than the way he killed animals in the stock yard, even though he found that work extremely traumatic: 'I think shooting would be better'n this way. That's the way they kill steers down at the stock-yards and I don't believe the Humane Society would let 'em hang 'em by the neck'.[38] Jackson further believes that his one redemptive characteristic is that he always treated his horse well and highlights this throughout his confessional narrative. In short, Darrow uses the just treatment of animals as a humanising factor in both his legal and literary work against the death penalty, while cruelty to animals and meat consumption reflects humanity's underlying animal nature and lack of free will.

Finally, in closing this section, it is worth a brief reflection on how a portion of Darrow's Leopold and Loeb defence speech directly alludes to Evans's work. Darrow uses Evans's book on animal punishment to demonstrate the absurdity of the precedents brought in support of the execution of minors and those with mental abnormalities:

> There was a time in England, running down as late as the beginning of the last century, when judges used to convene court and call juries to try a horse, a dog, a sow for crime. I have in my library a story of judges and juries and lawyers, trying and convicting an old sow for lying down on her ten pigs and killing them. And they stuck her. What does it mean? Animals were tried. I know that one of two things happened to this boy: that this terrible crime was inherent in his organism, and came from some ancestor, or that it came through his education and his training after he was born. Do I need to prove it?[39]

As in *Crime: Its Cause and Treatment*, Darrow here animal analogies to make human rational justice appear absurd and instinctive, driven by the same forces as the unthinking violence of animals. Reik would quickly go on to use the Leopold and Loeb case to prove his theory of self-betrayal and the compulsion to confess, showing a reciprocal interplay between law and psychoanalysis in an anti-death penalty context in the period.[40] The arguments Darrow makes here about how animal executions show the irrational nature of talionic law would also be repeated by abolitionists across the twentieth century: for example, Arthur Koestler in *Reflections on Hanging* (1956) makes exactly the same point in his chapter on pig executions.

Animals and Execution Technology

As I have shown, even those in favour of capital punishment, including Evans, Shaw and Inge asserted the wrongness of violence against animals. But it is important to acknowledge that many innovations in capital punishment were first tested on animals in order to test whether they would be effective and 'humane', even into the twentieth century. In the 1880s the Buffalo branch of the American Society for the Prevention of Cruelty to Animals (ASPCA), because of their search for a humane method of animal euthanasia, had become involved in the first experiments towards the development of electric chair, eventually electrocuting hundreds of stray dogs. Some of these dogs were also vivisected to show the effect of electricity on the heart's action. The judge Elbridge Gerry, author of the Gerry Report (1888) which recommended a change from hanging to electrocution in the State of New York, had also served as the attorney for the ASPCA and remained involved in its activities throughout this process.[41] In 1888, at the height of the 'war of currents', Gerry was present at experiments in which two calves and a horse were electrocuted in Edison's West Orange Laboratory.[42]

As Kelly Oliver has explored, the technology of execution and of representation developed in tandem in the twentieth century, coalescing around Thomas Edison's 1903 execution of Topsy, a mistreated circus elephant who had previously killed three of her keepers. This event was filmed for the kinetoscope and released within days of the animal's death. Oliver points out that 'many early films feature executions', whether real executions of animals or reenacted executions of humans.[43] It is also particularly striking that this one minute film clip does not present itself as a scientific experiment, but rather specifically as an *execution*. The Edison Catalogue summary of the film uses the word 'execution' twice:

> Topsy, the famous "Baby" elephant, was electrocuted at Coney Island on January 4, 1903. We secured an excellent picture of the execution. The

> scene opens with keeper leading Topsy to the place of execution. After copper plates or electrodes were fastened to her feet, 6600 volts of electricity were turned on. The elephant is seen to become rigid, throwing her trunk in the air, and then is completely enveloped in smoke from the burning electrodes. The current is cut off and she falls forward to the ground dead.[44]

Michael Punt suggests that the main reason that Topsy was executed in this way was that the ASPCA believed that the original plan to garotte her was cruel and would lead to unnecessary suffering, but their recommendation may simply have reflected their investment in a technology they had help to develop.[45]

In Topsy's case, because of lingering doubts about the effectiveness and humaneness of electrocution, technologies of execution were overlaid, with two fail-safes built in to ensure her death. In the film, there is the obvious and spectacular presence of the electrodes, but we can also see winches which would have been used for a form of hanging in the event of an electrical failure. Invisibly, Topsy had also been fed a carrot laced with potassium cyanide just before the switch was thrown.[46] Oliver also highlights the 1916 execution of another elephant 'Murderous Mary' in Erwin, Tennessee, where the method of hanging from a railroad crane was used (the chain broke on the first attempt, prolonging the elephant's suffering). She further explores how this execution is confused in the American popular imagination with memories of lynching; in relation to this connection between racial violence and violence against animals, see my reading of Orwell's 'Shooting an Elephant' in Chap. 8.[47] The layers of apparatus in Topsy's death might appear to point to the wish to make her death humane and avoid such accidents. Likewise, the ASPCA vivisection of individual dogs during the process of electrocution to provide assurance that it was a good, painless method of euthanasia to use when it was necessary to destroy strays may have felt justified. But the way the different forms of violence insure each other might also be read as baroque, brutal or unreasonable.[48]

While the American context of the development of electrocution is a very stark example, debate also raged in Britain about the rightness of animal vivisection and euthanasia, exemplified particularly in the Brown Dog affair (1903–1910), in parallel to the debates about the death penalty which I have been discussing. Susan Hamilton has recently explored how, in late nineteenth-century Britain, the method of euthanasia or execution at Battersea Dogs' Home was a 'lethal chamber' filled with chloroform gas and Philip Howell has written about Battersea as a carceral institution characterised by 'policing, incarceration, and execution'.[49] The scientist Ernest Starling, one the scientists accused of cruelty in the Brown Dog affair, justified his medical experiments on dogs because of this very practice at Battersea: he argued that anti-vivisectionists' efforts to save dogs from dissection would only lead to more strays killed by lethal gas at the Dogs' Home. He claimed that dogs were simply 'obtaining euthanasia at the hands of the physiologist'.[50]

In arguing against vivisection in the wake of the Brown Dog affair, in *Vivisection: A Heartless Science* (1916), Stephen Coleridge cited progress in human rights in the nineteenth century as an argument for the development of animal rights in the twentieth century:

> When my grandfather was called to the Bar, over a hundred years ago, men were hanged for offences which now entail no more than three or four months' imprisonment, and the slave-trade was a reputable avenue of commerce. When men exhibited the most atrocious barbarity to each other, they were not likely to trouble themselves much about cruelty to animals.[51]

While Lizzie Seal has persuasively argued for the influence of suffragette practice upon anti-death penalty campaigners such as Violet Van der Elst, another important influence was the kind of animal activism practised in relation to the Brown Dog affair. Van der Elst refers to anti-vivisection and anti-blood sports movements in her polemic *On the Gallows*, including a substantial digression on the subject of fox hunting.[52] In highlighting the interpenetration of arguments about abolition of the death penalty and the abolition of cruelty to animals in Van der Elst and Coleridge, we should consider the influence of the Humanitarian League, which I have previously discussed in relation to Shaw, which opposed the capital and corporal punishment of humans as well as fighting animal campaigns around blood sports and vivisection.

Although the American experiments on animals I have described as leading to the development of the electric chair might seem especially grisly, some similar experiments also appear to have been carried out in Britain. For example, the executioner James Berry wrote of the impact of electrocution on British execution culture and reflects on his involvement in experiments on animals who were to be euthanised:

> When particulars of the method that was to be adopted for executions in New York were first published, I was with a small committee of gentlemen in Manchester who were investigating the subject. They made all arrangements for experiments to test the reliability of the method. Two animals were obtained that had to be killed in any case, namely, a calf and an old dog of a large breed. In the case of the calf the connections were made in the manner prescribed, and the current was turned on. This was repeated twice, but the only result was to cause the calf to drop on its knees and bellow with fear and pain, and the butcher at once killed it in the ordinary way with his poleaxe. When the shock was applied to the dog he fell down and seemed to be paralysed, but it was some time before life was extinct.[53]

Berry used this anecdote to prove that hanging is the most humane method and that American execution practice is behind that of Britain, turning from this story to consider the botched electrocution of William Kemmler in 1891. Still, the deaths of the calf and dog recounted here should be placed in the context of the opening section of this chapter, in which psychoanalysts and anthropologists explored the impulse to subject the animal to forms of sacrifice directly or indirectly linked to the death penalty. It is especially interesting to note the overlaid methods (as in the execution of Topsy) and to compare the way the two species in Berry's story are treated when the experiment fails: in the case of the calf, the traditional method of killing ('the butcher's poleaxe') is resorted to 'in the usual way', but this method is not used on the dog even if it might spare it pain. It appears to have just been left to die. In this case, unlike in the case of 'Topsy' or 'Murderous Mary', Berry calls this is an 'experiment' and he is clear that the animals concerned bear no guilt themselves, though they 'had to be killed in any case', and are thus being euthanised. Unlike in Freud's paradigm of the totem animal, the sacrifice of the calf and the dog in Berry's anecdote can only prevent this *method* of execution being adopted in Britain through the failure of the experiment, rather than their deaths being sacrificially on *behalf* of condemned criminals who will still die on the gallows. And in that sense the suffering they experienced might be said to be all in vain.

Vivisection and Euthanasia in Golden Age Death Penalty Fiction

In Shaw's use of mad dog and poisonous snake analogies, there is an intertwining of rhetorical arguments for the necessity of certain forms of theriocide and for certain forms of the death penalty which writers such as Darrow, Van der Elst and Coleridge sought to unpick. This final section will examine how the death penalty is caught up, both explicitly and implicitly, in arguments about scientific experiments upon and euthanasia of animals for the good of society outlined in the previous section. These debates are primarily about cruelty: at several points across the chapter so far, I have touched on the question of 'humane' punishment. In fact, in the literature of the period we constantly find vivisection and animal euthanasia being brought into contact with the treatment of capital offenders, reflecting a history outlined above in which execution technologies were tested on animals. Until the 1861 Offences Against the Person Act, science had relied on the interchangeability of vivisected animals or dissected executed criminals and the distant memory of this practice may have shaped these symbolic connections.

In a range of both canonical and non-canonical detective fiction to be discussed in this section, including Dorothy L. Sayers's *Whose Body?* (1923), Raymond Postgate's *Verdict of Twelve* (1940), Freeman Wills Crofts's *Antidote to Venom* (1938), Alan Melville's *Death of Anton* (1936) and Christie's *Curtain* (written during World War II), we find concerns about the meaning of theriocide within a narrative about capital crime. Amongst the deaths depicted in each of these narratives, there is, alongside the traditional murder victim and perpetrator, a mix of animal victims: including unidentified lab animals (Sayers and Christie); a small boy's pet rabbit named in homage to Saki's short story about a vengeful pet (Postgate); a Russell's viper snake killed for its venom as part of a murder plot (Crofts); a tiger called Peter, who is put down after killing the man who he believed had killed his trainer (Melville). Animal rights and human rights (particularly in relation to gender, class and race) are deliberately entangled by the texts and authors I examine here as case studies.

In *Whose Body?* and *Curtain*, vivisection is itself part of the motive for murderous violence, becoming a source of anxiety about connections between medicine and the death penalty. Intriguingly, a copy of Freud's *Totem and Taboo* (discussed earlier) is preserved in Sayers's library, reflecting her interest in connections between animal and human sacrifice.[54] Dr Freke, already discussed in previous chapters, a psychoanalyst, medical researcher and vivisectionist, whose interest in hormones constitutes Sayers's own allusion to the Brown Dog affair discussed above, chooses to frame the hapless Mr. Thipps because Thipps has in the past given him anti-vivisection literature. Freke reflects, when looking for somewhere to dispose of a dead body: 'I remembered [Thipps's] silly face, and his silly chatter about vivisection. It occurred to me pleasantly how delightful it would be to deposit my parcel with him and see what he made of it'.[55] In addition to this, Sayers cements her reference to the Brown Dog affair by basing the action of much of her narrative in Battersea, a key battleground for pro- and anti-vivisection campaigners. The hospital where Freke works and disposes of much of the evidence of his killing, as well as performing dissection and vivisection, is 'St. Luke's Hospital, Battersea'.[56] Furthermore, Sayers's culprit has chosen his victim, Sir Reuben Levy, because of personal animosity but also for eugenic reasons: Levy is Jewish and is treated by Freke as having lesser claims to humanity because of his race. Levy is not only murdered: Freke's plot depends upon his body being degradingly dissected by medical students at the hospital. A recent essay by Eric Sandberg has productively highlighted the shocking and unusual character of the crime in *Whose Body?*, even in comparison to other Golden Age works.[57] Freke's confession asserts that he conceives his crime as an experiment—on the hapless victim, on the London Police force and, finally, on himself. Freke wishes his brain to be donated to science after his execution to be studied as an example of criminal psychology, recalling a longer history of dissecting criminal corpses. Sayers implies that Freke's science, as well as his rejection of Freud (discussed in Chap. 2), allows him to develop a twisted version of medicine that supports all forms of killing, including vivisection, theriocide, euthanasia, murder and the death penalty.

Similarly, in *Curtain*, a key sub-plot and motive for Poirot's murder of Norton is the fact that Captain Hastings's daughter Judith, working for a scientist who practises vivisection, is in love with her employer and is tempted to murder his invalid wife to facilitate his work on tropical diseases. Dr. Franklin, Judith's employer, has fitted up part of the boarding house where the story is set as a lab: Mrs. Lutrell, the owner of the house, reflects to Hastings that 'Hutches of guinea pigs he's got there, the poor creatures, and mice and rabbits. I'm not sure I like all this science, Captain Hastings'.[58] Indeed, a whole chapter of the novel is devoted to a debate between Christie's characters on the merits of euthanasia.[59] For example, Franklin asserts explicitly that 'about eighty per cent of the human race ought to be eliminated. We'd get on much better without them' and Judith echoes him, 'Only people who can make a decent contribution to the community ought to be allowed to live. The others ought to be put painlessly away'.[60] They are, of course, thinking of Franklin's invalid wife (she is not as helpless or harmless as she seems, however). Poirot implies in his last letter to Hastings that Judith has been brutalised by her scientific work with Franklin and that his murder of Norton is required to reduce the risk his friend's daughter poses to others. In *Curtain*, a last connection with vivisection is cemented in Christie's explanation of Norton's fixation with crime and punishment, as Poirot considers a story about his childhood squeamishness and sense of threatened masculinity in relation to animals:

> *One of the most significant things you told me was a remark about him having been laughed at at school for nearly being sick when seeing a dead rabbit. There, I think, was an incident that may have left a deep impression on him. He disliked blood and violence and his prestige suffered in consequence. Subconsciously, I should say, he has waited to redeem himself by being bold and ruthless [...] And little by little developing a morbid taste for violence at second-hand.*[61]

Poirot suggests that because Norton was teased by his classmates for being unable to participate in animal experiments at school, he has developed a sadistic wish to experiment on human subjects by torturing and manipulating them. In this sense he replaces one form of vivisection with another (we see Sayers's Freke make a similar move). Therefore, in these Golden Age narratives, medical attitudes to the disposability of human and animal life are shown to underpin drives both towards murder and the death penalty. Vivisection in these novels thus supports eugenic thinking which is as much death-dealing as it is life-giving.

This formulation, in which the death penalty is reinterrogated through symbolic linkage to animal death, vivisection and euthanasia, is also shared across less famous Golden Age narratives. For example, in Crofts' *Antidote to Venom* (1938), the murder victim, the elderly Professor Burnaby, performs animal experiments to test the effect of snake venom on cancer cells: George Surridge, who runs the nearby zoo, is persuaded to commit the crime by Burnaby's nephew Capper, who has embezzled Surridge's money. While Burnaby is a victim of crime, rather than a culprit or potential culprit (as in Sayers or Christie), Crofts does encourage us to consider whether these experiments are justified, given Burnaby's lack of success and his declining health, when set alongside the suffering of the lab animals involved in the work. Additionally, Surridge uses eugenic arguments to rationalise the murder and argue that Burnaby's death would be a form of euthanasia (we saw the same impulse at work in *Curtain*):

> Really the old man had one foot in the grave. He could not be enjoying his life and he was a danger to his fellow men [...] the man's death would be nothing but a blessing for himself and everyone around him.[62]

Burnaby's age and illness are used here to dehumanise him, while the idea of him as 'a danger' justifies his killing, mirroring ironically the public safety arguments in favour of the death penalty examined in a previous section of the chapter. As in Postgate's novel, *Antidote to Venom* also gives theriocide serious ethical consideration, partly because Surridge betrays his duty of care to the animal as its keeper. In the account of the murder are told of the snake's 'rage and fear' and that 'snakes were hard to drown', while the reality and cruelty of the snake's death is driven home by the post-mortem report on the snake's body given at the coroner's court which highlights the unique reality of the animal:

> a female Russell's viper, three feet one inch long [...] in a good state of health. It had died as a result of drowning. Its neck was somewhat bruised and swollen, presumably from being held in a snake tongs.[63]

While the snake is here only evidence about a murder, Crofts provides detail beyond what is necessary for the plot, suggesting that the snake is likewise a victim of human violence. Beyond the importance of animals in the narrative, Crofts's text triangulates criminal psychology, care for animals and the death penalty.

Readers of these texts might therefore become uncomfortable about links between vivisection, euthanasia, murder and capital punishment. A childhood incident involving animal cruelty drives the plot of Raymond Postgate's *Verdict of Twelve* (1940): after a sickly boy's pet rabbit is deliberately killed by his unsympathetic guardian, Mrs. Van Beer, on the pretext that it is unhealthy, the child becomes determined to take revenge. The rabbit's death is claimed by his guardian as a form of euthanasia, but Postgate describes the animal's suffering in great detail: 'the rabbit was kicking and fighting in the oven [...] it gave that high scream of terror which rabbits only give under the fear of death'.[64] J. C. Bernthal argues that 'gassing the rabbit has uncanny echoes of Nazi Germany's use of gas chambers on individuals deemed undesirable from a eugenicist perspective'; given the novel's theme of the death penalty, this method also directly echoes the American use of the gas chamber in the period.[65] The unhappy boy then takes poison leaving clues that frame Mrs. Van Beer for his murder, hoping she will be executed after his death. The rest of the narrative follows the unsympathetic Mrs. Van Beer's trial for the murder which, as Bernthal points out, includes expert psychoanalytic evidence of the boy's relationship with his rabbit in relation to fetishism, sadomasochism and the Oedipus Complex.[66] After her acquittal, Van Beer reveals to her legal team that she in fact knew her ward's plan all along and deliberately allowed him to kill himself. The narrative's final twist, which blurs murder, suicide and the death penalty, is driven by animal cruelty as Postgate seeks to prove connections between theriocide, homicide and the death penalty which are particularly significant in a wartime context. We find versions of this narrative across crime writing in the period: authors including Susan Glaspell in 'A Jury of Her Peers' (1917)[67] and F. Tennyson Jesse in *A Pin to See the Peepshow* (1934)[68] address the killing of a loved companion animal as a potential motive for murder, even when it places the owner at risk of the death penalty.

Though so far I have theorised animals as victims in these narratives, we should close this section by considering a text where an animal must be 'destroyed', rather than vivisected or euthanised, because it has caused harm to humans, as in Shaw's arguments for public safety. In Melville's *Death of Anton* (1936), circus tigers are traumatised by the disposal of their murdered trainer (the eponymous Anton) in their cage. The murderer had shot Anton and believed that the tigers would savage his body, destroying this evidence: the tigers' failure to do this marks the power of their relationship with Anton over human estimates of their violent instincts. Later in the narrative, the tigers kill their replacement trainer, someone suspected of this killing: Peter, the male tiger and the only one given a name, is shot and killed in the circus ring. Peter's death and that of the replacement trainer are enabled by the obsession of Melville's detective (Mr. Minto) that the tigers know who the culprit is and will attempt to avenge their trainer: indeed, he thinks of them as taking deliberate revenge when the remaining six tigers eventually attack the true culprit, Dodo the clown. In this case, because Dodo's guilt is confirmed, the surviving tigers are not punished for their violence: the main concern is saving

Dodo's life so that he can receive judicial execution. Minto simply says, 'Take good care of him [...] He's got an appointment with the hangman, and he'll have to be back in his usual health for that'.[69] For the plot's resolution, the sacrifice of Peter's life, as well as the trauma the tigers have suffered in their life at the circus, must be forgotten.

The Golden Age authors discussed in this section thus appear to share an anxiety about the instrumentalisation of violence and how reduction of the value of life applies across species boundaries and across the legal-illegal divide. These authors use psychoanalytic and anthropological techniques and concepts to explore connections of animal sacrifice and animal cruelty with violent crimes and punishments, through a study of the mind and character of the violent person. The modernist framework of psychoanalysis and the thrilling genre of crime fiction thus permit authors like Sayers, Christie, Crofts, Postgate and Melville to evade accusations of sentimentality or conservatism when expressing anxiety about connections between crime and cruelty. However, despite their awareness of the symbolic and literal dependence of the death penalty on cruelty to animals and of activism by the Humanitarian League which asserted the equal importance of human and animal rights, the authors I have examined here appear to primarily support the death penalty, with more urgent questions asked about vivisection, euthanasia and animal cruelty. I would argue this ethical blindspot is mainly due to the richness and polyvalence of animal figures in both pro- and anti- death penalty activism, as these metaphors drew attention away from the real animal and human victims of the *lex talionis*.

Notes

1. See the Palgrave book series called 'Green Criminology', as well as the recent special issue edited by Samantha Walton and Joseph Walton on the topic of 'Crime Fiction and Ecology', *Green Letters*, Vol. 22, No. 1 (2018). See also Samantha Walton's chapter, 'Studies in Green: Teaching Ecological Crime Fiction', *Teaching Crime Fiction* ed. by Charlotte Beyer, Houndsmills: Palgrave, 2018: 115–130.
2. Jacques Derrida, *The Beast and the Sovereign Volume I*, trans. by Geoffrey Bennington, Chicago and London: University of Chicago Press, 2009, 17.
3. Jacques Derrida, *The Death Penalty: Volume I* trans. by Peggy Kamuf, Chicago: University of Chicago Press, 2014, 231.

4. See David Nibert's *Animal Rights/Human Rights: Entanglements of Oppression and Liberation*, Oxford: Rowman and Littlefield, 2002 and his *Animal Oppression and Human Violence*, New York: Columbia University Press, 2013, as well as the two volumes of *Animal Oppression and Capitalism* ed. by Nibert, Santa Barbara, California: Praeger, 2017.
5. Greta Olson, *Criminals as Animals from Shakespeare to Lombroso*, Berlin/Boston: DeGruyter, 2013 and Piers Beirne, *Murdering Animals: Writings on Theriocide, Homicide and Nonspeciesist Criminology*, Houndsmills: Palgrave, 2018.
6. Sigmund Freud, *Totem and Taboo (1913), The Standard Edition of the Complete Psychological Works of Sigmund Freud, Volume XIII (1913–1914)*, trans. by Strachey et al., London: Vintage, 2001: ix–164 (151).
7. Freud, *Totem and Taboo*, 154–155.
8. Theodor Reik, *The Unknown Murderer, The Compulsion to Confess: On the Psychoanalysis of Crime and Punishment*, New York: Grove Press, 1961, 108.
9. Dr Hanns Sachs, *Does Capital Punishment Exist?*, Territet: POOL Group Pamphlet 1930, 16.
10. Freud, *Totem and Taboo*, 41.
11. Freud, *Totem and Taboo*, 146.
12. Freud, *Totem and Taboo*, 126–132.
13. James Frazer, *Folklore in the Old Testament: Stories in Comparative Religion, Legend and Law*, London: Macmillan, 1919, 415–445.
14. Frazer, *Folklore*, 424.
15. Frazer, *Folklore*, 438.
16. Frazer, *Folklore*, 447.
17. E. P. Evans, *The Criminal Prosecution and Capital Punishment of Animals*, London: Heinemann, 1906, 313–335. For a recent account of broader questions about Evans's historical accuracy and implications for animal rights, see Piers Beirne 'On the Geohistory of Justiciable Animals: Was Britain a Deviant Case?' in *Murdering Animals: Writings on Theriocide, Homicide and Nonspeciesist Criminology*, Houndsmills: Palgrave, 2018: 17–134; 'Law is an Ass: Reading E.P. Evans' The Medieval Prosecution and Capital Punishment of Animals' in *Society and Animals*, Vol. 1, No. 2 (1994): 27–46; Lesley Bates MacGregor, 'Criminalising Animals in Medieval France: Insights from Records of Executions', *Open Library of Humanities*, Vol. 5, No. 1 (2019): 15, https://doi.org/10.16995/olh.319.
18. Evans, *Criminal Prosecution*, 384.
19. Evans, *Criminal Prosecution*, 193.
20. Evans, *Criminal Prosecution*, 201.
21. Evans, *Criminal Prosecution*, 256.

22. George Bernard Shaw, *Doctors' Delusions: Crude Criminology and Sham Education*, London: Constable, 1950, 231–232.
23. Bernard F. Dukore, *Crimes and Punishments and Bernard Shaw*, Houndsmills: Palgrave, 2017, 201 and 205.
24. George Bernard Shaw, 'Capital Punishment (December 5th, 1947)', *The Letters of Bernard Shaw to The Times* ed. by Ronald Ford, Dublin: Irish Academic Press, 2007: 268–269 (268).
25. Shaw, 'Capital Punishment (December 5th, 1947)', 269.
26. George Bernard Shaw, *Collected Letters 1911–1925 Volume 3* ed. by Dan H. Laurence, London: Max Reinhardt, 1985, 56.
27. Dukore, *Crimes and Punishments and Bernard Shaw*, 202. Orwell wrote more sympathetically about the same case in his famous essay 'The Decline of the English Murder', blaming the public's eagerness to hang Jones on the violent and degrading atmosphere established by World War II.
28. Shaw writes, 'A vitriol thrower should be got rid of as ruthlessly as a cobra or a mad dog. A man who lives by promising to marry women and deserting them as soon as he has spent all their money is a social weed to be uprooted no less than if he drowned them in their baths' (*Collected Letters*, 56).
29. Rod Preece, *Animal Sensibility and Inclusive Justice in the Age of Bernard Shaw*, Vancouver: UBC Press, 2011, 137.
30. W. R. Inge, *Christian Ethics and Moral Problems*, London: 1930, 271.
31. Inge, *Christian Ethics*, 278.
32. Clarence Darrow, *Crime: Its Cause and Treatment*, New York: Thomas Y Crowell Company, 1922, 97.
33. Darrow, *Crime: Its Cause and Treatment*, 13.
34. Clarence Darrow, 'Attorney Clarence Darrow's Plea for Mercy in the Franks Case', *Attorney Clarence Darrow's Plea for Mercy and Prosecutor Robert E. Crowe's Demand for the Death Penalty in the Loeb-Leopold Case – The Crime of a Century*, Chicago: Wilson Publishing Company, 1924, 40.
35. Darrow, 'Attorney Clarence Darrow's Plea', 40.
36. Clarence Darrow, *An Eye for an Eye*, New York: Duffield and Co, 1920, 12.
37. Darrow, *An Eye for an Eye*, 30.
38. Darrow, *An Eye for an Eye*, 68.
39. Darrow, 'Attorney Clarence Darrow's Plea', 54.
40. Reik, *The Compulsion to Confess, The Compulsion to Confess: On the Psychoanalysis of Crime and Punishment*, New York: Grove Press, 1961, 258–259.
41. Jill Jonnes, *Empires of Light: Edison, Tesla, Westinghouse, and the Race to Electrify the World*, New York: Routledge, 2004, 176.
42. Jonnes, *Empires of Light*, 176–177.

43. Kelly Oliver, 'See Topsy "Ride the Lightning": The Scopic Machinery of Death', *The Southern Journal of Philosophy*, Vol. 50 (2012): 74–94 (83–84).
44. Anon. 'Electrocuting an Elephant', Edison Films No. 168, February 1903.
45. Michael Punt, 'The Elephant, the Spaceship and the White Cockatoo: An Archaeology of Digital Photography' in *The Photographic Image in Digital Culture* ed. by Martin Lister, Abingdon: Routledge, 1995: 55–76 (63).
46. Punt, 'The Elephant, the Spaceship and the White Cockatoo', 63.
47. Oliver, 'See Topsy "Ride the Lightning"', 79.
48. Oliver, 'See Topsy "Ride the Lightning"', 92.
49. Susan Hamilton, 'Dogs' Homes and Lethal Chambers, or, What Was it Like to be a Battersea Dog?', *Animals in Victorian Literature and Culture: Contexts for Criticism*, ed. by Laurence W. Mazzeno and Ronald D. Morrison, Houndsmills: Palgrave, 2017: 83–108. Phillip Howell, *At Home and Astray: The Domestic Dog in Victorian Britain*, Charlottesville: University of Virginia Press, 2015, 99.
50. See Hilda Kean, *Animal Rights: Political and Social Change in Britain Since 1800*, London: Reaktion, 1998, 142.
51. Stephen Coleridge, *Vivisection: A Heartless Science*, London: John Lane The Bodley Head, 1916, 6–7.
52. Violet Van der Elst, *On the Gallows*, London: The Doge Press, 1937, 31 and 285.
53. James Berry, *My Experiences as an Executioner*, London: Peter Lund & Co, 1892, 55. I have searched in vain for a newspaper report on this experiment: as a failed experiment it would have been less likely to be communicated to journalists.
54. See Sayers's archive at Wheaton College: https://www.wheaton.edu/media/wade-center/files/collections/author-library-listings/Sayers_Library_20180426.pdf [Accessed 9th August 2018].
55. Dorothy L. Sayers, *Whose Body?*, London: Hodder, 2016, 202.
56. Sayers, *Whose Body?*, 9.
57. Eric Sandberg, '"The Body in the Bath": Dorothy L. Sayers's *Whose Body?* and Embodied Detective Fiction', *Journal of Modern Literature*, Vol. 42, No. 2 (2019): 1–20.
58. Agatha Christie, *Curtain: Poirot's Last Case*, London: Harper Collins, 2002, 12.
59. Christie, *Curtain*, 145–151.
60. Agatha Christie, *Curtain*, 76.
61. Christie, *Curtain*, 262–263, Christie's italics.
62. Freeman Wills Crofts, *Antidote to Venom*, London: The British Library, 2015, 106.
63. Crofts, *Antidote to Venom*, 168.
64. Raymond Postgate, *Verdict of Twelve*, London: British Library, 2017, 120.

65. J. C. Bernthal, 'Killing Innocence: Obstructions of Justice in Late-Interwar British Crime fiction', *CLUES: A Journal of Detection*, Vol. 17, No. 2 (Fall 2019): 31–39 (38).
66. Bernthal, 'Killing Innocence', 38.
67. Susan Glaspell, 'A Jury of Her Peers', *Her America: "A Jury of Her Peers" and Other Stories*, ed. by Patricia L. Bryan and Martha C. Carpentier, Iowa City: University of Iowa Press, 2010: 81–102. Glaspell's story remains important to Law and Literature practice today, as Greta Olson notes in 'Futures of Law and Literature: A Preliminary Overview from a Culturalist Perspective', *Recht und Literatur im Zweischenraum/Law and Literature In-Between*, Bielefield: transcript 2015: 37–69 (60).
68. F. Tennyson Jesse, *A Pin to See the Peepshow*, London: Virago, 1988.
69. Alan Melville, *Death of Anton*, London: The British Library, 2015, 273.

CHAPTER 6

Sex, Gender and the Death Penalty in James Joyce, W. B. Yeats and the 1916 Generation

Introduction

This chapter will explore how writing by Joyce, W. B. Yeats and the 1916 revolutionaries converge around the Robert Emmet and Sarah Curran myth. While Roger Casement's 1916 execution for treason has frequently been viewed through the lens of queer theory, I will contend that the masochistic drives inherent in the death penalty as theorised by Freud, Reik and Derrida bring death and sex into close contact with all the Easter Rising executions.[1] In so doing, I will bring texts by Joyce, Yeats and the writers of the 1916 generation into dialogue through a focus on gender, sexuality and the death penalty. Through consideration of concepts of blood sacrifice and Christ-like iconography, gendered ideas of women's fidelity to their executed men beyond the death sentence and last letters sent by rebels, this chapter will assess representations of the death penalty as a source of masochistic pleasure in the context of Irish national struggle.

In this new section of this book themed around 'Conflict', moving away from a death sentence conceptualised as a natural punishment for murder, we enter a more complex area of twentieth-century thought where the continued appropriateness of execution in wartime and for political offences was assumed but seldom discussed. In this context it is noteworthy that the Gowers Commission report, despite coming immediately after a run of post-war executions, never discuss capital punishment

K. Ebury, *Modern Literature and the Death Penalty, 1890–1950*, Palgrave Studies in Literature, Culture and Human Rights, https://doi.org/10.1007/978-3-030-52750-1_6

outside of murder. They state merely that 'In England since 1861 the sentence of death has been executed only for murderer, except in one case of treason during the First World War and in two cases of treason and 15 cases of offences under the Treachery Act, 1940' and thus never give the military or political death penalty sustained attention.[2] Their figures include Casement who was hanged for treason, but exclude the 14 Easter Rising leaders executed by firing squad under the authority of the Defence of the Realm act for the offence of 'Armed Rebellion': Patrick Pearse, Thomas Clarke, Thomas MacDonagh, Joseph Plunkett, Edward Daly, Michael O'Harahan, Willie Pearse, John Macbride, Eamonn Ceannt, Michael Mallin, Sean Heuston, Con Colbert, Sean Mac Diarmada and James Connolly. A 15th man, Thomas Kent, was executed in Cork. That these rebel leaders were treated as enemy combatants rather than rebellious citizens is evident in the execution method itself—they were not hanged, but rather shot by firing squad—while their in-camera trials soon led to legal challenges[3] and parliamentary questions.[4] Details in the Court Martial files further add to a sense of comparative irregularity: for example, the 'Certificate of Execution' for John MacBride gives the anomalous time of execution as 3.47a.m. on the 5th of May, 1916.[5]

The Easter Rising had little public support before the hasty execution of its leaders. The idea of masochism underlying concepts of political martyrdom is therefore particularly fitting in thinking about the death penalty and heroism in Irish modernist culture. Freud asserted of masochism in 1924 that 'even the subject's destruction of himself cannot take place without libidinal satisfaction', mixing the eros and thanatos drives which had been central to *Beyond the Pleasure Principle* (1920).[6] In *Civilization and its Discontents* (1930), Freud further refines a definition of masochism which contrasts it with sadism but does not fully separate these drives: 'In sadism [...] we should have before us a particularly strong alloy of this kind between trends of love and the destructive instinct; while its counterpart, masochism, would be a union between destructiveness directed inwards and sexuality'.[7] Freud argues that the destructive impulse associated with the death drive, whether in sadism, masochism or even in non-pathological behaviour, goes alongside pleasure caused by the apparent fulfilment of fantasies of omnipotence.[8]

Connecting to his 'primal horde' theory, Freud links masochism of the ego to the unconscious guilt associated with Christianity: for Freud, a masochistic individual might therefore connect their destructive impulses (in the form of violence and/or punishment) or metaphorical omnipotence (at the hands of the super-ego) with Christ's experience of the death penalty.[9] In his earlier essay on 'Dostoyevsky and Parricide' (1928), Freud investigated the Russian author's 'very strong destructive impulse' which 'might easily have made him a criminal' but was 'in his actual life directed mainly against his own person'.[10] Freud regarded Dostoyevsky as a natural case study of masochism, an artist who channelled his Oedipal impulses into violent representations of crime and punishment and the rebellious political activities for which he was almost executed in 1849. (Dostoyevsky's death sentence was commuted at the last moment to exile in Siberia). This view of Dostoyevsky fits thus both with Freud's sense of his death drive, as well as with the abolitionist attitude to the death penalty previously expressed by him (through Reik) in the 1926 'View on Capital Punishment'.[11]

While Lucy McDiarmid powerfully links sexuality with the act of revolution, my particular concern here is the melodramatic effect of the death penalty itself in catalysing sexual and national desire.[12] In his landmark study *States of Ireland*, Conor Cruise O'Brien famously argued that Patrick Pearse had fused Catholicism and nationalism to develop the concept of 'blood sacrifice'.[13] As R. F. Foster notes, these twentieth-century rebels had consciously chosen to model their rebellion on the urban risings of 1798 and 1803, rather than less successful rural risings of 1848 and 1867; they had also, consciously or unconsciously, chosen to model it upon romantic, sexualised discourses of sacrifice and waste, betrayal and fidelity, that came directly from the Robert Emmet/Sarah Curran myth of lovers parted by revolution and the scaffold.[14] This melodramatic, romantic narrative is linked explicitly to the Irish memorialisation of 1803: in fact, a first generation of dramas about Emmet, not knowing the facts very well, *invented* a very similar romance independently. As Maureen Hawkins argues, the authors of early theatrical versions of the Robert Emmet story in America, N. H. Bannister's *Robert Emmet, the Irish Patriot* (1840) and James Pilgrim's *Robert Emmet, the Martyr of Irish Liberty* (1853) did not know about Sarah Curran, but invented a romantic interest all the same.[15] Tice L. Miller emphasises that dramatists 'had learned to frame [Emmet's] story within the conventions of domestic melodrama'.[16] This was continued in Dion Boucicault's *Robert Emmet* (1884), where Emmet is captured during an attempt to marry Curran. At the end of the play, Emmet avowedly regards the eve of his execution as 'the eve of my wedding night':

CUR. Give me some ground to plead upon. Will you not promise to forsake the cause that has betrayed you?

ROBT. Ask me to forsake your daughter, and be foresworn to my love. Bear with me, sir—and let me live out my life—what is left of it is full of her. Her dear image is before me. I have no other care—no other thought—this is the eve of my wedding-night. I lie down in my grave to dream of her until I wake to meet my bride at the altar of heaven. Tell her I wait her there.[17]

Realism ('my grave') and symbolism ('the altar of heaven') clash awkwardly in these lines: Boucicault would resolve this tension on the side of symbolism with a tableau in which a female figure of Ireland appears to comfort Emmet in his dying moments.[18] As Hawkins reminds us in her genealogy of Emmet plays, Emmet 'is not treated as a self-conscious martyr until Boucicault's [play], in which he rejects a pardon'.[19] It is therefore significant that this version of Emmet, a deliberate martyr who engages in what Derrida calls 'auto-execution', is the one Joyce and the 1916 generation were most familiar with.[20]

Foster has also recently highlighted the latent queerness of Pearse's and Casement's hero worship of Emmet, and this extends to their other sacrificial role models including Cúchulainn and Christ for both men.[21] Indeed, far beyond 1916, through what David Doyle refers to as Irish political 'martyrology', the Irish public practised an eroticised hero worship of condemned men, such as Robert Emmet, Michael Larkin, Kevin Barry and Roger Casement, as a way of thinking not only about the death penalty but also more broadly about Irish sovereignty and masculinity.[22] From the perspective of historical criminology, Doyle suggests that the deterrence argument for the death penalty became particularly weak in an Irish culture that had created rhetorics of heroic martyrdom which extended both to the spectacular execution and to the subtler hunger strike tradition.[23]

Likewise, the women of the Rising noted the example of women like Sarah Curran in supporting their men to undergo the death penalty: as Catriona Kennedy notes, in a 1930s official witness statement about the events of 1916, Eily O'Reilly reported reassuring her brother Michael O'Hanhrahan as part of a last visit before his execution that 'we would be all right' as 'the women of '98 had had to endure that too'.[24] Just as Eily O'Reilly makes the romantic sacrifice of wives like Curran, Matilda Tone and Pamela Fitzgerald fit, however awkwardly, with the loss of a beloved brother, the men of the 1916 generation also attempted to place themselves in the roles of the United Irishmen. In fact, a widespread public attachment to melodrama and romance responded to, but also obscured, the reality of the lives of the men and women of 1916, who were often non-conforming in various ways (suffragettes, trade unionists, LGBTQ+) before the traumatic events of the Rising.

Casement, for example, had also internalised fantasies of the United Irishmen's movement, despite the lack of a natural fit between his own queer life story and more standard nationalist fantasies of marriage with Cathleen ni Houlihan. Casement chose to model his own 'Speech from the Dock' upon Emmet's as a precedent, saying explicitly 'My lord, I have done', deliberately evoking Emmet's famous conclusion.[25] To this Casement adds, from Emmet's life story rather than his words, a concept of national loyalty as a form of love:

> Loyalty is a sentiment, not a law. It rests on love, not on restraint. The government of Ireland by England rests on restraint, and not on law; and since it demands no love, it can evoke no loyalty.[26]

He adds towards the conclusion of the speech that this love is not merely a metaphor for national allegiance but is instead like other kinds of love:

> Self-government is our right, a thing born in us at birth, a thing no more to be doled out to us, or withheld from us, by another people than the right to life itself—than the right to feel the sun, or smell the flowers, or to love our kind.[27]

Casement's assertion of love and the right to self-government in the context of a right to life is, of course, especially highly charged and potentially even ironic, in a speech that explains his actions and implicitly pleads for reprieve.[28] It is also, as Alison Garden suggests, a 'national feeling, a sentiment propelled forward by love, [that] is tinged with queerness'.[29] But we should not simply assume that Casement is politically naïve in arguing for rights to life, love and self-determination in the midst of his own disgrace and sentencing to death. As Michael G. Cronin has highlighted, across Casement's writings about pain and pleasure, from the official reports on colonial abuses to the private diaries, there is a constant masochistic interpenetration of pleasure and pain in writing the body.[30] In short, Casement's understanding of love and revolution had its own unique politics of embodiment.

Casement also emphasises love, foreshadowing his Speech from the Dock, in 'The Nameless One', a 1900 poem discovered by Lucy McDiarmid: as she has argued, here Casement 'attempted to articulate and defend his homosexuality in a discourse both religious and romantic'.[31] So, for example, in this stanza, we see a similar consciousness of transgression and pride expressed in his 'Speech from the Dock', through a conflict between love as a source of life-giving potential and as a path to death:

> I only know 'tis Death to give
> My love, —yet loveless can I live?
> I only know I cannot die
> And leave this love God made, not I.

In this poem too, the expression of his love risks a death sentence, "tis death', but death is also linked to its non-expression, 'yet loveless can I live?'.[32] By the 1930s, those famous observers who remembered both sets of events unconsciously blurred Casement's trial for treason with the Wilde trial for indecency in 1895. For example, Yeats would write in 1937 to Dorothy Wellesley, conflating the diaries and the trial: 'the Casement evidence was not true…it was one of a number of acts of forgery committed at that time'.[33] As Kathryn Conrad notes, Yeats's 'statement presents an odd conflation of the sexual and political acts of which Casement was accused', but, as I have argued, this conflation is set up in discourses related to the Rising far beyond Casement himself.[34] The conflation of the offences, as well as the prurient examination of his body for evidence of homosexuality after his execution, also reflects a buried memory of sodomy as a capital offence until 1861.[35]

Thus, while a queer reading of love in relation to Casement is undoubtedly appropriate, I differ from previous critics in highlighting how James Joyce's deployment of concepts of sexuality to explore the death penalty in *Ulysses* episodes including 'Sirens', 'Cyclops' and 'Circe' reflects his critical awareness of a longer history of perversity and masochism within heterosexual desire and within an Irish tradition of male political martyrdom. Susan de Sola Rodstein has noted how Joyce renders the Rising in 'Cyclops' through a parallel with 1798 and 1803;[36] similarly, Tracey Schwartze has suggested that 'Emmet arguably serves Joyce not only as himself but also as a Casement surrogate'.[37] Alison Garden has recently traced Joyce's interest in the Rising via Casement as far as *Finnegans Wake* (1939), which foreshadows World War II, exploring the way he is crossed with Parnell as a sexually and politically transgressive figure.[38] However, Joyce criticism has not so far addressed that this connection comes as much from the lives and texts of the Easter rebels themselves, as Joyce's artistic decision-making. Casement makes a direct appearance in the text towards the end of Joyce's 'Cyclops' episode (composed 1919), in his 1904 role as an Irish anti-imperialist humanitarian:

> — Well, says J. J., if they're any worse than those Belgians in the Congo Free State they must be bad. Did you read that report by a man what's this his name is?
> — Casement, says the citizen. He's an Irishman.
> — Yes, that's the man, says J. J. Raping the women and girls and flogging the natives on the belly to squeeze all the red rubber they can out of them.
> — I know where he's gone, says Lenehan, cracking his fingers.
> — Who? says I.
> — Bloom, says he, the courthouse is a blind. He had a few bob on Throwaway and he's gone to gather in the shekels.[39]

The passage shows a strange collapse between Casement's exposure of the abuse and the abuse itself: the citizen names Casement and claims him as Irish, J. J. O'Molloy agrees, but then he does not return to 'the Belgians'. Rather, the sentence develops as though Casement himself is 'the man' who is 'raping the women and girls and flogging the natives'; the next slippage, the 'he' who has 'gone', is between Casement and Joyce's hero Leopold Bloom. This collapse between Casement and Bloom reflects Patrick Mullen's argument for the influence of Casement's 'Speech from the Dock' on Bloom's emphasis on love in his refusal of physical force nationalism in the episode.[40] Mullen argues that in Casement's or Bloom's example 'the productive or generative capacities of love—which outside the properly heterosexual model of the Irish nation register as perverted—threaten the citizen's conception of the world by continually creating novel forms of social value'.[41] But Mullen and the citizen miss some subtleties about concepts of blood sacrifice, which depends precisely upon the loss of life of young men and which might render courtship and sexual congress between revolutionaries transgressive: they might not live to be married, might not have children, might not live to provide for any children in a nuclear family structure. Revolutionary love is more scandalous, in fact, than the citizen in his emphasis on fidelity and infidelity might suspect, as Joyce will imply elsewhere.

As I will show in my final section, last letters of the revolutionary generation before their execution are shot through with these anxieties. Emmet is influential on this pattern of romantic and personal closure deferred, as the famous last words in his 'Speech from the Dock' assert:

> I have parted with everything that was dear to me in this life for my country's cause, and abandoned another idol I adored in my heart—the object of my affections. My race is run—the grave opens to receive me, and I sink into its bosom [...] When my country takes her place among the nations of the earth, then, and not till then, let my epitaph be written. I have done.[42]

Direct quotation of Emmet's words permeates the end of the 'Sirens' episode of *Ulysses*, prepared for by Bloom observing Miss Douce's masturbatory response to Ben Dollard's rendition of 'The Croppy Boy', a traditional song about 1798 executions, in the bar of the Ormond Hotel:

> On the smooth jutting beerpull laid Lydia hand lightly, plumply, leave it to my hands. All lost in pity for croppy. Fro, to: to, fro: over the polished knob (she knows his eyes, my eyes, her eyes) her thumb and finger passed in pity: passed, repassed and, gently touching, then slid so smoothly, slowly down, a cool firm white enamel baton protruding through their sliding ring.[43]

As he leaves the Ormond, the anal-erotic Bloom sees an image of Emmet's last words in a shop window and responds through flatulence:

> Seabloom, greaseabloom viewed last words. Softly. When my countrytakes her place among.
> Prrprr.
> Must be the bur.
> Fff. Oo. Rrpr.
> Nations of the earth. No-one behind. She's passed. Then and not till then. Tram. Kran, kran, kran. Good oppor. Coming. Krandlkrankran. I'm sure it's the burgund. Yes. One, two. Let my epitaph be. Karaaaaaaa. Written. I have.
> Pprrpffrrppfff.
> Done.[44]

In considering the death penalty in Joyce's work in relation to 1916, I therefore wish to build on Mullen's point by exploring how the pressure and pleasure of execution for revolutionary activities sweeps many kinds of love into the pathological and the perverted, as in Miss Douce's or Bloom's case.

The reference to 'The Croppy Boy' in 'Sirens' shows Joyce's deployment of the concept of love to explore the melodrama of the Irish death penalty by placing it a longer history. In *Ulysses*, the famous lovers Emmet and Curran enter 'Cyclops' immediately after the famous, more scandalous, passage about execution and erection:

> — There's one thing it hasn't a deterrent effect on, says Alf.
> — What's that? says Joe.
> — The poor bugger's tool that's being hanged, says Alf.
> — That so? says Joe.
> — God's truth, says Alf. I heard that from the head warder that was in Kilmainham when they hanged Joe Brady, the invincible. He told me when they cut him down after the drop it was standing up in their faces like a poker.
> — Ruling passion strong in death, says Joe, as someone said.
> [...] So of course the citizen was only waiting for the wink of the word and he starts gassing out of him about the invincible and the old guard and the men of sixtyseven and who fears to speak of ninety-eight and Joe with him about all the fellows that were hanged, drawn and transported for the cause by drumhead courtmartial and a new Ireland and new this, that and the other. [...] And the citizen and Bloom having an argument about the point, the brothers Sheares and Wolfe Tone beyond on Arbour Hill and Robert Emmet and die for your country, the Tommy Moore touch about Sara Curran and she's far from the land.[45]

Thus, as this 'Cyclops' conversation implies, Sarah Curran is a focal point that converts the grotesque, wasteful and brutal aspects of the death penalty into a narrative of melodramatic heroism: the passage moves rhetorically from the troublesome 'ruling passion' of the unexplained erection of the generic hanged man to the national and romantic identifications that ought to be its proper target. Joyce recognises the way that romance and melodrama legitimises masochism in Irish culture, creating slippage between love interest and nation, between sex and death, between marriage and execution.

Yeats and 'The Vertigo of Self-Sacrifice'

I have already shown across this book how psychoanalytic theorists such as Freud, Reik and Sachs explored the complex motives, both conscious and unconscious, by which subjects might seek out the death penalty. These theorists also asserted the connection of fantasies of punishment with the normal sexual life of the subject. Derrida summarises these forces specifically in relation to the death penalty:

> The death penalty can seduce…There are those who desire it…There are those who may love it. And not only in life, but in the afterlife, those who want to remain, who will beyond the grave, a feeling that accompanies men beyond the grave. This is very powerful. So, this is the risk that the death penalty encourages, that there are those who may cultivate this, who may not only let themselves be fascinated, but do everything necessary to take maximum pleasure from [*jouir de*] the death penalty in the present and in the future. Not in the future of what may happen to them when they are killed, but after death. So, one must not give them the bonus of immortality, of afterlife.[46]

Derrida's insight is valuable in addition to a simpler Freudian formulation of masochism discussed earlier, because of his emphasis on sovereignty: the biopolitics of the sovereign state (or in the case of Rising, the mere idea of an Irish state) that validates pathological drives is not sufficiently present in Freud's theory to explain the way that symbolism of sexuality and the death penalty interpenetrate each other in the Irish context. Here Derrida's emphasis is not merely upon the erotic potential of the death penalty, in language such as 'seduce', 'desire' and 'pleasure', but also the more ambiguous 'love'—which we have seen already in Casement's 'Speech from the Dock' and in Joyce's *Ulysses*—that he imagines that men may feel for the death penalty.

Derrida's multiplicity of language allows us to conceptualise this positive affect around capital punishment in several ways, including as a version of the 'excess of love' found in Yeats's 'Easter, 1916'. Using very similar language about the seductive potential of the death penalty in an Irish context, Yeats wrote to his sister Lolly in the aftermath of the Rising, before the execution of the leaders, describing Patrick Pearse as 'a man made dangerous by the Vertigo of Self-Sacrifice. He has moulded himself upon Emmet'.[47] Pound also summarised Yeats's view of Pearse as a man obsessed by both Emmet and the death penalty simultaneously, going back years before the Rising, in a letter to John Quinn: Yeats had 'said for years that Pearse was half-cracked and that he wouldn't be happy until he was hanged. He seemed to think Pearse had Emmet mania, same as some other lunatics think they are Napoleon or God'.[48]

Yeats's phrase, 'the Vertigo of Self-Sacrifice', is often quoted but little examined. Yeats's word choice suggests something more double-edged than simple meanings such as 'dizziness' or 'disorientation' or 'fear of heights'. In Freud's work, vertigo is associated with anxiety neurosis and appears in response to the death drive even before he fully formulates this concept. Danielle Quinodoz reminds us that Freud's key examples of vertigo are cases of patients who experienced a conscious impulse to throw themselves out of a high window: she explains of cases dating from 1896, 1922 and 1926 that 'the instinctual demand before whose satisfaction the ego recoils is a masochistic one' and so the concept of vertigo is not unconnected with pleasure.[49] Yeats is thinking of something like the French *vertige* which can include more pleasurable usages such as 'intoxication', 'exaltation' and even 'pleasure'. This positive meaning of vertigo, alongside Freud's connection with anxiety, is also to be found in Kierkegaard, especially *The Book on Adler* (1872), which is a possible influence for Yeats's phrase.[50]

Yeats used exactly the same concept of 'vertigo' in relation to the death penalty in his letter to Asquith of 14 July 1916 asking for a reprieve for Casement. Arguing for the negative effect of Casement's execution on Irish public opinion, he suggested that 'young people...are less likely to be restrained by fear than excited by sympathy. There is such a thing as the vertigo of self-sacrifice'.[51] Given the relationship of sexuality and the death penalty that I am tracing in this chapter, it is especially important that this letter was written in Calvados during the period of Yeats's famous double proposal to Maud Gonne and her daughter Iseult. The letter was discredited by Ernley Blackwell, then legal adviser to cabinet, on these grounds.[52] While Blackwell's nota bene annotation on the file containing the letter is mostly written in pencil, he writes 'Madam Maud Gonne McBride' [sic] in red ink, underlined.[53] Ethel Mannin, a later love interest, would claim that Yeats only 'gave his signature to the appeal [...] to please Maud Gonne, who nagged him into it': and yet, his phrase about the death penalty and the 'vertigo of self-sacrifice' is clearly his own.[54] It is thus likely that Casement's reprieve letter was collaborative, inscribed equally in the context of Yeats's past romance with Maud and his hopes for a future one with Iseult.

The initial response of Yeats's own circle to the Rising was determined by discourses of gender and sexuality as shaped by its impact on Maud Gonne. For example, Lady Gregory writes of MacBride's execution as 'the best event that cd. come to him, giving him dignity—And what a release for her!', while Lily Yeats puts it more starkly, 'Maud Gonne is at last a widow, made so by an English bullet'.[55] And of course, MacBride primarily remains Gonne's estranged husband in the stanza of 'Easter 1916' devoted to him. In the poem, the Rising and his death sentence just about transfigure him from 'a drunken, vain-glorious lout' to a part of the 'terrible beauty' Yeats identifies, as 'He, too, has been changed in his turn'.[56] In a letter to Yeats, Gonne rejected this portrayal of MacBride: 'As for my husband he has entered Eternity by the great door of sacrifice'.[57] She also objected more widely to the lines that reflect on the desiring hearts of those executed in the Rising, such as 'Too long a sacrifice / Can make a stone of the heart':

> No I don't like your poem, it isn't worthy of you & above all it isn't worthy of the subject—Though it reflects your present state of mind perhaps, it isn't quite sincere enough for you who have studied philosophy and know something of history that sacrifice has never yet turned a heart to stone though it has immortalized many…you could never say that MacDonagh & Pearse & Conally [sic] were sterile fixed minds, each served Ireland…with varied faculties & vivid energy! Those three were men of genius, with large comprehensive & speculative & active brains.[58]

Gonne's letter is intriguing, especially in the context of my discussion of Derrida on 'love' of the death penalty, as she challenges Yeats first about feeling and the heart, but then quickly moves to the 'minds' and the 'brains' of the executed men, apparently to show their sacrifice had been consciously and rationally calculated. Iseult Gonne's judgement is perhaps the most profound: 'Your poem […] has been the cause of great argument in our household as to the nature and value of sacrifice. [Mother] who cannot accept art for art's sake would willingly admit sacrifice for sacrifice's sake, and I have come to admit neither exactly'.[59]

Yeats's phrase about the 'vertigo of self-sacrifice' is ultimately an appropriate description of his own poetry about the Rising and is also valuable for interpreting the work of other Rising poets, such as Joseph Plunkett, in its masochistic linking of death and sexuality. For Sarah Cole, the key to Plunkett's writing is 'a Christian-leaning eroticism', highlighting the 'apolitical' character of his work except as it applies to death, in an implicit invocation of concepts such as biopolitics and necropolitics.[60] My focus on the death penalty per se allows us to see Plunkett's dependence on death as a politically and psychologically symbolic event in melodramatic, punning poems for Grace Gifford such as 'My Lady Has the Grace of Death':

My lady has the grace of Death
Whose charity is quick to save,
Her heart is broad as heaven's breath,
Deep as the grave.

She found me fainting by the way
And fed me from her babeless breast
Then played with me as children play,
Rocked me to rest.

When soon I rose and cried to heaven
Moaning for sins I could not weep,
She told me of her sorrows seven
Kissed me to sleep.

And when the morn rose bright and ruddy
And sweet birds sang on the branch above
She took my sword from her side all bloody
And died for love.[61]

Yeats's interpretive phrase about the Rising and the 'vertigo of self-sacrifice' is certainly appropriate to this poem. Here Plunkett's feeling is projected onto the female figure and her 'little death'/murder at the hands of the speaker: here the violence of heterosexual desire is reciprocal, as her heart is also a 'grave' for him. Indeed, we might hear a direct echo of Boucicault's *Robert Emmet* in this line.

Similarly, Plunkett's sonnet, 'The Little Black Rose Shall Be Red At Last', written on the last night of his life when he also married Gifford, is less directly violent than 'My Lady Has the Grace of Death' but continues the pattern of eroticised martyrdom or 'enchanted violence' as Cole calls it in her own close reading.[62] The poem is dedicated to Cathleen ni Houlihan and is in dialogue with the song 'Róisín Dubh', although the beloved is clearly specifically imagined as Gifford:

Because we share our sorrows and our joys
And all your dear and intimate thoughts are mine
We shall not fear the trumpets and the noise
Of battle, for we know our dreams divine,
And when my heart is pillowed on your heart
And ebb and flowing of their passionate flood
Shall beat in concord love through every part
Of brain and body—when at last the blood
O'erleaps the final barrier to find
Only one source wherein to spend its strength
And we two lovers, long but one in mind
And soul, are made one only flesh at length;
Praise God if this my blood fulfils the doom
When you, dark rose, shall redden into bloom.[63]

The frank sexuality of this poem, alongside its nationalist and Catholic iconography, queers marriage and heterosexual desire in bringing together of the act of marriage and the act of the death penalty. In these poems, despite Plunkett's heterosexuality, we find the same triangulation of sexual love, mystical religion and death as in Casement's poem about his sexuality, 'The Nameless One', discussed in the previous section. The future tense in 'The Little Black Rose' defers and makes virtual both future sexual satisfaction and the blood sacrifice of execution, implying through the deictic 'this my blood', which is the only implied present, a profound connection between execution and marriage. Although it would have been scandalous to have said so at the time, revisionist historians such as McDiarmid believe that one reason Plunkett and Gifford were allowed to marry by the authorities was that Grace was pregnant. This would add an extra dimension to the final line of 'The Little Black Rose', 'When you, dark rose, shall redden into bloom' linking the birth of a new Ireland with that of their potential child.[64]

While Plunkett's poetry is rarely subject to close analysis, we can see his direct influence on Yeats's 'The Rose Tree', written in April 1917:

'But where can we draw water,'
Said Pearse to Connolly,
'When all the wells are parched away?
O plain as plain can be
There's nothing but our own red blood
Can make a right Rose Tree.'[65]

'The Little Black Rose' is a culmination of Plunkett's response to the eroticised Rosicrucianism of Yeats's 1890s period, in poems such as 'To the Rose upon the Rood of Time', 'The Secret Rose', 'The Rose of Peace' and 'The Rose of Battle', and includes a similar run of poems published posthumously in 1916 including 'The Little Black Rose, with 'I see His Blood upon the Rose' and 'The Claim that has the Canker on the Rose'. In 1916 alone, Plunkett's poems appeared in several editions with three presses, one English (Unwin), one Irish (Talbot Press) and one American (Frederick A. Stokes Company), so Yeats's 'Rose Tree' is clearly a direct response to Plunkett's work, although he is not named in the poem, closing this circle of influence.

Fidelity Beyond the Death Sentence

As Joyce was no doubt aware and as is clear from his hyperbolic portrayal of the female figure's engagement on the scaffold in 'Cyclops', nationalist biographies of Emmet have always had trouble with the part of Curran's story that deals with her marriage to another man. Emmet's Victorian biographers shorten the Curran/Robert Sturgeon marriage to 'a few months' and make no mention of their child together, whereas in fact Curran and Sturgeon were married for around two years before her death and they had a son who died in infancy.[66] Madden's biography of Emmet tells the story of Curran's marriage in Chapter XVI *before* he gives his account of Emmet's execution in Chapter XVII, so as not to overshadow the account of his martyrdom.[67] His deliberate obfuscation of the timeline might well have influenced Joyce's own ridiculous version of the engagement story in 'Cyclops'. Curran's remarriage caused tensions in nationalist identifications with her example and in literary representations of their story. In many plays about Emmet and Curran, her disappointed love rival betrays Emmet; H. C. Mangan depicts her as explicitly anti-nationalist, refusing to escape with him and thereby causing his death.[68]

While Joyce generally ironises aspects of the Emmet/Curran myth, the subtle misogyny of the historical and literary representation of Curran lingers. In a dream-sequence execution scene at the heart of the 'Cyclops' episode, the beloved ('Sheila') and an unnamed Englishman become engaged before the execution of the Emmet figure even begins:

> A most romantic incident occurred when a handsome young Oxford graduate, noted for his chivalry towards the fair sex, stepped forward and, present-

> ing his visiting card, bankbook and genealogical tree solicited the hand of the hapless young lady, requesting her to name the day, and was accepted on the spot. Every lady in the audience was presented with a tasteful souvenir of the occasion in the shape of a skull and crossbones brooch, a timely and generous act which evoked a fresh outburst of emotion: and when the gallant young Oxonian (the bearer, by the way, of one of the most time-honoured names in Albion's history) placed on the finger of his blushing fiancée an expensive engagement ring with emeralds set in the form of a fourleaved shamrock excitement knew no bounds.[69]

Outside of this interpellated execution scene and within the citizen's very different perspective, we also see an identification of sexuality, marriage, betrayal and fidelity at the heart of Irish colonial and revolutionary history:

> — The strangers, says the citizen. Our own fault. We let them come in. We brought them. The adulteress and her paramour brought the Saxon robbers here.
> — Decree nisi, says J. J.
> And Bloom letting on to be awfully deeply interested in nothing, a spider's web in the corner behind the barrel, and the citizen scowling after him and the old dog at his feet looking up to know who to bite and when.
> — A dishonoured wife, says the citizen, that's what's the cause of all our misfortunes.[70]

Dervorgilla is widely known as 'Helen of Ireland', and by the twentieth century a substantial historiography had arisen around the question of whether she was abducted from her husband Tigernán Ua Ruairc by Diarmait Mac Murchada in 1152, whether she went willingly as part of an affair or finally whether she was used to secure a dynastic alliance. The story was so contested because Diarmait Mac Murchada would subsequently ask for English help in this dispute from Henry II leading to a continuing colonial interference from this time.

Anxiety about fidelity would be a feature of the aftermath of the Easter Rising.[71] Yeats began working on his verse play 'The Dreaming of the Bones' in summer 1917, and it was first performed in 1919: this play features a young Easter Rising gunman haunted during his escape from Dublin by the ghosts of Dermot and of Dervorgilla, those very figures cursed by the citizen in 'Cyclops'. In Yeats's play these transgressive lovers plead forgiveness, but the young man repeatedly calls their love a 'crime' and several times utters as a refrain 'Oh, never, never / Will Dermot and Dervorgilla be forgiven'.[72] Claire Nally writes that 'The Young Man's denial of his origins in the rejection of Dermot and Dervorgilla is also a theoretical suppression of the genesis of the nationalist ideology in Ireland, a disavowal of nationalism's emulative and aggressively masculinist creed which emerged from English imperialism'.[73] This critical judgement connects with Yeats's anxiety in 'Easter, 1916' that 'Too long a sacrifice / Can make a stone of the heart', as he implies that the masochistic drives at work in a fixation on the death penalty could lead to a similarly masochistic focus on betrayal.

It is thus worth asking whether the melodramatic 'Cyclops' execution fantasy is located within the citizen's imagination, or in Bloom's own? I have shown how the unnamed narrator of 'Cyclops' places the citizen and Bloom's argument about execution and Emmet/Curran as the most significant context for the beginning of the execution scene. The question of Sheila's fidelity is as likely to come from Bloom's particular anxieties about his wife Molly's infidelity with Blazes Boylan, one of the most important events in the narrative, as from the citizen's misogynistic denunciation of Dervorgilla.[74] Bloom's obsessive concerns about fidelity and betrayal as well as masochistic or non-productive sexuality are certainly present. Later in *Ulysses*, in 'Circe', another threatened execution scene, this time of Bloom, is framed by the key symbol of Molly's infidelity—the jingling quoits of their Eccles Street bed. In fact, this moment from 'Circe' is powerful evidence that the whole 'Cyclops' execution scene and its diagnosis of links between masochistic sexuality and the death penalty were originally located in Bloom's fantasy:

> (The brass quoits of a bed are heard to jingle.)
>
> THE QUOITS Jigjag, Jigajiga. Jigjag.
> [...]
> THE CRIER (Loudly.) Whereas Leopold Bloom of no fixed abode is a well-known dynamitard, forger, bigamist, bawd and cuckold and a public nuisance to the citizens of Dublin and whereas at this commission of assizes the most honourable.
> [...]

> THE RECORDER I will put an end to this white slave traffic and rid Dublin of this odious pest. Scandalous! (He dons the black cap.) Let him be taken, Mr Subsheriff, from the dock where he now stands and detained in custody in Mountjoy prison during His Majesty's pleasure and there be hanged by the neck until he is dead and therein fail not at your peril or may the Lord have-mercy on your soul. Remove him. (A black skullcap descends upon his head.)[75]

Here, the death sentence is pronounced on Bloom for a mixture of sexual offences (he is called bigamist, bawd, cuckold, white slaver) and for crimes related to treason (such as 'dynamitard', recalling earlier Fenian cases such as the Clerkenwell executions in 1867). Similarly, the execution of the 'Croppy Boy' figure in 'Circe' is likely to be located within the consciousness of Stephen Dedalus, the other main character of the novel. Bloom and Stephen, while refusing violence and physical force nationalism, have thus fallen victim, at least for now, to a masochistic and misogynistic response to imperialism and nationalism. But these fantasies of inhabiting the death penalty go alongside Joyce's frankness about the perversity of Irish history and willingness to pastiche the forces of melodrama and masochism found within the 1916 generation. Unlike historians of 1798, 1803 and 1916, Joyce refuses to exclude direct representations of sexuality from his versions of Irish martyrology, and he also reflects self-conscious performances of gender and sexuality in the writings of the Easter Rising participants themselves.

Last Letters

If Irish masculinity was often fired by masochistic drives in relation to revolution and the death penalty, I have also begun to uncover very real anxieties about the place of women and female sexuality beyond the death sentence. Within this economy of betrayal, fidelity and the death penalty, represented particularly by Sarah Curran but also by Maud Gonne, Grace Gifford and Joyce's 'Sheila', I must then consider the private last letters that executed rebels sent to their wives, which included private feeling among wider statements of national commitment intended to be read by the Irish public. While McDiarmid has recently focused on the strength shown by women of the Rising as they visited death cells in Kilmainham, their stories and behaviour were circumscribed to an extent by the duality of the Sarah Curran myth.[76] Joyce is obviously satirising both of these tendencies in his 'Cyclops' scene; his female figure is both hysterical and unfaithful, her affect in relation to the death sentence both too much and not enough.[77]

1916 rebels inscribe these anxieties about fidelity into texts of their own, especially their last letters. The rhetoric of last letters is thus overdetermined, leading necessarily to a loss of identity and to unconscious or conscious role play around fidelity, even in more complex cases such as Casement's where a protracted legal process left a long trail of letters to diverse correspondents. Casement's last letters feature an anxiety about whether he could live up to Emmet's standard of masculinity in facing his execution. He writes to his cousins that 'If it be said I shed tears—remember tears come not from cowardice, but from sorrow'.[78] Casement responds to this anxiety through deliberate reference to Emmet, 'It is a glorious death for Ireland's sake with Allen, Larkin, and O'Brien and Robert Emmet'.[79] He had previously made a suicide attempt while awaiting trial in the Tower, which suggests a contrasting identification with Wolfe Tone, as well as his intense unhappiness after his capture.[80] Similarly, Casement's last letter to his sister Nina addresses her quite romantically, suggesting that near his execution he needs this rhetorical style, inflected by his knowledge of Emmet's famous last letter to Sarah Curran, just as his speech from the dock was linked to Emmet's:

> Emmet to CurranFor God's sake, write to me by the bearer one line to tell me how you are in spirits. I have no anxiety, no care, about myself; but I am terribly oppressed about you. My dearest love, I would with joy lay down my life, but ought I to do more?[81]

> Casement to NinaNow dearest do you know what I feel for you? My eyes are blinded with tears and I can scarcely write. All my selfishness has passed away, and I see you plain and clear—your face—your eyes—your heart, and I can only sob and say that you are more to me than all else on earth.[82]

His very last letter, destroyed by the Prison Authorities (see Chap. 2), was more political but still shaped by rhetorics of sacrifice, as he compared himself to Christ and directly asked his friends to 'roll away the stone from his grave'.[83]

Even in the extreme case of a marriage overshadowed by the planned Rising and his own serious illness (he had tuberculosis), Plunkett's original December 1915 proposal letter forcefully demands both marriage to

Gifford and makes a claim to future fidelity, 'Darling Grace You will marry me and nobody else'.[84] The tone of his final letter's demand, written in blue pencil in his field notebook on the Saturday of the surrender, 'the 6th Day of the Irish Republic', is softer but equally insistent upon fidelity: 'Love me always as I love you'.[85] Thomas Macdonagh's last letter begins as a public impersonal statement, 'I, Thomas MacDonagh, having now heard the sentence of the Court Martial held on me today, declare…', discussing his wife and children in the third person, 'Never was there a better, truer, purer woman than my wife Muriel, or more adorable children than Don and Barbara'.[86] But the final two paragraphs pivot towards a direct address to his wife and children, 'Good bye my love, till we meet again in Heaven. I have a sure faith of our union there'. The letter is signed, 'Your loving husband Thomas MacDonagh' as though it were only addressed to Muriel, without the impersonal or historical national audience conjured in the opening of the letter.[87]

In several of these last letters, the sense of masochistic pleasure in sacrifice highlighted throughout this chapter is qualified: MacDonagh writes to Muriel that 'But for your suffering, this would be all joy and glory'. Both MacDonagh and Pearse try to include their loved ones in the sacrifice involved in the death sentence: 'My wife and I have given all for Ireland' (MacDonagh), while Pearse asks his mother to 'think of it [his death] as a sacrifice which God asked of me *and of you*'.[88] Rebels who did not have close romantic relationships are able to write more 'soldierly' last letters: for example, Sean Mac Diarmada writes to his IRB friend John Daly 'I have been sentenced to a soldier's death, to be shot to-morrow morning. I have nothing to say about this only that I look on it as a part of the day's work. We die that the Irish Nation may live, our blood will re-baptise and reinvigorate the old land',[89] while J. J. Heuston writes even more baldly to his colleague at the Great Southern and Western Railway that 'I have thank God no vain regrets. After all, it is better to be a corpse than a coward'.[90]

To give a final example of how discourses of necessary sacrifice and pointless waste conflict with each other within a single text, we should consider Michael Mallin's remarkable last letter to his wife Agnes. He writes in almost stream-of-consciousness style, with very little punctuation and with, often, direct contradictions between his reflections. Mallin uses this letter to say goodbye and to justify his actions but also ask Agnes not to remarry after his execution:

> I would ask a special favour of you wife of my heart, but I leave you absolutely free in the matter dont give your love to any other man you are only a girl yet and perhaps it is selfish of me to ask it of you but my darling this past forghnight [sic] has taught me that you are my only love my only hope. I have sinned against you many times in the fulness [sic] of your pure holy love for me you will forgive me my many transgressions against you.[91]

The letter is simultaneously a public and private document. Though it is full of sensitive detail including an apparent admission of infidelity, it also seems intended for a wider audience, reflecting more broadly on a sense of posthumous patriotism, 'I do not believe our Blood has been shed in vain'.[92] Passages were published in *The Catholic Bulletin* in the months after the Rising.[93] A sense of vacillation is created by the lack of punctuation, 'I would ask a special favour' / 'I leave you absolutely free'.[94]

Perhaps the strangest thing about the address to the family in this context is the official signature; it is not 'Michael' asking Agnes to remain faithful, nor is it 'Father' asking his children to join the church, rather the signature is the impersonal, 'Michael Mallin Commandant Stephens Green Command'.[95] It is a signatory of the Proclamation who is asking these things. A sense of the awkwardness of this request is reflected in the removal of much of the content of this letter within Piarais MacLochlainn's *Last Words*, a 1970s book of letters from those executed during the Rising.[96] Even today, while many of the 1916 letters that I have referred to in this chapter are available digitally, it cannot be a coincidence that Mallin's is not amongst them. In summing up the letter, Brian Hughes explores Mallin's ambivalence about the discourses of sacrifice that have led him to this point: 'Mallin looked on death as a punishment rather than a sacrifice [...] Mallin shows a far more developed sense of the loss and sadness that his imminent execution would cause for others, and significantly, for which he accepts full responsibility himself'.[97] We might therefore say that the letter is less masochistic than some Easter Rising texts I have examined here: but the content of Mallin's letter still demands significant painful sacrifice of others.

This chapter has shown how the idea of masochism underlying concepts of political martyrdom allows us to think again about the death penalty and masculinity in Irish modernist culture. Freud's idea of the perverse temporality of masochism in a reactivated Oedipus complex in which, as

Amber Musser aptly puts it, 'the subject seeks to produce a future in the image of the past' reflects the way that masochism underpins the whirlpool of temporalities at work in the texts under examination here: 1916 rebels look back nostalgically at 1798 and 1803 and seek to reactivate that cultural moment but also leap forward to a future specific moment of self-sacrifice as well as a hazier projected future of a postcolonial Ireland and of families reunited in heaven.[98]

Beyond the Rising

It is worth closing this chapter by highlighting how connections between execution and romance persist in the Irish death penalty debate far beyond the Rising. For example, in May 1925 the Free State Senate rejected an amendment proposed by Senator Harrington that would have reformed the death penalty, replacing it in cases of treason with penal servitude but retaining it for murder. In summarising his position, *The Manchester Guardian* noted:

> Mr Harrington gave a list of countries in which the death penalty for all crimes had been abolished, and said that the Free State should not follow the example of Great Britain, which was one of the States now in a minority in retaining capital punishment. They all now regretted the loss of the young lives of those who were executed in recent years. *Catholic priests who had ministered to prisoners at their executions had told him that those men went to their deaths with a lightness of heart such as they would have if they were going to a marriage.*[99]

In relation to this quotation, we might think of Joseph Plunkett and Grace Gifford planning a double wedding with Geraldine Plunkett and Thomas Gifford for the Easter Sunday of 1916, as both a diversionary tactic and a symbolic act; we think of the later eve-of-execution wedding between those two; finally, and perhaps more strangely, we think of John MacBride wearing the suit that he had donned to be the best man at his brother's wedding throughout the Rising. But, of course, by 1925, when Harrington makes this claim, he is using the romantic image of the Rising executions to obscure the controversy of the executions of the Irish Civil War (1922–1923) even as his amendment implicitly responds to it.

Though a draft of the 1922 Constitution of the Irish Free State had included a ban on the death penalty, the Civil War meant that British laws on capital punishment remained in force. In fact, although W. T. Cosgrave, head of the new government, claimed to oppose capital punishment in principle, he allowed many executions during this period. In the 1920s, Yeats defended the value of capital punishment despite his hesitating arguments about deterrence and vertigo in the aftermath of the Rising: after the execution of 77 Republican prisoners during the Civil War, Yeats commented that 'The Government of the Free State has been proved legitimate by the one effective test; it has been permitted to take life'.[100] Gavin Foster notes that in response to the final period of guerrilla Civil War by the IRA, the Free State had created oppressive new judicial institutions which, in their recourse to internment, military courts and the death penalty, mirrored the British response to 1916, including 'roughly 150 extra-judicial murders of republican prisoners and unarmed political activists'.[101] Similarly, Doyle and O'Donnell note the irony that de Valera relied on the political death penalty, though he had been at risk of being executed for similar actions after the Rising.[102]

Doyle and O'Donnell assert that while successive governments following the Civil War defended the death penalty because of the dangers of treason and subversion, in fact 'the vast majority of executions involved killings that had no conceivable political dimension and yet a situation was allowed to persist where capital punishment was mandatory for all murders'.[103] When Harrington had claimed euphemistically in 1925 that those who were executed in recent years' had gone 'to their deaths with a lightness of heart such as they would have if they were going to a marriage', he misses an opportunity to distinguish civil war executions and implies that they were comparably consensual sacrifices to those made by the 1916 generation.[104] This form of fidelity to the memory of those executed in 1916 allowed the death penalty to be maintained until the final abolition of the death penalty in Ireland (last execution 1954; abolition 1964): the emphasis in commemoration is on the symbolic, masochistic force of capital punishment itself rather than the value of the lives that were sacrificed for Ireland.

Notes

1. In the aftermath of Casement's death sentence, his diaries were copied and shared with prominent people in England, Ireland and the US to discourage them from linking their names to his reprieve campaign. The authenticity of the diaries was challenged in the 1930s, but they are now accepted to be genuine. They are best read alongside his 'White Diaries', a more public record of his political activities: *Roger Casement's Diaries 1910: The Black and the White*, ed. by Roger Sawyer, London: Pimlico, 1997. For an excellent reading of Casement, nationalist heroism and contemporary representations of Irish American gay and lesbian identities, see Kathryn Conrad, 'Queer Treasons: Homosexuality and Irish National Identity', *Cultural Studies*, Vol. 15, No. 1 (2001): 124–137. For an understanding of Casement's legacy within and beyond modernism, see Lucy McDiarmid 'The Afterlife of Roger Casement', *The Irish Art of Controversy*, Ithaca and London: Cornell University Press, 2005, and Alison Garden *The Literary Afterlives of Roger Casement, 1899–2016*, Liverpool: Liverpool University Press, 2020.
2. Sir Ernest Arthur Gowers et al. *Royal Commission on Capital Punishment, 1949–1953, REPORT, Presented to Parliament by Command of Her Majesty September 1953* (also known as Gowers Commission Report), London: Her Majesty's Stationery Office, 1953, paragraph 18, page 5.
3. Gavan Duffy, who defended Casement, summarised in the autumn the legal controversies involved in in-camera trials in an October 1916 letter which aimed to prevent any more executions and preserve the rights of those imprisoned and interned (George Gavan Duffy, 'Letter from George Gavan Duffy to Messrs Corrigan & Corrigan, 4th October 1916' Letters of 1916 (Schreibman, Susan, Ed.) Maynooth University: 2016. Website. [Accessed 19th June 2018]).
4. For example, during a House of Lords debate, Lord Charnwood, though supportive of the government's response to the Rising, argued against the secrecy of these trials and executions ('THE SINN FEIN REBELLION', House of Lords Debate 11th May 1916 Vol. 21 cc1002–36 (1014)).
5. See National Archives, Courts Martial Proceedings, for example, WO 71/350 (Macbride, John. Offence: Armed Rebellion), WO71/345, (Pearse, P. H., Offence: Armed Rebellion) or WO71/349 (Plunkett, Joseph. Offence: Armed Rebellion). Hansard gives the figures of those punished in the immediate aftermath of the Rising as 14 executed, 2 sentenced to death but not executed, 73 sentenced to penal servitude, 6 imprisoned with hard labour, 1706 deported/interned ('NUMBER OF EXECUTIONS', House of Commons Debate 11th May 1916 Vol. 82 cc886–7).

6. Sigmund Freud, 'The Economic Problem of Masochism', *The Standard Edition of the Complete Psychological Works of Sigmund Freud, Volume XIX*, trans. by Strachey et. al, London: Vintage, 2001: 159–172 (170).
7. Sigmund Freud, *Civilization and its Discontents* (1930 [1929]), *The Standard Edition of the Complete Psychological Works of Sigmund Freud Volume XXI* (1927–1931), trans. by Strachey et. al, London: Hogarth/ Vintage, 2001: 59–148 (119).
8. Freud, *Civilization and its Discontents*, 121.
9. Freud, *Civilization and its Discontents*, 136.
10. Freud, 'Dostoyevsky and Parricide', *The Standard Edition of the Complete Psychological Works of Sigmund Freud Volume XXI* (1927–1931), London: Hogarth/Vintage, 2001: 175–196 (178).
11. Reik and Freud, 'View on Capital Punishment' (1926), in *The Compulsion to Confess*, New York: Grove Press, 1961: 469–474. Freud would include an exchange of letters with Reik about the essay in subsequent editions of 'Dostoyevsky and Parricide'.
12. Lucy McDiarmid, *At Home in the Revolution*, Dublin: Royal Irish Academy, 2015, 91.
13. Conor Cruise O'Brien, *States of Ireland* 2nd edn, London 1974, 247. For a broader summary of the historiography of Irish political violence, see Ian McBride, 'The Shadow of the Gunman: Irish Historians and the IRA', *Journal of Contemporary History*, Vol. 46, No. 3 (2011): 686–710. For a literary studies examining similar texts and contexts to this chapter, see Nicholas Allen, *Modernism, Ireland and Civil War*, Cambridge: Cambridge University Press, 2009, as well as Sarah Cole, 'Cyclical Violence: The Irish Insurrection and the Limits of Enchantment', *At the Violet Hour: Modernism and Violence in England and Ireland*, Oxford and New York: Oxford University Press, 2012: 131–197.
14. R. F. Foster, *Vivid Faces: The Revolutionary Generation in Ireland, 1890–1923*, London: Penguin, 2015, iv.
15. Maureen Hawkins, 'The Dramatic Treatment of Robert Emmet and Sarah Curran', *Women in Irish Legend, Life and Literature* ed. by S. F. Gallagher, Gerrards Cross: Colin Smythe, 1983: 125–137 (130).
16. Tice L. Miller, *Entertaining the Nation: American Drama in the Eighteenth and Nineteenth Centuries*, Carbondale: Southern Illinois University Press, 2007, 88.
17. Dion Boucicault, 'Robert Emmet' (1884), *Selected Plays of Dion Boucicault*, ed. by Colin Smythe, Washington, D.C.: The Catholic University of America Press, 1987, Act IV: Scene II, 387–388.
18. Boucicault, *Robert Emmet*, Act IV: Last Tableau, 396–397.
19. Hawkins, 'The Dramatic Treatment of Robert Emmet and Sarah Curran', 128. See Deirdre McFeely who has recently argued that this play is too

violent and nihilistic for Boucicault to have had a substantial role in the authorship (*Dion Boucicault: Irish Identity on Stage*, Cambridge: Cambridge University Press, 2012, 169–172).

20. Jacques Derrida, *The Death Penalty: Volume II* ed. by Geoffrey Bennington and Marc Crépon/trans. by Elizabeth Rottenberg, Chicago: University of Chicago Press, 2017, 67.
21. Foster, *Vivid Faces*, 135–136.
22. David Doyle, 'Republicans, Martyrology, and the Death Penalty in Britain and Ireland, 1939–1990', *Journal of British Studies*, Vol. 54 (2015): 703–722 (704).
23. Doyle, 'Republicans', 705.
24. Caitriona Kennedy, 'The Names that Stilled Her Childish Play: The Women of 1916 and '98', Conference of Irish Historians in Britain, website, n.pag. [Accessed 13th June 2018].
25. Casement, 'The Prisoner's Speech', *The Trial of Sir Roger Casement* (ed. by George H. Knott) Edinburgh and London: William Hodge & Company, 1917, 205.
26. Casement, 'The Prisoner's Speech', 198.
27. Casement, 'The Prisoner's Speech', 204.
28. As Derrida reminds us that even within the Universal Declaration of Human Rights (1948) 'the right to life, liberty, and security of the person' allowed the death penalty to sit alongside it. Jacques Derrida, *The Death Penalty: Volume I* (trans. by Peggy Kamuf) Chicago: University of Chicago Press, 2014, 81.
29. Garden, *The Literary Afterlives of Roger Casement*, 89.
30. Michael G. Cronin, 'Pain, Pleasure and Revolution: The Body in Roger Casement's Writings', *The Body in Pain in Irish Literature and Culture* ed. by Fionnuala Dillane, Naomi McAreavey and Emilie Pine, Houndsmills: Palgrave, 2016: 135–148 (142). See also Siobhán Kilfeather, 'Remembering Pleasure and Pain: Roger Casement's Diaries', *Perversions 2* (1994): 4–22.
31. Lucy McDiarmid, *The Irish Art of Controversy*, Ithaca and London: Cornell, 2005, 175.
32. McDiarmid, *Irish Art*, 176–178.
33. W. B. Yeats, *The Letters of W. B. Yeats*, ed. by Allan Wade, New York: Macmillan, 1955, 870.
34. Kathryn Conrad, 'Foreign Bodies: Representations of Homosexuality and the Irish Body Politic', *Locked in the Family Cell: Gender, Sexuality, and Political Agency in Irish National Discourse*, Madison: University of Wisconsin Press, 2004, 21–63 (29).
35. See National Archives, HO 144/1637/311643/141 for details of this prurient extra post-mortem conducted by Dr Percy R. Mander (Medical

Officer of Pentonville) for Sir Herbert Smalley (Medical Commissioner of Prisons) and kept thereafter in Home Office files.

36. Susan de Sola Rodstein, 'Back to 1904: Joyce, Ireland and Nationalism', *Joyce: Feminism, Postcolonialism*, Amsterdam: Rodopi, 1998: 145–186 (148).
37. Tracey Schwartze '"Fabled by the Daughters of Memory": Roger Casement, James Joyce and the Irish Nationalist Hero', *Memory Ireland Volume 4: James Joyce and Cultural Memory* ed. by Oona Frawley and Katherine O'Callaghan, Syracuse: Syracuse University Press, 2014: 79–94 (92).
38. Garden, '"Piously forged palimpsests" and the "pelagiast pen": Casement and *Finnegans Wake*', *The Literary Afterlives of Roger Casement*: 136–145.
39. James Joyce, *Ulysses*, ed. by Hans Walter Gabler, London: The Bodley Head, 2002, 12.1542–1550.
40. Joyce, *Ulysses*, 12.1481–1492.
41. Patrick R. Mullen *The Poor Bugger's Tool: Irish Modernism, Queer Labor, and Postcolonial History*, Oxford: Oxford University Press, 2012, 111.
42. Richard Robert Madden, *The United Irishmen: Their Lives and Times*, London: The Catholic Publishing and Bookselling Company Limited, 1860, 455.
43. Joyce, *Ulysses*, 11.1111–1117.
44. Joyce, *Ulysses*, 11.1283–1294.
45. Joyce, *Ulysses*, 12.454–501.
46. Derrida, *The Death Penalty: Volume II*, 94.
47. R. F. Foster, *W. B. Yeats: A Life II: The Arch-Poet 1915–1939*, Oxford: Oxford University Press, 2003, 46.
48. Foster, *W. B. Yeats: A Life II*, 46.
49. Danielle Quinodoz, 'Chapter 11: Vertigo in the work of Sigmund Freud and Melanie Klein', *Emotional Vertigo: Between Anxiety and Pleasure*, London and New York: Routledge, 1997: 136–151 (137).
50. See John M. Hoberman, 'Kierkegaard on Vertigo', *International Kierkegaard Commentary: The Sickness unto Death*, ed. by Robert L. Perkins, Macon, Georgia: Mercer University Press, 1987: 185–208.
51. Seán McConville, *Irish Political Prisoners, 1848–1922: Theatres of War*, London: Routledge, 2003, 578.
52. McConville, *Irish Political Prisoners*, 578.
53. The National Archives, HO 144/1636/311643/45.
54. Foster, *W. B. Yeats: A Life II*, note 28, 683.
55. Foster, *W. B. Yeats: A Life II*, 47, 49.
56. Yeats, 'Easter, 1916', *The Collected Works of W. B. Yeats: Volume I: The Poems*, 2nd Edition ed. by Richard Finneran, New York: Scribner, 1997: 182–184 (183).

57. Foster, *W. B. Yeats: A Life II*, 63.
58. Foster, *W. B. Yeats: A Life II*, 63.
59. Foster, *W. B. Yeats: A Life II*, 63.
60. Sarah Cole, 'Cyclical Violence: The Irish Insurrection and the Limits of Enchantment', *At the Violet Hour: Modernism and Violence in England and Ireland*, Oxford and New York: Oxford University Press, 2012: 131–197 (145).
61. Joseph Plunkett, *The Poems of Joseph Mary Plunkett*, ed. by Geraldine Plunkett Dillon, New York: Frederick A. Stokes Company, 1916, 62.
62. Cole, 'Cyclical Violence', 145.
63. Plunkett, *The Poems*, 59.
64. Joseph Plunkett's sister wrote in her memoirs that she had witnessed Grace experience a miscarriage (McDiarmid, *At Home in the Revolution*, 127–129).
65. Yeats, 'The Rose Tree', *The Poems*, 185.
66. R. R. Madden *The life and times of Robert Emmet, Esq.*, Dublin: James Duffy, 1847, 269–270 and Thomas Sherlock, *Robert Emmet: The Story of His Life and Death*, Dublin: T.D. Sullivan, 1878, 28–29.
67. Madden, *The life and times of Robert Emmet, Esq* 269–270.
68. H. C. Mangan, *Robert Emmet: A History Play in Three Acts*, Dublin: M. H. Gill & Son, 1904.
69. Joyce, *Ulysses*, 12.658–669.
70. Joyce, *Ulysses*, 12.1156–1164.
71. For a broader focus on Joyce's specific investments in betrayal, see James Fraser, *Joyce and Betrayal*, Houndsmills: Palgrave, 2016. For a response to the question of the Blooms' marriage plot, see Peter *Kuch, Irish Divorce/Joyce's Ulysses*, Houndsmills: Palgrave, 2017.
72. W. B. Yeats, 'The Dreaming of the Bones', *The Collected Works of W.B. Yeats Volume II: The Plays*, New York: Scribner, 2001: 307–316 (314).
73. Claire Nally, *Envisioning Ireland: W.B. Yeats's Occult Nationalism*, Bern, Switzerland: Peter Lang, 2010, 209.
74. Joyce, *Ulysses*, 12.676.
75. Joyce, *Ulysses*, 15.1137–1174.
76. McDiarmid, *At Home in the Revolution*, 2015.
77. Joyce, *Ulysses*, 12.658–669.
78. Herbert O. Mackey, *The Life and Times of Roger Casement*, Dublin: C.J. Fallon, 1954, 134.
79. Mackey, *The Life and Times*, 135.
80. The National Archives, HO 144/1636/311643/7A.
81. Robert Emmet, 'Letter to Sarah Curran', *Women of 'Ninety-Eight* ed. by Helena Walsh Concannon, Dublin: M. H. Gill and Son, 1919, 273.

82. Roger Casement. 'Letter from Roger Casement to Nina Casement, 25th July 1916' *Letters of 1916*, ed. by Susan Schreibman, Maynooth University, 2016. Website. [Accessed 20th June 2018].
83. The National Archives, HO 144/1637/311643/182.
84. Anne Clare, *Unlikely Rebels: The Gifford Girls and the Fight for Irish Freedom*, Cork: Mercier Press, 2011, 145.
85. Joseph Plunkett, 'Letter by Plunkett to his fiancé Grace Gifford', National Library of Ireland, NLI.MS.20.858.
86. Thomas MacDonagh, 'Typescript of last letter and will of Thomas MacDonagh, 2nd May 1916', *Letters of 1916*, ed. by Susan Schreibman, Susan, Maynooth University, 2016. Website. n.pag. [Accessed 20th July 2018].
87. MacDonagh, 'Typescript of last letter and will of Thomas MacDonagh, 2nd May 1916', n.pag.
88. MacDonagh, 'Typescript of last letter and will of Thomas MacDonagh, 2nd May 1916', n.pag. Pearse, 'Letter from Patrick Pearse to his mother Margaret Pearse, 3 May 1916' *Letters of 1916*, ed. by Susan Schreibman, Maynooth University, 2016. Website. [Accessed 19th June 2018]. My italics.
89. Seán Mac Diarmada, 'Letter from Seán Mac Diarmada to John Daly, 10th May 1916', *Letters of 1916*, ed. by Susan Schreibman, Maynooth University, 2016. Website. [Accessed 19th June 2018].
90. J.J. Heuston. 'Letter from J.J. Heuston to Mr. E. Walsh, 7th May 1916', *Letters of 1916*, ed. by Susan Schreibman, Susan, Maynooth University, 2016. Website. [Accessed 19th June 2018].
91. Michael Mallin, 'Appendix 1: Michael Mallin's last letter to his wife Agnes, Kilmainham Gaol, 7th May 1916', *Michael Mallin: 16 Lives* ed. by Brian Hughes, Dublin: The O'Brien Press, 2013, 231.
92. Mallin, 'Appendix 1: Michael Mallin's last letter', 232.
93. *The Catholic Bulletin* Vol. VI, No. VII (July 1916) 399 and Vol. VI, No. XII (Dec. 1916) 700.
94. Mallin, 'Appendix 1: Michael Mallin's last letter', 231.
95. Mallin, 'Appendix 1: Michael Mallin's last letter', 233.
96. Piaras F. Mac Lochlainn, *Last Words: Letters and Statements of the Leaders Executed after the Rising at Easter 1916*, Dublin: Stationery Office, 1990.
97. Brian Hughes, *Michael Mallin: 16 Lives*, Dublin: The O'Brien Press, 2013, 184–185.
98. Amber Musser, *Sensational Flesh: Race, Power, and Masochism*, New York: New York University Press, 2014, 103.
99. Anon. 'CAPITAL PUNISHMENT IN IRELAND: Strong Opposition', *The Manchester Guardian* May 7, 1925, 9, my italics.

100. Yeats, 'Ireland 1921–1931' *The Collected Works of W. B. Yeats, Volume X: Later Articles and Reviews*, ed, by Colton Johnson, New York: Scribner, 2000, 487.
101. Gavin Foster, The Irish Civil War and Society: Politics, Class and Conflict, Houndsmills: Palgrave, 2015, 5–6.
102. David Doyle and Ian O'Donnell, 'The Death Penalty in Post-Independence Ireland', The Journal of Legal History, Vol. 33, No. 1 (2012): 65–91 (68).
103. Doyle and O'Donnell, 'The Death Penalty', 68.
104. Anon. 'CAPITAL PUNISHMENT IN IRELAND', 9.

CHAPTER 7

The Legacy of World War I Court Martial in Interwar Death Penalty Writing

Introduction

This chapter will examine how a range of British publications inflected by the diagnostic logic of psychoanalysis helped to facilitate a cultural processing of the widespread use of the military death penalty during World War I. Freudian thought, transmitted by the work of the famous shell shock doctor W. H. R. Rivers, influenced the representations of the effect of the military death penalty in an impressive array of popular texts from various genres, including A. P. Herbert's novels *The Secret Battle* (1919) and *The House by the River* (1921), the Labour M. P. Ernest Thurtle's testimony pamphlet *Shootings at Dawn* (1924), A. D. Gristwood's novella *The Coward* (1927), Patrick Hamilton's play *Rope* (1929) and Dorothy L. Sayers's detective novel *Busman's Honeymoon* (1937). This chapter will thus respond to Christie Davies's suggestion that the reform of military and civilian capital punishment ought to be studied together by examining literary works that speak to this interdependence.[1] Rivers argues in the context of military medicine that if Freud's theory of the unconscious is true, then it has very wide implications and 'must be taken into account not only by the physician, but by the teacher, by the politician, the moralist, the sociologist, and every other worker who is concerned with the study of human conduct'.[2] The first half of this chapter will examine the serving soldier, and how their psychology was affected by the threat of the

K. Ebury, *Modern Literature and the Death Penalty, 1890–1950*, Palgrave Studies in Literature, Culture and Human Rights, https://doi.org/10.1007/978-3-030-52750-1_7

military death penalty, whether as a victim, as a participant in the firing squad or merely as a witness. The second half of the chapter will then explore attitudes to civilian capital crimes, especially murder, considering whether the death penalty looked uniquely different to the shell shocked veteran.

During World War I, there was roughly one military execution for every week of the war for offences including cowardice, desertion, mutiny, murder, disobedience, assisting the enemy and striking a senior officer.[3] Desertion was the most common offence for which death sentences were passed: Teresa Iacobelli suggests that cowardice was a rarer charge because it was a more subjective crime and thus harder to prove for the authorities.[4] About 11% of the death sentences passed were carried out, with the other sentences being commuted: this figure appears to have been a deliberate strategy, as a '"safe" level politically speaking' for the army to demonstrate its ability to show mercy and understanding.[5] This limitation of the number of actual executions was as much directed externally, at the government and public at home, as internally within the army to maintain consent for discipline.[6] The military death penalty was disproportionately used by Britain and its Empire compared to other countries: figures provided by Beckett et al. suggest that the US Army executed only 35 men; the Belgian Army executed 18; the German Army, despite its abiding militaristic reputation, executed 48.[7] The British had 27 capital offences in their military code during the war, compared to 11 capital offences in the German Army and 2 in the French Forces:[8] 12 offences were always punishable by death and 15 were capital if committed while on active duty.[9] Due to a culture of restriction and official secrecy around the military death penalty, it is difficult to find an agreed definitive figure for exactly how many soldiers were executed for military offences by Britain during World War I. Ernest Thurtle claims 261 executions in *Shootings at Dawn*, but in the 1930 debates about military death penalty reform, he gives different and more precise figures, claiming 'There were 287 men executed in the last War. Two of them for striking officers, two for sleeping at posts; 18 for cowardice and 264 for desertion'.[10] As these figures are accepted even by those MPs who were opposed to Thurtle's campaign for the abolition of the military death penalty, I will therefore rely on Thurtle's numbers as reflective of informed public knowledge in the interwar period, though most contemporary historians believe there were at least three hundred executions.[11] According to Iacobelli, Generals 'believed that executions were an effective punishment' because of an overemphasis on the death penalty in the British civilian penal code.[12] Beyond the attitudes of Generals, the use of the death penalty is also indicative of Divisional Commanders' views on deterrence, as they made the decision to charge and shaped the sentence.[13] In short, during World War I, Britain 'remained exceptional in its reliance on the death penalty' in both civilian and military contexts.[14]

Derrida makes space for a brief consideration of those killed during World War I within his death penalty project: the death penalty is, he says, not merely a question of punishment but 'rather [...] of the different ways the state has of affirming its sovereignty by disposing of the life of certain subjects, foreign subjects (the enemy soldier, sometimes the enemy civilian) but also its own soldiers sent to the front or even condemned to death in wartime for treason or desertion'.[15] His key examples of executions with only 'the appearance of legality' include the specific example of the battles fought at Chemin des Dames during World War I, as well as a more general anecdotal response to the conflict, in which 'those who did not move to the front quickly enough during a WWI offensive' were liable to both execution and extrajudicial killing.[16] These state actions, and their radical challenge to conventional legal practice, take us from a Foucauldian biopolitical paradigm to a more drastic use of sovereignty closer to Achille Mbembe's concept of necropolitics. For Mbembe, the concept of necropolitics is required to understand war: 'War, after all, is as much a means of achieving sovereignty as a way of exercising the right to kill. Imagining politics as a form of war, we must ask: What place is given to life, death, and the human body (in particular the wounded or slain body)? How are they inscribed in the order of power?'.[17] While Mbembe's examples are drawn mostly from a sense of contemporary emergency, his concept is undoubtedly useful for examining the necropolitics of World War I and its aftermath.

Post-war reports examining a selection of cases of the execution of minors found that shell shock defences were rejected in around a third of cases.[18] Similarly, the report by the 1922 government committee on shell shock asserted that 'some "injustices" had been done in the early years of the war when psychoneurotic soldiers might have been court-martialed and executed for cowardice before the phenomenon was understood'.[19] This report indeed strongly suggested that the shell shocked soldier might not be criminally responsible: Ted Bogacz argues that it offered a direct line to the eventual abolition of the death penalty for cowardice in 1930.[20] Throughout the interwar years, forms of military death sentence were gradually removed, until by 1930 only treason and mutiny remained as capital offences in military law. These reforms of the military death penalty, which came out of debates questioning broader principles of punishment in general—including deterrence, premeditation and the psychology of the offender—undoubtedly had a huge influence on public opinion about the death penalty in civil society, as I will show in subsequent sections by examining the role of a range of literary works.

The Military Death Penalty in World War I Fiction and Life-Writing

To sum up the key aspects of the historical context, the rise of psychoanalysis, as well as a widespread public perception that shell shock was a factor in unjust use of the military death penalty, was directly influential on parliamentary debates about capital punishment in the war's aftermath.[21] At the same time, shell shock's resistance to treatment would change psychoanalysis itself, leading to Freud's post-war emphasis on the death drive, as well as to the emphasis of his followers such as Sachs and Reik on the need for psychoanalysis to combat the death penalty. In dealing with literature responding to the military death penalty, we find ambiguity even in straightforwardly polemical texts, as authors respond to various pressures of censorship and restriction. For example, while it would have been easy to always use the term 'shell shock' as a humanising factor, this language is rare in the texts I consider here. These texts are also moderate in not interrogating the value of concepts of military crime per se but simply questioning the use of capital punishment in cases of impaired responsibility. In A. P. Herbert's novel *The Secret Battle* (1919), the narrator uses the language of 'battle-psychology' in examining the chain of events that led his friend Harry Penrose to be executed for desertion.[22] The novel's form combines the combat memoir, the case history, the courtroom drama and the death penalty narrative.[23] Herbert is influenced by psychoanalysis but, as I have already noted, he avoids using the term 'shell shock': this is striking because the novel is a fictive version of a real court martial case, that of Temporary Sub-Lieutenant Edwin Dyett. Dyett was executed for desertion in 1917 despite a diagnosed history of shell shock which had long preceded his offence, but his medical record is not referenced in his court martial paperwork, where the comments are brief and stereotyped.[24]

Similarly, shell shock is not the focus of Ernest Thurtle's influential pamphlet *Shootings at Dawn* (1924) where he publishes witness statements about the effect of military executions as a form of testimony (or 'plain, unvarnished tales', as he puts it).[25] Those executed are instead described in the witness statements in euphemistic language such as 'a bundle of nerves'.[26] Finally, the language of 'shell shock' is not used by the main character of A. D. Gristwood's 1927 novella *The Coward*, in which he recounts to the unnamed frame narrator who receives his confession that he used a self-inflicted wound to escape from the Front, even though he is acutely conscious that his crime merits the death penalty. Despite the even wider dissemination of the idea of shell shock by the late 1920s, Gristwood's character still uses emotional language, rather than medical or psychological terms, including 'desperation', 'shame' and 'pride'.[27] He accepts the rightness of the death penalty for his offence and has internalised the language of crime.[28] As with Herbert, Gristwood's depiction of his protagonist implies diminished responsibility due to shell shock. The character believes that 'the uncanny spell of calmness that possessed'[29] him in planning to shoot himself in the hand suggests that 'I cannot have been entirely responsible for my actions'.[30] Despite the lack of psychological terminology in Gristwood's text, he shows very effectively that the effect of war trauma is profound long after his protagonist's crime and beyond even the end of the war. For example, he has nightmares in which he is executed:

> Terrified by my dread of the death penalty, night after night I dreamed that the worst had befallen me. I pictured to myself the firing-party and the word of command: the crash of the volley and "the nothing all things end in".[31]

Indeed, Gristwood's whole story is occasioned by his character's need to confess his crime to a stranger in a railway carriage, reflecting concepts such as Reik's compulsion to confess and Freud's repetition compulsion discussed in earlier chapters. Gristwood's unnamed character's internalised acceptance that he is worthy of the death penalty is reflected in the novel's ending, 'the coward is a coward still, and nothing can exonerate him', changing his experience of temporality and preventing him from processing his war trauma.[32]

Thurtle's witnesses register extreme physical and emotional reactions to the military death penalty, including anger, tears, nightmares, vomiting and fainting among witnesses and the firing party. For example, one witness records that 'we stood in silence for what seemed hours, although only minutes', while 'one of the Yorkshires fainted, the strain was that great'.[33] As the testimony highlights, the firing squad would always not kill the condemned man outright, and the commanding officer would then need to 'administer the coup de grâce'.[34] This cruelty in carrying out the sentence, which falls far short of the humane standard of punishment explored in civilian life, is noted in 'Letter No. 1' in Thurtle's pamphlet, as the soldier testifies that his comrade 'poor "A."' was executed early in the war (on 30 September 1914) before effective execution protocols were established. 'A.' had attempted escape by running away from the firing squad: 'The firing party fired at him on the run, wounding him in the shoulder', and then 'the sergeant of the guard was ordered by the Provost-Marshal to finish him off as he lay wounded'.[35] In 'Letter No. 3', the witness 'heard another shot, which I afterwards ascertained was the doctor's shot to make sure he was dead'.[36] The letters register the traumatic effect of this responsibility on both ordinary soldiers and commanding officers. The language of murder is directly used,[37] and in one letter, two men from the firing party who fail to shoot at the condemned man are eventually court martialled themselves for disobeying orders but 'found mentally unfit'.[38] One officer in charge of a firing party concludes his statement, 'I think these terrible things should be abolished, and so would everyone else who had witnessed a "Shooting at Dawn" affair'.[39]

While, at the time, Thurtle's accounts of the military death penalty were felt to have been sensationalised, they are in fact very similar to unpublished (and thus non-polemic) witness accounts. For example, preserved in the Edwin Dyett Home Office file is a moving unpublished account of his death:

> the eyewitness states that his end was "an inspiration to those present" so much so that two officers absolutely collapsed and had to be medically treated. He addressed the firing party and told them, inter alia, he had nothing to fear, and he did not blame them; saying they were only obeying their orders, and concluded "don't muddle it boys, shoot straight".[40]

Other unpublished life-writing held at the Imperial War Museum emphasises the traumatic effect of executions on witnesses. For example, from the private diary of A. P. Roberts:

> July 16, 1915, 4.a.m.: I have a very pathetic incident to relate. We had the order to stand to arms at 2.45am, parade 3am. We formed up on parade to hear one of our own men being shot for cowardice, we did not see him, but we heard the report of the rifles at 3.45am. The CO then came out and read to us the sentence of the court martial, and the cause of the sentence of death. I must say it had a very depressing effect on the whole battalion.[41]

The 'depressing effect' of the death penalty is writ large in Roberts's brief account of the rest of the day: by 10am he has already punished a man for insubordination and reported sick himself. Traumatic accounts of the military death penalty are quite commonplace within the Imperial War Museum Archive.[42]

In contrast to these real accounts, Herbert's novel demonstrates deliberate restraint in its representation of the execution scene in a way that appears to minimise its traumatic effect:

> The thing was done seven mornings later, in a little orchard behind the Casquettes' farm. The Padre told me he stood up to them very bravely and quietly. Only he whispered to him "For God's sake make them be quick." That is the worst torment of the soldier from beginning to end—the waiting. He was shot by his own men, by men of D Company.[43]

Indeed, *The Secret Battle*'s influence was primarily secured by a few influential readers and by the parliamentary debates that echo it. The novel was read by the Prime Minister (David Lloyd George) and the Secretary of State for War (Winston Churchill). Herbert's narrator's final summary deliberately denies the novel's claims to be a polemic and refuses judgement:

> This book is not an attack on any person, on the death penalty, or on anything else, though if it makes people think about these things so much the better. I think I believe in the death penalty—I do not know. But I did not believe in Harry being shot. That is the gist of it; that my friend Harry was shot for cowardice—and he was one of the bravest men I ever knew.[44]

Herbert also dramatises a broader debate around the death penalty in a concluding fictional debate held between the soldiers of Penrose's platoon, which in many ways set the tone for future parliamentary debates of the 1920s, both for and against the military death penalty.[45] One soldier suggests that no one who *volunteers* to fight ought to be executed; another soldier that the Court Martial is justified as there should be 'some sort of standard'; another soldier focuses on the role of self-knowledge, suggesting that Penrose should not have volunteered because of the risk to others; another soldier suggests the Court Martial ought to consider the offender's mental and physical health before deciding sentence; another soldier suggests that it is unfair that Australian soldiers cannot be executed for similar offences; a last voice expresses his hope that mercy will be shown. Each of these points, initially raised in Herbert's text, appears in the mouths of MPs during the interwar period. For example, Sir Gerald Hurst and Major Hills would argue against the execution of volunteers in the 1930 debate about cowardice and desertion;[46] in the same debate, Sir Hugh O'Neill would argue for the value of the military death penalty in maintaining military standards and ensuring success in future wars.[47] Lieutenant-Colonel Spender-Clay argued for the risk to others posed by those who committed military offences.[48] Ernest Thurtle himself offers two of the arguments posed by soldiers in Herbert's novel, suggesting that he may have been directly influenced by *The Secret Battle*. Firstly, in a 1928 debate, like Herbert's soldier who suggested that cowardice should be seen in the context of a soldier's mental and physical health, Thurtle argues that:

> The Government have not been able to show that the men who are convicted of these offences are culpable or criminal in any real sense of the word. They have fallen because of the imperfections of their nervous and physical endowment, and enlightened public opinion to-day does not regard that as sufficient reason for imposing the death penalty.[49]

Secondly, in the 1930 debate on cowardice, like Herbert's soldier who argued for a more enlightened approach based on the exemption from punishment of Australian soldiers, Thurtle argued:

> I say, that if it is demonstrated that the Australian troops could fight gallantly and courageously, as they did, without the death penalty, then it is a libel on the courage of other British troops to say that they will not fight without the death penalty.[50]

Herbert's novel's non-polemic character, which I have highlighted, also allowed Winston Churchill to vote against the 1930 bill removing the death penalty for the offences of cowardice and desertion, despite the fact that he had in 1928 contributed a moving preface to Herbert's book. Churchill did not speak in the debate, but he is listed among the 'Noes' in the parliamentary record.[51]

The contrasting reception history of *The Secret Battle* and *The Coward* also reflects divisions within a wider literary culture about the military death penalty, similar to those I have shown in these parliamentary debates. For example, a reviewer in *The Observer* notes that 'Mr. Herbert is not a propagandist' as the novel is 'a faithful and balanced view of war as it is, its psychology and its setting'.[52] Similarly, in the *Times Literary Supplement*, the reviewer linked the book with 'medical research' and the 'psychoanalytical treatment of shell-shock' suggesting that Herbert's novel is the first war chronicle to deal with 'the many subtle ways that fear has of getting at a man' from a 'scientific understanding'.[53] At the same time, the reviewer struggles with the wider implications of the novel, claiming 'a certain perversity', comparing Herbert to Thomas Hardy: in designing the tragedy of Harry Penrose, the novelist 'has left no stone unturned to ensure the full measure of calamity'.[54] And yet, the reviewer also feels that 'one's discomfort in reading the book is enhanced by the certainty that something very like it must have happened over and over again'.[55] The reviewer's evasive 'it', meaning war trauma, the military death penalty and injustice all at the same time, avoids spoiling the story for the reader and also escapes the need to directly respond to the problem of court martial execution. The reviewer's whole response to the novel is simultaneously euphemistic and appalled.

By contrast, the more shocking nature of Gristwood's representation of shell shock in the shadow of the death penalty is reflected in the fact that although it was quite successful (it sold about 2100 copies), his publishers quickly decided not to keep the book in print. This decision perhaps responds to the harsh judgement of hostile reviewers such as the individual in the *New Statesman* who asserts that 'Mr Gristwood's propagandistic journalese certainly does not deserve to be read [...] by future generations'.[56] Reviewers of Gristwood's work were usually ex-servicemen themselves: for them, 'the book spoke for "the trench malingerer", who, unless silenced, could unman his comrades'.[57] For example, Cyril Falls expresses anxiety that 'The writer does not tell us that he sympathises with this person, but he allows no hint of reprobation or contempt to escape him'.[58] In short, reviewers' beliefs about the natural justice of the military death penalty were challenged by these fictions: Harry Penrose was felt to be too sympathetic to be executed, while Gristwood's narrator was too unsympathetic not to be.

In these examples, refusing straightforward arguments about shell shock allows authors such as Herbert, Gristwood and Thurtle to explore a more complex version of the influence of psychoanalysis on ideas of trauma and criminal responsibility, which applied far beyond a war-time situation. I have argued that all these texts represent, but refuse to explicitly diagnose, soldiers who grapple with shell shock. These authors mobilise this shared resistance to articulate surprisingly different attitudes towards the military death penalty. Indeed, we might say that Thurtle and Gristwood diagnose injustice, while Herbert suggests reform. Thurtle's pamphlet directly indicts the military death penalty through claims about its effects on witnesses. Gristwood's novella is more oblique than Thurtle's but still represents military justice as nightmarish and psychologically harmful. Overall, the military death penalty is shown to be an inappropriate punishment because it fails to deter, because of the unevenness of its application and because of its lingering effects on post-war civil society. Arguments about court martial executions dramatise and prepare the ground for a wider questioning of the death penalty, but it would take 35 more years to get to the same result with civilian capital punishment. As I will show in the next section, throughout the interwar period, war trauma remained loosely and metaphorically connected with the trauma of the death penalty, but in ways that seemed as likely to lead to further war, mental illness and capital crimes rather than to pacifism and abolitionism.

Shell Shock, Murder and the Civilian Death Penalty in Interwar Literature

In the previous section I examined how parliamentary debates and literary texts about the death penalty were informed by the impact of a new science, the psychology of shell shock and a new historical pressure, the reality of World War I court martial. Many of the tensions identified were eased by the successful passing of legislation removing the death penalty for most military offences (except treason and mutiny) by 1930. However, there remained the problem of the civilian death penalty, which was exacerbated by wider social concerns about how wounded, traumatised men could be reintegrated into civilian society. One of the more common uses of the military death penalty was for the offence of murder (5th behind Desertion, Sleeping at post, Cowardice, and Disobedience), and this was also a crime that was less commonly reprieved by commanding officers (118 sentences were passed and 74 were carried out), which is useful for judging a continuity between violence among serving troops and demobilised soldiers adapting to civilian life.[59] Indeed, from the end of the war onwards, shell shock was an important component in legal debates and crime reporting about capital crimes and the insanity defence.

Many of the implications of the intersection of psychoanalysis, war trauma and the death penalty were only gradually absorbed into literary representations of justice. The concept of shell shock, alongside a more complex understanding of mental illness and psychoanalysis, acutely troubled the M'Naghten Rules, which symbolically determined who would be executed and who would be sent for treatment. The most famous example of a post-war case that challenged M'Naghten was that of Ronald True (1922). Though True was never a conventional shell shock victim, an important part of his defence for his murder of Gertrude Yates was his physical and mental trauma from plane crashes during his wartime training as a pilot, as well as a morphine addiction resulting from his treatment.[60] Another distinctive feature of True's legal case is its detailed engagement with psychoanalytic thought: in one obvious measure, variants of the word 'psychoanalysis' ('psychology', 'psycho-analyst', 'psychological') appear more than 20 times across the published transcript of the True trial.[61] But it was ultimately True's war service that seems to have led to his reprieve. An earlier case, which has not had the same historical longevity, had prepared the ground for the True reprieve: in 1919, Colonel Rutherford was found 'guilty but insane' of the murder of Major Cariston Seton. Despite the violence of Rutherford's murder and substantial evidence of premeditation, Rutherford was not executed because expert witnesses diagnosed him with shell shock and character references from brother officers attested to Rutherford's war record. Rutherford, like True, was committed to Broadmoor.

The cases of True and Rutherford achieved public notoriety and had a substantial literary influence, but I have found legal reporting of everyday capital cases highlighting shell shock extremely frequently, in a wide range of case outcomes. For example, in just four years, 1918–1921, shell shock is reported as factor across a wide range of capital trials including David Greenwood (1918, death sentence commuted);[62] Harold Chennells (1919, died by suicide);[63] Arthur Beard (1919, death sentence commuted);[64] Charles Tellett (1921, death sentence commuted);[65] George Henry Rodolph (1920, found 'guilty but insane');[66] Frederick Holt (1920, executed);[67] Joseph Hutty (1919, death sentence commuted)[68] and Edward Charles Semmens (1920, found 'Not guilty').[69] Most of these cases were domestic or sexual crimes, where a traumatised former soldier killed a woman in their life. Clive Emsley describes, with a focus on 1919, a wide cultural unease about the perception of returning soldiers committing capital crimes, showing that the reason this unease did not develop into a full-scale 'moral panic' was partly due to a wide sense of public compassion for the trauma suffered by these soldiers.[70] Emsley argues explicitly that 'the press and the courts may have used shell-shock as a way of explaining violence among men from the respectable classes'.[71] The law might therefore perpetuate class and military hierarchies in dividing those crimes worthy of the death penalty from those that were more excusable.

This is noteworthy because the protagonists of the texts I will examine here are all members of the officer class: it is their trauma and their affective response to the death penalty which will be an index for an interwar reconsideration of the purpose of punishment. While many examples could be given, in this section I have chosen to focus on narratives where war trauma is central to the whole narrative: A. P. Herbert's *The House by the River* (1921), Patrick Hamilton's *Rope* (1929) and Dorothy L. Sayers's *Busman's Honeymoon* (1937). The death penalty and its interaction with war trauma is central to the characterisation and psychology of Herbert's Stephen Byrne, Hamilton's Rupert Cadell and Sayers's Lord Peter Wimsey, cutting across their different functions within each narrative: Byrne is a murderer who is subject to the death penalty; Cadell is first an inadvertent accomplice of the perpetrators and eventually an agent of the law; Wimsey is a veteran detective who is harmed by capital punishment as the outcome of his work.

The Colonel Rutherford and Ronald True cases show a more nuanced public understanding of connections between war trauma, murder and the death penalty, which fed into the literature of the period. For example, A. P. Herbert's abiding interest in capital punishment extended into the interwar period and into a consideration of civilian crime and punishment, via his second novel, *The House by the River* (1920), a social satire. In this novel a war poet, Stephen Byrne, commits an accidental murder but is unable to face justice because of fear and shame focused especially on the death penalty. Byrne is at first introduced by Herbert as 'one of a few men who had been able in a few fine poems to set free for the nation a little of the imprisoned grandeur, the mute emotion of that time'.[72] The opening chapter of the novel features a performance at a party of Byrne's musical setting of Asquith's 'We shall not sheathe the sword' speech.[73] Herbert uses this incident to suggest the psychology of his society remains unbalanced by the war: when the song is finished, the party guests feel like crying, but instead the silence is 'broken with peals of insane laughter'.[74] When, in the next chapter, Byrne suddenly kills Emily Gaunt, his housemaid, after drunkenly assaulting her, his violence is triggered by a sense of trauma at hearing her scream: 'What he wanted was silence...complete silence, that was it...screams and gasps, they were all dangerous...'.[75]

Herbert's most direct inspiration for *The House by the River*, because of this combination of a sexual motive alongside war trauma and drunkenness as mitigating factors, appears to have been the Arthur Beard trial, rather than Rutherford or True. Beard was a recently demobbed Navy veteran who had raped and murdered a 13-year-old girl. Beard's lawyers did not make his war trauma a significant part of his defence strategy, focusing instead on his drunkenness: but trial reports note that Beard 'either had trench fever or was gassed' and his war record was widely reported and included in petitions for reprieve.[76] Trial reports kept in his Home Office file show how the newspapers chose to include images of Beard in uniform.[77] He was initially convicted of murder and sentenced to death; then the Court of Appeals quashed the murder sentence and substituted manslaughter on the grounds that he was too drunk to premeditate the crime; finally, the House of Lords (very unusually) intervened to reverse the Appeal decision. The sentence was ultimately commuted because of the awkwardness of the legal process. A legal focus on drunkenness as an early form of the diminished responsibility defence formed an interesting challenge to M'Naghten, and the drawn-out legal case was a cause célèbre. Ten thousand people signed the petition for Beard's reprieve, reflecting the cultural sympathy for the shell shocked murderer explored by Emsley among others.

While Herbert represents Byrne's state of mind as falling outside the legal definition of insanity, Byrne's war trauma, alongside the aggravating factor of drunkenness, is shown to make him susceptible to capital crimes. In contrast with Byrne, his friend Egerton, who helps him conceal his crime, is terrified by the murder and its implications. Egerton has not seen war service and thus offers a 'normal' response to the crime as a foil to Byrne's abnormal, unbalanced response:

> [Egerton] was a highly sensitive man and easily shocked. He had not been, like Stephen, to the war—being a Civil Servant and imperfect in the chest—

> and in an age when the majority of living young men have looked largely on, and become callous about, death, John Egerton had never seen a dead body.[78]

Indeed, Egerton will be suspected of the murder because of his guilty reaction to becoming an accomplice, in contrast with Byrne who is psychologically incapable of these conventional responses. Byrne is unable to feel guilt for his murder because of his war experience: he 'had seen too much of death in the war to be much distressed by the fact of death'.[79] Throughout the novel Byrne also attempts to repress the reality of his crime because of the punishment attached to it:

> He would not be afraid now. He would give himself up. No, no! He couldn't do that. Not fair to Margery—a long wait, prison, trial, the dock, hanging! Aah! He made a shuddering cry at that thought, and he lashed out with the stick in his hand, beating at the withes in a fury of fear. No, no! by God, no!—hanging—the last morning! Not that. But still, he must be brave. No more cowardice. That was the worst of all he had done this summer—the cowardice.[80]

Here, Byrne is attempting to persuade himself either to give himself up to justice or to write a confession and commit suicide, but ironically the 'worst' thing he can accuse himself of is 'cowardice', showing the skewed perspective in which he is unable to bring his crime of murder into focus. Herbert's deployment of the opposed ideas of masculine honour and cowardice offers an important continuity with *The Secret Battle*. In both *The Secret Battle* and *The House by the River*, then, capital punishment is shown to be an impediment to natural justice and becomes part of the 'tragic' structure of each novel's examination of flawed masculinity. However, Herbert nonetheless depicts Byrne as a very different character to the brave Harry Penrose: Byrne instead dies in an undignified accidental drowning accident after fighting with Egerton. The final words of *The House by the River* offer a direct contrast with the parallelism of the final words of *The Secret Battle* ('my friend Harry was shot for cowardice—and he was one of the bravest men I ever knew'[81]): the inscription on Byrne's memorial asserts that he 'was a great poet; it did not say he was a good man'.[82]

The original publicity notice for *The House by the River* encourages readers to identify with the character of Stephen Byrne in his quest to escape the death penalty: it asks simply, 'What would you do if you, a respectable and popular young Poet, had committed a murder? The question is answered in "The House by the River"'.[83] Similarly, *The New York Times* reviewer calls this a work of 'genuine, high-grade psychology' and asks again for sympathy: 'Those of us who are entirely honest with ourselves can only watch his twistings and turnings, his futile regrets and perpetual yielding to temptation, and ask very humbly, whether we, in his place, could or would have acted differently'.[84] An *Observer* reviewer notes that while 'the murder is a very grim murder', nevertheless 'It is the attitude of Stephen towards his crime, and towards his friend who is entangled in it, that makes the story, and it is a very good story indeed'.[85] We should note the contrast between the reviewers' call for compassionate feeling and my earlier examination of reviewers' contemptuous rejection of Gristwood's cowardly character. This identification reflects Emsley's argument that a wide sense of public guilt and compassion for the trauma suffered by soldiers led to more sympathetic attitudes when they committed civilian capital crimes.

A review of the 1938 theatrical adaptation Herbert's *The House by the River*, which was called *Flood Tide*, directly compared the play's themes and atmosphere with Patrick Hamilton's *Rope*. The reviewer suggests that with some small improvements 'this play can easily be transformed into a highly intelligent thriller in the same class as Mr. Patrick Hamilton's unforgettable "Rope"'.[86] The critical history of Hamilton's *Rope* (1929) has so far been too focused on the influence of the Leopold and Loeb case (1924) on the play, obscuring the World War I context which is central to its drama.[87] In fact, I would argue that the main source of conflict within Hamilton's play is the veteran Rupert Cadell's change of heart about murder and the death penalty, rather than the actions of the killers, his friends and former students Wyndham Brandon and Charles Granillo. Cadell starts from a nihilistic position shaped by his war wounds, where murder might be analogous to wartime killing and where capital punishment might well be unjustly imposed:

> RUPERT I think, possibly, I approve of murder too much to approve of capital punishment [...] I have already committed murder myself. [...] It is all simply a question of scale. You, my friends, have, paradoxically, a horror of murder on a small scale, a veneration for it on a large scale. That is the difference between what we call murder and war. One gentleman murders another in a back alleyway in London for, let us say, since you have suggested it, the gold fillings in his teeth, and all society shrieks out for vengeance on the miscreant. They call that murder. But when the entire youth

> and manhood of a whole nation rises up to slaughter the entire youth and manhood of another, not even for the gold fillings in each other's teeth, then society condones and applauds the outrage, and calls it war. How, then, can I say that I disapprove of murder, seeing that I have, in the last Great War, acted on these assumptions myself?[88]

Indeed, Brandon and Granillo initially considered including Cadell in their plan for a perfect murder because of these views. But when Cadell realises that Brandon and Granillo have murdered Ronald Kentley and he witnesses the shocking reality of Kentley's dead body, Cadell immediately changes his mind.

Brandon at first attempts to lead Cadell progressively towards condoning the crime he has discovered: 'You're not a man of morals, are you?', 'And you do not rate life as a very precious thing, do you?', and 'You read Nietzsche, don't you, Rupert?'.[89] Brandon offers a self-serving argument against the death penalty, calculated to appeal to Cadell's sense of war trauma and disillusionment: 'Two lives can't recall one. It'd just be triple murder [...] You can't kill us. You can't kill. You're not a murderer, Rupert'.[90] Cadell feels confronted by Brandon's statement of his recent nihilism and turns in shocked reaction to the rhetorics of the normative morality which maintained the death penalty, such as 'sin' and 'blasphemy'.[91] But Cadell's final speech ultimately suggests that his response to Kentley's murder is still shaped by the trauma of his war experience. Alerting the police, Cadell storms:

> RUPERT It is not what *I* am doing, Brandon. It is what society is going to do. And what will happen to you at the hands of society I am not in a position to tell you. That's it's own business. But I can give you a pretty shrewd guess, I think. *(He moves forward to the chest and swings back the lid)* You are going to hang, you swine! Hang! Both of you! Hang! *(Whistle in hand, he runs hobbling to the window, throws it open, leans out, and sends three piercing whistles into the night)*
>
> *Curtain.*[92]

While, unlike Byrne, Cadell has committed no crime himself, his change of heart is still unsettling as his awakening to the value of justice and human life takes a violently retributive form. As in the reception of *The House by the River*, while reviews of the play note Cadell's status as 'a psychological curio', references to capital punishment and to war trauma are again omitted.[93]

Finally, recent work by modernist critics has identified Sayers's detective, Lord Peter Wimsey, as, like Byrne and Cadell, a victim of the lingering effects of shell shock and war trauma.[94] However, absent the detailed historical context explored across this chapter, these past critics have also failed to identify the extent to which Wimsey's neurotic symptoms are triggered specifically by the death penalty. In fact, Wimsey's work as a detective fits in with the Freudian concept of a repetition compulsion as a response to trauma: therefore, Wimsey cannot simply use his talents as a detective to 'provide a treatment for shell shock that enables him to recoup his masculinity'.[95] As a 'character who vacillates between surface and depth', and who is perceptively compared by Ariela Friedman to P. G. Wodehouse's Bertie Wooster, Wimsey's mix of dangerousness and foppishness is also very much like Sir Percy Blakeney of Baroness Orczy's *Scarlet Pimpernel* series of novels.[96] The comparison with Wooster points to the frequently comic texture of Sayers's work and her engagement with the novel of manners, but the second reference point of Blakeney allows a darker picture of historical crisis and the death penalty to emerge.[97] And yet, as Sayers must have been aware in invoking the character, while The Scarlet Pimpernel saves people from execution, Wimsey uneasily leads criminals towards their death. As Kathryn Henrickson has recently argued, Wimsey's 'authority over the outcome of the case, and with it the ending of another person's life, returns him to the responsibilities of war'.[98]

My focus on the death penalty, rather than war trauma per se, allows us to see exactly how each case Wimsey solves instead merely opens his wounds afresh. While some of Sayers's private letters suggest that she was not a whole-hearted abolitionist, her writing also vividly represents the death penalty as traumatic.[99] Throughout Sayers's Wimsey series, her character experiences shell shock symptoms, including mania, hysteria and catatonia, in response to the resolution of the case: I argue that his illness comes from guilt that the perpetrator he has caught must be executed. Wimsey's psychological responses to the death penalty are particularly acute in *Whose Body?* and *Busman's Honeymoon*, the first and last novels, though they are alluded to throughout the series, including in *Unnatural Death*, *Murder Must Advertise* and *Gaudy Night*. These plots also often imply the failure of deterrence: Wimsey's investigations often lead to more murders, as the culprit's overwhelming fear of the death penalty leads them to kill witnesses and bystanders. For example, Wimsey is haunted long term by the escalating murder plot of *Unnatural Death* (1927) where an elderly woman who is killed by her great-niece. As he describes in *Gaudy Night* (1935), showing a similar unease to Cadell's initial nihilistic feelings about retributive justice,

> As soon as I started to meddle, the girl set to work again, killed two innocent people to cover her tracks and murderously attacked three others. Finally she killed herself. If I'd left her alone, there might have been only one death instead of four.[100]

From *Unnatural Death* onwards, Sayers provided a biographical note about Wimsey, ostensibly written by his uncle, which was also added to all reprints, confirming the connection between his war trauma and capital punishment:

> The only trouble about Peter's new hobby was that it had to be more than a hobby if it was to be any hobby for a gentleman. You cannot get murderers hanged for your private entertainment. Peter's intellect pulled him one way and his nerves another, till I began to be afraid they would pull him to pieces. At the end of every case we had the old nightmares and shell-shock over again.[101]

This addition of the biographical note implies Sayers's deliberate preparation for the death penalty plot of *Busman's Honeymoon*, resetting the novel series in a more abolitionist mode.[102]

In *Busman's Honeymoon*, using garbled language from psychoanalysis ('inhibition' or 'exhibition'), Wimsey's mother explains his traumatised response to the death penalty to his new bride Harriet Vane as a crisis of wartime responsibility: 'I suppose if you've been giving orders for nearly four years to people to go and get blown to pieces it gives you a—an inhibition, or an exhibition, or something, of nerves'.[103] In this last novel, Wimsey's marriage to Vane, who had herself almost been wrongly executed in the novel *Strong Poison* (1930), causes him to accuse himself of being a murderer or executioner himself. Thinking about the way their wedding night was quickly overshadowed by capital crimes, Vane reflects: 'His hands, so gentle and experienced…With what sort of experience?…', while Wimsey immediately leaps to self-accusation: '"These hangman's hands," he said, watching her. "You knew that, though, didn't you?"'.[104] Wimsey is also conscious that his distress does harm to Vane, reminding her that she herself might have died on the gallows: her apparent function as a straightforwardly comforting female presence is qualified by her symbolic alliance with those condemned to death.[105]

Busman's Honeymoon concludes as Wimsey experiences a much more severe psychological breakdown in response to the execution of the culprit, the gardener Frank Crutchley. This last scene deserves substantial quotation, because of its lack of euphemism regarding the trauma of the death penalty and because it unfolds in real time alongside the execution, which will occur with the dawn at eight o'clock in the morning. In this moment, Sayers's detective feels literal sympathy, as if by telepathy, not just with the condemned man but with the other prisoners forced to be symbolically present at the execution:

> "They hate executions, you know. It upsets the other prisoners. They bang on the doors and make nuisances of themselves. Everybody's nervous.... Caged like beasts, separately....That's the hell of it....we're all in separate cells....I can't get out, said the starling....If one could only get out for one moment, or go to sleep, or stop thinking....Oh, damn that cursed clock!...Harriet, for God's sake, hold on to me....get me out of this...break down the door..."
>
> "Hush, dearest. I'm here. We'll see it out together."
>
> Through the eastern side of the casement, the sky grew pale with the forerunners of the dawn. "Don't let me go." [...]
>
> The light grew stronger as they waited. Quite suddenly, he said, "Oh, damn!" and began to cry—in an awkward, unpractised way at first, and then more easily. So she held him, crouched at her knees, against her breast, huddling his head in her arms that he might not hear eight o'clock strike.[106]

In this passage, Sayers uses ellipsis to convey Wimsey's state of anxiety and hysteria as well as a sense of the urgency of passing time. None of the original reviews of the novel highlight this transformative moment in the novel, and, indeed, it is comparatively understudied by critics today as well. Sayers's specific focus on the principle of the death penalty is heightened by her design of Crutchley as the most unsympathetic of all her murderers: he murdered only for money, and after capture he remains unrepentant and cruel to the other people involved in the case.[107] In Sayers's theatrical version of the story, she writes in Crutchley's character note that he is 'definitely of the post-war breed', refusing to extend to him the psychological extenuation of violence offered to some other villains in her novels.[108] In short, it is not that Crutchley himself is deserving of Wimsey's sympathy, or that of Sayers's readers, rather it is the penalty itself that is unjust and traumatic. This case is the breaking of Wimsey's career, as the death penalty ultimately tests Sayers's middlebrow modernism to destruction.

Notes

1. Christie Davies, 'The British State and the Power of Life and Death' in *The Boundaries of the State in Modern Britain* ed. by S. J. D. Green and R. C. Whiting, Cambridge: Cambridge University Press, 2002: 341–375 (342).
2. W. H. R. Rivers, 'Freud's Psychology of the Unconscious', *The Lancet* Vol. 189 (16th Jun 1917): 912–914 (912).
3. Teresa Iacobelli, *Death or Deliverance: Canadian Courts Martial in the Great War*, Vancouver: UBC Press, 2013, 24.
4. Iacobelli, *Death or Deliverance*, 24.
5. Gerard Oram, *Military Executions During World War I*, Houndsmills: Palgrave, 2003, 130.
6. Executions that were perceived to be unjust could lower morale, instead of maintaining discipline, and might even lead to further military crimes (Oram, *Military Executions*, 92–93).
7. Ian Beckett, Timothy Bowman and Mark Connelly, 'Citizen Soldiers: Discipline, Morale and the Experience of War', *The British Army and the First World War*, Cambridge: Cambridge University Press, 2017: 135–169 (156–157).
8. Beckett et al., 'Citizen Soldiers', 156–157.
9. See Table 1.2 and discussion in Oram, *Military Executions*, 30–32.
10. Mr. Thurtle, Speech on CLAUSE 5.—(Abolition of death penalty in certain cases.) House of Commons Debate 03 April 1930 Vol. 237 cc1564-6271564 (1309).
11. Davies suggests 278 men were executed (Davies, 'The British State', 342); Hugh McManners gives the total of 312 executions and 3080 commutations (Hugh McManners, *The Scars of War*, London: Harper Collins, 1994); Anthony Babington claims 346 executions (Anthony Babington, *For the Sake of Example: Capital Courts-Martial 1914–1920*, London: Leo Cooper, 1983); while Cathryn Corns and John Hughes-Wilson give the figure of 351 executed (Cathryn Corns and John Hughes-Wilson, *Blindfold and Alone: British Military Executions in the Great War*, London: Cassell, 2001). Iacobelli gives a broader figure, including the wider Empire, of 361 executions and 2719 commuted sentences (Iacobelli, *Death or Deliverance*, 4). Ian Beckett, Timothy Bowman and Mark Connelly give a broader figure of 438 executions during World War I and its immediate aftermath and including the execution of civilians and POWs (Ian Beckett, Timothy Bowman and Mark Connelly, *The British*

Army and the First World War, Cambridge: Cambridge University Press, 2017). Oram's figures also refer to the whole Empire and go up to 1924, including treason and espionage charges: he claims 455 executions and 3362 commutations (Gerard Oram, *Death sentences passed by military courts of the British Army 1914–1924*, London: Francis Boutle, 1998). Beyond the difficulties identified above, there is considerable anecdotal evidence of summary execution that is not captured in these figures.

12. Iacobelli, *Death or Deliverance*, 32.
13. Oram, *Military Executions*, 100–101.
14. Oram, *Military Executions*, 32–34.
15. Jacques Derrida, *The Death Penalty: Volume II* ed. by Geoffrey Bennington and Marc Crépon/trans. by Elizabeth Rottenberg, Chicago: University of Chicago Press, 2017, 19–20.
16. Derrida, *The Death Penalty Volume II*, 19–20.
17. Achille Mbembe, 'Necropolitics', trans. by Libby Meintjes, *Public Culture*, Vol. 15, No. 1 (2003): 11–40 (12).
18. Oram, *Military Executions*, 62.
19. Caroline Cox, 'Invisible Wounds: The American Legion, Shell-Shocked Veterans, and American Society, 1919–1924', *Traumatic Pasts: History, Psychiatry, and Trauma in the Modern Age, 1870–1930*, ed. by Mark S. Micale and Paul Lerner, Cambridge: Cambridge University Press, 2001: 280–306 (291).
20. Ted Bogacz, 'War Neuroses and Cultural Change in England, 1914–1922: The Work of the War Office Committee of Enquiry into Shell Shock', *Journal of Contemporary History* 24 (1989): 227–256 (250).
21. See, for example, newspaper articles from during World War I including 'The Death Penalty in the Army', *The Times*, 1st October 1917, 8; Frederick Milner, 'Letter to the Editor: Insanity and the War', *The Times*, 19 September 1917, 7; 'Shellshock and Desertion', *The Times*, 20th February 1918, 8; 'Procedure in Courts-Martial', *The Times*, 15th March 1918, 12.
22. A. P. Herbert, *The Secret Battle*, London: Methuen, 1936, 71.
23. Marzena Sokołowska-Paryě, *Reimagining the War Memorial, Reinterpreting the Great War: The Formats of British Commemorative Fiction*, Newcastle: Cambridge Scholars Publishing, 2012, 60–61.
24. Edwin Dyett Court Martial File, The National Archives, WO339/87122.
25. Ernest Thurtle, *Shootings at Dawn: The Army Death Penalty at Work*, London: Victoria House Printing Co. 1924, 3.
26. Thurtle, *Shootings at Dawn*, 4.
27. A. D. Gristwood, *The Coward* (1927), in *The Somme including also The Coward*, Columbia: The University of South Carolina Press, 2006: 117–189.
28. Gristwood, *The Coward*, 152.
29. Gristwood, *The Coward*, 153.

30. Gristwood, *The Coward*, 152.
31. Gristwood, *The Coward*, 186.
32. Gristwood, *The Coward*, 188.
33. Thurtle, *Shootings at Dawn*, 5–7.
34. Oram, *Military Executions*, 91.
35. Thurtle, *Shootings at Dawn*, 4.
36. Thurtle, *Shootings at Dawn*, 5.
37. Thurtle, *Shootings at Dawn*, 6.
38. Thurtle, *Shootings at Dawn*, 8.
39. Thurtle, *Shootings at Dawn*, 8.
40. Edwin Dyett Court Martial File, The National Archives, WO339/87122.
41. A. P. Roberts Diary Documents 4616, Imperial War Museum.
42. See, for example, in the Imperial War Museum, Private Papers of E. Beer 695; Private Papers of A. Smith Box 15/10/01; W. Kimberley papers, Documents 7017.
43. Herbert, *The Secret Battle*, 215.
44. Herbert, *The Secret Battle*, 215–216. Many of the testimonies in Thurtle's pamphlet also see the executed soldier as brave: 'a braver man at that moment wasn't to be found in France' (4) or 'a braver man never went on active service' (6).
45. Herbert, *The Secret Battle*, 205–213.
46. CLAUSE 5.—(Abolition of death penalty in certain cases.) House of Commons Debate 03 April 1930 Vol. 237 cc1564-1627 (1572).
47. CLAUSE 5.—(Abolition of death penalty in certain cases.), 1618–1619.
48. CLAUSE 5.—(Abolition of death penalty in certain cases.), 1619.
49. CLAUSE 4.—(Abolition of death penalty in certain cases.) House of Commons Debate 17 April 1928 Vol. 216 cc31-83 (47).
50. CLAUSE 5.—(Abolition of death penalty in certain cases.), 1613.
51. CLAUSE 5.—(Abolition of death penalty in certain cases.) cc1564-1627.
52. Anon. '*THE SECRET BATTLE*', *The Observer*, 27th July 1919, 5.
53. R. O. Morris, 'Book Review: *The Secret Battle*', *The Times Literary Supplement* Issue 911, 3rd July 1919, 356.
54. Morris, 'Book Review', 356.
55. Morris, 'Book Review', 356.
56. Hugh Cecil, *Flowers of Battle: How Britain Wrote the Great War*, South Royalton, Vermont: Steerforth Press, 1996: 89–106 (106).
57. Cecil, *Flowers of Battle*, 106.
58. Falls, *War Books*, 276.
59. Oram, *Military Executions*, 15.
60. On True and M'Naghten see Samantha Walton, *Guilty But Insane: Mind and Law in Golden Age Detective Fiction*, Oxford: Oxford University Press, 2015: 94–134.

61. Donald Carswell (ed.), *Ronald True: Notable British Trials Series*, London: William Hodge and Company, 1925.
62. Anon. 'Eltham Murder Arrest', *The Daily Telegraph*, 15th February 1918, 5.
63. Anon. 'Athlete's Unhappy Married Life', *The Times*, 17th May 1919, 9.
64. Anon. 'The Hyde Murder Appeal', *The Observer*, 15th November 1919 and 'Conviction Quashed: Rex v. Beard', *The Times*, 25th November 1919.
65. Anon. 'Women Jurors in Tears', *The Daily Telegraph*, 11th February 1921, 7.
66. Anon. 'Doctor's Insanity', *The Times*, 24th January 1920, 14.
67. Anon. 'Sandhills Murder', *The Daily Telegraph*, 30th March 1920, 7.
68. Anon. 'Liverpool Nurse's Death', *The Times*, 7th August 1919, 12.
69. Anon. 'Paddington Hotel Tragedy: Committal for Trial', *The Daily Telegraph*, 9th July 1920, 15.
70. Clive Emsley, 'Violent crime in England in 1919: post-war anxieties and press narratives', *Continuity and Change*, Vol. 23, No. 1 (2008): 173–195.
71. Emsley, 'Violent crime', 188.
72. A. P. Herbert, *The House by the River*, New York: Alfred A. Knopf, 1921, 12.
73. Herbert, *The House by the River*, 21–25.
74. Herbert, *The House by the River*, 26.
75. Herbert, *The House by the River*, 39.
76. Arthur Beard file, The National Archives, HO 144/20991.
77. Arthur Beard file, The National Archives, HO 144/20991.
78. Herbert, *The House by the River*, 46.
79. Herbert, *The House by the River*, 85.
80. Herbert, *The House by the River*, 257–258.
81. Herbert, *The Secret Battle*, 216.
82. Herbert, *The House by the River*, 292.
83. 'MESSRS. METHUEN'S NEW BOOKS: The HOUSE by the RIVER', *The Times Literary Supplement*, September 23rd, 1920, 613.
84. Anon. 'Latest Works of Fiction: The House by the River', *The New York Times*, 11th January 1920, 69.
85. Anon. 'Humour and Thrills: The House by the River', *The Observer*, 12th September 1920, 4.
86. A.D. '*Flood Tide* at The Phoenix', *The Manchester Guardian*, 24th March 1938, 10.
87. While it is certainly true that Hamilton responds to the Leopold and Loeb case, Hitchcock's 1948 adaptation of the play has deformed its critical legacy by amplifying this element. In Hitchcock's film, Cadell has served and been injured in the war, but speeches identifying his embittered,

disillusioned attitudes to crime and punishment as sourced in war experience are removed.

88. Patrick Hamilton, *Rope*, Act II, London and New York: Samuel French, 61–62.
89. Hamilton, *Rope*, 87–88.
90. Hamilton, *Rope*, 88.
91. Hamilton, *Rope*, 89.
92. Hamilton, *Rope*, 90.
93. I.B. 'A "SHOCKER" THAT REALLY SHOCKS: *Rope* at the Ambassadors Theatre', *The Manchester Guardian*, April 26, 1929, 6. Other original reviews further support this sense of deliberate omission of the wartime and punishment plots focusing instead on the murder itself: St. J. E. '"*ROPE*" BY PATRICK HAMILTON', *The Observer*, April 28, 1929, 15; Sydney W. Carroll 'ANOTHER YOUNG DRAMATIST: MOTIVELESS MURDER: Anon. "*ROPE*" A REAL TRAGEDY', *The Daily Telegraph*, May 9, 1929, 17. All of these reviews allude to Leopold and Loeb.
94. Kelly C. Connelly, 'From Detective Fiction to Detective Literature: Psychology in the Novels of Dorothy L. Sayers and Margaret Millar', *Clues*, Vol. 25, No. 3 (2007): 35–47 (38); Ariela Friedman, 'Dorothy Sayers and the Case of the Shell-Shocked Detective', *Partial Answers*, Vol. 8. No. 2 (2010): 365–387; Monica Lott, 'Dorothy L. Sayers, the Great War, and Shell Shock', *Interdisciplinary Literary Studies*, Vol. 15, No. 1 (2013): 103–126; Matthew Levay, *Violent Minds: Modernism and the Criminal*, Cambridge: Cambridge University Press, 2019; Kathryn Hendrickson, 'Whose Trauma? Dorothy L. Sayer's Use of Shell Shock and the Role of Memory in Interwar Detective Fiction', *CLUES: A Journal of Detection*, Vol. 37, No. 2 (2019): 51–60.
95. Lott, 'The Great War, and Shell Shock', 104.
96. Levay, *Violent Minds*, 57 and Friedman, 'The Case of the Shell-Shocked Detective', 380.
97. While Orczy is not substantially discussed in this book because of her focus on historical fictions, her series featuring the Scarlet Pimpernel (1903–1940) did undoubtedly shape attitudes to the death penalty during this period. Alison Light compares Wimsey with Blakeney, but in the context of post-war masculinity rather than punishment and revolution contexts ('Agatha Christie and conservative modernity', *Forever England: Femininity, literature and conservatism between the wars*, London and New York: Routledge, 1991: 61–113 (72)).
98. Hendrickson, 'Whose Trauma? Dorothy L. Sayer's Use of Shell Shock', 53 and 56.

99. See Sayers's 1945 correspondence about capital punishment with the church organist Herbert Byard ('Capital Punishment', DLS 38, Marion E. Wade Centre, Wheaton College), where Sayers argues that capital punishment has a psychological effect slightly different to conventional deterrence: she suggests it creates an inhibition preventing capital crimes. In this exchange of letters, she defends the value of the death penalty to more abolitionist correspondent.
100. Dorothy L. Sayers, *Gaudy Night*, London: Hodder and Stoughton, 2016, 367.
101. Dorothy L. Sayers, 'Biographical Note: Communicated by Paul Austin Delgardie', *Unnatural Death*, London: Hodder and Stoughton, 2016, 300–307 (305).
102. The issue of Sayers's intention to end the novel series on this note is complicated by the fact that *Busman's Honeymoon* was originally written as a collaborative play, with her friend Muriel St Clare Byrne. However, even the play itself, which offers a watered-down view of these issues, had a troubling effect on the actor Peter Haddon, who rejected the role of Wimsey, explaining that, in comparison to the previous novels, 'The Peter of *Busman's Honeymoon* rather frightens me' (Alzina Stone Dale, 'Introduction', Dorothy L. Sayers and Muriel St. Clare Byrne, *Love All together with Busman's Honeymoon*, Kent, Ohio: The Kent State University Press, 1985, xxv).
103. Dorothy L. Sayers, *Busman's Honeymoon*, London: Hodder and Stoughton, 2016, 431.
104. Sayers, *Busman's Honeymoon*, 343.
105. Sayers, *Busman's Honeymoon*, 450.
106. Sayers, *Busman's Honeymoon*, 451.
107. Sayers, *Busman's Honeymoon*, 439, 449.
108. Dorothy L. Sayers and Muriel St. Clare Byrne, *Love All together with Busman's Honeymoon*, Kent, Ohio: The Kent State University Press, 1985, xxix, my italics.

CHAPTER 8

Race, Lynching and the Colonial Death Penalty

Introduction

In twentieth-century Britain and America, the domestic logic of the death penalty, including its public safety and deterrence arguments, was underpinned by a need to maintain law and order across a wider colonial and frontier space. The target of this judicial violence was often non-white subjects. Even in mainland Britain, criminologists such as Lizzie Seal and Alexa Neale have investigated race as a factor within capital punishment and, especially, the insanity defence and have frequently found racism at work in judges' summing up and sentencing.[1] Additionally, as Stacey Hynd has shown, 'State executions were stark enactments of colonial power': in British territories these punishments remained public spectacles long after 1868, and this form of punishment in particular was 'differentiated on racial lines'.[2] Recently Howard W. Allen and Jerome M. Clubb also identified similar forces at work within the American context: they found that spikes in executions of non-white groups, including African Americans, Native Americans, Hispanic Americans and Chinese Americans, generally 'reflect patterns of national expansion and settlement'.[3] Further, as James W. Clarke points out, American southern states, border states and frontier states always 'had the most extensive capital statutes, often stipulating the death penalty for theft'.[4] Capital punishment, once exported into colonial situations, would often remain long after it was abandoned

K. Ebury, *Modern Literature and the Death Penalty, 1890–1950*, Palgrave Studies in Literature, Culture and Human Rights, https://doi.org/10.1007/978-3-030-52750-1_8

by former colonisers and would continue to be used, often still on racialised lines, in semi-colonial and postcolonial situations from America to the Far East.

A key influence on this chapter is Achille Mbembe's conception of necropolitics as a refinement of Foucauldian biopower, which was briefly introduced in the previous chapter. Mbembe, powerfully influenced by Fanon's postcolonial inheritance of Freud, argues that:

> If the relations between life and death, the politics of cruelty, and the symbolics of profanity are blurred in the plantation system, it is notably in the colony and under the apartheid regime that there comes into being a peculiar terror formation I will now turn to. The most original feature of this terror formation is its concatenation of biopower, the state of exception, and the state of siege. Crucial to this concatenation is, once again, race. In fact, in most instances, selection of races, the prohibition of mixed marriages, forced sterilization, even the extermination of vanquished peoples are to find their first testing ground in the colonial world. Here we see the first syntheses between massacre and bureaucracy, that incarnation of Western rationality.[5]

Across his identification of necropolitics as a death-dealing force within a colonial state of exception, Mbembe reconfigures biopower both towards race and towards death. This makes his work particularly appropriate for an examination of how racism shaped capital punishment in both Britain and America, moving from the necropolitics of slavery and forced colonisation through the law and order associated with an uneasy social apartheid and state of siege.

Though the specific concept of necropolitics was missing, Mbembe's diagnosis was anticipated by twentieth-century anti-colonial and anti-racist discourses. For example, Nancy Cunard referred, in the introduction to *Negro: An Anthology* (1933), to a crisis in the racialised use of the death penalty: she addresses an increase in lynchings and executions of black Americans, especially the case of the Scottsboro Boys, as reflecting a white desire 'to force into the dumbest and most terrified form of subjection all Negro workers who dare to aspire to live otherwise than as virtual slaves'.[6] Using the tools of anthropology, ethnography and psychoanalysis and turning them against the dominant white culture, this diagnosis is repeated throughout *Negro*, comparing the American context with European colonialism. For example, in 'Murderous Humanitarianism', an essay by the

French Surrealist Group translated by Samuel Beckett, colonial war is implicitly identified as a form of necropolitics within white psychology: 'With his psalms, his speeches, his guarantees of liberty, equality and fraternity, he seeks to drown out the noise of his machine-guns'.[7] As Priyamvada Gopal points out, Cunard's anthology was banned by several British colonial administrations because of passages such as these.[8]

So far, this book has centred the progressive aspects of psychoanalytic thought and its challenge to the death penalty, but here I must highlight Freud's explanation of and critique of murder and the death penalty through reference to so-called 'primitive societies' in *Totem and Taboo* (1913). Freud here and elsewhere sought to identify the origin of these violent behaviours in the tribal societies out of which Western society developed, as is obvious from its controversial subtitle 'Some Points of Agreement between the Mental Lives of Savages and Neurotics'.[9] The dual ramifications of Freud's approach included (1) a recognition of these repressed 'primitive' impulses towards violence and sacrifice in his Western patients as sources of psychological illness and (2) a hierarchical view of race which implicitly justified colonial interventions in the areas of the world which were the targets of anthropological knowledge.[10] *Totem and Taboo* is known to be influenced by colonial anthropology, such as James Frazer's *Totemism and Exogamy* (1910), and these sources undoubtedly shaped Freud's racial imagination and implicit support for European imperialism, despite his own experience of anti-Semitism.[11] As Stephen Frosh has recently explored, these aspects of Freud's thought left postcolonial theory and psychoanalysis at variance for decades, despite the determined boundary-crossing work of critics including Frantz Fanon and Gayatri Chakravorty Spivak.[12]

The first half of this chapter will address British white-authored fictions which reflect substantially on how a racialised death penalty contributed to the psychology of the modern literature of Empire; all of the texts examined in this first section reflect an interwar crisis in imperialism. These 1930s narratives represent the colonies as a space of conflict, where a fear of insurrection led to a rate of capital punishment much higher than in the colonial centre. The texts discussed in detail will include a range of modernist and middlebrow literature in which a colonial rhetoric is used to examine the death penalty: Graham Greene's *It's a Battlefield* (1934); George Orwell's 'A Hanging' (1931) and 'Shooting an Elephant' (1936); and, finally, Agatha Christie's *And Then There Were None* (1939, famously first published in Britain as *Ten Little N*ggers*). In the second half of this chapter I will build on this literature of the colonial death penalty to examine similarities and differences between this and the American context. My special focus is the interplay between lynching and a racialised death penalty which became central to American modernity within Richard Wright's *Native Son* (1940). Wright's intense focus on various forms of a racialised death penalty is unparalleled and makes him worthy to be the key author within my chapter, representative of the whole American scene.[13] The narrative of *Native Son* reflects Wright's awareness of a specific historical transfer of racist necropolitics, since during his lifetime lynching gave way to capital punishment as the dominant biopolitical force shaping black lives.

Race and the Colonial Death Penalty in British 1930s Writing

Despite complacency in the British establishment about the colonial death penalty, from very early in the twentieth century, activist groups had sought to develop local campaigns against the death penalty across the Empire, as well as to generate data on the ethnic and religious make-up of those executed. For example, in the British Library I found a clutch of campaigning leaflets from 1909 produced by the Society for the Abolition of Capital Punishment (founded in 1901 by Josiah Oldfield). The leaflet A announces the establishment of an 'Indian and Colonial Committee', chaired by Sir Henry Cotton, inviting the support of 'persons living in the colonies' to campaign for 'the abolition of the death penalty in the various parts of the British Empire'; leaflet B targets the excessive use of the death penalty in Ceylon/Sri Lanka and provides an ethnic breakdown of those executed; leaflet C offers a summary of those executed in all British colonies and protectorates in 1908.[14] Leaflet C shows the highest numbers of executions in Southern Nigeria (42), followed by Ceylon (23) and Northern Nigeria (20). These figures also show that some countries with lower numbers of executions such as Fiji (11) or the East African Protectorate (13) never reprieved anyone sentenced to death. This suggests a vastly different legal standard to the colonial centre, where around 45% of capital offenders were reprieved in England and about 60% in Scotland.[15] Similarly, the Society's breakdown of figures for Ceylon in leaflet B shows significant racial and religious disparities with 49 Singhalese and 41 Buddhists executed in 1907, but only 1 Mohammedan (Muslim) and 11 Roman Catholics. This is the context in which I will address the importance of colonial capital punishment for white psychology in fictions by Greene, Orwell and Christie. It was therefore important to set out by highlighting the work of the colonial committee of the Society for the Abolition of Capital Punishment in order to show that these authors' works, however critical of Empire, are actually quite regressive in comparison to this activist work produced by the Society for the Abolition of Capital Punishment and to other anti-colonial movements of the day described by Gopal and others.

Even though there is valuable work on Graham Greene, race and colonialism, most critics have so far missed Greene's literary concern with the colonial death penalty per se.[16] This interest is demonstrated most clearly by his early novel *It's a Battlefield* (1934). This interwar novel is focused on the effect on the London scene of the imminent execution and eventual reprieve of Jim Drover, a communist bus driver who accidentally killed a police officer during a protest. Greene's novel's title and plot implies that a state of emergency extends beyond the violence of Imperial conquest. Greene's London, an imperial centre, forms the backdrop for a governmental crisis of confidence about the value of the death penalty in Drover's particular case. Greene's central character, the Assistant Commissioner (whose real name we never learn, reflecting his institutional authority), is newly returned from colonial policing and has been asked by the Home Secretary to give a view, based on public opinion, on whether Drover should be reprieved or not. But the Assistant Commissioner resents the question, reflecting that 'one left justice to magistrates, to judges and juries, to members of Parliament, to the Home Secretary'.[17] The Assistant Commissioner feels that police work was meant 'simply to preserve the existing order, and it made no odds to him whether justice condemned a man to live in a common cell in a small tropical prison [...] or in a private cell in Block C with a table for library books'.[18] While I have already highlighted a disparity between justice conducted in the colonies compared to the colonial centre, the Assistant Commissioner has brought back a brutal model of policing as colonial occupation to London and is uninfluenced by the developments in criminology described elsewhere in this book.

Indeed, Greene immediately depicts the Assistant Commissioner as highly accustomed to the violence of the colonial death penalty: at the opening of the novel, his central character feels 'suddenly old and dusty; as if he had just returned from one of his torrid tedious marches, with a man left dangling in the jungle for the birds to peck'.[19] Greene also introduces him, ironically, as racially othered by his colonial experience with a 'narrow yellow face' and 'a plodding jungle step' which forms the rhythm of both his body and his mind.[20] Unable to retire, or to move on from a martial law model of policing, the Assistant Commissioner thinks of London as a 'battlefield' several times throughout the novel. One specific occurrence explicitly links the metaphor with race and the colonial death penalty:

> It was hard, he thought, to get any clear idea of a war carried on in this piecemeal way throughout a city. He was not used yet to visualising a situation from a policeman's colourless report; he had been accustomed in the East to seeing with his own eyes the casualties of law: the stabbed soldier, the smouldering hut, the body hanging from a branch.[21]

The Assistant Commissioner thinks of 'casualties of law', rather than 'casualties of war', reflecting his complex awareness of the violence of his past administration of summary capital punishment. Beyond the brown body hanging from the branch in the Assistant Commissioner's memory, 'the smouldering hut' suggests a deliberate reprisal which goes beyond conventional justice, while in the earlier passage he remembered disgracing the victim of colonial violence in leaving the body unburied.

The details of the Assistant Commissioner's memory reflect the iconography of lynching in American culture, rather than the legalised, medicalised and private rituals of the domestic British death penalty. None of the Assistant Commissioner's violent memories feature a specific crime or legal process that led to these killings. It is this extreme experience which means that he believes that Drover's suffering in relation to his impending execution is 'not the worst pain', but only 'the outer circle'.[22] This particular memory of 'smouldering huts' occurs in a moment in which the Assistant Commissioner ought to be considering 'colourless' reports on the likely effects of Drover's reprieve: the memory arises as an excuse for setting the question of mercy aside and for turning to evidence in the Streatham murder case he is also investigating.[23] While Greene presents the Assistant Commissioner as a comparatively humane and sympathetic character, seeing himself clear-sightedly as 'a mercenary soldier'[24] and 'the paid servant of an unpopular government',[25] he also feels complacent nostalgia for harsher colonial justice in which racially othered criminals can be more promptly dispatched. Without a justifying belief in Empire, seeing imperialism straightforwardly as 'an old-fashioned war', the Assistant

Commissioner's passivity and acceptance of the status quo, alongside his understated racism, points to his settler and frontier approach to justice.[26]

In the novel's main thriller plot, a sense of the injustice of capital punishment will radicalise Drover's brother Conrad, who is obviously named in honour of Joseph Conrad. Conrad will attempt to assassinate the Assistant Commissioner, both as a private revenge and as a political act. Greene's novel thus combines the imperial concerns of Conrad's *Heart of Darkness* with the portrait of the city housing the 'enemy within' central to his *The Secret Agent*.[27] Though this is only implicit in Greene's text, the importance of Communist movements in the 1920s and 1930s in relation to anti-colonial and anti-racist activity, as well as the corresponding incitement of 'Red Scare' in official attempts to maintain consent for empire, places Conrad's assassination attempt on a former colonial official on behalf of his brother within a particular historical and political context.[28] Throughout the novel, Drover, as a communist, is also othered and made not fully English because he is 'a Red'. This adds another layer to the imperial and racial overtones applied to London by the Assistant Commissioner's simultaneously traumatised and self-satisfied memories of the East: as reflected in Greene's choice of an epigraph from Alexander Kinglake's *The Invasion of the Crimea* (1854), London, Russia and the Orient are triangulated within Greene's portrait of the 1930s death penalty. Greene's novel ends unhappily, with Conrad dying accidentally during the murder attempt, while Drover is reprieved by the Home Secretary and then immediately attempts suicide because of the length of the prison sentence he must serve instead. The Assistant Commissioner returns doubtfully to the Streatham murder and the capture of capital offenders. Thus Greene's novel, more broadly, describes the state of emergency arising from a crisis in imperialism by which the law and the death penalty is maintained in the face of implicitly allied dissent within the nation in the form of the Communist Party and without it in the non-white resistance to Empire which the Assistant Commissioner remembers.

While we never learn exactly where the Assistant Commissioner completed his brutal colonial service, Orwell's short prose piece 'A Hanging' (1931) more directly reflects on the 'more than 150 executions a year' carried out in colonial Burma during Orwell's time there.[29] These extreme figures of 150 executions per year during the period from 1922–1927 are noticeably higher numbers than in Britain, the imperial centre, where information provided to the Gowers Commission suggests just 138 executions across the whole decade.[30] Peggy Kamuf reflects that in 'A Hanging' capital punishment resembles 'some ancient rite of sacrifice'.[31] While Kamuf's diagnosis accurately reflects the arbitrariness and ritual nature of white colonial violence, she does not notice Orwell's use of eugenic necropolitical discourses. Orwell racialises the death penalty well beyond the victim of the hanging, a 'Hindu, a puny wisp of a man, with a shaven head and vague liquid eyes'.[32] Indeed, the narrator's racialising gaze is unusually precise and stereotyped, in direct contrast with Greene's Assistant Commissioner's blurred memories. Orwell's eye absorbs in a very short space the 'brown silent men' who are 'due to be hanged within the next week or two'; 'six Indian warders'; the European superintendent of the jail, with his 'grey toothbrush moustache'; the head jailer, Francis, who despite his English name is 'a fat Dravidian' with a 'black hand'; a 'young Eurasian jailer'; and even the cross-breed dog, 'half Airdale, half pariah', who disrupts the execution throughout.[33] In this detailed eugenic thinking within the execution scene, Orwell is at pains to highlight the complicity of both the colonised and the coloniser in the execution, although the native hangman is in fact an unwilling convict held prisoner in the jail. The reality of the execution supposedly generates a feeling of horrified solidarity: 'Everyone had changed colour', Orwell notes ironically.[34] And when the execution is safely over, everyone is linked through Western rituals of masculinity—cigarettes and whisky and awkward laughter—so that an anecdote of a botched execution eventually 'seemed extraordinarily funny. We all had a drink together, native and European alike, quite amicably. The dead man was a hundred yards away.'[35]

In Orwell's later 'Shooting an Elephant' (1936), the narrator, a colonial police officer, 'executes' an elephant which has been on a rampage, destroying property and killing a local man by trampling.[36] By the time he kills the elephant, it is no longer a threat, taking Orwell's narrator's actions into the realm of the death penalty as he responds to the crowd's demands for the elephant to be punished.[37] The narrator has prefaced the story with an account of colonial conditions in which 'anti-European feeling was very bitter', which perhaps accounts for his feeling that he is under siege by his audience, a 'sea of yellow faces' with 'garish clothes'.[38] The elephant is sacrificed as a kind of sacrificed totem animal (see Chap. 5): its life is the price by which British power is maintained in the area, even though the narrator himself has already 'made up my mind that imperialism was an evil thing and the sooner I chucked up my job [...] the better'.[39] His botched killing of the elephant represents his simultaneous rational critique of empire alongside an affective drive to murder deeply connected to racism, both of which he terms 'the normal by-products of imperialism': 'With one part of my mind I thought of the British Raj as an unbreakable tyranny [...] with another part I thought that the greatest joy in the world would be to drive a bayonet into a Buddhist priest's guts'.[40] The death of the elephant is undoubtedly connected with the second drive towards violence, but the close of the story reveals a more extreme colonial necropolitics surrounding the narrator, expressed through a sudden outbreak of explicit racism at the Colonial Club:

> The older men said I was right, the younger men said it was a damn shame to shoot an elephant for killing a coolie, because an elephant was worth more than any damn Coringhee coolie. And afterwards I was very glad that the coolie had been killed; it put me legally in the right and it gave me a sufficient pretext for shooting the elephant. I often wondered whether any of the others grasped that I had done it solely to avoid looking a fool.[41]

Orwell's direct experience of maintaining law and order in Burma inflects his work with a more fully anti-imperial and anti-death penalty character. Nonetheless, he cannot apparently—at least in these two examples—neutralise the racial imagination which legitimises the disparity between the high numbers of executions in Burma compared to Britain and which is tempted to fully dehumanise colonial citizens.

Indeed, postcolonial sociologists such as Ranajit Guha and Barry Hindess have used 'Shooting an Elephant' as a way of critiquing philosophies of anti-colonial liberalism. For them, despite his irony and his self-contempt, Orwell's narrator shows 'a cultivated liberal's distaste, on the one hand, for working with and living among people he clearly regarded as inferior and, on the other, for the dirty work of paternalistic rule': for them, Orwell's affective responses offer a case study for liberalism's failure to value freedom within a colonial situation.[42] While it is clear that both Greene and Orwell intend to critique injustice, they still end up reinforcing colonial necropolitics. I wish to highlight the role of toxic white masculinity in these texts: in both Greene and Orwell, these critical, even traumatised witnesses of the colonial death penalty are also privileged perpetrators of violence. Further, as none of these authors is specific about the crimes committed by the non-white men they are involved in executing, the reality is that these narratives appear to depict not a *lex talionis*, with a straightforward equivalence between crime and punishment, but a more ambiguous and eugenic state of emergency in which to be non-white might in itself be criminalised. The limitation and indirectness of this critique of colonial necropolitics is clear in the context of Gopal's recent account of a anti-colonial activism that centred non-white voices in the 1920s and 1930s via her investigations of the League against imperialism and the literary activism that surrounded it, including Cunard's collaborative *Negro: An Anthology*, discussed earlier.[43]

By contrast, in the final text I will examine in this section, Agatha Christie's *And Then There Were None* (1939), racially othered characters are only symbolically present, but the death penalty itself is explicitly racialised and black subjects are metaphorically the targets of the novel's violence. By the end of the interwar period, racial and colonial anxieties were especially acute, as reflected in Christie's original title, *Ten Little N*ggers*. It is noteworthy that this title was felt to be too controversial for the US context even at the time of its first publication, while since 1985 this novel has also been published under the title of the US edition. Early reviewers understood the role of capital punishment in the plot: a *Times* reviewer suggests that the novel's victims must 'pay the penalty for a murder committed in intention, if not in deed'.[44] Yet contemporary reviews are unable to keep questions of race and colonialism in focus even while conscious of the novel's 'baleful' atmosphere.[45]

I argue that while Christie conceives of the death penalty as explicitly the stuff of a thriller or even a horror narrative (albeit without taking an abolitionist stance), the novel also implicitly reflects on colonial summary justice. As readers eventually learn at the end of the novel, Christie's perpetrator, Judge Wargrave, has purchased an island, called either 'N*gger Island' (until 1985 in the UK) or 'Indian Island' (in the play version) or 'Soldier Island' (in the American edition and later UK editions), in order to kill or, as he sees it, 'execute' the murderers he has invited as his guests. Within the main story, each of the ten guests is murdered by an unseen perpetrator who comes to seem supernatural. The reader initially believes that Wargrave himself was an early victim of this serial killer, though in fact he faked his own death and committed suicide at the end of his 'experiment'. However, Wargrave is ultimately not content with creating a 'perfect murder': while there is no detective figure and readers witness the failure of the conventional police investigation, at the end of the narrative readers are given his confession from a message in a bottle which had only just been found.

Wargrave's crime points towards lynching, given the quasi-judicial framework set up to justify the crime: but of course, this is not 'mob justice' but rather a serial killer acting alone. Instead of a mob, these killings are supported by financial capital: it is Wargrave's personal fortune, acquired through his legal work as a 'hanging judge', that provides the opportunities to kill, in the hire of the house and island. As in Greene's novel, where the Assistant Commissioner was nostalgic for a simpler colonial duty which would not include mercy, in his confession Wargrave describes how he felt constrained by the reality of his role in administering justice. While the Assistant Commissioner's more humane instincts means he experiences the questions at stake in Drover's case as a reluctant reawakening even though he has been involved in colonial violence, Wargrave, by contrast, has always felt a desire to kill which was ultimately unfulfilled by the symbolism of the black cap and the rituals of the capital sentence.[46] He reflects that 'For some years past I have been aware of a change within myself, a lessening of control—a desire to act instead of to judge. I have wanted—let me admit it frankly—*to commit murder myself*'.[47] Once he receives a terminal diagnosis, he chooses victims who are 'beyond the reach of the law' and imposes an imperialist, racist symbolism on his project based on 'A childish rhyme of my infancy [...] It had fascinated me as a child of two—the inexorable diminishment—the sense of inevitability'.[48]

We should not be fooled by the fact that all of Wargrave's victims are white. Wargrave's childhood rhyme, the inspiration for his crimes and for the novel, has always been racist: originating in the American context, a ballad published in 1868 by Septimus Winner is believed to be the first version entitled 'Ten Little "Injuns"', while a parallel version of the song arose as early as 1869 with the target of its spectacular violence changed to 'n*ggers'. Both versions of the rhyme describe a gradual, though mostly accidental, extinction of an othered group, and both versions continued to circulate widely until Christie's novel appeared. The American theatrical adaptation of Christie's novel appeared under the title *Ten Little Indians* in 1944, implying the greater acceptability of violence against Native Americans compared to African Americans in the period. As J. C. Bernthal points out, tensions between Wargrave's 'conscientious obeying of rules and his carnal desires' lead to 'what Wargrave calls "murder on a grand scale"—almost the expression first used by Joseph Conrad to describe colonization'.[49] Though Bernthal does not explore this insight further, seeing the novel primarily as a response to the crisis of World War II, he nevertheless argues that 'It also was in the mid- to-late 1930s that British and American crime fiction began, still largely unengaged with international politics, to question its own self-containedness on matters of justice'.[50]

It is therefore important to note that, via his childhood rhyme, Wargrave embraces a eugenic premise of gradual colonial racial extinction, sourced initially in the American context, as central to his plan of summary execution. In a macabre twist, he designs the methods of each killing to reflect the rhyme; after each death, he destroys one of the China figures of black children which he originally left in the dining room as a warning (these ornaments are soldiers in later versions). Wargrave's psychology—combining the symbolism of white supremacy rooted in childhood with a desire to murder which does not extend to compassionate understanding of these impulses in others—is especially shocking in a judge who throughout his life has taken on a sovereign power over life and death, fitting in with Reik's diagnosis of the pathology of capital sentencing. Indeed, Reik claims in *The Unknown Murderer* that narcissistic and sadistic impulses are often the basis of judgement, especially in capital cases, arguing that 'the authorities of the law prefer judicial murder to anything that may compromise them'.[51] Discussing the reluctance of most judges to admit a miscarriage of justice due to the 'principle of the omnipotence of thought', alongside unconscious guilt and narcissism, Reik shows that faced with ambiguity, judges construct an unassailable belief that they understand what really happened, so that from circumstantial evidence, judges adjust the facts in directing the jury: 'he is, like a god, reshaping reality according to his will'.[52] While Reik argues elsewhere that 'No earthly judge will attain the strictness of the superego in many persons', Wargrave does appear to be the embodiment of this punitive, patriarchal and primitive force of the law which underpinned colonialism.[53] In response to their situation, from the moment their peril is revealed, his victims' sense of their own humanity is reduced. They experience themselves as racially othered and as animalised: Christie's narrator reflects 'And all of them, suddenly, looked less like human beings. They were resorting to more bestial types',[54] while another character reflects '*We're the Zoo*...Last night, we were hardly human anymore. *We're the Zoo*'.[55]

While Wargrave's actions are undoubtedly informed by a racist logic in which white murderers are reduced to the 'bare life' associated with colonial subjects, nevertheless an extra layer of racial complexity is added by the nature of Phillip Lombard's crime, which he freely admits (unlike other characters). In the gramophone recording that Wargrave sets up at the beginning of his murder plot, Lombard is indicted of murders connected explicitly with colonialism: 'Philip Lombard, that upon a date in February, 1932, you were guilty of the death of twenty-one men, members of an East African tribe'.[56] A colonial adventurer, Lombard grinned and explained:

> Story's quite true! I left 'em! Matter of self-preservation. We were lost in the bush. I and a couple other fellows took what food there was and cleared out [...] Not quite the act of a *pukka sahib*, I'm afraid. But self-preservation's a man's first duty. And natives don't mind dying, you know. They don't feel about it as Europeans do.[57]

Lombard and Wargrave share an acute understanding of the colonial underpinning of each other's psychology of violence, as Lombard is the only character to suspect Wargrave as the persecutor of those on the island.[58] It is thus especially troubling that Lombard, paired to a certain extent with Wargrave (in their investments in racism and in the severity of their crimes), is chosen by Christie in her theatrical adaptation of the novel to be (with Vera Claythorne) a character who is ultimately proven innocent and allowed to survive.[59] This suggests that—as in Greene and Orwell—Christie's attitude to colonial violence is, at the very least, unresolved.

All these representations of the colonial death penalty—in Greene, Orwell and Christie—exploit the problem of race primarily to illuminate the psychology of white male central characters. While these texts might lead readers towards an anti-colonial and/or anti-death penalty position, this does not appear to be the primary aim: instead we find connections to primitivism and atavism, as shared by modernism and psychoanalysis, and to traditional colonial anxieties about 'going native', especially within the traces of Conrad's *Heart of Darkness* identifiable as an influence in all three texts.[60] These British 1930s writers all emphasise emotional and psychological responses to the highly charged political and ethical context of the colonial death penalty, reducing the colonised subjects who are the victims of white violence to mere objects or metaphors. Nevertheless, as Stephen Frosh has argued, 'perhaps because it does speak from the heart of colonialism, psychoanalysis offers a route toward explicating the workings of the colonial mind and its legacy in the postcolonial world'.[61] Here, the affective force of these representations of necropolitics—including trauma and ambivalence in the case of Greene's and Orwell's characters, and horror, pleasure and identification in relation to Christie's Judge

Wargrave—ask valuable questions about colonial psychology even though they require 'a parasitic relationship to blackness'.[62]

Race, Lynching and the Death Penalty in Richard Wright's *Native Son* (1940)

The second half of this chapter will examine the American death penalty in the first half of the twentieth century, investigating how a history of slavery and lynching shapes black writers' representations of capital crime and punishment. My particular focus will be on Richard Wright's *Native Son* (1940), but I will also consider the wider historical and cultural context around race, lynching and the American death penalty which the novel distils. Wright's work differs from the fictions of colonialism discussed above, and is also distinct from most representations of lynching in which the victim is often still voiceless and objectified, in depicting a complex picture of a black subjectivity torn between victim and perpetrator status. Within the novel, Wright's protagonist Bigger Thomas commits two crimes: the murder of his white employer's daughter, Mary Dalton, and the rape and murder of his black girlfriend Bessie Mears. But white Chicago society is only concerned with Mary's fate. In his preface to *Native Son*, 'How Bigger Was Born', Wright combines his inheritance of Marxist and psychoanalytic thought to reveal Bigger's accidental murder of Mary and deliberate rape and killing of Bessie as the narrative product of his own real experiences of death-dealing racism. Wright's novel depends, first, upon the racialising of the death penalty for rape and, second, upon the historical switch from lynching to the death penalty as the predominant biopolitical force shaping black masculinity.

Eli Zaretsky has argued that Wright combined a Marxist view of culture with his unique status as 'the first African American intellectual to fully engage with Freud' during a period in which psychoanalysis was changing its emphasis 'from a theory of the unconscious to a theory of the resistance'.[63] Wright, indeed, had a copy of Reik's *The Unknown Murderer* in his personal library and, as I will show later, had substantial contact with psychoanalysts such as Benjamin Karpman and Frederic Wertham about racism and crime after *Native Son* was published.[64] In Bigger Thomas, Wright sacrifices a version of himself deemed by society to be worthy of the electric chair, which Wright sees as simply more psychologically damaged than himself. By the time Wright was born, in 1908, the historical peak of lynching had already been reached (in 1892), and in his youth in the 1920s, as James W. Clarke notes, 'executions of black people exceeded lynchings for the first time'.[65] Clarke argues that 'lynching's decline was hastened by a pernicious system of court-ordered executions that served the same purpose', as states with large black populations switched from extrajudicial killing to capital punishment, with southern states explicitly calling executions 'legal lynchings'.[66] By the 1930s in these southern states '75 per cent of all persons put to death [...] were black'.[67] Maggie E. Morris Davis has recently traced this shift from lynching to execution within African American poetry of the period, suggesting that poets gave new expression to the lynched subject's suffering in response to the change.[68] We see something similar in the free verse of Wright's own lynching poem, 'Between the World and Me' (1935), where the victim speaks through the poet who comes across the scene of violence.

A symbiosis of concepts of lynching and of lawful execution, with the formal death penalty maintained through a fear of mob violence, is also reflected in debates outside the US context. For example, in British parliamentary debates about the military death penalty in the 1920s, several of the MPs arguing for the maintenance of the status quo suggested that if capital offences were removed, then soldiers might bring in mob justice, while in a 1938 debate on civilian capital punishment it was argued that because public opinion lagged far behind parliamentary feeling, if the death penalty were to be abolished, it would risk Britain being 'exposed for the first time in its history to the horrors of lynch law'.[69] At the same time, British abolitionist campaigners such as Violet Van der Elst also used anxieties about lynching, racism and mob justice within the American system as an emotive part of her appeal against the practice of capital punishment in Britain.[70]

Native Son is directly focused on the interdependence of lynching and the death penalty, building on Davis's final claim that 'There is more at stake as racism becomes invisible, silently and arrogantly parading as justice'.[71] While the texts examined in the previous section focused on contemporary British colonialism, Abdul R. JanMohamed has located the root of Wright's depiction of death in the older paradoxes of colonial slavery in which the slave is obliged 'to live under a conditionally commuted death sentence', which involves a 'social-death'.[72] The slave, or the subject who inherits this history, must adjust his aspirations for life to live in the narrow space of social death at risk of actual death. Lacking Mbembe's neat concept of necropolitics, JanMohamed responds to

Wright's work by developing his own innovative concepts such as the 'death-bound-subject' and the 'death-dream-work' to express the effect of the terror of lynching on black subject formation.[73] Indeed, Bigger's crime and his punishment is presented as being inevitable within the structure of the novel's famous subsections, its progression through Fear and Flight to Fate. Bigger's mother believes that her son's pettiest transgressions could one day be punishable by death: 'You think I don't know what you boys is doing, but I do. And the gallows is at the end of the road you traveling, boy. Just remember that'.[74] She believes her warning will keep her child safe, but in fact it overshadows and overdetermines his existence: Bigger is conscious 'that the moment he allowed what his life meant to enter fully into his consciousness, he would either kill himself or someone else'.[75] While his mother's warning cannot help him, as death lies down every path, Bigger's first thought on accidentally killing Mary is nonetheless of the electric chair, inducing him to exacerbate an accidental crime by dismembering and burning the body.[76] By doing so, Bigger also arouses the racialised suspicion that he raped Mary before killing her.

The American death penalty was very different than that practiced in Britain and its colonies at the time in allowing a wider range of executions for nonlethal offences including, especially, rape. As explored in the previous chapter, in Britain after 1930 the only nonlethal capital offences in either civilian or military law were treason, treachery and mutiny. Allen and Clubb show 'a clear ethnic bias' in sentencing for these offences, with African Americans proportionately far more likely to be executed for rape.[77] Cutler's 1905 book on lynching, the first study of the topic, perpetuated the myth of the black rapist even while arguing against the practice.[78] In the twentieth century, while lynchings did eventually reduce, this aspect of the African American experience substantially worsened as the century advanced with a spike in executions for nonlethal offences, especially rape, in the period 1936–1945.[79] In literary works of the period, the myth of the black rapist was so powerful that, as Sondra Guttman has argued, the rapist in Faulkner's *Sanctuary* (1931), Popeye Pumphrey, whose actions also provoke the lynching of an innocent man before his execution for other crimes, is obsessively coded as black through phrases such as 'Popeye's black presence' and references to his 'black and nameless threat'.[80] Popeye's 'blackness' allows Faulkner to simultaneously racialise and de-racialise the death penalty, engaging in a critique of lynching culture via the death of the white Lee Goodwin, who takes the blame for Popeye's crime, but without questioning the appropriateness of the execution of the African American wife-murderer also depicted in the novel, even though he appears to be mentally ill.

In terms of the broader theme of this book, the use of the death penalty as punishment for rape breaks the tidy equivalence of the *lex talionis*; even when capital punishment was fiercely contested by authors and campaigners, they often found their hands tied by the 'natural' and 'common sense' logic which demands one life in exchange for another. In this American context I am examining, the racist application of the death penalty for the crime of rape in the twentieth century reveals the way that 'natural' and 'common sense' logic in these cases is not the *lex talionis*, but rather different forms of necropolitics. In 'How Bigger Was Born', Wright suggests a racist American society deliberately maintains the death penalty for sex crimes because it allows punishment for the subversion of Jim Crow racial hierarchies, especially in the case of consensual mixed-race couples: 'If a Negro rebels against rule and taboo, he is lynched and the reason for the lynching is usually called rape'.[81]

Native Son was undoubtedly shaped by the trials of the Scottsboro Boys, nine African American teenagers accused of a 1931 rape, which dragged on throughout the 1930s with prosecutors aggressively seeking the death penalty in each individual case. The Scottsboro case is also directly referred to in the novel.[82] Scottsboro had also involved an attempted lynching soon after the accused were arrested, while those supportive of their cause, including the modernist writers published in Nancy Cunard's *Negro* anthology, explicitly compared the legal proceedings, involving all-white juries, to 'legal lynching'.[83] The event became, as Gopal suggests, 'metonymic' of the death-dealing role of racism in both colonialism and the American system.[84] As Gopal has argued, the *Negro* anthology and other British, European and American activist collaboration against Scottsboro 'represented, not least through its transatlantic dimension, the yoking together of anti-racism and anti-colonialism in a global frame'.[85] While black poets such as T. Thomas Fortune Fletcher and Carrie Williams Clifford contribute a sense of the voices of victims to the anthology in 'That Other Golgotha' and 'The Black Draftee from Dixie', Cunard's poem 'Southern Sheriff' ventriloquises and critiques the white racist logic in which lynching and the death penalty are interchangeable weapons for oppressing African Americans, concluding '*That* is the Southern justice/ Not lynch-mobs, but part of the law speaking'.[86]

Wright's novel, and especially, the trial scene in the final 'Fate' section, ultimately examines the triangulation of race, rape and the death penalty in the Northern, 'progressive' state of Illinois. While Cunard's anthology explicitly targeted the southern states, in Wright's text we see exactly the phenomenon of executions with only a pretence of legality identified by Clarke, in which 'only the form of violence changed' as lynching declined: 'after swift and superficial trials before white judges and juries, the outcomes could never be in doubt'.[87] Bigger understands clearly the role of rape discourse in his fate. For example, even before his arrest he panics when he sees the loaded phrase 'AUTHORITIES HINT SEX CRIME' in the journalistic reporting of Mary's murder. He fully understands that he will not now receive a fair trial, with either capital punishment or lynching his 'natural' fate:

> Those words excluded him utterly from the world. To hint that he had committed a sex crime was to pronounce the death sentence; it meant a wiping out of his life even before he was captured; it meant death before death came, for the white men who had read those words would at once kill him in their hearts.[88]

Buckley's arguments as the State's Attorney and prosecutor in the case exactly reflect the symbolic switch from lynching to capital punishment from the 1920s onwards and the spike in African American executions for rape in the period 1936–1945 discussed above. Buckley sees the death penalty as a form of mercy in comparison with lynching and immediately weaponises the threat of summary justice to secure Bigger's confession:

> Buckley led Bigger to a window through which he looked and saw the streets below crowded with masses of people in all directions. 'See that boy? Those people would like to lynch you. That's why I'm asking you to trust me and talk to me.'[89]

Later in the novel, Buckley's words are shown to be more than mere brutal tactics to secure a confession, but rather, much more uncomfortably, his sincerely held beliefs about the legal system. At Bigger's trial, Buckley offers several similar arguments, asserting that the death penalty is a lenient sentence compared to the mob justice that he has helped to mobilise, using racist stereotypes to leverage the maximum punishment: for example, 'The law is strong and gracious enough to allow all of us to sit here in this courtroom today and try this case with dispassionate interest, and not tremble with fear that at this very moment some half-human black ape may be climbing through the windows of our homes to rape, murder and burn our daughters!'[90] and 'That treacherous beast must have known that if the marks of his teeth were ever seen on the white flesh of her breasts, he would not have been accorded the high honour of sitting here in this court of law!'.[91] Our continued access to Bigger's perspective during his crimes exposes this dehumanising rhetoric as the mere pathological fantasies of American white masculinity. Indeed, Bigger's lawyer Max explicitly analyses the origins of vigilantism and lynching in pathological white guilt:

> There is guilt in the rage that demands that this man's life be snuffed out so quickly! There is fear in the hate and impatience which impels the action of the mob congregated upon the streets beyond that window! All of them [...] know and feel that their lives are built upon a historical deed of wrong against many people, people from whose lives they have bled their leisure and their luxury.[92]

In designing the character of Max, Wright was also inspired by Darrow's work on the Leopold and Loeb trial.[93] And yet, in direct contrast with the successful Leopold and Loeb defence, Wright's judge will consider Max's plea for only one hour before deciding, inevitably, to end Bigger's life.[94]

Further, while the trial awakens important self-reflective aspects of Bigger's character, he is increasingly exposed to racism before his execution, in an experience of what he calls 'death before death came'.[95] This experience leads to a nihilistic revelation on the night before Bigger's execution, which humbles and alienates Max, his last defender:

> What I killed for must've been good! [...] I didn't know I was really alive in this world until I felt things hard enough to kill for 'em...It's the truth, Mr Max. I can say it now, 'cause I'm going to die.[96]

Max's response to Bigger is primarily physical—he backs away, 'his body moved nervously' and his 'eyes were wet': though racially othered as Jewish and Communist in some contexts, Max feels his whiteness and, crucially, his status as a living man who will not be executed, too viscerally to respond to Bigger fully.[97] Eli Zaretsky argues that across his work Wright 'articulated a principle of negativity' rooted in trauma, citing Paul Gilroy's emphasis on a 'repeated choice of death rather than bondage', 'which did not so much oppose as deepen and complicate the affirmative ideal of culture laid down by the dominant (white) culture'.[98] This principle of negativity as expressed by Bigger is precisely what Max cannot cope with, even with his Marxist principles, and the scene in fact foreshadows Wright's own break from communism.

Wright's Anti-Racist Criminal Psychology

Despite Wright's critique of the capacity of psychoanalysis to challenge the intersection of racism and the death penalty, as medical experts in *Native Son* express virulent prejudice against Bigger, his depiction of black capital crime would eventually change the analytic practice itself, moving the conversation on from a Reikian view of generalised unconscious guilt as the cause of crime to a focus on internalised racism. Many of Wright's most important experiences with psychoanalysis and the death penalty would occur after *Native Son*, inspired by his work on that novel. Wright's engagement took the form of 'highly personal encounters with psychoanalysis'[99] and included meetings and shared political projects with psychoanalysts, such as Frederic Wertham and Benjamin Karpman, who transcended many of Freud's limitations with regard to race. These analysts provided treatment adapted to black social conditions via institutions such as the Lafargue Clinic in Harlem, as well as expert study of, and testimony on behalf of, African American capital criminals.[100] Wertham also argued against segregation in Delaware, in a prelude to Brown v. The Board of Education.[101] These influences on Wright have long been noted by scholars but have never before been directly connected with his attitude to the death penalty.

Native Son also formally enters the history of postcolonial psychoanalysis in Frantz Fanon's citation of the novel in his famous 1952 essay, *The Fact of Blackness.* Faced by the power of the horror of the 'myth of the Negro' and the white world's expectation of black violence, Fanon argues that Bigger responds through an irrational death drive: 'To put an end to his tension, he acts, he responds to the world's anticipation', drawing the wider psychological conclusion from the novel that 'The Negro is a toy in the white man's hands; so, in order to shatter the hellish cycle, he explodes'.[102] In closing this chapter, I thus want to recognise Wright's influence on postcolonial theory and anti-racist psychoanalysis, as well as to acknowledge the importance of his move to France in 1947 to engage in anti-colonial struggle. Wright's later activism is the culmination of intellectual and emotional connections developed in response to the Scottsboro case between death-dealing racism in both the colonial and the American contexts. In his post-World War II experience, this more internationalist shift in thought—which ultimately places Bigger's experience and Wright's own reading in psychoanalysis within a larger struggle against a law shaped by a white settler cultural project—is shaped by Wright's recognition that, as Zaretsky argues, 'ethnocide is not a violation of the emancipatory project of modernity, but its defining characteristic.[103]

Notes

1. Lizzie Seal and Alexa Neale, 'Race, Racialisation and "Colonial Common Sense" in Capital Cases of Men of Colour in England and Wales, 1919–1957', 'Special Collection: Literature, Law and Psychoanalysis', *Open Library of Humanities*, 5.1 (2019): 1–21. DOI: https://doi.org/10.16995/olh.471.
2. Stacey Hynd, 'Killing the Condemned: The Practice and Process of Capital Punishment in British Africa, 1900–1950s' *The Journal of African History*, Vol. 49, No. 3 (2008): 403–418 (403, 406).
3. Howard W. Allen and Jerome M. Clubb, *Race, Class and the Death Penalty: Capital Punishment in American History*, New York: State University of New York Press, 2008, 12.
4. James W. Clarke 'Without Fear or Shame: Lynching, Capital Punishment and the Subculture of Violence in the American South', *British Journal of Political Science*, Vol. 28, No. 2 (1998): 269–289 (286).
5. Achille Mbembe, 'Necropolitics', trans. by Libby Meintjes, *Public Culture*, Vol. 15, No. 1 (2003): 11–40 (22–23). See also his more recent full-length book on this topic: *Necropolitics*, trans. by Steve Corcoran, Durham, N.C.: Duke University Press, 2019.
6. Nancy Cunard, 'Foreword', *Negro: An Anthology*, New York: London, 1970, xxxi-xxxii (xxxi).
7. SURREALIST GROUP, 'Murderous Humanitarianism', trans. by Samuel Beckett, *Negro: An Anthology*, 352–353 (353).
8. Priyamvada Gopal, *Insurgent Empire: Anticolonial Resistance and British Dissent*, London, Verso, 2019, 306.
9. Sigmund Freud, *Totem and Taboo (1913), The Standard Edition of the Complete Psychological Works of Sigmund Freud, Volume XIII (1913–1914)*, trans. by Strachey et al., London: Vintage, 2001: ix–164.
10. Freud, *Totem and Taboo*, 1.
11. For a reflection on how Freud's Jewish identity inflected his attitudes to race and settler colonialism, see Edward Said, *Freud and the Non-European*, London: Verso, 2004.

12. Stephen Frosh, 'Psychoanalysis, colonialism, racism', *Journal of Theoretical and Philosophical Psychology*, Vol. 33, No. 3 (2013): 141–154.
13. Abdul R. JanMohamed, *The Death-Bound-Subject: Richard Wright's Archaeology of Death*, Durham and London: Duke University Press, 2005, 1.
14. [Three leaflets ([A]-C) issued by the Society for the Abolition of Capital Punishment, Indian and Colonial Committee], Society for the Abolition of Capital Punishment, Indian and Colonial Committee, [London], [1909], The British Library, General Reference Collection 8425.h.(13–15).
15. Sir Ernest Arthur Gowers et al. *Royal Commission on Capital Punishment, 1949–1953, REPORT, Presented to Parliament by Command of Her Majesty September 1953* (also known as Gowers Commission Report), London: Her Majesty's Stationery Office, 1953, paragraph 606, page 212.
16. See, for example, James Scannell, 'The Method is Unsound: The Aesthetic Dissonance of Colonial Justification in Kipling, Conrad, and Greene', *Style*, Vol. 30, No. 3 (1996): 409–432 and Valerie Kennedy, 'Conradian quest versus dubious adventure: Graham and Barbara Greene in West Africa', *Studies in Travel Writing*, Vol. 19, No. 1 (2015): 48–65.
17. Graham Greene, *It's a Battlefield*, Kingswood: The Windmill Press, 1952, 2.
18. Greene, *It's a Battlefield*, 16.
19. Greene, *It's a Battlefield*, 4.
20. Greene, *It's a Battlefield*, 1.
21. Greene, *It's a Battlefield*, 146–147.
22. Greene, *It's a Battlefield*, 19.
23. Greene, *It's a Battlefield*, 147.
24. Greene, *It's a Battlefield*, 146.
25. Greene, *It's a Battlefield*, 189.
26. Greene, *It's a Battlefield*, 194–195.
27. See Lynne Cheney, 'Joseph Conrad's *The Secret Agent* and Graham Greene's *It's a Battlefield*: A Study in Structural Meaning', *Modern Fiction Studies*, Vol. 16 (1970): 117–131; Robert Pendleton, 'Arabesques of Influence: The Repressed Conradian Masterplot in the Novels of Graham Greene', *Conradiana*, Vol. 25, No. 2 (1993): 83–98; Malika Rebai Maamri, 'Cosmic Chaos in *The Secret Agent* and Graham Greene's *It's a Battlefield*', *Conradiana*, Vol. 40, No. 2 (2008): 179–192.
28. Gopal, *Insurgent Empire*, 244–278 and 279–318.
29. John Rodden and John Rossi, *The Cambridge Introduction to George Orwell*, Cambridge: Cambridge University Press, 2012, 64.

30. Gowers et al. 'Table I Recommendations to Mercy (England and Wales)' and 'Table II Recommendations to Mercy (Scotland)', *Royal Commission*, paragraphs 31–35, pages 9–10.
31. Peggy Kamuf, *Literature and the Remains of the Death Penalty*, New York: Fordham University Press, 58.
32. Orwell, 'A Hanging', *Shooting an Elephant: and Other Essays*, London: Secker and Warburg, 1950, 11.
33. Orwell, 'A Hanging', 11–12.
34. Orwell, 'A Hanging', 15.
35. Orwell, 'A Hanging', 17.
36. Critics call 'Shooting an Elephant' and 'A Hanging' variously essays or short stories. John Rodden suggests that 'the consensus today is that "A Hanging" is "faction", an autobiography based essay' ('"A Hanging" Circa 80', *The MidWest Quarterly*, Vol. 56, No. 1 (2014): 70–85 (78)).
37. George Orwell, 'Shooting an Elephant', *Shooting an Elephant: and Other Essays*, London: Secker and Warburg, 1950, 6.
38. Orwell, 'Shooting an Elephant', 1.
39. Orwell, 'Shooting an Elephant', 1.
40. Orwell, 'Shooting an Elephant', 2.
41. Orwell, 'Shooting an Elephant', 10.
42. See Ranajit Guha, 'Not at Home in Empire', *Critical Inquiry*, Vol. 23, No. 3 (1997): 482–493 and Barry Hindess, 'Not at Home in the Empire', *Social Identities: Journal for the Study of Race, Nation and Culture*, Vol. 7, No. 3 (2001): 363–377 (363).
43. See Gopal, *Insurgent Empire*, 244–278 and 279–318.
44. Anon. 'Detective Stories', *Times*, 2nd January 1940, 3. Isaac Anderson, 'New Mystery Stories', *New York Times*, 25th February 1940, 86.
45. Maurice Richardson, 'The Crime Ration', *The Observer*, 5th November 1939, 6.
46. Agatha Christie, *And Then There Were None*, New York: Harper Collins, 2011, 36, 286.
47. Agatha Christie, *And Then There Were None*, 287.
48. Christie, *And Then There Were None*, 287.
49. J. C. Bernthal, 'Killing Innocence: Obstructions of Justice in Late-Interwar British Crime fiction', *CLUES: A Journal of Detection*, Vol. 17, No. 2 (Fall 2019): 31–39 (36).
50. Bernthal, 'Killing Innocence', 32.
51. Theodor Reik, *The Unknown Murderer, The Compulsion to Confess: On the Psychoanalysis of Crime and Punishment*, New York: Grove Press, 1961, 161.
52. Reik, *The Unknown Murderer*, 158–159.

53. Theodor Reik, *The Compulsion to Confess, The Compulsion to Confess: On the Psychoanalysis of Crime and Punishment*, New York: Grove Press, 1961, 268.
54. Christie, *And Then There Were None*, 211.
55. Christie, *And Then There Were None*, 248 and 250.
56. Christie, *And Then There Were None*, 47.
57. Christie, *And Then There Were None*, 67.
58. Christie, *And Then There Were None*, 169.
59. Agatha Christie, *And Then There Were None: A Play in Three Acts*, London: Samuel French, 1944.
60. For an overview, see Michael Bell, 'Primitivism: Modernism as Anthropology', *Oxford Handbook of Modernisms*, ed. by Peter Brooker et al., Oxford: Oxford University Press, 2010. For case studies of particular contexts, see Sinéad Garrigan Mattar, *Primitivism, Science and the Irish Revival*, Oxford: Oxford University Press, 2004; Carole Sweeney, *From Fetish to Subject: Race, Modernism, and Primitivism, 1919–1935*, Westport and London: Praeger, 2004; Gina M. Rossetti, *Imagining the Primitive in Naturalist and Modernist Culture*, Columbia and London: University of Missouri Press, 2006.
61. Frosh, 'Psychoanalysis, colonialism, racism', 145.
62. Liam Kennedy, *Race and Urban Space in American Culture*, New York and London: Routledge, 2000, 132.
63. Eli Zaretsky, 'Beyond the Blues: Richard Wright, Psychoanalysis, and the Modern Idea of Culture', *The Transnational Unconscious: Essays in the History of Psychoanalysis and Transnationalism*, ed. by Joy Damousi and Mariano Ben Plotkin, Houndsmills: Palgrave Macmillan, 2009: 43–70 (47).
64. Joyce Ann Joyce, 'Richard Wright's *A Father's Law* and *Black Metropolis*: Intellectual Growth and Literary Vision', *Richard Wright: New Readings in the 21st Century*, ed. by Alice M. Craven and William E. Dow, New York: Palgrave Macmillan, 2011: 129–146 (137).
65. Clarke, 'Without Fear or Shame', 286.
66. Clarke, 'Without Fear or Shame', 289 and 284.
67. Clarke, 'Without Fear or Shame', 287.
68. Maggie E. Morris Davis, 'Sound and Silence: The Politics of Reading Early Twentieth-Century Lynching Poetry', *Canadian Review of American Studies*, Vol. 48, No. 1 (2018): 40–60 (52).
69. Anon. 'The Case For Abolition', *The Manchester Guardian*, 17th November 1938, 14.

70. Violet van der Elst, *On the Gallows*, London: Doge Press, 1937. This thread of argument is widespread across her polemic, but see especially 96, 214–223.
71. Davis, 'Sound and Silence', 57.
72. JanMohamed, *Death-Bound-Subject*, 19.
73. JanMohamed, *Death-Bound-Subject*, 7.
74. Richard Wright, *Native Son*, London: Vintage, 2000, 39.
75. Wright, *Native Son*, 40.
76. Wright, *Native Son*, 121.
77. Allen and Clubb, *Race, Class and the Death Penalty*, 23.
78. James Cutler, *Lynch-law: an investigation into the history of lynching in the United States*, New York: Longmans, Green, and co., 1905, 214–217.
79. Allen and Clubb, *Race, Class and the Death Penalty*, 23.
80. Sondra Guttman, 'Who's Afraid of the Corncob Man? Masculinity, Race, and Labor in the Preface to Sanctuary', *Faulkner Journal* Vol. 15, No. 1–2 (1999): 15–34 (25).
81. Richard Wright, 'How Bigger Was Born', *Native Son*, London: Vintage, 2000: 1–31 (7).
82. Wright, *Native Son*, 106.
83. Cunard, 'Scottsboro—and other Scottsboros', *Negro: An Anthology*, 155–174.
84. Gopal, *Insurgent Empire*, 306.
85. Gopal, *Insurgent Empire*, 298.
86. Carrie Williams Clifford, 'The Black Draftee from Dixie', *Negro*, 261; T. Thomas Fortune, 'That Other Golgotha', *Negro*, 261; Cunard, 'Southern Sheriff', *Negro*, 265–266.
87. Clarke, 'Without Fear or Shame', 282–285.
88. Wright, *Native Son*, 273.
89. Wright, *Native Son*, 333.
90. Wright, *Native Son*, 432.
91. Wright, *Native Son*, 436.
92. Wright, *Native Son*, 415.
93. Toru Kiuchi and Yoshinobu Hakutani, *Richard Wright: A Documented Chronology, 1908–1960*, Jefferson, N.C.: McFarland, 2013, 79.
94. Wright, *Native Son*, 439.
95. Wright, *Native Son*, 366–369.
96. Wright, *Native Son*, 453.
97. Wright, *Native Son*, 453–454.
98. Zaretsky, 'Beyond the Blues', 45
99. Zaretsky, 'Beyond the Blues', 47.
100. Zaretsky, 'Beyond the Blues', 65.

101. Jay Garcia, *Psychology Comes to Harlem: Rethinking the Race Question in Twentieth-Century America*, Baltimore, Maryland: John Hopkins University Press, 2012, 60.
102. Frantz Fanon, 'The Fact of Blackness', *Theories of Race and Racism: A Reader* ed. by Les Back and John Solomos, London: Routledge, 2000: 257–266 (265).
103. Zaretsky, 'Beyond the Blues', 48.

CHAPTER 9

The Political Death Penalty in World War II Writing

Introduction

Derrida argues that in examining the political death penalty, we must consider 'what defines an enemy, a stranger, a state of war—civil war or not; the criteria have always been difficult to determine and are becoming so more and more'.[1] This chapter will focus on representations of British civilians who are threatened with the death penalty by legislation including the Emergency Powers (Defence) Act 1939, the Treachery Act 1940 and the Treason Act 1945. Each of the texts examined in this chapter will problematise the concept of the 'public enemy', reflecting Kristine A. Miller's sense that authors such as Greene, Christie and others successfully 'manipulated the conventions of detective and spy fiction in order to attract a diverse reading public desperate not for escape from the Blitz but for understanding of it'.[2] These texts—including Agatha Christie's *N or M?* (1941), Graham Greene's *The Ministry of Fear* (1943) and Elizabeth Bowen's *The Heat of the Day* (1949)—demonstrate anxieties around whether the death penalty is an appropriate punishment for 'the enemy within', whether they are a disloyal British citizen or foreign patriot. In these narratives, spies commit a range of capital offences (including passing information to the enemy, sabotage and even murder) for diverse reasons. The perpetrator in these texts might have a patriotic connection to the enemy country, or they might be forced to betray, without wishing to,

K. Ebury, *Modern Literature and the Death Penalty, 1890–1950*, Palgrave Studies in Literature, Culture and Human Rights, https://doi.org/10.1007/978-3-030-52750-1_9

through blackmail and other forms of coercion. These culprits might also unconsciously wish to avenge their own trauma, disillusionment and rootlessness by acting treacherously.

Much of the energy coming from this questioning of the political death penalty came from the legacy of Irish World War I treason and rebellion. Despite the diversity of these texts, each narrative includes symbolic discussion of Ireland and direct invocation of Roger Casement in particular. Perhaps surprisingly, none of the texts directly allude to the Irish campaign of terrorism and sabotage carried out by the IRA from 1939 to 1940 (called variously the S-Plan, the Sabotage Campaign or England Campaign), which was targeted at the issue of partition and which predated the declaration of war.[3] They also fail to address the many instances of Irish service on the Allied side during World War II.[4] Instead these texts are backward-turned, drawing on an older tradition of Irish treason from the Easter Rising and earlier.[5] Mo Moulton argues that 'the Irish are important both as reality and as metaphor' during the interwar period, and this situation would intensify during World War II.[6] Even as my chosen authors attempt to imagine the traitor's point of view and question the violent tactics used by those pursuing him, they also consistently 'other' the traitor.

Ireland and the Irish therefore become an important reference point for imagining a treacherous subject who might 'pass' as British but also retain their essential difference: the paradigmatic case here remained Roger Casement, an Easter Rising revolutionary who had previously been knighted for his colonial service and who is repeatedly referred to in World War II texts and laws. The return to Casement reflects Shoshana Felman's emphasis on legal history as trauma, as a difficult case might return and repeat.[7] During World War II the traumatic case of Casement returns first as government policy and as treason law, and second as fictional and non-fictional writing about the political death penalty. Within the chapter as a whole, we witness a fragmentation of the Kantian view that treason should always be punishable by death: the justice of capital punishment for political crimes instead appears to depend on a broader context for the act, such as whether other capital crimes are committed.[8] In particular, I will identify an interpenetration of capital crimes: treason and treachery are frequently conceptualised symbolically as forms of killing and, indeed, literal homicide often becomes part of the plot. These authors leave unresolved the question of whether the death penalty for political crimes *causes* murders (as fear of the punishment leaves traitors desperate to remove witnesses) or whether the Fascist politics inspiring their characters simply reduces the value of human life.[9] Finally, while questioning the inflexibility of the law, these authors will also construct narratives that are 'death traps' for treacherous characters, in which very few of those guilty of such a betrayal will survive to the end of the story.[10]

Treason, Treachery and the Death Penalty

In this section I will explore why executions for treason, treachery and related offences are a key concern of British World War II writing and consider the place of Ireland within that national conversation. The concept of the death penalty for offences other than murder was profoundly affected by the Treachery Act 1940. This legislation was introduced because, until the Treason Act 1945, the offence of treason had quite technical rules of evidence, including a requirement that two witnesses of treasonous behaviour be produced. Between 1940 and 1946, 20 spies and saboteurs were sentenced to death under the Treachery Act (with one sentence commuted to life imprisonment). The crime of treachery was also designed to punish disloyalty and espionage from those who were not citizens and who owed no allegiance to Britain or its Empire. But not all those executed under the Treachery Act 1940 were foreign nationals; three of them were British, and prosecution for treachery was presumably chosen because of the special rules of evidence in a treason trial.[11] The Treason Act 1945 amended the evidentiary and procedural requirements for treason to bring it in line with murder, by then the only other mandatory capital offence.[12] The trials of William Joyce and John Amery, to be discussed later in relation to Rebecca West's work, were conducted under this new treason legislation.

The Treachery Act 1940 provided for in-camera trials, with only limited reporting of each case after sentence was carried out. The legal historian A. W. Brian Simpson notes that 'Most of those liable to the death penalty had done no harm whatever; the function of liability was to coerce agents into providing information or joining the double cross system'.[13] Public anxiety about these secret trials was found to be justified in the post-war period. For example, Pierrepoint, in his minutes of evidence to the Gowers Commission, reflected that one of these hangings under the Treachery Act 1940, identifiable as Karel Richard Richter in December 1941, was the worst in his career. Pierrepoint reflected that Richter panicked and resisted the execution: 'He was rough. It was unfortunate; he was not an Englishman, he was a spy and he kicked up rough'.[14] It is a historical curiosity—but one which would shape her expressed view of treason—that because of her work as part of the Gowers Commission, Elizabeth Bowen would be in the room when Pierrepoint gave this evidence of his most traumatic execution.[15]

Because the political death penalty reached the mid-century without effective cultural, legal and political examination, instead, reference to past precedent, and especially to the Easter Rising, was an important way that debates about the World War II death penalty were short-circuited during the war. In arguing for the new Treachery Bill, the Secretary of State for the Home Department (Sir John Anderson) refers explicitly to this longer history and to Casement in arguing for the necessity of a wartime state of emergency and an increased liability to suffer the death penalty:

> In the course of the last war 10 persons—all, I think, aliens—were dealt with by court-martial under the Regulations made in accordance with these provisions. [...] Hon. Members will recollect that when proceedings were taken against Roger Casement he was put on trial for high treason before a civil court, and was sentenced to death under the Treason Acts. [...] The Treason Acts apply to all British subjects, wherever they may be, and also—by reason of a doctrine known as the doctrine of local allegiance—to aliens resident within His Majesty's jurisdiction. I am advised, however, that this doctrine of local allegiance could not reasonably be held to apply to aliens who had come to this country in a clandestine way for a hostile purpose intending, whether by espionage or by committing acts of sabotage, to undermine our system of national defence. It is obviously desirable that all classes of aliens in this country, whether they are normally resident here or have come here solely for a hostile purpose, should be made equally liable to the death penalty, if they commit offences of this kind.[16]

Within the Home Secretary's summary of the issues addressed by the Treachery Act, the legislation is explicitly turned towards the successful implementation of the death penalty itself, rather than justice or public safety concerns: variants of the phrase 'death penalty' are repeated several times within this short summing up. His reference to Casement and Ireland also aimed to shore up a consensus that it is 'obviously desirable' to be able to execute enemy aliens. This presentation of the Treachery Bill is not exceptional in its reference to Casement; indeed, a brief reference to Casement is present in every parliamentary debate about treason and treachery legislation I have consulted in my research.[17] Despite the controversy around the justice of Casement's sentence then and now, for Britain in the 1940s he becomes the paradigmatic traitor who must be executed and for whom treason and treachery legislation is designed.

Newspaper articles reporting the wartime execution of spies and traitors also frequently included either a coded or more obvious reference to Casement and the Easter Rising in order to leverage public consent for this version of the death penalty and to smooth differences between legal practices in each case. For example, a 1941 article describes the execution for treachery of a parachutist, Josef Jakobs, and then lists the executions of four other parachutists between 1940 and 1941 but concludes more strangely: 'More than 150 years passed without an execution in the Tower. The interval was broken during the last war. Carl Hans Lody, a former German naval officer, who was shot there, was one of 19 spies executed. His was the first execution in the Tower for more than 150 years. During the Great War Sir Roger Casement was hanged at Pentonville as a traitor'.[18] The short report rushes from a German executed at the Tower in 1941, to a German spy similarly executed in 1914, to Casement, who was not German, nor a parachutist, nor executed at the Tower. Under the cluster of context linked by the concepts 'treason and the death penalty in war-time', the article signals a certain amount of ambivalence about wartime execution in the 1940s by using Ireland's past to fill a linguistic and symbolic paralysis in representing the political death penalty. This narrative of seamless continuity between World War I and World War II execution also obscures the important differences between the capital offences of treason and treachery outlined above, with the latter a new crime that had only just been introduced. A final connection between Casement's legacy and World War II treason is that several traitors, including John Amery, were inspired by Casement's work on the 'Irish Brigade' (which had aimed to turn Irish P.O.Ws to German service) to create the British Free Corps, a unit of the Waffen SS made up of disaffected British and Dominion P.O.Ws. Casement was thus an extremely complex figure during World War II: he was a focus for the design of treason and treachery legislation; an inspiration for British traitors, even those without sympathy for Ireland and its independence struggles; and a literary and psychological precedent for the revolutionary/traitor binary which informed a cultural understanding of conflicted allegiance.

Reflecting on this period in British history, Rebecca West's post-war creative nonfiction *The Meaning of Treason* (1947) used reference to Casement and Ireland to sketch the contours of her psychological portrait of William Joyce, the Nazi radio propagandist executed for treason in 1946 after a lengthy trial which included proceedings in the Court of Appeals and the House of Lords. As part of creating this portrait of Joyce as 'The Revolutionary' in contrast with those who had committed similar offences, West reflected 'like the great treason trial of the First World War, when Sir Roger Casement went to the gallows, was an Irish drama'.[19] As Eva Horn puts it pithily, West 'views treason as the tragedy of severed home ties'.[20] In this example, West's reference to conjures in just three words, 'Sir Roger Casement', a resonant psychodrama of treason and the death penalty, as well as supporting her narrative of the origins of William Joyce's treason in his conflicted Irish identity, via his childhood collaboration with the British paramilitary organisation the 'Black and Tans' during the Irish War of Independence (1919–1921).[21] As part of this focus on Ireland, West explains William Joyce's treason using a psychoanalytically inflected theory of conflicted national allegiance originating in his relationship with his father. West also implies that an insanity defence might have been appropriate for Joyce, alluding to Freudian concepts of masochism and the death drive.

In contrast to the hostility shown towards Casement in government legislation and newspaper reports, West's choice of Casement is connected with her decision to render William Joyce as a sympathetic character, gifted with a nobility and eloquence that he is unable to display during his trials.[22] In her account of William Joyce, West directly echoes Casement's 'Speech from the Dock' in repeatedly emphasising the importance of love in Joyce's life and politics. For example, West imagines Joyce's realisation that Germany would not win the war and renders his likely feelings about his own self-sacrifice in words that directly echo (and mangle) Casement's: 'If a man does not love his country enough to concede its right to self-government, he will end by not loving it at all, by hating it'.[23] While West's intervention does not quite coalesce into a direct critique of the M'Naghten Rules or the mandatory death sentence for treason, her reflections on the effect of the trial on those present are clearly very uneasy. As West notes, much of the public mood during and after the William Joyce trial wished to see him 'get away with it': 'The public who cried out that William Joyce should not have been hanged' wanted 'the perverse satisfaction of a seeing a man whose crime it knew by the testimony of its own ears go unpunished'.[24] Through her reference to both the historical and psychological complication of Ireland in Joyce's life and crimes, West manages to raise anxiety about the commonplace view of treason and treachery as capital offences in specific cases, but these shorthand references allow the justice of the political death penalty to continue to be unexamined.

In the next sections of this chapter, I will examine how West's psychoanalytically shaped ideas of guilt and desire, and her problematic identification of treason as distinctively Irish, are shared across fictional narratives by Christie, Greene and Bowen. These fictions of the World War II death penalty were also inescapably shaped by the legacy of World War I, especially the Easter Rising. Reference to Ireland fills a sense of linguistic aphasia in which the political death penalty cannot *quite* be argued against.

A 'Very Sharp-Pointed Entertainment': Agatha Christie's *N or M?* (1941)

In my first example, Christie's *N or M?* (1941), a thriller published early in World War II, a husband and wife detective team, Tommy and Tuppence Beresford, hunt a spy ring centred upon a seaside boarding house in the fictional town of Leahampton (based on Bournemouth).[25] The two key perpetrators sought are a male spy (codename N) and a female one (codename M), who are passing information to the enemy. It seems likely that the novel, with its seaside boarding house setting and the comparatively unusual emphasis on women as traitors and spies, was inspired by the Dorothy O'Grady case (1940): O'Grady had been a landlady in an Isle of Wight boarding house before her arrest as a saboteur. As the original reviewers noted, in the context of a fear of a German invasion, the novel induces a heightened form of the usual paranoid reading associated with detective fiction, offering a 'very sharp-pointed entertainment',[26] as 'each character in turn sheds clues that give cause for alarm'.[27] 'In other words', the reviewer concludes, the novel 'gets you'.[28] Christie's *N or M?* is particularly designed for conditions in which detective novels and thrillers might be sought as much for cultural self-examination, as for pleasure and patriotism. Miller argues that in Christie's fictions of World War II, including *And Then There Were None* and *Curtain*, 'murder in wartime was no longer a drawing-room puzzle; instead, it was an institutionalized mandate that made assassins and victims of all who fought'.[29]

The boarding house under investigation by Tommy and Tuppence, called Sans Souci, is owned by Mrs Perenna, an Irish woman who is suspected of being the female traitor (M) because of her mysterious past: Mrs Perenna is eventually revealed to be part of the IRA, but not involved in active espionage activities. In symbolic centre of Christie's novel, Perenna's daughter Sheila responds angrily to a dinner table discussion of Edith Cavell:

> Mrs Sprot had just said in her thin fluting voice: 'Where I do think the Germans made such a mistake in the last war was to shoot Nurse Cavell. It turned everybody against them.'
> It was then that Sheila, flinging back her head, demanded in her fierce young voice: 'Why shouldn't they shoot her? She was a spy, wasn't she?'
> 'Oh, no, not a spy.'
> 'She helped English people to escape—in an enemy country. That's the same thing. Why shouldn't she be shot?'
> 'Oh, but shooting a woman—and a nurse.'
> Sheila got up.
> 'I think the Germans were quite right,' she said.
> She went out of the window into the garden.[30]

Mention of Cavell is traumatic for Sheila because of the legacy of World War I treason and rebellion in her family. She tearfully confides in Christie's male detective Tommy, pathologising her father's actions, and seeing the story of his life and death as one of neglect of domestic, affectionate forms of love:

> 'Yes, I hate patriotism, do you understand? All this *country, country, country*! Betraying your country—dying for your country—serving your country. Why should one's country mean anything at all?'
> Tommy said simply: 'I don't know. It just does.' [...]
> 'You believe in the British Empire—and—and—the stupidity of dying for one's country... *Nothing's* worth dying for...Do you know who my father was?'
> 'No!' Tommy's interest quickened.
> 'His name was Patrick Maguire. He—he was a follower of Casement in the last war. He was shot as a traitor! All for nothing! For an idea—he worked himself up with those other Irishmen. Why couldn't he just stay at home quietly and mind his own business? He's a martyr to some people and a traitor to others. I think he was just—*stupid*. [...] I–I don't know why I've been telling you all this. I got worked up. Where did it all start?'
> 'A discussion on Edith Cavell.'
> 'Oh yes—patriotism. I said I hated it.'
> 'Aren't you forgetting Nurse Cavell's own words?'
> 'What words?'
> 'Before she died. Don't you know what she said?' He repeated the words:

> '*Patriotism is not enough...I must have no hatred in my heart.*'
> 'Oh.' She stood there stricken for a moment.
> Then, turning suddenly, she wheeled away into the shadow of the garden.[31]

Because of Sheila's father's execution after the Easter Rising, a state of emergency has existed in her family throughout the interwar period. Sheila's alienation from her father's sacrifice of his life and from filial and national allegiances is represented by the distancing reference to 'those other Irishmen' and to her advocating the death of Cavell and, implicitly, her own father. Sheila's outburst about her past places her and her mother at present risk of the death penalty as Tommy and Tuppence begin to investigate them. She is therefore unconsciously rebelling against her mother's fidelity to her husband by continuing his nationalist work. A final layer of irony is eventually added to this dinner table scene and its aftermath because the vapid young mother Mrs Sprot is finally revealed to be the female Fifth Columnist: Sprot's views on Cavell and Germany are thus eventually shown to have been rehearsed to support her persona. Within the broader narrative and its themes, Christie's double, comparative allusion to Cavell and Casement implicitly disputes the conventional English pieties that would excuse Cavell's actions while condemning Casement and Sheila's father to death.

Another innocent suspect that Tommy and Tuppence identify is, like Sheila and her mother, again superficially 'othered': Carl von Deinim, a German refugee in a romantic relationship with the conflicted Sheila, which adds to the cloud of suspicion surrounding him. When von Deinim asserts his confused sense of national allegiance ('Germany is still my country') and explains that he is considering suicide because of the suspicion he is living under, Christie again alludes to Cavell's words.[32] When von Deinim is eventually arrested, Sheila begs Tuppence to prevent his execution: Tuppence refuses but asserts that although the death penalty is traumatic, it ultimately removes the threat posed by the spy and ennobles them into a patriot.[33] Christie's sense of the horror of the wartime death penalty comes forcefully through Sheila's perspective:

> Sheila flung her head up. She said passionately: 'Then there's no hope for us. They'll take him away and shut him up, and one day, early in the morning, they'll stand him up against a wall and shoot him—and that will be the end.'
> She went out, shutting the door behind her.[34]

Sheila's emotional response, inspired by the World War I death penalty and her memory of her father, reflects a specific fear of the in-camera trials and secret executions associated with the Treachery Act 1940. She fears particularly that she will not know when the person she loves has been killed. In response to Sheila, Tuppence momentarily abandons conventional euphemisms about service to one's country, to assert internally that von Deinim surely '*deserves* to be shot':

> 'Oh, damn, damn, damn the Irish!' thought Tuppence in a fury of mixed feelings. 'Why have they got that terrible power of twisting things until you don't know where you are? If Carl von Deinim's a spy, he deserves to be shot. I must hang onto that, not let this girl with her Irish voice bewitch me into thinking it's the tragedy of a hero and a martyr.'[35]

Her more extreme reaction to Sheila's 'Irish' provocation to empathise with treason leaves Tuppence wishing that von Deinim might be innocent. Christie therefore raises anxiety about the political death penalty in specific cases (von Deinim, Sheila's father, Cavell, perhaps Casement) but does not touch the principle that a spy 'deserves to be shot'. However, von Deinim is eventually revealed to be a British intelligence agent.[36] The real male culprit was the apparently bluff and trustworthy Commander Haydock, rather than a more obvious suspect: Haydock has been merely posing as English, as von Deinim was pretending to be German.[37] Revealing the limitations of Tommy and Tuppence's investigation, they do not suspect Sprot, or Haydock or, worse, the serviceman Anthony Marsden (their own daughter's boyfriend) who eventually lures Tuppence into a trap that could have led to her death.[38]

While the sympathetic characters of von Deinim, Sheila and her mother are ultimately exonerated and saved from execution, narrative closure is apparently achieved by the implied execution of Haydock, Marsden, Mrs Sprot and others. But, crucially, this closure is linked with Christie's rendering of their guilt for the core capital crime of murder. Tuppence had directly witnessed Mrs Sprot kill someone in a situation that had initially seemed to be self-defence,[39] while Haydock and Marsden certainly planned to murder both Tommy and Tuppence.[40] While in reality none of those convicted and executed under the Treachery Act 1940 or the Treason Act 1945 were actually accused of exacerbating violent crimes, in *N or M?* Christie's spies have also committed murder, kidnapping and attempted murder. In common with Greene's *Ministry of Fear*, as I will shortly discuss, Christie therefore designs unusual treason cases in which spies are also guilty of murder in order to reduce readers' possible ambivalence about the death penalty as a punishment for treason and treachery. However, it is also true that references to Casement and Ireland in *N or M?* raise more questions about the political death penalty—predominantly associated with the character of Sheila—than Christie is able to adequately answer, so that psychologically complex characters such as Sheila and von Deinim *cannot* be executed, while treason *must be* bolstered by murder to avoid the reader experiencing a potential sense of injustice.

'A Piece of Grit in the State Machinery': Graham Greene's *The Ministry of Fear* (1943)

While Christie as author made no public remark on the subject of treason and the death penalty, the other two authors examined in this chapter, Graham Greene and Elizabeth Bowen, directly intervened on this topic. For example, Greene argued for the value of a sympathetic literary understanding of the traitor in a 1948 BBC debate, which included Bowen and which was subsequently published as *Why Do I Write*. In expressing his views on this topic, Greene depends on the language of psychoanalysis, of which he had a sound understanding: indeed, his craft as a writer was directly shaped by his experience of analysis with Dr Kenneth Richmond in his youth.[41] In his remarks, Greene writes movingly about how the state 'poisons the psychological wells' to restrict human sympathy, while the writer is engaged in a guerrilla war to restore a political openness to humanity.[42] He asks further,

> [H]ave any writers at all been lucky enough to die by the rope or by a firing squad? I can think of none, for the world knows only too well that given time the writer will be corrupted into loyalty. Ezra Pound therefore goes to an asylum… (the honourable haven of the uncorruptible—Smart, Cowper, Clare and Lee). Loyalty confines us to accepted opinions: loyalty forbids us to comprehend sympathetically our dissident fellows; but disloyalty encourages us to roam experimentally through any human mind: it gives to the novelist the extra dimension of sympathy. […] I hope I am making clear that I'm not advocating a conscious advocacy of the dispossessed, in fact I am not advocating propaganda at all, as it was written by Dickens, Charles Reade or Thomas Hood […] Propaganda is only concerned to elicit sympathy for the innocent or those whom the propagandist likes to regard as

> innocent: he too poisons the wells. But the novelist's task is to draw his own likeness to any human being, the guilty as much as the innocent. Isn't our attitude to all our characters more or less—There, and may God forgive me, goes myself? If we can only awaken sympathetic comprehension in our readers, not only for our most evil characters (that is easy: there is a cord there fastened to all hearts that we can twitch at will), but of our smug, complacent, successful characters, we have surely succeeded in making the work of the State a degree more difficult—and that is a genuine duty we owe society, to be a piece of grit in the state machinery.[43]

For Greene, at least in this essay, to die by the death penalty for one's beliefs is not a sign of imbalance or pathology but rather a badge of honour. His emphasis on disloyalty and resistance to the state and to social norms takes his art very close to a symbolic identification of the writer with the traitor. Some of Greene's implied questioning of the death penalty emerges from a critique of Fascist or Communist misuse of the state's sovereign right to kill its citizens: Greene quickly moves from the above extremely subversive claim into a standard critique of Russian government control of art and individual liberty. Greene's attitudes towards treason, as Michael Brennan has argued, were also powerfully shaped by his own intelligence work for MI6 and by the detention of his cousin, Ben Greene, as a Fifth Columnist in 1940.[44]

Many of the same issues are raised in Greene's novel *The Ministry of Fear* (1943), which extends the serious focus on the death penalty begun in *It's A Battlefield* (discussed in Chap. 8). The novel is set, like Christie's, during the Blitz, dating it to the period immediately after the Treachery Act 1940. *The Ministry of Fear* (1943) is far more directly concerned with capital punishment as a theme than Christie's *N or M?* because of the choice of protagonist. Greene's central character, Arthur Rowe, is directionless and newly released from an institution after the murder of his wife in a mercy killing. Rowe accidentally stumbles into the centre of a spy ring passing stolen information, a missing roll of microfilm which would be used to assist the German invasion. However, unlike Tommy and Tuppence, Rowe's fear of and desire for the death penalty forms a psychological barrier which prevents him from realising the nature of the treason surrounding him. Indeed, the language of psychoanalysis is especially highlighted in reviews of Greene's novel: William DuBois argued in *The New York Times* that Greene is 'a writer who might have been a poet or a psychoanalyst', referring to Rowe's 'clouded subconscious' and suggesting that as a character he is primarily designed as 'Mr. Greene's illustration of the schizophrenia that is corroding the world today'.[45] R. D. Charques, the *TLS* reviewer, wrote less admiringly that despite the urgency of wartime 'this author's characteristic of obscure, complex and under-toned psychological motivation is as pronounced as ever', though he also admits that the story has 'a sharply teasing psychological suspense'.[46]

As in Christie, reference to Ireland remains important as a context for Greene's thriller plot. Greene's most direct reference to Casement occurs towards the middle of the narrative. Rowe has been involved in an explosion engineered by the spy ring and loses his memory. Rechristened Digby, he is institutionalised in a mental hospital run by the Fifth Columnist, Dr Forester. Rowe/Digby has been permitted to read the newspapers, and Johns, an attendant in the institution, uses Casement as a way of explaining the role and motivations of traitors in the present war:

> This morning as he was reading [the newspaper] Johns came in for a chat, and Digby looking up from the paper asked, 'What's a Fifth Column?'
>
> There was nothing Johns liked better than giving information. He talked for quite a while, bringing in Napoleon.
>
> 'In other words people in enemy pay?' Digby said. 'That's nothing new.'
>
> 'There's this difference,' Johns said. 'In the last war—except for Irishmen like Casement—the pay was always cash. Only a certain class was attracted. In this war there are all sorts of ideologies.'[47]

This reference to Casement is a revealing moment in the wider narrative and should alert Rowe/Digby to the fact that he should be suspecting his apparent friends, the Austrian refugees Willi Hilfe and his sister Anna. Johns reflects in explaining the psychology of treason that Fascism '*is* attractive to men who are not tied—to a particular village or town they don't want to see scrapped. People with unhappy childhoods, progressive people who learn Esperanto, vegetarians who don't like shedding blood'.[48] As in Christie's *N or M?*, where immigrants and refugees were most powerfully threatened by the political death penalty, Greene's novel represents the Hilfes as mostly sympathetic characters but also as a dispossessed enemy within: the Hilfes' displaced status creates the conditions for their treachery.[49]

The language of love, as in Casement's 'Speech From the Dock', is also central to Rowe's theory of crime and punishment in wartime, and this is placed into close contact with the direct allusion to Casement. Rowe/Digby has come to care for the Hilfes, especially Anna, who he has romantic feelings for:

> Wasn't it better to take part even in the crimes of people you loved, if it was necessary hate as they did, and if that were the end of everything suffer damnation with them, rather than be saved alone? But that reasoning, it could be argued, excused your enemy. And why not? he thought. It excused anyone who loved to kill or be killed.[50]

This theory of love, transgression and the death penalty, influenced by Casement's words and legacy, is an early admission that he knows on some level of Anna's connection with treason, murder and death. As this reflection on love suggests, Rowe/Digby will become as eager to save Anna from the death penalty, in part because of his guilt about the murder of his wife, as he is to have her brother Willi executed for the same crime. Remembering his real identity, Rowe justifies his plan to have Willi hanged by highlighting that he has committed *two* different capital crimes:

> Spies, like murderers, were hanged, and in this case there was no distinction. [Willi] lay asleep in there and the gallows was being built outside.[51]

While Willi will not be the direct cause of all of these murders, 'the last clarification' of Greene's plot is preceded by a 'massacre on an Elizabethan scale'.[52] Just as in Christie's narrative, then, Greene smooths over the issue of the rightness of the wartime death penalty by depicting treacherous characters committing murder in addition to their political crimes.

This identification of the refugee as the enemy is quite disappointing in comparison with Christie's exploding of this plot, as Greene's narrative apparently demands the sacrifice and scapegoating of particular groups in order to preserve the status quo.[53] However, Greene introduces different layers of complication because his hero may be worthy of the death penalty himself. Further, as Brian Diemert points out, Prentice, the policeman Rowe works with to clear up the spy ring, is as tainted as Rowe or Hilfe.[54] Greene goes further than Christie in depicting the secrecy of wartime justice associated with the Treachery Act 1940, especially the practice of in-camera trials and suppressed reporting of execution. In a particularly dark scene from *The Ministry of Fear* where a key member of the spy ring Rowe uncovers, Mrs Bellairs, is arrested by Prentice, Greene directly alludes to the government's suppression of information about capital sentences in the newspapers:

> 'Oh no, ma'am, it's you who'll suffer. Giving information to the enemy is a hanging offence.'
> 'They don't hang women. Not in this war.'
> 'We may hang more people, ma'am,' Mr Prentice said, speaking back at her from the passage, 'than the papers tell you about.'[55]

Willi Hilfe will eventually commit suicide because he fears torture rather than the gallows: 'I don't want to be beaten up [...] I know what they do to spies. They'll think they can make me talk—they will make me talk'.[56] Despite Rowe's naïve assertion that 'We don't beat up prisoners here', the atmosphere of Greene's novel suggests that Hilfe is right to fear wartime punishment above and beyond the death penalty itself.[57]

Willi further challenges Rowe's naïve belief that only spies who are also murderers will be executed. In threatening Rowe, he reminds him that his efforts to punish the ring of Fifth Columnists will put his beloved Anna at risk of the death penalty, even though she is not guilty of murder:

> 'They probably wouldn't hang her. Of course that would depend on what I say. Perhaps it would be just an internment camp until the war's over—and then deportation if you win. From my point of view,' he explained drily, 'she's a traitor, you know.'[58]

While murder is, as in Christie, used to leverage readerly consent for executions for political crimes, Rowe's belief on the justice of the death penalty in Willi's case is tainted by his own links to capital crimes and self-serving because his priority is his love for Anna. Rowe eventually learns to weaponise his fear of and desire for the death penalty by coercing Willi's suicide. The novel closes with Rowe's determination to protect Anna from the return of his memory and from the consequences of her treachery in the context of a love shot through with secrecy and unhappiness.[59]

'What about the Conscience of the Unstable Person': Elizabeth Bowen's *The Heat of the Day*

The use of Casement as a foundation for a psychologically complex approach to the political death penalty during World War II is also central to Elizabeth Bowen's understanding of treason. In August 1952, Bowen's participated in a BBC broadcast called 'Conversation on Traitors'—a debate between herself, Nigel Balchin (a novelist), Alan Moorehead (a journalist and nonfiction writer) and Noel Annan (a Cambridge politics lecturer). Bowen had been invited to appear on the programme on the strength of *The Heat of the Day*, published three years before and, like *N or M?* or *The Ministry of Fear*, set during the Blitz. Beyond her fiction, Bowen's participation must have been sought because she was serving on the Gowers Commission, as the questions addressed to her are often focused on punishment. It is unclear whether the BBC producers would also have known that Bowen (like Greene) had also been a spy herself during World War II and thus had an intimate understanding of conflicted allegiance.[60] In this sense, Bowen is uniquely qualified for reflecting on the intersection of treason and the death penalty by both her wartime and her post-war experience.[61]

The BBC broadcast shows that Bowen's thinking about Casement is foundational in her attitude to both treason and the death penalty. The introduction to the broadcast, voiced by Noel Annan, names Alan Nunn May (convicted 1946 under the Official Secrets Act), Klaus Fuchs (1950 under the Official Secrets Act), William Joyce (convicted of high treason 1945) and Ezra Pound (indicted of treason 1943, found unfit to plead 1946, indictment dismissed 1958), as recent topical cases of treason that they wish to address. Two of these men were sentenced to imprisonment (Nunn May and Fuchs); one was institutionalised to avoid the death penalty (Pound); one was, as we know, executed (Joyce). In a revised edition of *The New Meaning of Treason* (1964), while William Joyce remained the core of the book, West would add in discussion of these same cases, as well as the Rosenberg trial (1953).

Just as West, Christie and Greene consider treason through reference to Casement, the first question of the 'Conversation on Traitors' broadcast asks Bowen for her views on the Easter Rising and World War I:

> Annan: ...We want to think about what we mean by the word "treason" and consider all sorts of questions about loyalty to one's country and the

> conflicting loyalties which come up and make one sometimes feel that a man, though he was a traitor to his country, had done the right thing. For instance, a controversial case which comes to my mind is one of Sir Roger Casement in the First World War. He was an Irishman. Can you tell us, Miss Bowen, about him?[62]

Bowen's response is factual and even-handed—Casement 'might be said to have betrayed' England. She notes his attempt to suborn the Irish brigade in Germany and records that he was 'trying to stop the Easter rising' at the point of capture. She sums up ambivalently that in Ireland he is viewed as 'a true patriot', while in England he is believed to have turned on a country that had honoured him.[63]

Beyond demonstrating the influence of the Casement case on her thinking, Bowen consistently psychoanalyses treason throughout the 'Conversation on Traitors' broadcast. Where Balchin and Moorehead use the language of reason, conscience and transgression even while taking a sympathetic view of treason, Bowen, like West in particular, insists instead upon the influence of pathology on the traitor and offers resistance to the view that they are rational actors who should be held responsible for their crimes. For example, she says that Klaus Fuchs 'returned [to treason] almost against his will, against his newly developing social conscience—as an addict returns to a drug or a person returns to a vice'.[64] When Balchin defends the right to freedom of conscience even in traitors, Bowen responds with both agreement and objection simultaneously, asking 'what about the conscience of the unstable person, which is bound to tilt and veer according to his emotional reactions?'.[65] In this sense she moves slightly beyond Casement as a springboard to consider the example of Ezra Pound's treason and his insanity defence. Although Bowen never recorded any direct account of her experience there, she had visited St Elizabeth's Hospital in the US, where Pound was being treated, in 1950 as part of her work with the Gowers Commission. On treason she says, showing the influence of the Gowers Commission experience:

> Suppose [traitors are] so unequally developed—to get back to my idea of the driving of an obsession which deforms the reasoning faculty, or which draws the natural emotion out of them—that you can have a person bordering on the insane who has the whole machinery for instance—who has the fine brain, but owing to some displacement of the normal faculties through being obsessed, through a single-minded burning thing which has—to put

> the thing practically—driven out this sense of cruelty or the sense of responsibility, or the sense of society—then you have in that person a particular case.[66]

Bowen's comments echo the psychiatric judgements given in the Pound case.[67] These claims about World War II treason also appear designed to trouble the M'Naghten Rules: while in *The Heat of the Day* her reference to the death penalty for political crimes is oblique compared to the other authors examined, this focus on treason and insanity is nonetheless a very important contribution to the problem. As she says, the traitor may be 'bordering on the insane' in one area of the mind only, but they still should not be held to be fully responsible for their actions, making the death penalty an inappropriate penalty for their crime. In her 'Frankly Speaking' interview, she also reflects directly on how the Gowers Commission 'spent a great deal of time naturally over the insanity laws and the MacNaughten rules';[68] she also believed her contribution to the report was a psychological one, in arguing for a broadening of the provocation defence.[69]

In *The Heat of the Day* (1949), Bowen's protagonist, Stella Rodney, learns her lover, Robert Kelway, is a Fascist spy only when Harrison, a counterspy, offers to keep this secret in exchange for sex with her. Bowen's novel was directly compared by a *New York Times* reviewer to Greene's *The Ministry of Fear* for its 'exciting and sinister' psychological texture, in which 'a discovery [is] made through the semi-obscurity of cryptic clues—an unfinished gesture, a discordant word, a familiar face sighted in an unlikely place'.[70] Similarly, the original *TLS* reviewer compares the novel to 'the thriller' but says that 'once she has established the melodramatic centre to her delicate design Miss Bowen is able to illuminate it by a series of approaches characteristically oblique'.[71] Indeed, it is worth remembering the melodramatic force of Stella's dilemma—to save Kelway from the death penalty, she would have to betray both her country *and* her love for Kelway by sleeping with Harrison: as she puts it succinctly, 'You propose that by becoming your mistress I buy out a man, in whom I have an interest, who is by your showing dangerous to the country'.[72] While Stella could free herself by reporting both Harrison and Kelway, her initial reaction is that her feelings for Robert trumps her 'duty' to the country despite her own intelligence work for the government.[73] Stella eventually comes to respond to the problem as an intellectual one, as much as an affective one, becoming an informal counterspy against Kelway by performing her own investigation of his crimes and his psychology.

While *The Heat of the Day* lacks a direct reference to Casement in the way that West, Christie and Greene allude to him by name, for Bowen Ireland and the history of Irish revolution is an extremely important reference point. As Megan Faragher argues, 'the political conflicts surrounding the Anglo-Irish experience aid in the aestheticization of the World War II experience'.[74] In her 'Frankly Speaking' interview, Bowen describes Ireland as 'a sort of terrain of imagination', which 'gave me the thing about seeing England from the outside'.[75] The parallel between England during the Blitz and an Irish colonial context is also a feature of the short fiction that Bowen published during World War II, as Thomas S. Davis argues with a particular focus on 'The Happy Autumn Fields' and 'Sunday Afternoon'.[76] In Bowen's BBC broadcast, she emphasised the idea of a 'perverted patriotism' based on ideas of love and emotion, recalling Casement's emphasis on love in his 'Speech from the Dock', as in the other texts I have examined. In *The Heat of the Day*, Bowen's key questions are also about love and treason: 'Could these two have loved each other better at a better time?...War at present worked as a thinning of the membrane between the this and the that, it was a becoming apparent—but then what else is love? No, there is no such thing as being alone together'.[77]

The connection to Ireland comes primarily from Stella's background rather than Kelway's as the traitor. This emphasis on Stella's Irish connection is appropriate because it is *her* attitude to the psychology and punishment of treason that the novel examines, with Kelway a mere cipher. In the centre of the novel, Stella goes to Ireland and visits Mount Morris, the house her son has inherited: she returns from Ireland determined to confront Kelway about his treason and to break with Harrison. Though she does neither of these things as decisively as she intended, the source of the plot development which leads to Kelway's death ultimately has its foundation in the Irish context. Stella's return to Ireland during World War II also reflects an intelligence mission Bowen had made under her married name, Mrs Cameron, to assess the value of Ireland's neutrality in the context of past colonial history. For Adam Piette, this visit, and Stella's broader relationship with Kelway, reflects the way that 'The "hybrid" Anglo-Irish self is capable of a double allegiance, to country and to that country's "enemy"'.[78] Further, Stella's son Roderick will recover from the revelation about Kelway's treason and death by planning a future in Ireland at Mount

Morris. In short, this novel of treason is structured by symbolic reference to Ireland.

When Stella investigates Kelway's childhood via a visit to Holme Dene, his family home, she is not considering *whether* he has committed treason (which is the received critical interpretation), but rather, like Rebecca West with William Joyce, to explore its background and origin and to consider whether an insanity defence might save him. Indeed, Alan Hepburn has compared Kelway to the William Joyce of West's *The Meaning of Treason*, suggesting the likely influence of West's trial reporting in the design of Bowen's psychological case study of treason.[79] This reflects Bowen's psychological understanding of treason and its punishment in her 'Conversation on Traitors'. Though Kelway will refuse all pathologising interpretations of his behaviour, he also acknowledges the root of his betrayal in his traumatic past. The climactic scene of *The Heat of the Day*, in which Kelway admits his treason to Stella before dying while attempting to escape arrest, is full of the language of insanity ('mad', 'besotted', 'malady').[80] Bowen presents one root of Kelway's treason in his oppressive middle-class home, anticipating the psychoanalytic interpretation offered by West in which treason is particularly focused on parental relationships. Kelway as a character accepts this reading of his suborned allegiance: his betrayal 'utterly undid fear. It bred my father out of me, gave me a new heredity'.[81] Kelway also explains his political crimes through his love for Stella: he says 'We've seen law in each other…'[82] and 'you have been my country'.[83] The final origin of Kelway's treason, to connect back to my earlier chapter on World War I, is his war trauma: Kelway has been radicalised by what he calls 'the extremity' of being wounded at Dunkirk, which makes him feel that he had been fighting on 'the wrong side'.[84] (Kelway's knee wound and his nihilism link him symbolically to Hamilton's Rupert Cadell in *Rope*.)[85] Indeed, Kelway's rapid descent from war trauma to treason reflects the historical forces which led to the creation of the Directorate of Army Psychiatry in 1942.[86]

Bowen's portrayal of Kelway is unique in the sense that he is the only traitor discussed in this chapter who has not, as far as we know, committed other capital crimes. Compared to West, or Christie, or Greene, Bowen is also idiosyncratic in her understatement of the threat of the political death penalty. In keeping with the subtlety of his manipulation of Stella, Harrison does not explicitly threaten Robert Kelway with the death penalty, instead using a common euphemism in explaining the stakes involved: 'Now the point is, he's being given rope', suggesting, of course, the idiom 'give a man enough rope and he'll hang himself'.[87] Bowen presents Kelway's drive towards Germany as a kind of death wish: he thinks of the possibility of a German victory as 'the conclusion', rather than a beginning.[88] Kelway's death is a possible suicide, 'a fall or leap from the roof' to escape the death penalty.[89] For other critics, including Faragher, Kelway's death by extrajudicial execution is also a possible reading of Bowen's text: 'Robert dies mysteriously while leaving Stella's flat—whether by suicide or at an agent's hand remains unclear'.[90]

Indeed, if we remember Bowen's interpretation in her BBC broadcast that most traitors are 'bordering on the insane' while still having 'the whole machinery', Kelway's death by accident or suicide in the novel is not so much an escape from punishment as a likely symptom of his imbalance and pathology, and the perversity of his love for Stella.[91] Further, because the novel is written later in the 1940s, we must consider Bowen's awareness of the post-war extrajudicial punishment and executions of collaborators in continental Europe which often targeted women like Stella whose loyalties had been compromised.[92] Nevertheless she does, as Garden points out, face a trial of sorts at Kelway's inquest, which becomes an 'inquest into Stella's moral character [which] actually operates as a trial for her sexuality, whereby her political morality becomes conflated with her sexual activities': she argues that 'parallels to the Casement trial seem palpable in this scene'.[93] Stella's eventual response to the aftermath of Kelway's death is to plan the kind of convenient cousin-marriage that ruined the lives of the former owners of Mount Morris and, simultaneously, to continue to deliberately court death in the Blitz. While Bowen keeps melodrama to a minimum in her representation of wartime treason, her oblique references to insanity, torture, execution and extrajudicial killing ensure that the novel is a reflection of the fates of those executed under the Treachery Act 1940 and the Treason Act 1945.

The End of the Death Penalty?

A change in public mood around the political death penalty is reflected in the fact that the executions of William Joyce and Theodore Schurch at Wandsworth and Pentonville on 3 and 4 January 1946 were the last executions for crimes other than murder which took place in Britain; Joyce was the last execution for treason and Schurch for treachery. It is also noteworthy that prison doctors after World War II found some of those prosecuted under the Treachery Act but not executed, such as Dorothy

O'Grady, to be suffering from intense psychological problems, proving the value of these literary interventions into a public debate about treason and mental illness.[94] From this date onwards, while treason would technically remain a capital crime (until 1998), only executions for murder would be carried out between 1946 and the abolition of the death penalty in 1965. The lack of sustained consideration given to the political death penalty by the Gowers Commission, however cynical in its repression of recent history, also reflects a sense that the conversation had genuinely moved on and that these executions for treason and treachery would not be repeated in British post-war life.

At the same time, this change of opinion was limited to treason. Indeed, in the texts we have examined in this chapter, while the political death penalty has been assailed from several directions, a sense of the natural justice of capital punishment in cases of murder remained largely unchallenged during wartime and its immediate aftermath. Although the abolition of capital punishment had been a long-term Labour policy,[95] the 1945 Labour government failed to follow through on its aims for abolition.[96] Lizzie Seal has recently examined how public attitudes to the death penalty in relation to murder hardened because of World War II, as reflected in individual letters to the Home Secretary which express strong support for the punishment.[97] The Nuremberg Trials were also a factor. Bailey describes how Sir Hartley Shawcross, the chief prosecutor at Nuremberg, though a Labour politician and a penal reformer associated with the Howard League from the 1920s onwards, would state his belief that the death penalty was justified in the case of Nazi war criminals.[98] This was how the Gowers Commission, which Bowen was part of, came to be explicitly prohibited from recommending the abolition of the death penalty, leading to a report that is complacent, or at least resigned. Similarly, the Universal Declaration of Human Rights in 1948 asserted the right to life in a way that left the principle of capital punishment untouched.

This book's natural end is 1950. In the aftermath of World War II, according to some definitions, we would see a definitive end of the first phase of psychoanalysis, of the Golden Age of crime fiction and of the modernist literary movement. Many writers important for this project would either die or cease writing during the conflict, including Sigmund Freud, James Joyce and Dorothy L. Sayers and although others including Theodor Reik, Agatha Christie and Richard Wright would produce more texts their impact on their culture was reduced. New activist literature about capital punishment would be produced by authors such as Brendan

Behan (*The Quare Fellow*, 1954), Arthur Koestler (*Reflections on Hanging*, 1956), Truman Capote (*In Cold Blood*, 1966) in ways that continued and changed the conversation I have analysed here. However, beyond this point, Anglophone cultural responses to the death penalty would diverge, with the US moving towards retention of the death penalty, largely due to the development of the lethal injection, and, with some complexities addressed above and at the end of Chaps. 6 and 7, Britain and Ireland progressing towards its abolition. At the time of writing, according to Amnesty International's most recent report, the death penalty exists in practice in Afghanistan, Antigua and Barbuda, Bahamas, Bahrain, Bangladesh, Barbados, Belarus, Belize, Botswana, Chad, China, Comoros, Cuba, the Democratic Republic of the Congo, Dominica, Egypt, Equatorial Guinea, Ethiopia, Gambia, Guyana, India, Indonesia, Iran, Iraq, Jamaica, Japan, Jordan, Kuwait, Lebanon, Lesotho, Libya, Malaysia, Nigeria, North Korea (Democratic People's Republic of Korea), Oman, Pakistan, Palestine, Qatar, Saint Kitts and Nevis, Saint Lucia, Saint Vincent and the Grenadines, Saudi Arabia, Singapore, Somalia, South Sudan, Sudan, Syria, Taiwan, Thailand, Trinidad and Tobago, Uganda, United Arab Emirates, the US, Vietnam, Yemen and Zimbabwe.[99] I am grateful to activists from the rights charities Amnesty and Reprieve for their perspective on my research project in the early days of its development.

Notes

1. Jacques Derrida, *The Death Penalty: Volume I*, trans. by Peggy Kamuf, Chicago: University of Chicago Press, 2014, 10.
2. Kristine A. Miller, *British Literature of the Blitz: Fighting the People's War*, Houndsmills: Palgrave Macmillan, 2009, 24.
3. Because the S-Plan is beyond the scope of my chapter, for more information see, for example, Mo Moulton, *Ireland and the Irish in Interwar England*, Cambridge: Cambridge University Press, 2014, 306–329.
4. Again, see Moulton, *Ireland and the Irish*, 306–329.
5. David Doyle, 'Republicans, Martyrology, and the Death Penalty in Britain and Ireland, 1939–1990', *Journal of British Studies*, 54 (2015): 703–722 (704).
6. Moulton, *Ireland and the Irish*, 2.
7. Shoshana Felman, *The Juridical Unconscious: Trials and Traumas in the Twentieth Century*, Cambridge, MA, and London: Harvard University Press, 2002, 57.

8. Derrida, *The Death Penalty: Volume II* ed. by Geoffrey Bennington and Marc Crépon/trans. by Elizabeth Rottenberg, Chicago: University of Chicago Press, 2017, 188.
9. On late modernism's politics of violence, see Allan Hepburn, *Intrigue: Espionage and Culture*, Yale: Yale University Press, 2005; Lisa Fluet, 'Hit-Man Modernism', *Bad Modernisms* ed. by Douglas Mao and Rebecca L. Walkowitz, Durham and London: Duke University Press, 2006: 269–297; Matthew Levay, 'Cases of Identity: Late Modernism and the Art of Crime', *Violent Minds: Modernism and the Criminal*, Cambridge: Cambridge University Press, 2019: 169–214.
10. The only exception to this rule I can think of is Greene's Anna Hilfe.
11. A. W. Brian Simpson, 'The Invention of Trials in Camera in Security Cases', *The Trial in History Volume II: Domestic and international trials, 1700–2000*, Manchester: Manchester University Press, 2003: 76–106 (95).
12. Hansard, 'Treason Bill', House of Commons Debate, 11th June 1945 Vol. 411 cc1393-8.
13. Simpson, 'The Invention of Trials', 96.
14. Mr. A Pierrepoint, 'MINUTES OF EVIDENCE TAKEN BEFORE THE ROYAL COMMISSION ON CAPITAL PUNISHMENT: TWENTY-EIGHTH DAY AND TWENTY-NINTH DAY', London: His Majesty's Stationery Office, 1951, 8404–8410. The inquest records show no trace of the traumatic execution that Pierrepoint recalled in his official evidence, suggesting deliberate suppression (The National Archives, PCOM 9/909).
15. As we saw in Chap. 3, Pierrepoint would also feel a sense of anxiety and constraint in describing his work because women had been appointed to the Gowers Commission.
16. 'TREACHERY BILL', Hansard, House of Commons Debate, 22nd May 1940 Vol. 361 cc185-95
17. See, for example, 'TREASON BILL', Hansard, House of Lords Debate, 30th May 1945, Vol. 136, 272–273 and 'TREASON BILL' Hansard, House of Commons Debate, 11th June 1945 Vol. 411, 1395–1396.
18. Anon. 'German Spy Shot: Meteorologist with Radio Set', *The Manchester Guardian*, August 16th 1941, 8.
19. Rebecca West, *The Meaning of Treason*, London: The Reprint Society, 1952, 6.
20. Eva Horn, *The Secret War: Treason, Espionage, and Modern Fiction*, trans. by Geoffrey Winthrop-Young, Evanston: Northwestern University Press, 2013, 75.
21. For a full picture of what participation in a guerrilla policing campaign might have meant for William Joyce, see D. M. Leeson's *The Black and Tans: British Police and Auxiliaries in the Irish War of Independence, 1920–1921*, Oxford: Oxford University Press, 2011.

22. West, *The Meaning of Treason*, 59.
23. West, *The Meaning of Treason*, 146–147.
24. West, *The Meaning of Treason*, 59.
25. Both Lucy McDiarmid (*The Irish Art of Controversy*, Ithaca: Cornell University Press, 2005, 249) and Alison Garden (*The Literary Afterlives of Roger Casement, 1899–2016*, Liverpool: Liverpool University Press, 2020, 129–130) have briefly addressed this allusion to Casement in Christie, but it has not previously been closely analysed.
26. Anon. 'New Mystery Stories', *New York Times*, 22nd June 1941, 17.
27. M. Willson Disher, 'Master Spies', *The Times Literary Supplement*, 29th November 1941, 589.
28. Disher, 'Master Spies', 589.
29. Miller, *British Literature of the Blitz*, 118.
30. Agatha Christie, *N or M?*, London: Harper Collins, 2015, 59.
31. Agatha Christie *N or M?*, 60–62.
32. Agatha Christie *N or M?*, 97–98.
33. Christie, *N or M?*, 147.
34. Christie, *N or M?*, 148.
35. Christie, *N or M?*, 148–149.
36. Christie, *N or M?*, 240–241.
37. Christie, *N or M?*, 217.
38. Christie, *N or M?*, 210–221.
39. Christie, *N or M?*, 134–135.
40. Christie, *N or M?*, 221–223.
41. Michael G. Brennan, *Graham Greene: Fictions, Faith and Authorship*, London: Continuum, 2010, xii and 75. Brennan argues that the treacherous Dr Forester in *The Ministry of Fear* is partially based on Kenneth Richmond.
42. Graham Greene, *Why Do I Write: An Exchange of Views Between Elizabeth Bowen, Graham Greene and V. S. Pritchett*, London: Percival Marshall, 1948, 47.
43. Greene, *Why Do I Write*, 47–48.
44. Brennan, *Graham Greene*, 74–81, 75.
45. William Du Bois, 'Graham Greene's Dark Magic: *The Ministry of Fear*', *The New York Times*, 23rd May 1942, 3.
46. R. D. Charques, 'Film in the Cake', *The Times Literary Supplement*, 29th May 1943, 257.
47. Graham Greene, *The Ministry of Fear*, London: Vintage, 2001, 120.
48. Greene, *Ministry of Fear*, 120
49. Newspaper reports of war-time executions frequently note a fear of 'bogus refugees' who were really spies (See, for example, the Waldberg/Lassudry file, The National Archives, PCOM 9/891).

50. Greene, *Ministry of Fear*, 132.
51. Greene, *Ministry of Fear*, 203
52. Charques, 'Film in the Cake', 257.
53. Miller, *British Literature of the Blitz*, 120–121.
54. Brian Diemert, *Graham Greene's Thrillers and the 1930s*, Montreal & Kingston: McGill-Queen's University Press, 1996, 172.
55. Greene, *Ministry of Fear*, 176
56. Greene, *Ministry of Fear*, 215.
57. For a rigorous investigation of the British torture of PoWs during World War II, see Helen Fry, *The London Cage: The Secret History of Britain's World War II Interrogation Centre*, New Haven and London: Yale University Press, 2017.
58. Greene, *The Ministry of Fear*, 213
59. West, *The Meaning of Treason*, 158–159 and 164–165.
60. Elizabeth Bowen, *'Notes on Eire': espionage reports to Winston Churchill, 1940–1942*, ed. by Jack Lane and Brendan, Clifford Aubane: Aubane Historical Society, 2009.
61. My reading of *The Heat of the Day* dovetails substantially, though our companion texts and overall framework are different, with Alison Garden's reading of the novel in her Casement book, which appeared after the manuscript of this book was finalised (*The Literary Afterlives of Roger Casement*, 146–154).
62. Elizabeth Bowen, 'Conversation on Traitors', *Listening In: Broadcasts, Speeches, and Interviews by Elizabeth Bowen*, ed. by Allan Hepburn, Edinburgh: Edinburgh University Press, 2010: 304–322 (304).
63. Bowen, 'Conversation on Traitors', 304–305.
64. Bowen, 'Conversation on Traitors', 311.
65. Bowen, 'Conversation on Traitors', 308.
66. Bowen, 'Conversation on Traitors', 314.
67. A. David Moody, *Ezra Pound: Poet A Portrait of the Man and his Work, III The Tragic Years 1939–1972*, Oxford: Oxford University Press, 2015, 187–188.
68. Bowen, 'Frankly Speaking', *Listening In: Broadcasts, Speeches, and Interviews by Elizabed Bowen*, ed. by Allan Hepburn, Edinburgh: Edinburgh University Press, 2010: 323–343 (336).
69. Bowen, 'Frankly Speaking', 337–338.
70. Alice S. Morris, 'Miss Bowen Illumines The Landscape of War', *New York Times*, 20th February 1949, 1.
71. Francis Wyndham, 'The Climate of Treason', *Times Literary Supplement*, 5th March 1949, 152.
72. Bowen, *The Heat of the Day*, 34.
73. Bowen, *The Heat of the Day*, 39.
74. Megan Faragher 'The form of modernist propaganda in Elizabeth Bowen's *The Heat of the Day*', *Textual Practice*, Vol. 27, No. 1 (2013): 49–68 (56).

75. Bowen, 'Frankly Speaking', 327.
76. Thomas S. Davis, 'Elizabeth Bowen's war gothic', *Textual Practice*, Vol. 27, No. 1 (2013): 29–47.
77. Bowen, *The Heat of the Day*, 195.
78. Adam Piette, *Imagination at war: British fiction and poetry, 1939–1945*, London: Papermac, 1995, 172.
79. Hepburn, *Intrigue: Espionage and Culture*, Yale: Yale University Press, 2005, 159.
80. Bowen, *The Heat of the Day*, 260 and 266.
81. Bowen, *The Heat of the Day*, 264.
82. Bowen, *The Heat of the Day*, 262.
83. Bowen, *The Heat of the Day*, 264.
84. Bowen, *The Heat of the Day*, 265.
85. Bowen, *The Heat of the Day*, 262.
86. For a full account of the role of psychiatric medicine during WWII, especially psychiatrists' involvement in 'battle schools', see Joanna Bourke, 'Psychiatry, Hate Training, and the Second World War', *Journal of Social History*, Vol. 52, No. 1 (2018): 101–120.
87. Bowen, *The Heat of the Day*, 33.
88. Bowen, *The Heat of the Day*, 264.
89. Bowen, *The Heat of the Day*, 281.
90. Faragher, 'The form of modernist propaganda in Elizabeth Bowen's *The Heat of the Day*', 57.
91. Bowen, 'Conversation on Traitors', 314.
92. Hepburn, *Intrigue: Espionage and Culture*, 141–142.
93. Garden, *The Literary Afterlives of Roger Casement*, 148.
94. See The National Archives, 'O'Grady, Dorothy Pamela' PCOM 9/1497 and PCOM 9/1497/1 'Psychological report dated 16/6/1944'.
95. In 1927, the Labour party had issued a petition which called capital punishment 'a relic of barbarism', the majority of the Labour leadership was supportive of abolition in the 1928 debate and at the 1934 party conference resolution was passed to abolish the death penalty.
96. Victor Bailey, 'The Shadow of the Gallows: The Death Penalty and the British Labour Government, 1945–1951', *Law and History Review*, Vol. 18, No. 2 (2000): 305–349 (309).
97. Seal, 'Perceptions of safety, fear and social change in the public's pro-death penalty discourse in mid twentieth-century Britain', *Crime, Histoire & Sociétés/Crime, History & Societies*, Vol. 21, No. 1 (2017) n.pag. paragraphs 1–40.
98. Bailey, 'The Shadow of the Gallows', Note 45, 323.
99. Amnesty International Global Report: Death Sentences and Executions 2019, 'Annex II: Abolitionist and Retentionist Countries as of 31 December 2019': https://www.amnestyusa.org/wp-content/uploads/

2020/03/Amnesty-Death-Sentences-and-Executions-2019.pdf [Accessed 27th July 2020]. The report also lists separately those countries which allow the death penalty only under military law or in exceptional circumstances (Brazil, Burkina Faso, Chile, El Salvador, Guatemala, Israel, Kazakhstan, Peru) and countries which retain the death penalty but have not executed anyone for 10 years (Algeria, Brunei Darussalam, Cameroon, Central African Republic, Eritrea, Eswatini (former Swaziland), Ghana, Grenada, Kenya, Laos, Liberia, Malawi, Maldives, Mali, Mauritania, Morocco/Western Sahara, Myanmar, Niger, Papua New Guinea, Russian Federation, Sierra Leone, South Korea (Republic of Korea), Sri Lanka, Tajikistan, Tanzania, Tonga, Tunisia and Zambia).

Bibliography

Archival Sources

Imperial War Museum

A P Roberts Diary Documents 4616.
Private Papers of E. Beer 695.
Private Papers of A. Smith Box 15/10/01.
W Kimberley papers, Documents 7017.

National Library of Ireland

Joseph Plunkett, 'Letter by Plunkett to his fiancé Grace Gifford', National Library of Ireland, NLI.MS.20.858.

The British Library

Three leaflets ([A]-C) issued by the Society for the Abolition of Capital Punishment, Indian and Colonial Committee], Society for the Abolition of Capital Punishment, Indian and Colonial Committee, [London], [1909], The British Library, General Reference Collection 8425.h.(13–15).

K. Ebury, *Modern Literature and the Death Penalty, 1890–1950*, Palgrave Studies in Literature, Culture and Human Rights, https://doi.org/10.1007/978-3-030-52750-1

The National Archives: Prison Commission and Home Office Papers

'Uniform pattern for all prisons: Execution Arrangements', Registered Papers, PCOM 8/185.

'Execution arrangements at Pentonville to be standardised', Registered Papers, PCOM 8/186.

'Executioner James Berry', Registered Papers, PCOM 8/191.

'Executions: parliamentary questions and debate arising from allegations about the execution of Mrs Edith Thompson', Registered Papers, PCOM 9/1983.

'Instructions to Governors of prisons attending inquests on executed prisoners', Registered Papers, PCOM 8/214.

'Letters written or received by prisoners', Registered Papers, PCOM 8/203.

'Previously closed extract: Psychological report [on Dorothy O'Grady] dated 16/6/1944', Registered Papers, PCOM 9/1497/1.

'Pierrepoint, Albert: former executioner; articles in Sunday Empire News; decision not to prosecute', Registered Papers, PCOM 9/2024.

'O'Grady Dorothy Pamela: convicted at Winchester', Registered Papers, PCOM 9/1497.

'Record of execution: 3rd August 1916 [Sir Roger Casement]', Registered Papers, PCOM 2331.

'Surveillance by prison officers: execution arrangements', Registered Papers, PCOM 8/200.

'Waldberg Jose: convicted at Central Criminal Court', Registered Papers, PCOM 9/891.

'Richter Karel Richard: convicted at Central Criminal Court', Registered Papers, PCOM 9/909.

Home Office Papers

'CAPITAL PUNISHMENT: Execution by hanging: procedure to be followed', Registered Papers, HO 45/25843.

'CAPITAL PUNISHMENT: Proposed abolition: comparison with countries where capital punishment already abolished; letters from members of the public', Registered Papers, HO 45/25084.

'CRIMINAL CASES: Beard, Arthur: convicted at Chester on 31st October 1919 for murder and sentenced to death (commuted), Registered Papers, HO 144/20991.

'TREASON: Sir Roger Casement: Miss Agnes O'Farrelly requests letter written by Casement shortly before execution: refused', Registered Papers, HO 144/1637/311643/182.

'TREASON: Sir Roger Casement: Mrs Green again wishes to visit Casement; his attempted suicide and subsequent supervision', Registered Papers, HO 144/1636/311643/7A.

'TREASON: Sir Roger Casement: Post-mortem examination of Casement's body: evidence of alleged homosexual activities', Registered Papers, HO 144/1637/311643/141.

'TREASON: Sir Roger Casement: WB Yeats urges that Casement be reprieved', Registered Papers, HO 144/1636/311643/45.

War Office Papers

'2/Lieutenant Edwin Leopold Arthur DYETT Royal Naval Division', War Office: Officers Services, First World War, Long Number Papers, WO339/87122.

'Macbride, John. Offence: Armed Rebellion', Judge Advocate General's Office: Courts Martial Proceedings and Board of General Officers' Minutes. IRELAND. FIELD GENERAL COURTS MARTIAL – CIVILIANS, WO 71/350.

'Pearse, P. H., Offence: Armed Rebellion', Judge Advocate General's Office: Courts Martial Proceedings and Board of General Officers' Minutes. IRELAND. FIELD GENERAL COURTS MARTIAL – CIVILIANS, WO71/345.

'Plunkett, Joseph. Offence: Armed Rebellion', Judge Advocate General's Office: Courts Martial Proceedings and Board of General Officers' Minutes. IRELAND. FIELD GENERAL COURTS MARTIAL – CIVILIANS, WO71/349.

Dorothy L. Sayers's Archive at Marion E. Wade Centre, Wheaton College

Sayers's correspondence, 'Capital Punishment' (1945), DLS 38, Marion E. Wade Centre, Wheaton College Dorothy L. Sayers Library. https://www.wheaton.edu/media/wade-center/files/collections/author-library-listings/Sayers_Library_20180426.pdf. [Accessed 9th August 2018].

Primary and Secondary Sources

Aberdare Committee, *Report of the Committee appointed to inquire into the Existing Practice as to carrying out of Sentences of Death, and the Causes which in several recent Cases have led either to failure or to unseemly occurrences; and to consider and report what arrangements may be adopted (without altering the existing Law) to ensure that all Executions may be carried out in a becoming manner without risk of failure or miscarriage in any respect*, London: Her Majesty's Stationery Office, 1888.

A.D. '*Flood Tide* at The Phoenix', *The Manchester Guardian,* 24th March 1938, 10.

Allen, Howard W. and Jerome M. Clubb, *Race, Class and the Death Penalty: Capital Punishment in American History*, New York: State University of New York Press, 2008.

Allen, Nicholas, *Modernism, Ireland and Civil War*, Cambridge: Cambridge University Press, 2009.

Anon. 'Athlete's Unhappy Married Life', *The Times*, 17th May 1919, 9.

Anon. 'The Case for Abolition', *The Manchester Guardian*, 17th November 1938, 14.

Anon. 'CAPITAL PUNISHMENT IN IRELAND: Strong Opposition', *The Manchester Guardian*, 7th May 1925, 9.

Anon. 'Conviction Quashed: Rex v. Beard', *The Times*, 25th November 1919.

Anon. 'The Death Penalty in the Army', *The Times*, 1st October 1917, 8.

Anon. 'Defence of the State', *Irish Independent*, 7th May 1925, 7.

Anon. 'Detective Stories', *Times*, 2nd January 1940, 3.

Anon. 'Doctor's Insanity', *The Times*, 24th January 1920, 14.

Anon. 'Electrocuting an Elephant', Edison Films No. 168, February 1903.

Anon. 'Eltham Murder Arrest', *The Daily Telegraph*, 15th February 1918, 5.

Anon. 'German Spy Shot: Meteorologist with Radio Set', *The Manchester Guardian*, 16th August 1941, 8.

Anon. 'Hangman's effects auctioned', *Manchester Evening News*, 18th April 2010 https://www.manchestereveningnews.co.uk/news/greater-manchester-news/hangmans-effects-auctioned-972869. [Accessed 13th May 2018].

Anon. 'Haunted by Ghosts of Men He Hanged', *San Francisco Call*, Vol. 86, No. 145, 23rd October 1899, 2.

Anon. 'The Haunting of Amos Lunt', *San Francisco Call*, Vol. 87, No 107, 15th September 1901a, 5.

Anon. 'The Hyde Murder Appeal', *The Observer*, 15th November 1919, 6.

Anon. 'Humour and Thrills: *The House by the River*', *The Observer*, 12th September 1920, 4.

Anon. 'Latest Works of Fiction: *The House by the River*', *The New York Times*, 11th January 1920, 69.

Anon. 'Liverpool Nurse's Death', *The Times*, 7th August 1919, 12.

Anon. 'MESSRS. METHUEN'S NEW BOOKS: *THE HOUSE BY THE RIVER*', *The Times Literary Supplement*, 23rd September 1920, 613.

Anon. 'New Mystery Stories', *New York Times*, 22nd June 1941, 17.

Anon. 'New Novels: A PIN TO SEE THE PEEPSHOW', *The Times*, 9th October 1934, 8.

———. 'Paddington Hotel Tragedy: Committal for Trial', *The Daily Telegraph*, 9th July 1920, 15.
———. 'Procedure in Courts-Martial', *The Times*, 15th March 1918a, 12.
———. 'To-night's Censored Play', *The Daily Telegraph*, 8th May 1951, 4.
———. 'Sandhills Murder', *The Daily Telegraph*, 30th March 1920, 7.
———. '*THE SECRET BATTLE*', *The Observer*, 27th July 1919, 5.
———. 'Shellshock and Desertion', *The Times*, 20th February 1918, 8.
———. 'The Slow Passing of Amos Lunt', *Sausalito News*, Vol. 17, No. 31, 31st August 1901b, 5.
———. 'Women Jurors in Tears', *The Daily Telegraph*, 11th February 1921, 7.
Babington, Anthony, *For the Sake of Example: Capital Courts-Martial 1914–1920*, London: Leo Cooper, 1983.
Bailey, Victor, 'The Shadow of the Gallows: The Death Penalty and the British Labour Government, 1945–51', *Law and History Review*, Vol. 18, No. 2 (2000): 305–349.
Baldwin, James, 'Everybody's Protest Novel', *Notes of a Native Son*, Boston: Beacon Press, 1984: 13–23.
Banner, Stuart, *The Death Penalty: An American History*, Cambridge (Mass.): Harvard University Press, 2002.
Barton, John Cyril, *Literary Executions: Capital Punishment and American Culture, 1820–1925*, Baltimore: John Hopkins University Press, 2014.
Bayard, Pierre, *Who Killed Roger Ackroyd?: The Murderer who Eluded Hercule Poirot and Deceived Agatha Christie*, trans. by Carol Cosman, London: Fourth Estate, 2000.
Beckett, Ian, Timothy Bowman and Mark Connelly, 'Citizen Soldiers: Discipline, Morale and the Experience of War', *The British Army and the First World War*, Cambridge: Cambridge University Press, 2017: 135–169.
Bell, Michael, 'Primitivism: Modernism as Anthropology', *Oxford Handbook of Modernisms*, ed. by Peter Brooker et al., Oxford: Oxford University Press, 2010: 351–367.
Benson, E. F. *The Room in the Tower and Other Stories*, London: Mills & Boon, 1912.
———. *More Spook Stories*, London: Hutchinson & Co. Ltd, 1934.
Bennett, Christopher, 'Considering Capital Punishment as a Human Interaction', *Criminal Law and Philosophy*, Vol. 7, No. 2 (2013): 367–382.
Bernthal, J. C., 'Killing Innocence: Obstructions of Justice in Late-Interwar British Crime fiction', *CLUES: A Journal of Detection*, Vol. 17, No. 2 (Fall 2019): 31–39.
Berrios, German E., *The History of Mental Symptoms: Descriptive Psychopathology Since the Nineteenth Century*, Cambridge: Cambridge University Press, 1996.
Berry, James, *My Experiences as an Executioner*, London: Peter Lund & Co, 1892.

Beirne, Piers. *Murdering Animals: Writings on Theriocide, Homicide and Nonspeciesist Criminology*, Houndsmills: Palgrave, 2018.

———. 'Is There a Progression from Animal Abuse to Interhuman Violence?', *Confronting Animal Abuse: Law, Criminology, and Human-Animal Relationships*, Lanham: Rowman & Littlefield, 2009.

———. 'Law is an Ass: Reading E.P. Evans' The Medieval Prosecution and Capital Punishment of Animals' in *Society and Animals*, Vol. 1, No. 2 (1994): 27–46.

Blanchot, Maurice, and Jacques Derrida, *The Instant of My Death/Demeure: Fiction and Testimony*, trans. by Elizabeth Rottenberg, Stanford: Stanford University Press, 2000.

Bland, Lucy, 'The Trials and Tribulations of Edith Thompson: The Capital Crime of Sexual Incitement in 1920s England', *Journal of British Studies*, Vol. 47, No. 3 (2010): 624–648.

Bogacz, Ted, 'War Neuroses and Cultural Change in England, 1914–1922: The Work of the War Office Committee of Enquiry into Shell Shock', *Journal of Contemporary History* Vol. 24 (1989): 227–256.

Bosworth, Mary, *Explaining U.S. Imprisonment*, London: Sage, 2010.

Boucicault, Dion, 'Robert Emmet' (1884), *Selected Plays of Dion Boucicault*, ed. by Colin Smythe, Washington, D.C.: The Catholic University of America Press, 1987.

Bourke, Joanna, 'Psychiatry, Hate Training, and the Second World War', *Journal of Social History*, Vol. 52, No. 1(2018): 101–120.

Bowen, Elizabeth. *Collected Stories*, London: Vintage, 1999.

———. 'Conversation on Traitors', *Listening In: Broadcasts, Speeches, and Interviews by Elizabeth Bowen*, ed. by Allan Hepburn, Edinburgh: Edinburgh University Press, 2010: 304–322.

———. 'Frankly Speaking: Interview, 1959', *Listening In: Broadcasts, Speeches, and Interviews by Elizabeth Bowen*, ed. by Allan Hepburn, Edinburgh: Edinburgh University Press, 2010: 323–343.

———. *The Heat of the Day*, London: Jonathan Cape, 1954.

———. *'Notes on Eire': espionage reports to Winston Churchill, 1940–2*, ed. by Jack Lane and Brendan Clifford, Aubane: Aubane Historical Society, 2009.

Brandon, Craig, *Murder in the Adirondacks: "An American Tragedy" Revisited*, Utica: North Country Books, 1986.

Brennan, Michael G., *Graham Greene: Fictions, Faith and Authorship*, London: Continuum, 2010.

Bright, Brittain, 'The Unshockable Mrs. Bradley: Sex and Sexuality in the Work of Gladys Mitchell', *Murder in the Closet: Essays on Queer Clues in Crime Fiction Before Stonewall*, ed. by Curtis Evans, Jefferson: McFarland & Company, 2017: 78–92.

Brooks, Peter, *Troubling Confessions: Speaking Guilt in Law and Literature*, Chicago and London: University of Chicago Press, 2000.

Bryan, Patricia L., 'Stories in Fiction and in Fact: Susan Glaspell's "A Jury of Her Peers" and the 1901 Murder Trial of Margaret Hossack' *Stanford Law Review*, Vol. 49, No. 6 (1997): 1293–1363.

Burt, E. S., 'The Autobiographical Subject and the Death Penalty', *The Oxford Literary Review*, Vol. 35, No. 2 (2013): 165–187.

Cadogan, Edward, *The Roots of Evil: Being a Treatise on the Methods of Dealing with Crime and the Criminal During the Eighteenth and Nineteenth Centuries in Relation to Those of a More Enlighted Age*, London: John Murray, 1937.

Canuel, Mark, *The Shadow of Death: Literature, Romanticism, and the Subject of Punishment*, Princeton: Princeton University Press, 2007.

Carroll, Sydney W., 'ANOTHER YOUNG DRAMATIST: MOTIVELESS MURDER: "ROPE" A REAL TRAGEDY', *The Daily Telegraph*, 9th May 1929, 17.

Carswell, Donald (ed.), *Ronald True: Notable British Trials Series*, London: William Hodge and Company, 1925.

Casement, Roger. 'Letter from Roger Casement to Nina Casement, 25th July 1916' *Letters of 1916*, ed. by Susan Schreibman, Maynooth University, 2016. Website. [Accessed 20th June 2018].

———. *Roger Casement's Diaries 1910: The Black and the White*, ed. by Roger Sawyer, London: Pimlico, 1997.

The Catholic Bulletin. Vol. VI, No. VII (July 1916a).

———. Vol. VI, No. XII (Dec. 1916b).

Cecil, Hugh, *Flowers of Battle: How Britain Wrote the Great War* South Royalton, Vermont: Steerforth Press, 1996: 89–106.

Charques, R. D., 'Film in the Cake', *The Times Literary Supplement*, 29th May 1943, 257.

Cheney, Lynne, 'Joseph Conrad's *The Secret Agent* and Graham Greene's *It's a Battlefield*: A Study in Structural Meaning', *Modern Fiction Studies*, Vol. 16, No. 2 (1970): 117–131.

Christie, Agatha. *And Then There Were None*, New York: Harper Collins, 2011.

———. *Curtain: Poirot's Last Case*, London: Harper Collins, 2002a.

———. *Five Little Pigs*, London: Harper Collins, 2007.

———. *The Murder of Roger Ackroyd*, London: Harper Collins, 2002.

———. *N or M?*, London: Harper Collins, 2015.

———. *Towards Zero*, London: Harper Collins, 2002.

Clare, Anne, *Unlikely Rebels: The Gifford Girls and the Fight for Irish Freedom*, Cork: Mercier Press, 2011.

Clarke, James W., 'Without Fear or Shame: Lynching, Capital Punishment and the Subculture of Violence in the American South', *British Journal of Political Science*, Vol. 28, No. 2 (1998): 269–289.

Clifford, Carrie Williams, 'The Black Draftee from Dixie', *Negro: An Anthology*, ed. by Nancy Cunard, New York: Frederick Unger, 1970, 261.

Cobain, Ian, *The History Thieves: Secrets, Lies and the Shaping of a Modern Nation*, London: Granta, 2016.

Cole, Sarah, *At the Violet Hour: Modernism and Violence in England and Ireland*, New York: Oxford University Press, 2012.

Cole, Simon A., and Michael C. Campbell, 'From subhumans to superhumans: Criminals in the evolutionary hierarchy, or what became of Lombroso's atavistic criminals?', *The Cesare Lombroso Handbook*, ed. by Paul Knepper and P.J. Ystehede, Abingdon: Routledge, 2013: 153–154.

Coleridge, Stephen. *Vivisection: A Heartless Science*, London: John Lane The Bodley Head, 1916.

Connelly, Kelly C., 'From Detective Fiction to Detective Literature: Psychology in the Novels of Dorothy L. Sayers and Margaret Millar', *Clues*, Vol. 25, No. 3 (2007): 35–47.

Conrad, Kathryn. 'Queer Treasons: Homosexuality and Irish National Identity', *Cultural Studies*, Vol. 15, No. 1 (2001): 124–137.

———. 'Foreign Bodies: Representations of Homosexuality and the Irish Body Politic', *Locked in the Family Cell: Gender, Sexuality, and Political Agency in Irish National Discourse*, Madison: University of Wisconsin Press, 2004: 21–63.

Corns, Cathryn, and John Hughes-Wilson, *Blindfold and Alone: British Military Executions in the Great War*, London: Cassell, 2001.

Cox, Caroline, 'Invisible Wounds: The American Legion, Shell-Shocked Veterans, and American Society, 1919–1924', *Traumatic Pasts: History, Psychiatry, and Trauma in the Modern Age, 1870–1930*, ed. by Mark S. Micale and Paul Lerner, Cambridge: Cambridge University Press, 2001: 280–306.

Crofts, Freeman Wills, *Antidote to Venom*, London: The British Library, 2015.

Cronin, Michael G., 'Pain, Pleasure and Revolution: The Body in Roger Casement's Writings', *The Body in Pain in Irish Literature and Culture* ed. by Fionnuala Dillane, Naomi McAreavey and Emilie Pine, Houndsmills: Palgrave, 2016: 135–148.

Cunard, Nancy. *Negro: An Anthology*, New York: Frederick Unger, 1970.

———. 'Southern Sheriff', *Negro: An Anthology*, New York: Frederick Unger, 1970b: 265–266.

Cutler, James, *Lynch-law: an investigation into the history of lynching in the United States*, New York: Longmans, Green, and co., 1905.

Darrow, Clarence. *An Eye for an Eye*, New York: Duffield and Co, 1920.

———. 'Attorney Clarence Darrow's Plea for Mercy in the Franks Case', *Attorney Clarence Darrow's Plea for Mercy and Prosecutor Robert E. Crowe's Demand for the Death Penalty in the Loeb-Leopold Case – The Crime of a Century*, Chicago: Wilson Publishing Company, 1924.

———. *Crime and Criminals: An Address Delivered to the Prisoners in the Chicago County Jail*, Chicago: Charles H. Kerr & Company, 1910.

Dailey, Anne C. 'Preface: Special Issue: Legal Analysis', *American Imago*, Vol. 64, No. 3 (2007): 291–295.

———. *Law and the Unconscious: A Psychoanalytic Perspective*, Yale: Yale University Press, 2017.

Davies, Christie, 'The British State and the Power of Life and Death' in *The Boundaries of the State in Modern Britain* ed. by S. J. D. Green and R. C. Whiting, Cambridge: Cambridge University Press, 2002: 341–375.

Davies, Owen, and Francesca Matteoni, *Executing Magic in the Modern Era: Criminal Bodies and the Gallows in Popular Medicine*, Houndsmills: Palgrave, 2017.

Davis, Thomas S., 'Elizabeth Bowen's war gothic', *Textual Practice*, Vol. 27, No. 1 (2013): 29–47.

Derrida, Jacques. *The Beast and the Sovereign Volume I*, trans. by Geoffrey Bennington, Chicago and London: University of Chicago Press, 2009.

———. *The Death Penalty: Volume I* trans. by Peggy Kamuf, Chicago: University of Chicago Press, 2014.

———. *The Death Penalty: Volume II* ed. by Geoffrey Bennington and Marc Crépon/trans. by Elizabeth Rottenberg, Chicago: University of Chicago Press, 2017.

Deane, Vincent, 'Bywaters and the Original Crime', *European Joyce Studies 4: Finnegans Wake: Teems of Times*, ed. by Andrew Treip, Amsterdam: Rodopi, 1994: 165–179.

Dernley, Syd, with David Newman, *The Hangman's Tale: Memoirs of a Public Executioner*, London: Robert Hale, 1989.

Diemert, Brian, *Graham Greene's Thrillers and the 1930s*, Montreal & Kingston: McGill-Queen's University Press, 1996.

Disher, M. Willson, 'Master Spies', *The Times Literary Supplement*, 29th November 1941, 589.

Doyle, David, 'Republicans, Martyrology, and the Death Penalty in Britain and Ireland, 1939–1990', *Journal of British Studies*, Vol. 54, No. 3 (2015): 703–722.

———. 'The Death Penalty in Post-Independence Ireland', *The Journal of Legal History*, Vol. 33, No. 1 (2012): 65–91.

Doyle, David, and Ian O'Donnell. 'A Family Affair: English Hangmen and a Dublin Jail, 1923–54', *New Hibernia Review*, Vol. 18, No. 8 (2014): 101–118.

Du Bois, William, 'Graham Greene's Dark Magic: *The Ministry of Fear*', *The New York Times*, 23rd May 1942, 3.

Duffy, George Gavan, 'Letter from George Gavan Duffy to Messrs Corrigan & Corrigan, 4th October 1916' Letters of 1916, ed. by Susan Schreibman, Maynooth University: 2016. Website. [Accessed 19th June 2018].

Dukore, Bernard F. *Crimes and Punishments and Bernard Shaw*, Houndsmills: Palgrave, 2017.

Eburne, Jonathan, *Surrealism and the Art of Crime*, Ithaca: Cornell University Press, 2008.

Ebury, Katherine, "Nothing in the world would save me from the gallows": O'Nolan and the death penalty', in Ruben Borg and Paul Fagan (eds.), *Flann O'Brien: Gallows Humour*, Cork: Cork University Press, 2020.

Editor, 'Review: *The Upas Tree* by Robert McMurdy', *The Virginia Law Register*, Vol. 19, No. 2 (1913): 160.

Eliot, T. S., 'Letter to the Editor', *The Daily Mail*, 8th January 1923, 8.

Elliott, Robert G. and Albert R. Beatty, *Agent of Death: The Memoirs of an Executioner*, London: John Long, 1940.

Ellis, John, *Diary of a Hangman*, London: Forum Press, 1996.

Emsley, Clive, 'Violent crime in England in 1919: post-war anxieties and press narratives', *Continuity and Change*, Vol. 23, No. 1 (2008): 173–195.

Emmet, Robert, 'Letter to Sarah Curran', *Women of 'Ninety-Eight* ed. by Helena Walsh Concannon, Dublin: M. H. Gill and Son, 1919.

Evans, E. P. *Evolutional Ethics and Animal Psychology*, New York: D. Appleton and Company, 1898.

———. *The Criminal Prosecution and Capital Punishment of Animals*, London: Heinemann, 1906.

Evers, Kai, *Violent Modernists: The Aesthetics of Destruction in Twentieth-Century German Literature*, Evanston: Northwestern University Press, 2013.

Faragher, Megan, 'The form of modernist propaganda in Elizabeth Bowen's *The Heat of the Day*', *Textual Practice*, Vol. 27, No. 1 (2013): 49–68.

Fanon, Frantz, 'The Fact of Blackness', *Theories of Race and Racism: A Reader*, ed. by Les Back and John Solomos, London: Routledge, 2000: 257–266.

Shoshana Felman, *The Juridical Unconscious: Trials and Traumas in the Twentieth Century*, Cambridge, Mass., and London: Harvard University Press, 2002.

Ferguson, Christine, 'Eugenics and the afterlife: Lombroso, Doyle, and spiritualist purification of the race', *Journal of Victorian Culture*, Vol. 12, No. 1 (2007): 64–85.

Fielding, Steve, *Pierrepoint: A Family of Executioners* (John Blake 2008, ebook, n.p.).

Foucault, Michel. *Discipline and Punish: The Birth of the Prison*, New York: Vintage Books, 1995.

———. *The History of Sexuality Volume 1*, trans. Robert Hurley, New York: Vintage, 1978.

Frazer, James, *Folklore in the Old Testament: Stories in Comparative Religion, Legend and Law*, London: Macmillan, 1919.

Freeman, R. Austin, 'The Art of the Detective Story', *Nineteenth century and after*, May 1924, 718.

Freud, Sigmund. 'Beyond the Pleasure Principle' (1920), *The Standard Edition of the Complete Psychological Works of Sigmund Freud, Volume XVIII*, trans. by Strachey et al., London: Vintage, 2001: 7–66.

———. *Civilization and its Discontents* (1930 [1929]), *The Standard Edition of the Complete Psychological Works of Sigmund Freud Volume* XXI (1927–1931), trans. by Strachey et al., London: Hogarth/Vintage, 2001: 59–148.

———. 'Dostoyevsky and Parricide', *The Standard Edition of the Complete Psychological Works of Sigmund Freud Volume* XXI (1927–1931), trans. by Strachey et al., London: Hogarth/Vintage, 2001: 175–196.

———. 'The Economic Problem of Masochism', *The Standard Edition of the Complete Psychological Works of Sigmund Freud, Volume XIX*, trans. by Strachey et al., London: Vintage, 2001: 159–172.

———. 'Psycho-Analysis and the Establishment of Facts in Legal Proceedings' (1906), *The Standard Edition of the Complete Psychological Works of Sigmund Freud, Volume IX*, trans. by Strachey et al., London: Vintage, 2001: 97–114.

———. *Totem and Taboo (1913), The Standard Edition of the Complete Psychological Works of Sigmund Freud, Volume XIII*, trans. by Strachey et al., London: Vintage, 2001: ix–164.

———. "Three Essays on the Theory of Sexuality', *The Standard Edition of the Complete Psychological Works of Sigmund Freud, Volume VII (1901–1905)*, trans. by Strachey et al., London: Vintage, 2001: 125–172.

———. 'Thoughts for the Times on War and Death', *On Creativity and the Unconscious*, ed. by Benjamin Nelson, New York: Harper & Row, 1965: 222–23.

Ferguson, Rex, 'Personal Impressions: Fingerprints, Freud and Conrad', *New Formations: a journal of culture/theory/politics*, 79 (2013): 43–62.

Fluet, Lisa, 'Hit-Man Modernism', *Bad Modernisms* ed. by Douglas Mao and Rebecca L. Walkowitz, Durham and London: Duke University Press, 2006: 269–297.

Fortune, T. Thomas, 'That Other Golgotha', *Negro: An Anthology*, ed. by Nancy Cunard, New York: Frederick Unger, 1970: 261.

Foster, Gavin, *The Irish Civil War and Society: Politics, Class and Conflict*, Houndsmills: Palgrave, 2015.

Foster, R. F. *Vivid Faces: The Revolutionary Generation in Ireland, 1890–1923*, London: Penguin, 2015.

———. *W. B. Yeats: A Life II: The Arch-Poet 1915–1939*, Oxford: Oxford University Press, 2003.

Fraser, James, *Joyce and Betrayal*, Houndsmills: Palgrave, 2016.

Friedman, Ariela, 'Dorothy Sayers and the Case of the Shell-Shocked Detective', *Partial Answers*, Vol 8. No. 2 (2010): 365–387.

Frosh, Stephen, 'Psychoanalysis, colonialism, racism', *Journal of Theoretical and Philosophical Psychology*, Vol. 33, No. 3 (2013): 141–154.

Fry, Helen, *The London Cage: The Secret History of Britain's World War II Interrogation Centre*, New Haven and London: Yale University Press, 2017.

Garcia, Jay, *Psychology Comes to Harlem: Rethinking the Race Question in Twentieth-Century America*, Baltimore, Maryland: John Hopkins University Press, 2012.

Garden, Alison, *The Literary Afterlives of Roger Casement, 1899–2016*, Liverpool: Liverpool University Press, 2020.

Garrigan Mattar, Sinéad, *Primitivism, Science and the Irish Revival*, Oxford: Oxford University Press, 2004.

Gates, Jay Paul, and Nicole Marafioti, *Capital and Corporal Punishment in Anglo-Saxon England*, Martlesham: Boydell Press, 2014.

Glaspell, Susan, 'A Jury of Her Peers', *Her America: "A Jury of Her Peers" and Other Stories*, ed. by Patricia L. Bryan and Martha C. Carpentier, Iowa City: University of Iowa Press, 2010: 81–102.

Gopal, Priyamvada, *Insurgent Empire: Anticolonial Resistance and British Dissent*, London, Verso, 2019.

Gould, Gerald, 'New Novels: A ROUND DOZEN', *The Observer*, 21st October 1934, 6.

Gowers et al. *Royal Commission on Capital Punishment, 1949–1953, REPORT, Presented to Parliament by Command of Her Majesty September 1953* (also known as Gowers Commission Report), London: Her Majesty's Stationery Office, 1953.

———. *Gowers Commission: Minutes of Evidence*, The National Archives, PCOM 9/1773.

Greene, Graham. *It's a Battlefield*, Kingswood: The Windmill Press, 1952.

———. *The Ministry of Fear*, London: Vintage, 2001.

———. with Elizabeth Bowen and V. S. Pritchett, *Why Do I Write: An Exchange of Views Between Elizabeth Bowen, Graham Greene and V. S. Pritchett*, London: Percival Marshall, 1948.

Gregory, James. *Victorians Against the Gallows: Capital Punishment and the Abolitionist Movement in the Nineteenth Century Britain*, New York: I.B. Tauris & Co Ltd, 2012.

Gristwood, A. D., *The Coward* (1927), in *The Somme including also The Coward*, Columbia: The University of South Carolina Press, 2006.

Guha, Ranajit, 'Not at Home in Empire', *Critical Inquiry* Vol. 23 No. 3 (1997): 482–493.

Guttman, Sondra, 'Who's Afraid of the Corncob Man? Masculinity, Race, and Labor in the Preface to Sanctuary', *Faulkner Journal* Vol. 15, Nos. 1–2 (1999): 15–34 (25).

Hamilton, Patrick, *Rope*, London and New York: Samuel French, 1929.

Hamilton, Susan, 'Dogs' Homes and Lethal Chambers, or, What Was it Like to be a Battersea Dog?', *Animals in Victorian Literature and Culture: Contexts for Criticism*, ed. by Laurence W. Mazzeno and Ronald D. Morrison, Houndsmills: Palgrave, 2017: 83–108.

Hansard. CLAUSE 4.—(Abolition of death penalty in certain cases). House of Commons Debate 17th April 1928 Vol. 216 cc31–83.

———. CLAUSE 5.—(Abolition of death penalty in certain cases). House of Commons Debate 3rd April 1930 Vol. 237 1564–1627.

———. 'THE SINN FEIN REBELLION', House of Lords Debate 11th May 1916a Vol. 21 1002–36.

———. 'NUMBER OF EXECUTIONS', House of Commons Debate 11th May 1916b Vol. 82 886–7.

———. TREACHERY BILL', House of Commons Debate, Deb 22nd May 1940 Vol. 361 185–95.

———. 'TREASON BILL', House of Lords Debate, 30th May 1945a, Vol. 136, 272–273.

———, House of Commons Debate, 11th June 1945b Vol. 411, 1395–1396.

Hawkins, Maureen, 'The Dramatic Treatment of Robert Emmet and Sarah Curran', *Women in Irish Legend, Life and Literature* ed. by S. F. Gallagher, Gerrards Cross: Colin Smythe, 1983: 125–137.

Hendrickson, Kathryn, 'Whose Trauma? Dorothy L. Sayer's Use of Shell Shock and the Role of Memory in Interwar Detective Fiction', *CLUES: A Journal of Detection*, Vol. 37, No. 2 (2019): 51–60.

Allan Hepburn, *Intrigue: Espionage and Culture*, Yale: Yale University Press, 2005.

Herbert, A. P. *The Secret Battle*, London: Methuen, 1936.

———. *The House by the River*, New York: Alfred A. Knopf, 1921.

Heuston, J. J., 'Letter from J.J. Heuston to Mr. E. Walsh, 7th May 1916', *Letters of 1916*, ed. by Susan Schreibman, Maynooth University, 2016. Website. [Accessed 19th June 2018].

Hindess, Barry, 'Not at Home in the Empire', *Social Identities: Journal for the Study of Race, Nation and Culture*, Vol. 7, No. 3. (2001): 363–377.

H. M. B. 'Review: *The Upas Tree* by Robert McMurdy', *Michigan Law Review*, Vol. 11, No. 2 (1912): 176–177.

Hoberman, John M., 'Kierkegaard on Vertigo', *International Kierkegaard Commentary: The Sickness unto Death*, ed. by Robert L. Perkins, Macon, Georgia: Mercer University Press, 1987: 185–208.

Houlbrook. Matt, '"A PIN TO SEE THE PEEPSHOW": CULTURE, FICTION AND SELFHOOD IN EDITH THOMPSON'S LETTERS, 1921–1922', *Past & Present*, No. 207 (2010): 215–249.

Hourigan, Daniel, 'Specters and Psychoanalysis in the Turn to Law and Affect', *Law & Literature* (2017): 1–17.

Horn, Eva, *The Secret War: Treason, Espionage, and Modern Fiction* trans. by Geoffrey Winthrop-Young, Evanston: Northwestern University Press, 2013.

Howell, Phillip, *At Home and Astray: The Domestic Dog in Victorian Britain*, Charlottesville: University of Virginia Press, 2015.

Hughes, Brian, *Michael Mallin: 16 Lives*, Dublin: The O'Brien Press, 2013.

Iacobelli, Teresa, *Death or Deliverance: Canadian Courts Martial in the Great War*, Vancouver: UBC Press, 2013.

I.B. 'A "SHOCKER" THAT REALLY SHOCKS: *Rope* at the Ambassadors Theatre', *The Manchester Guardian*, 26th April 1929, 6.
Iles, Francis, *Malice Aforethought*, London: Orion, 2005.
Inge, W. R., *Christian Ethics and Moral Problems*, London: 1930.
Inglis, Brian, *Roger Casement*, London: Penguin, 2002.
Isaac Anderson, 'New Mystery Stories', *New York Times*, 25th February 1940, 86.
JanMohamed, Abdul R., *The Death-Bound-Subject: Richard Wright's Archaeology of Death*, Durham and London: Duke University Press, 2005.
James, M. R., *Collected Ghost Stories*, Oxford: Oxford University Press, 2013.
J. C. A. 'Review: *The Upas Tree* by Robert McMurdy', *University of Pennsylvania Law Review and American Law Register*, Vol. 62. No. 5 (1914): 404–405.
Jeffrey, Evie, 'Capital Punishment and Women in the British Police Procedural: Josephine Tey's *A Shilling for Candles* and *To Love and Be Wise*', *CLUES: A Journal of Detection*, Vol. 37, No. 2 (Fall 2019): 40–50.
Joyce, James, *Ulysses*, ed. by Hans Walter Gabler, London: The Bodley Head, 2002.
Joyce, Joyce Ann, 'Richard Wright's A Father's Law and Black Metropolis: Intellectual Growth and Literary Vision', *Richard Wright: New Readings in the 21st Century* ed. by Alice M. Craven and William E. Dow, New York: Palgrave, 2011: 129–146.
Jesse, F. Tennyson, *A Pin to See the Peepshow*, London: Virago, 1988.
Jolly, Margaretta, and Liz Stanley, 'Letters As/Not a Genre', *Life Writing*, Vol. 2, No. 2 (2005): 91–118.
Jones, Paul Christian, *Against the Gallows: Antebellum American Writers and the Movement to Abolish Capital Punishment*, Iowa City: University of Iowa Press, 2011.
Jonnes, Jill, *Empires of Light: Edison, Tesla, Westinghouse, and the Race to Electrify the World*, New York: Routledge, 2004.
Kamuf, Peggy, *Literature and the Remains of the Death Penalty*, New York: Fordham University Press, 2018.
Kean, Hilda, *Animal Rights: Political and Social Change in Britain Since 1800*, London: Reaktion, 1998.
Kelleher, Margaret, *The Maamtrasna Murders: Language, Life and Death in Nineteenth-Century Ireland*, Dublin: University College Dublin Press, 2018.
Kennedy, Caitriona, 'The Names that Stilled Her Childish Play: The Women of 1916 and '98', Conference of Irish Historians in Britain, website, n.pag. [Accessed 13 June 2018].
Kennedy, Liam, *Race and Urban Space in American Culture*, New York and London: Routledge, 2000, 132.
Kennedy, Rosanne, 'Affecting Evidence: Edith Thompson's Epistolary Archive', *Australian Feminist Law Journal*, Vol. 40, No. 1(2014): 15–34.
Kennedy, Valerie, 'Conradian quest versus dubious adventure: Graham and Barbara Greene in West Africa', *Studies in Travel Writing*, Vol. 19, No. 1 (2015): 48–65.

Kilfeather, Siobhán, 'Remembering Pleasure and Pain: Roger Casement's Diaries', *Perversions 2* (1994): 4–22.

Kiuchi, Toru, and Yoshinobu Hakutani, *Richard Wright: A Documented Chronology, 1908–1960*, Jefferson, N.C.: McFarland, 2013.

Knott, George H. (ed.), *The Trial of Sir Roger Casement*, Edinburgh and London: William Hodge & Company, 1917.

Kuch, Peter, *Irish Divorce/Joyce's Ulysses*, Houndsmills: Palgrave, 2017.

Lacan, Jacques, *The Seminar of Jacques Lacan: Book II: The Ego in Freud's Theory*, ed. by Jacques-Alain Miller and trans. by Sylvana Tomaselli, New York and London: Norton, 1991.

Lawrence, Margery, 'Abolish the Death Penalty!', *Psychic Journal*, No. 22, May 1948.

Leeson, D. M., *The Black and Tans: British Police and Auxiliaries in the Irish War of Independence, 1920–1921*, Oxford: Oxford University Press, 2011.

Levay, Matthew, *Violent Minds: Modernism and the Criminal*, Cambridge: Cambridge University Press, 2019.

Light, Alison, 'Agatha Christie and conservative modernity', *Forever England: Femininity, literature and conservatism between the wars*, London and New York: Routledge, 1991: 61–113.

Lott, Monica, 'Dorothy L. Sayers, the Great War, and Shell Shock', *Interdisciplinary Literary Studies*, Vol. 15, No. 1 (2013): 103–126.

Lovitt, Carl R., 'The Rhetoric of Murderers' Confessional Narratives: The Model of Pierre Riviere's Memoir', *The Journal of Narrative Technique*, Vol. 22, No. 1 (1992): 23–34.

Maamri, Malika Rebai, 'Cosmic Chaos in *The Secret Agent* and Graham Greene's *It's a Battlefield*', *Conradiana*, Vol. 40, No. 2 (2008): 179–192.

MacDonagh, Thomas, 'Typescript of last letter and will of Thomas MacDonagh, 2nd May 1916', *Letters of 1916*, ed. by Susan Schreibman, Maynooth University, 2016. Website. n.pag. [Accessed 20th July 2018].

Mac Diarmada, Seán, 'Letter from Seán Mac Diarmada to John Daly, 10 May 1916', *Letters of 1916*, ed. by Susan Schreibman, Maynooth University, 2016. Website. [Accessed 19th June 2018].

MacGregor, Lesley Bates, 'Criminalising Animals in Medieval France: Insights from Records of Executions', *Open Library of Humanities*, 5(1) (2019): 15. https://doi.org/10.16995/olh.319.

Mackey, Herbert O., *The Life and Times of Roger Casement*, Dublin: C.J. Fallon, 1954.

Mac Lochlainn, Piaras F., *Last Words: Letters and Statements of the Leaders Executed after the Rising at Easter 1916*, Dublin: Stationery Office, 1990.

Madden, Richard Robert, *The United Irishmen: Their Lives and Times*, London: The Catholic Publishing and Bookselling Company Limited, 1860.

Mallin, Michael, 'Appendix 1: Michael Mallin's last letter to his wife Agnes, Kilmainham Gaol, 7 May 1916', *Michael Mallin: 16 Lives* ed. by Brian Hughes, Dublin: The O'Brien Press, 2013.

Mangan, H. C., *Robert Emmet: A History Play in Three Acts*, Dublin: M. H. Gill and Son, 1904.

Marcus, Laura, 'Cinema and Psychoanalysis: Introduction', *Close Up 1927–1933: Cinema and Modernism*, ed. by James Donald et al., Princeton: Princeton University Press, 1998: 241–247.

Mbembe, Achille. 'Necropolitics', trans. by Libby Meintjes, *Public Culture*, Vol. 15, No. 1 (2003): 11–40 (12).

———. *Necropolitics*, trans. by Steve Corcoran, Durham, N.C.: Duke University Press, 2019.

McBride, Ian, 'The Shadow of the Gunman: Irish Historians and the IRA', *Journal of Contemporary History* Vol. 46, No. 3 (2011): 686–710.

McConville, Seán, *English Local Prisons 1860–1990*, London and New York: Routledge, 1995.

McCormack, W. J., *Roger Casement in Death: or, Haunting the Free State*, Dublin: University College Dublin, 2002.

McDiarmid, Lucy. *At Home in the Revolution*, Dublin: Royal Irish Academy, 2015.

———. 'The Afterlife of Roger Casement: Memory, Folklore, Ghosts, 1916–', *The Irish Art of Controversy*, Ithaca and London: Cornell University Press, 2005: 167–210.

McFeely, Deirdre, *Dion Boucicault: Irish Identity on Stage*, Cambridge: Cambridge University Press, 2012.

McManners, Hugh, *The Scars of War*, London: Harper Collins, 1994.

McMurdy, Robert, *The Upas Tree*, Chicago: F. J. Schulte & Company, 1912.

Melville, Alan, *Death of Anton*, London: The British Library, 2015.

Meranze, Michael, 'Michel Foucault, the Death Penalty and the Crisis of Historical Understanding', *Historical Reflections / Réflexions Historiques* Vol. 29, No. 2 (2003): 191–209.

Meredith, Anne, *Portrait of a Murderer*, London: British Library, 2017.

Miller, Kristine A., *British Literature of the Blitz: Fighting the People's War*, Houndsmills: Palgrave, 2009.

Miller, Tice L., *Entertaining the Nation: American Drama in the Eighteenth and Nineteenth Centuries*, Carbondale: Southern Illinois University Press, 2007.

Milner, Frederick, 'Letter to the Editor: Insanity and the War', *The Times*, 19th September 1917, 7.

Mitchell, Gladys. *The Saltmarsh Murders*, London: Vintage, 2009.

———. *Speedy Death*, London: Vintage, 2014.

Moody, A. David, *Ezra Pound: Poet A Portrait of the Man and his Work, III The Tragic Years 1939–1972*, Oxford: Oxford University Press, 2015.

Morris, Alice S., 'Miss Bowen Illumines The Landscape of War', *New York Times*, 20th February 1949.
Morris Davis, Maggie E., 'Sound and Silence: The Politics of Reading Early Twentieth-Century Lynching Poetry', *Canadian Review of American Studies*, Vol. 48, No. 1 (2018): 40–60.
Morris, R. O., 'Book Review: *The Secret Battle*', *The Times Literary Supplement*, 3rd July 1919, 356.
Moulton, Mo, *Ireland and the Irish in Interwar England*, Cambridge: Cambridge University Press, 2014: 306–329.
Mullen, Patrick R., *The Poor Bugger's Tool: Irish Modernism, Queer Labor, and Postcolonial History*, Oxford: Oxford University Press, 2012.
Musser, Amber, *Sensational Flesh: Race, Power, and Masochism*, New York: New York University Press, 2014.
Naas, Michael, 'THE PHILOSOPHY AND LITERATURE OF THE DEATH PENALTY: TWO SIDES OF THE SAME SOVEREIGN', *The Southern Journal of Philosophy*, Vol. 50, No. 1 (2012): 39–55.
Nally, Claire, *Envisioning Ireland: W.B. Yeats's Occult Nationalism*, Bern, Switzerland: Peter Lang, 2010.
Newquist, Roy, 'A Rainy Afternoon with Truman Capote' (1964), *Truman Capote: Conversations*, ed. by M. Thomas Inge, Jackson and London: University Press of Mississippi, 1987: 33–46.
Nibert, David. *Animal Rights/Human Rights: Entanglements of Oppression and Liberation*, Oxford: Rowman and Littlefield, 2002.
———. *Animal Oppression and Human Violence* New York: Columbia University Press, 2013.
———. *Animal Oppression and Capitalism*, Santa Barbara, California: Praeger, 2017.
O'Brien, Conor Cruise, *States of Ireland*, 2nd edn, London 1974.
O'Brien, Flann, *The Third Policeman, The Complete Novels*, New York: Everyman's Library, 2007.
O'Donnell, Ian, *Justice, Mercy, and Caprice: Clemency and the Death Penalty in Ireland*, Oxford: Oxford University Press, 2017.
Oliver, Kelly, 'See Topsy "Ride the Lightning": The Scopic Machinery of Death', *The Southern Journal of Philosophy*, Vol. 50, No. 1 (2012): 74–94.
Olson, Greta. *Criminals as Animals from Shakespeare to Lombroso*, Berlin/Boston: DeGruyter, 2013.
———. 'De-Americanizing Law and Literature Narratives: Opening Up the Story', *Law and Literature*, Vol. 22, No. 2 (2010): 338–364.
———. 'The Turn to Passion: Has Law and Literature become Law and Affect?', *Law & Literature*, Vol. 28, No. 3 (2016): 335–353.

———. 'Futures of Law and Literature: A Preliminary Overview from a Culturalist Perspective', *Recht und Literatur im Zweischenraum/Law and Literature In-Between*, Bielefield: transcript 2015: 37–69.

Oram, Gerard. *Death sentences passed by military courts of the British Army 1914–1924*, London: Francis Boutle, 1998.

———. *Military Executions During World War I*, Houndsmills: Palgrave, 2003.

Orlov, Peter, *An American Tragedy: the Perils of the Self-Seeking Success*, Cranbury, NJ: Associated University Press, 1998.

Orwell, George, *Shooting an Elephant: and Other Essays*, London: Secker and Warburg, 1950.

Our London Staff, 'PSYCHO-ANALYSIS AND CRIME: SUBCONSCIOUS MIND THAT STRAYS CRIMINOLOGISTS', *The Manchester Guardian*, 21st November, 1923, 10.

Past, Elena, 'Cesare Lombroso Vivisects the Criminal', *Methods of Murder: Beccarian Introspection and Lombrosian Vivisection in Italian Crime Fiction*, Toronto: University of Toronto Press, 2012: 135–170.

Pearse, Patrick, 'Letter from Patrick Pearse to his mother Margaret Pearse, 3 May 1916' *Letters of 1916*, ed. by Susan Schreibman, Maynooth University, 2016. Website. [Accessed 19/06/2018].

Pendleton, Robert, 'Arabesques of Influence: The Repressed Conradian Masterplot in the Novels of Graham Greene', *Conradiana*, Vol. 25, No. 2 (1993): 83–98.

Peppis, Paul, 'Querying and queering golden age detection: Gladys Mitchell's *Speedy Death* and popular modernism', *Journal of Modern Literature*, Vol. 40, No. 3 (2017): 120–13.

Pethica, James. '"Easter, 1916" at its Centennial: Maud Gonne, Augusta Gregory and the Evolution of the Poem', *International Yeats Studies*, Vol. 1, No. 1 (2016): 30–48.

Phelps, W. M. Lyon, 'Review: *The Upas Tree* by Robert McMurdy', *The Yale Law Journal*, Vol. 24, No. 2 (1914): 172.

Pierrepoint, Albert. *Executioner Pierrepoint*, Random Acres: Eric Dobby Press, 2005.

———. 'Ellis', The National Archives, PCOM 9/1773, 1–11.

———. 'Heath', The National Archives, PCOM 9/1773, 1–8.

Piette, Adam, *Imagination at war: British fiction and poetry, 1939–1945*, London: Papermac, 1995.

Plain, Gill, *Twentieth-century Crime Fiction: Gender, Sexuality and the Body*, Edinburgh: Edinburgh University Press, 2001.

Plunkett, Joseph, *The Poems of Joseph Mary Plunkett*, ed. by Geraldine Plunkett Dillon, New York: Frederick A. Stokes Company, 1916.

Pontalis, J. B., 'On Death-work', *Frontiers in Psychoanalysis: Between the Dream and Psychic Pain*, London: The Hogarth Press, 1981: 184–194.

Postgate, Raymond. *Verdict of Twelve*, London: British Library, 2017.

Potter, Harry, *Hanging in judgement: religion and the death penalty in England from the bloody code to abolition*, London: SCM Press, 1993.

Poulosky, Laura, *Severed Heads and Martyred Souls: Crime and Capital Punishment in French Romantic Literature*, New York: Peter Lang, 2003.

Preece, Rod. *Animal Sensibility and Inclusive Justice in the Age of Bernard Shaw*, Vancouver: UBC Press, 2011.

Punt, Michael, 'The Elephant, the Spaceship and the White Cockatoo: An Archaeology of Digital Photography' in *The Photographic Image in Digital Culture* ed. by Martin Lister, Abingdon: Routledge, 1995: 55–76.

Quinodoz, Danielle, 'Chapter 11: Vertigo in the work of Sigmund Freud and Melanie Klein', *Emotional Vertigo: Between Anxiety and Pleasure*, London and New York: Routledge, 1997: 136–151.

Reid, B. L., *The Lives of Roger Casement*, New Haven and London: Yale University Press, 1976.

Reik, Theodor. *The Unknown Murderer, The Compulsion to Confess: On the Psychoanalysis of Crime and Punishment*, New York: Grove Press, 1961a.

———. *The Compulsion to Confess, The Compulsion to Confess: On the Psychoanalysis of Crime and Punishment*, New York: Grove Press, 1961b.

———. *The Compulsion to Confess: On the Psychoanalysis of Crime.* With Sigmund Freud, 'View on Capital Punishment' (1926), in *The Compulsion to Confess: On the Psychoanalysis of Crime and Punishment*, New York: Grove Press, 1961c, 469–474.

Richardson, Maurice, 'The Crime Ration', *The Observer*, 5th November 1939, 6.

Rivers, W. H. R., 'Freud's Psychology of the Unconscious', *The Lancet*, Vol. 189, 16 Jun 1917: 912–914.

Rodden, John. and John Rossi, *The Cambridge Introduction to George Orwell*, Cambridge: Cambridge University Press, 2012.

———. '"A Hanging" Circa 80', *The MidWest Quarterly*, Vol. 56, No. 1 (2014): 70–85.

Rodstein, Susan de Sola, 'Back to 1904: Joyce, Ireland and Nationalism', *Joyce: Feminism, Postcolonialism*, Amsterdam: Rodopi, 1998: 145–186.

Rossetti, Gina M., *Imagining the Primitive in Naturalist and Modernist Culture*, Columbia and London: University of Missouri Press, 2006.

Roudinesco, Élisabeth, *Freud: In His Time and Ours*, trans. by Catherine Porter, Harvard: Harvard University Press, 2016.

Rowland, Anthony, 'The Oasis Poets: Perpetrators, Victims, and Soldier Testimony', *Poetry as Testimony: Witnessing and Memory in Twentieth-century Poems*, New York and London: Routledge, 2014: 41–69.

Ryan, Katy, *Demands of the Dead: Executions, Storytelling, and Activism in the United States*, Iowa City: University of Iowa Press, 2012.

Sachs, Hanns, *Does Capital Punishment Exist?*, Territet: POOL Group Pamphlet, 1930.
Said, Edward. *Freud and the Non-European*, London: Verso, 2004.
Sandberg, Eric, '"The Body in the Bath": Dorothy L. Sayers's *Whose Body?* and Embodied Detective Fiction', *Journal of Modern Literature*, Vol. 42, No. 2 (2019): 1–20.
Sanson, Henry, *Memoirs of the Sansons (1688–1847)*, London: Chatto and Windus, 1881.
Sarat, Austin, *Gruesome Spectacles: Botched Executions and America's Death Penalty*, Stanford: Stanford University Press, 2014.
Sayers, Dorothy L. *Busman's Honeymoon*, London: Hodder and Stoughton, 2016a.
———. *Gaudy Night*, London: Hodder and Stoughton, 2016b.
———. With Muriel St. Clare Byrne, ed. by Alzina Stone Dale, *Love All together with Busman's Honeymoon*, Kent, Ohio: The Kent State University Press, 1985.
———. *Strong Poison*, London: Hodder and Stoughton, 2003.
———. *The Unpleasantness at the Bellona Club*, London: Hodder and Stoughton, 2016c.
———. *Whose Body?*, London: Hodder and Stoughton, 2016d.
———. 'Biographical Note: Communicated by Paul Austin Delgardie', *Unnatural Death*, London: Hodder and Stoughton, 2016e: 300–307.
Scannell, James. 'The Method is Unsound: The Aesthetic Dissonance of Colonial Justification in Kipling, Conrad, and Greene', *Style*, Vol. 30, No.3 (1996): 409–432.
Schmeiser, Susan R., 'Punishing Guilt', 'Special Issue: Legal Analysis', *American Imago*, Vol. 64, No. 3 (2007): 317–337.
Schwartze, Tracey, '"Fabled by the Daughters of Memory": Roger Casement, James Joyce and the Irish Nationalist Hero', *Memory Ireland Volume 4: James Joyce and Cultural Memory* ed. by Oona Frawley and Katherine O'Callaghan, Syracuse: Syracuse University Press, 2014: 79–94.
Seal, Lizzie. *Capital Punishment in Twentieth-Century Britain: Audience, Justice, Memory*, Abingdon: Routledge, 2014.
———. 'Perceptions of safety, fear and social change in the public's pro-death penalty discourse in mid twentieth-century Britain', *Crime, Histoire & Sociétés / Crime, History & Societies* Vol. 21, No.1 (2017) website, n.pag. paragraphs 1–40.
———. and Alexa Neale, 'Race, Racialisation and "Colonial Common Sense" in Capital Cases of Men of Colour in England and Wales, 1919–1957', 'Special Collection: Literature, Law and Psychoanalysis', ed. by Katherine Ebury and Samraghni Bonnerjee, *Open Library of Humanities*, Vol 5, No.1 (2019): 1–21. https://doi.org/10.16995/olh.471.

Serafini, Stefano, "The Ghost of Dr. Freud Haunts Everything Today": Criminal Minds in the Golden Age Psychological Thriller', *CLUES: A Journal of Detection*, Vol. 37, No. 2 (Fall 2019): 20–30.

Shapira, Michal, *The War Inside: Psychoanalysis, Total War, and the Making of the Democratic Self in Postwar Britain*, Cambridge: Cambridge University Press, 2013.

Shaw, George Bernard. *Doctors' Delusions: Crude Criminology and Sham Education*, London: Constable, 1950.

———. 'Capital Punishment (5th December, 1947)', *The Letters of Bernard Shaw to The Times*, ed. by Ronald Ford, Dublin: Irish Academic Press, 2007.

———. *Collected Letters 1911–1925 Volume 3* ed. by Dan H. Laurence, London: Max Reinhardt, 1985.

Sheehan, Paul *Modernism and the Aesthetics of Violence*, Cambridge: Cambridge University Press, 2013.

Sherlock, Thomas, *Robert Emmet: The Story of His Life and Death*, Dublin: T.D. Sullivan, 1878.

Simpson, A. W. Brian, 'The Invention of Trials in Camera in Security Cases', *The Trial in History Volume II: Domestic and international trials, 1700–2000*, Manchester: Manchester University Press, 2003: 76–106.

Smith, Andrew, 'M. R. James's Gothic Revival', *The ghost story 1840–1920: A cultural history*, Manchester: Manchester University Press, 2013: 168–185.

Sokołowska-Paryě, Marzena, *Reimagining the War Memorial, Reinterpreting the Great War: The Formats of British Commemorative Fiction*, Newcastle: Cambridge Scholars Publishing, 2012.

Steffens, Lincoln, 'Lynching by Law or by Lustful Mob North and South: Red and Black', (*Contempo* 1.13, 1).

Stewart, Victoria, *Crime Writing in Interwar Britain: Fact and Fiction in the Golden Age*, Cambridge: Cambridge University Press, 2017.

St. J. E. '"ROPE" BY PATRICK HAMILTON', *The Observer*, April 28, 1929, 15.

SURREALIST GROUP, 'Murderous Humanitarianism', trans. by Samuel Beckett, *Negro: An Anthology*, New York: Frederick Unger: 352–353.

Sweeney, Carole, *From Fetish to Subject: Race, Modernism, and Primitivism, 1919–1935*, Westport and London: Praeger, 2004.

Tarlow, Sarah, *The Golden and Ghoulish Age of the Gibbet in Britain*, Houndsmills: Palgrave, 2017.

Terpstra, Nicholas. *The Art of Executing Well: Rituals of Execution in Renaissance Italy*, Kirksville: Truman State University Press, 2008.

Thurston, Luke, 'Double-crossing: Elizabeth Bowen's ghostly short fiction', *Textual Practice*, Vol. 27, No. 1 (2013): 7–28.

Thurtle, Ernest, *Shootings at Dawn: The Army Death Penalty at Work*, London: Victoria House Printing Co. 1924.

Tiernan, Sonja. *Eva Gore-Booth: An image of such politics*, Oxford: Oxford University Press, 2013.

T. W. M. 'INSANITY AND CRIME: MEANING OF FREUDIAN DOCTRINE WHAT IT REALLY SAYS', *The Manchester Guardian*, 4th July 1922, 8.

Van der Elst, Violet. *On the Gallows*, London: Doge Press, 1937a.

———. *The Torture Chamber and Other Stories*, London: Doge Press, 1937b.

von Rothkirch, Alyce, '"His face was livid, dreadful, with a foam at the corners of his mouth": a typology of the villains in Detective Fiction', *Modern Language Review* Vol. 108 (2013): 1042–1063.

Voss, Ralph F., *Truman Capote and the Legacy of* In Cold Blood, Tuscaloosa, Alabama: University of Alabama Press, 2011.

Walton, Samantha. *Guilty But Insane: Mind and Law in Golden Age Detective Fiction*, Oxford: Oxford University Press, 2015.

———. 'Studies in Green: Teaching Ecological Crime Fiction', *Teaching Crime Fiction* ed. by Charlotte Beyer, Houndsmills: Palgrave, 2018: 115–130.

Walton, Samantha, and Joseph Walton, 'Crime Fiction and Ecology' *Green Letters* 22.1 (2018).

West, Rebecca, *The Meaning of Treason*, London: The Reprint Society, 1952.

Wilde, Oscar, 'The Ballad of Reading Gaol', *Oscar Wilde: Complete Poetry*, Oxford: Oxford World's Classics, 2009: 152–171.

Williams, Orlo, 'A Pin to See the Peepshow', *The Times Literary Supplement*, 11th October 1934, 692.

Wood, John Carter, 'The Third Degree': Press Reporting, Crime Fiction and Police Powers in 1920s Britain', *Twentieth Century British History*, Vol. 21, No. 4, 2010: 464–485.

Woolf, Virginia, *The Diary of Virginia Woolf: Volume II, 1920–1924*, ed. by Anne Olivier Bell, London: The Hogarth Press, 1978.

Wordsworth, William, *The Thirteen-Book Prelude* ed. by Mark L. Reed, Ithaca: Cornell University Press, 1991.

Wright, Richard. 'How Bigger Was Born', *Native Son*, London: Vintage, 2000a: 1–31.

———. *Native Son*, London: Vintage, 2000b.

Wyndham, Francis, 'The Climate of Treason', *Times Literary Supplement*, 5th March 1949, 152.

Yeats, W. B. *The Collected Works of W. B. Yeats: Volume I: The Poems*, 2nd Edition ed. by Richard Finneran, New York: Scribner, 1997.

———. 'The Dreaming of the Bones', *The Collected Works of W.B. Yeats Volume II: The Plays*, ed. by Richard Finneran and George Mills Harper, New York: Scribner, 2001: 307–316.

The Collected Works of W.B. Yeats Volume II: The Plays, . Ireland 1921–1931' *The Collected Works of W. B. Yeats, Volume X: Later Articles and Reviews*, ed, by Colton Johnson, New York: Scribner, 2000.

———. *The Letters of W. B. Yeats*, ed. by Allan Wade, New York: Macmillan, 1955.

Zaretsky, Eli, 'Beyond the Blues: Richard Wright, Psychoanalysis, and the Modern Idea of Culture', *The Transnational Unconscious: Essays in the History of Psychoanalysis and Transnationalism*, ed. by Joy Damousi and Mariano Ben Plotkin, Houndsmills: Palgrave, 2009: 43–70.

Index[1]

[1] Note: Page numbers followed by 'n' refer to notes.

K. Ebury, *Modern Literature and the Death Penalty, 1890–1950*, Palgrave Studies in Literature, Culture and Human Rights, https://doi.org/10.1007/978-3-030-52750-1

The manufacturer's authorised representative in the EU is Springer Nature Customer Service Centre GmbH, Europaplatz 3, 69115 Heidelberg, Germany. If you have any concerns regarding our products, please contact ProductSafety@springernature.com

Printed and bound by CPI Group (UK) Ltd, Croydon, CR0 4YY

30/09/2026

02225457-0009